PRAXIS II®
MATHEMATICS

CONTENT KNOWLEDGE
AND PEDAGOGY
(5161/0065)

LEARNINGEXPRESS®

NEW YORK

Cataloging-in-Publication Data is on file with the Library of Congress.

Printed in the United States of America

9 8 7 6 5 4 3 2 1

ISBN 978-1-57685-977-3

For information on LearningExpress, other LearningExpress products, or bulk sales, please write to us at:
   80 Broad Street
   4th Floor
   New York, NY 10004

Or visit us at:
   www.learningexpressllc.com

CONTENTS

INTRODUCTION TO THE PRAXIS II® MATHEMATICS: CONTENT KNOWLEDGE (5161) AND PEDAGOGY (0065) TESTS

CHAPTER SUMMARY

The Praxis® Series of tests are administered by the Educational Testing Service (ETS). (See www.ets.org/praxis for complete information.) This chapter discusses information about the Praxis II® Mathematics exams, including test formats and content.

The Praxis® Series of Tests

All the exams in the Praxis® Series of tests are designed to measure the scholastic and pedagogical capability of teachers at different stages of their careers. As you probably remember, the first exam in the Praxis® Series, the Praxis I® Pre-Professional Skills Test (PPST), may be taken early in a student's college career to qualify for entry into a teaching credential program. It is also taken by prospective teachers to be considered for a license in states not requiring education degrees.

The Praxis I® PPST is composed of individual tests that measure basic skills in reading, mathematics, and writing. The second group of exams in the Praxis® Series, the Praxis II®, is taken by individuals entering the teaching profession as part of their state's teacher licensing and certification process. The Praxis II® consists of three groups of tests that measure subject-specific content knowledge, general pedagogical knowledge, and teaching foundations.

STATES USING THE PRAXIS® SERIES OF TESTS

Each state sets its own requirements for which tests to take and what score will be accepted as passing. Information regarding specific state or organization requirements may change from time to time. For accurate, up-to-date information, refer to the official Praxis website at www.ets.org/praxis and your state's Education Department.

About the Praxis II® Mathematics Tests

The Praxis II® Subject Assessments include more than 120 tests. These tests measure knowledge of specific K–12 content areas, from Agriculture to World and U.S. History. They also test teaching knowledge and skills. The Praxis II® Mathematics tests covered in this book (Content Knowledge, 5161, and Pedagogy, 0065) test the knowledge and competencies for teaching secondary school mathematics.

Praxis II® Mathematics test takers generally have a bachelor's degree with a math major. The Content Knowledge test is administered on a computer and takes 150 minutes. There are 60 questions: About two-thirds are allotted to number and quantity, algebra, functions, and calculus; the balance cover geometry, probability and statistics, and discrete mathematics.

Answer formats include:

- multiple choice with one or more selections
- numeric entry
- drag-and-drop
- text completion

The Pedagogy test takes an hour and consists of three equally weighted essay questions on planning instruction, implementing instruction, and assessing instruction. The level of math called for by the test is no higher than first-year algebra. Questions may ask you to include informal geometry, probability, and proof information in your answers.

To earn a high score on this test, you must demonstrate a mastery of math pedagogy, including the ability to identify, analyze, and improve upon student errors; knowledge of how to differentiate instruction based on gender, ethnic, or socioeconomic status; a knowledge of the appropriate use of technology in lesson planning and implementation; the appropriate use of forms of representation; the ability to assess skills; and ability with identifying multiple problem-solving strategies. The one hour provided for all three essays covers your brainstorming, prep work, *and* writing your response.

CALCULATORS ON THE PRAXIS II® MATHEMATICS TESTS

Please note: You *will* have access to an on-screen graphing calculator for the duration of the Praxis II® Mathematics: Content Knowledge test. Note *that no other* calculator use is allowed—you will not be able to bring a calculator from home.

You are allowed to bring a graphing calculator to the Praxis II® Mathematics: Pedagogy test. Please note that test administrators will clear the memory of your calculator when you arrive at the testing site and when you leave.

The Computer-Delivered Test

Praxis II® tests are available as computer-delivered tests in more than 300 locations throughout the United States. They are given frequently. You don't have to know much about computers to take the computer-based version—each test begins with a tutorial on the use of the computer. You are encouraged to spend as much time as needed on the tutorial.

With the exception of the numeric entry and drag-and-drop mathematics questions, all questions for the Content Knowledge test are in multiple-choice format. The questions are presented on the computer screen, and you choose your answers by selecting one by clicking in the oval next to the correct choice or choices (for multiple-answer math questions). For numeric entry questions, you will be asked to type your answer into a box or boxes provided, and for drag-and-drop questions, you will need to move an item or items with the mouse and drop it or them into an appropriate place on the screen.

The computer-based tests now have a special "mark" function, which allows you to "mark" a question that you would like to skip temporarily and come back to at a later time during the same section on the test. Test takers will have a review screen to see whether a question has been answered, not seen yet, or "marked."

The computer-based test is designed to ensure fairness, because each test taker receives:

- the same distribution of content
- the same amount of testing time
- the same test directions
- the same tutorials on computer use

Test Scoring

Each question on the Content Knowledge exam has equal worth. There may be a few questions that won't count toward your score, but you won't know which those will be. There is no guessing penalty, which means you will not lose points for getting a question wrong. Thus, you should always guess on a question, even if you are not sure what the correct answer is. Even though there are 60 questions, your final score is not based on 60 points. ETS counts the number of questions you answered correctly and then translates that number into a scaled score. Each state accepts a different scaled score as "passing"—refer to www.ets.org/praxis and your state's Education Department to find out what score you must earn to pass the exams.

If you take the computer version of the test, you will receive your score right away, immediately after you have completed the exam. Your official score will then be reported to you and the organizations you designate about two to three weeks after your test date.

Each of the three questions in the Pedagogy exam is scored on a scale from 0 to 5. Each question is weighted the same toward your final score. Refer to the Sample Answers section of Chapters 13, 14, and 15 to see what an essay at each level contains.

Registering for the Test

You can register for both exams online at www.ets.org/praxis/register. On the site, you can also check test dates and center locations most convenient to you. You can register for the computerized test electronically using a credit or debit card, and for the paper test by mailing in a hard copy form with a check or credit/debit card information.

Your next step is learning all about test-taking strategies in Chapter 2. Then, go on to take the diagnostic test in Chapter 3 to find out your strengths and weaknesses so you can plan your course of study.

You're on the way to becoming a math teacher—congratulations and good luck!

SPECIAL ACCOMMODATIONS FOR THE PRAXIS® TESTS

ETS offers some accommodations for students with disabilities. For example, students may have extended time or additional rest breaks. Some students may take the Praxis II® test in a large print, Braille, or audio format.

You can view the testing arrangements and registration procedures at www.ets.org/praxis/prxdsabl.html. To find out if you are eligible for the special accommodations, you can contact ETS Disability Services directly:

Phone: Monday through Friday, 8:30 A.M. to 4:30 P.M. Eastern Time
1-866-387-8602 (toll free) from the United States, U.S. territories, and Canada
1-609-771-7780 (all other locations)
TTY: 1-609-771-7714
Fax: 1-609-771-7165
E-mail: stassd@ets.org
Mail: ETS, Disability Services, P.O. Box 6054, Princeton, NJ 08541-6054

2 ▶ THE LEARNINGEXPRESS TEST PREPARATION SYSTEM

CHAPTER SUMMARY

The Praxis® Series of tests can be challenging. A great deal of preparation is necessary for achieving top scores and advancing your career. The LearningExpress Test Preparation System, developed by leading experts exclusively for LearningExpress, offers strategies for developing the discipline and attitude required for success.

Fact: Taking the Praxis II® Elementary Education: Curriculum, Instruction, and Assessment test is not easy, and neither is getting ready for it. Your future career as a teacher depends on getting a passing score, but an assortment of pitfalls can keep you from doing your best. Here are some of the obstacles that can stand in the way of success:

- being unfamiliar with the exam format
- being paralyzed by test anxiety
- leaving your preparation to the last minute
- not preparing at all(!)
- not knowing vital test-taking skills: how to pace yourself through the exams, how to use the process of elimination, and when to guess
- not being in tip-top mental and physical shape
- messing up on test day by arriving late at the test site, having to work on an empty stomach, or feeling uncomfortable during the exams because the room is too hot or too cold

What is the common denominator in all these test-taking pitfalls? One word: control. Who's in control, you or the exam? Here's some good news: The LearningExpress Test Preparation System puts *you* in control. In nine easy-to-follow steps, you will learn everything you need to know to make sure that you are in charge of your preparation and your performance on the exams. Other test takers may let the tests get the better of them; other test takers may be unprepared or out of shape, but not you. You will have taken all the steps you need to take to get a high score on the Praxis® tests.

Here's how the LearningExpress Test Preparation System works: Nine easy steps lead you through everything you need to know and do to get ready to master your exams. Each of the following steps includes both reading about the step and one or more activities. It's important that you do the activities along with the reading, or you won't be getting the full benefit of the system. Each step tells you approximately how much time that step will take you to complete.

Step 1: Get Information	50 minutes
Step 2: Conquer Test Anxiety	20 minutes
Step 3: Make a Plan	30 minutes
Step 4: Learn to Manage Your Time	10 minutes
Step 5: Learn to Use the Process of Elimination	20 minutes
Step 6: Know When to Guess	20 minutes
Step 7: Reach Your Peak Performance Zone	10 minutes
Step 8: Get Your Act Together	10 minutes
Step 9: Do It!	10 minutes
Total	**3 hours**

We estimate that working through the entire system will take you approximately three hours, though it's perfectly okay if you work faster or slower. If you take an afternoon or evening, you can work through the whole LearningExpress Test Preparation System in one sitting. Otherwise, you can break it up, and do just one or two steps a day for the next several days. It's up to you—remember, you are in control.

Step 1: Get Information

Time to complete: 50 minutes
Activity: Read Chapter 1, "Introduction to Praxis II® Mathematics Tests."

Knowledge is power. The first step in the LearningExpress Test Preparation System is finding out everything you can about the Praxis® tests. Once you have your information, the next steps in the LearningExpress Test Preparation System will show you how to apply it.

Straight Talk about the Praxis II®

Why do you have to take rigorous exams, anyway? It's simply an attempt to be sure you have the knowledge and skills necessary to be a teacher. It's important for you to remember that your scores on the Praxis® tests do not determine how smart you are or even whether you will make a good teacher. There are all kinds of things exams like these can't test, such as whether you have the drive, determination, and dedication to be a teacher. Those kinds of things are hard to evaluate, while a test is easy to evaluate. This is not to say that the exams are not important! The knowledge tested on the exams is knowledge you will need in order to do your job. And your ability to enter the profession you've trained for depends on passing. And that's why you are here—using the LearningExpress Test Preparation System to achieve control over the exams.

What's on the Tests

If you haven't already done so, stop here and read Chapter 1 of this book, which gives you an overview of the Praxis® Series of tests. Then, go online and read the most up-to-date information about your exam directly from the test developers at www.ets.org/praxis.

Step 2: Conquer Test Anxiety

Time to complete: 20 minutes
Activity: Take the Test Anxiety Test.

Having complete information about the exams is the first step in getting control of them. Next, you have to overcome one of the biggest obstacles to test success: test anxiety. Test anxiety not only impairs your performance on the exams, but also keeps you from preparing. In Step 2, you will learn stress management techniques that will help you succeed. Learn these strategies now, and practice them as you work through the exams in this book so that they will be second nature to you by exam day.

Combating Test Anxiety

The first thing you need to know is that a little test anxiety is a good thing. Everyone gets nervous before a big exam—and if that nervousness motivates you to prepare thoroughly, so much the better. It's said that Sir Laurence Olivier, one of the foremost British actors of the twentieth century, felt ill before every performance. His stage fright didn't impair his performance; in fact, it probably gave him a little extra edge—just the kind of edge you need in order to do well, whether on a stage or in an examination room. The Test Anxiety Test is on the next page. Stop and answer the questions to find out whether your level of test anxiety is something you should worry about.

Stress Management before a Test

If you feel your level of anxiety getting the best of you in the weeks before a test, here is what you need to do to bring the level down again:

- **Get prepared.** There's nothing like knowing what to expect and being prepared for it to put you in control of test anxiety. That's why you are reading this book. Use it faithfully, and remind yourself that you are better prepared than most of the people taking the test.
- **Practice self-confidence.** A positive attitude is a great way to combat test anxiety. This is no time to be humble or shy. Stand in front of the mirror and say to your reflection, "I am prepared. I am full of self-confidence. I am going to ace this test. I know I can do it." Record this affirmation and play it back once a day. If you hear it often enough, you will believe it.
- **Fight negative messages.** Every time someone starts telling you how hard the exam is or how it's almost impossible to get a high score, start telling them your self-confidence messages you learned about in the previous entry. Don't listen to the negative messages. Turn on your recorder and listen to your self-confidence messages.
- **Visualize.** Imagine yourself reporting for duty on your first day as a teacher or in your teacher training program. Visualizing success can help make it happen—and it reminds you of why you are doing all this work preparing for the exam.
- **Exercise.** Physical activity helps calm your body down and focus your mind. Besides, being in good physical shape can actually help you do well on the exam. Go for a run, lift weights, or go swimming—and do it regularly.

Stress Management on Test Day

There are several ways you can bring down your level of anxiety on test day. They will work best if you practice them in the weeks before the test so that you know which ones work best for you.

- **Practice deep breathing.** Take a deep breath while you count to five. Hold it for a count of one, then let it out on a count of five. Repeat several times.

You need to worry about test anxiety only if it is extreme enough to impair your performance. The following questionnaire will provide a diagnosis of your level of test anxiety. In the blank before each statement, write the number that most accurately describes your experience.

0 = Never
1 = Once or twice
2 = Sometimes
3 = Often

___ I have gotten so nervous before an exam that I simply put down the books and didn't study for it.

___ I have experienced disabling physical symptoms such as vomiting and severe headaches because I was nervous about an exam.

___ I have simply not shown up for an exam because I was afraid to take it.

___ I have experienced dizziness and disorientation while taking an exam.

___ I have had trouble filling in the little circles because my hands were shaking too hard.

___ I have failed an exam because I was too nervous to complete it.

___ **Total: Add up the numbers in the blanks.**

Your Test Anxiety Score

Here are the steps you should take, depending on your score. If you scored:

- **Below 3**, your level of test anxiety is nothing to worry about; it's probably just enough to give you that little extra edge.

- **Between 3 and 6**, your test anxiety may be enough to impair your performance, and you should practice the stress management techniques in this section to try to bring your test anxiety down to manageable levels.

- **Above 6**, your level of test anxiety is a serious concern. In addition to practicing the stress management techniques listed in this section, you may want to seek additional, personal help. Call your local high school or community college and ask for the academic counselor. Tell the counselor that you have a level of test anxiety that sometimes keeps you from being able to take an exam, or impairs your performance. The counselor may be willing to help you or may suggest someone else you should talk to.

- **Move your body.** Try rolling your head in a circle. Rotate your shoulders. Shake your hands from the wrist. Many people find these movements very relaxing.
- **Visualize again.** Think of the place where you are most relaxed: lying on the beach in the sun, walking through the park, or wherever. Now close your eyes and imagine you are actually there. If you practice in advance, you will find that you only need a few seconds of this exercise to experience a significant increase in your sense of well-being.

When anxiety threatens to overwhelm you right there during the exam, there are still things you can do to manage your stress level:

- **Repeat your self-confidence messages.** You should have them memorized by now. Say them quietly to yourself, and believe them!
- **Visualize one more time.** This time, visualize yourself moving smoothly and quickly through the test, answering every question right and finishing just before time is up. Like most visualization techniques, this one works best if you have practiced it ahead of time.
- **Find an easy question.** Find an easy question, and answer it. Getting even one question finished gets you into the test-taking groove.
- **Take a mental break.** Everyone loses concentration once in a while during a long test. It's normal, so you shouldn't worry about it. Instead, accept what has happened. Say to yourself, "Hey, I lost it there for a minute. My brain was taking a break." Put down your pencil, close your eyes, and do some deep breathing for a few seconds. Then you are ready to go back to work.

Try these techniques ahead of time, and see if they work for you.

Step 3: Make a Plan

Time to complete: 30 minutes
Activity: Construct a study plan.

Maybe the most important thing you can do to get control of yourself and your exams is to make a study plan. Too many people fail to prepare simply because they fail to plan. Spending hours on the day before the exam poring over sample test questions not only raises your level of test anxiety, but also is simply no substitute for careful preparation and practice over time.

Don't fall into the cram trap. Take control of your preparation time by mapping out a study schedule. On the following pages are two sample schedules, based on the amount of time you have before you take the Praxis II®. If you are the kind of person who needs deadlines and assignments to motivate you for a project, here they are. If you are the kind of person who doesn't like to follow other people's plans, you can use the suggested schedules here to construct your own.

Even more important than making a plan is making a commitment. You have to set aside some time every day for study and practice. Try for at least 20 minutes a day. Twenty minutes daily will do you much more good than two hours on Saturday.

Don't put off your study until the day before the exam. Start now. A few minutes a day, with half an hour or more on weekends, can make a big difference in your score.

Schedule A: The 30-Day Plan

If you have at least a month before you take the Praxis II®, you have plenty of time to prepare—as long as you don't waste it! If you have less than a month, turn to Schedule B.

TIME	PREPARATION
Days 1–4	Skim over any other study materials you may have. Make a note of areas you expect to be emphasized on the exam and areas you don't feel confident in. On Day 3, read "Mathematics Pedagogy Review" (Chapter 12). On Day 4, concentrate on your weakest content areas (select from Chapters 4 through 10).
Day 5	Take the content knowledge diagnostic test in Chapter 3.
Day 6	Score the test using the answers at the end of Chapter 3. Identify two areas that you will concentrate on before you take the first practice exam. Also on Day 6, take your first pedagogy practice test, Chapter 13.
Days 7–10	Study one of the areas you identified as a weak point for content knowledge.
Days 11–14	Study any other areas you identified as weak points.
Day 15	Take the first practice exam in Chapter 11.
Day 16	Score the practice exam. Identify one area to concentrate on before you take the next practice exam. Take another pedagogy practice test, Chapter 14.
Days 17–21	Study the one content knowledge area you identified for review.
Days 22–23	Take the second practice exam online. Score it and note any areas in which you need improvement.
Days 24–28	Study any remaining topics you still need to review. Take your last pedagogy practice test, Chapter 15. Use the review chapters for help.
Day 29	Take an overview of all your study materials, consolidating your strengths and improving on any weaknesses. Review the sample scoring and responses for the pedagogy test; remind yourself to address all parts of the question and to be thorough in your explanations.
Day before the exam	Relax. Do something unrelated to the exam, and go to bed at a reasonable hour.

Schedule B: The Ten-Day Plan

If you have two weeks or less before you take the exam, use this ten-day schedule to help you make the most of your time.

TIME	PREPARATION
Day 1	Take the diagnostic test in Chapter 3 and score it using the answers at the end of the chapter. Note which topics you need to review most. Read the pedagogy review, Chapter 12.
Day 2	Review one content knowledge area that gave you trouble on the diagnostic test. Take a pedagogy practice test, Chapter 13.
Day 3	Review another content knowledge area that gave you trouble on the pretest.
Day 4	Take the first practice exam in Chapter 11 and score it.
Day 5	If your score on the first practice exam doesn't show improvement on the two areas you studied, review them again. If you did improve in those areas, choose a new weak area to study today. Take a second pedagogy test, Chapter 14.
Days 6–7	Continue to review chapters to improve some skills and reinforce others.
Day 8	Take the second practice exam online and score it.
Day 9	Choose your weakest area from the second practice exam to review. Take your last pedagogy practice test, Chapter 15.
Day 10	Use your last study day to brush up on any areas that are still giving you trouble. Use the review chapters. Review the sample scoring and responses for the pedagogy test; remind yourself to address all parts of the question and to be thorough in your explanations.
Day before the exam	Relax. Do something unrelated to the exam, and go to bed at a reasonable hour.

Step 4: Learn to Manage Your Time

Time to complete: 10 minutes to read; many hours of practice!

Activity: Practice these strategies as you take the sample tests in this book.

Steps 4, 5, and 6 of the LearningExpress Test Preparation System put you in charge of your exams by showing you test-taking strategies that work. Practice these strategies as you take the sample tests in this book, and then you will be ready to use them on test day.

First, take control of your time on the exams. It's a terrible feeling to know there are only five minutes left when you are only three-quarters of the way through a test. Here are some tips to keep that from happening to you:

- **Follow directions.** You may choose to take the computer-based Praxis® exam. You should take your time taking the computer tutorial before the exam. Read the directions carefully and ask questions before the exam begins if there's anything you don't understand.
- **Pace yourself.** If there is a timer on the screen as you take the exam, keep an eye on it. This will help you pace yourself. For example, when one-quarter of the time has elapsed, you should be a

quarter of the way through the test, and so on. If you are falling behind, pick up the pace a bit. If you do not take your exam on a computer, use your watch or the clock in the testing room to keep track of the time you have left.

- **Keep moving.** Don't waste time on one question. If you don't know the answer, skip the question and move on. You can always go back to it later.
- **Don't rush.** Although you should keep moving, rushing won't help. Try to keep calm and work methodically and quickly.

Step 5: Learn to Use the Process of Elimination

Time to complete: 20 minutes
Activity: Complete the worksheet on Using the Process of Elimination.

After time management, your next most important tool for taking control of your exam is using the process of elimination wisely. It's standard test-taking wisdom that you should always read all the answer choices before choosing your answer. This helps you find the right answer by eliminating wrong answer choices. And, sure enough, that standard wisdom applies to your exam, too.

You should always use the process of elimination on tough questions, even if what seems to be the right answer jumps out at you. Sometimes the answer that jumps out isn't right after all. You should always proceed through the answer choices in order. You can start with answer choice **a** and eliminate any choices that are clearly incorrect.

If you are taking the test on paper, like the practice exams in this book, it's good to have a system for marking good, bad, and maybe answers. We're recommending this one:

    X = bad
    ✔ = good
    ? = maybe

If you don't like these marks, devise your own system. Just make sure you do it long before test day—while you're working through the practice exams in this book—so you won't have to worry about it just before the exam.

Even when you think you are absolutely clueless about a question, you can often use the process of elimination to get rid of one answer choice. If so, you are better prepared to make an educated guess, as you will see in Step 6. More often, the process of elimination allows you to get down to only two possibly right answers. Then you are in a strong position to guess.

And sometimes, even though you don't know the right answer, you find it simply by getting rid of all the wrong ones.

Try using your powers of elimination on the questions in the worksheet Using the Process of Elimination on the next page. The questions aren't about teaching; they're just designed to show you how the process of elimination works. The answer explanations for this worksheet show one possible way that you might use the process to arrive at the right answer. The process of elimination is your tool for the next step, which is knowing when to guess.

Step 6: Know When to Guess

Time to complete: 20 minutes
Activity: Complete the worksheet on Your Guessing Ability.

Armed with the process of elimination, you are ready to take control of one of the big questions in test taking: Should I guess? The answer is: Yes. Some exams have a guessing penalty, in which a fraction of your wrong answers is subtracted from your right answers, but the Praxis® Series of tests does *not* work like that. The number of questions you answer correctly yields your raw score. So you have nothing to lose and everything to gain by guessing.

USING THE PROCESS OF ELIMINATION

Use the process of elimination to answer the following questions.

1. Ilsa is as old as Meghan will be in five years. The difference between Ed's age and Meghan's age is twice the difference between Ilsa's age and Meghan's age. Ed is 29. How old is Ilsa?
   a. 4
   b. 10
   c. 19
   d. 24

2. "All drivers of commercial vehicles must carry a valid commercial driver's license whenever operating a commercial vehicle."
   According to this sentence, which of the following people need NOT carry a commercial driver's license?
   a. a truck driver idling his engine while waiting to be directed to a loading dock
   b. a bus operator backing her bus out of the way of another bus in the bus lot
   c. a taxi driver driving his personal car to the grocery store
   d. a limousine driver taking the limousine to her home after dropping off her last passenger of the evening

3. Smoking tobacco has been linked to
   a. increased risk of stroke and heart attack.
   b. all forms of respiratory disease.
   c. increasing mortality rates over the past ten years.
   d. juvenile delinquency.

4. Which of the following words is spelled correctly?
   a. incorrigible
   b. outragous
   c. domestickated
   d. understandible

Answers

Here are the answers, as well as some suggestions as to how you might use the process of elimination to find them.

1. d. You can eliminate choice **a** right off the bat. Ilsa can't be four years old if Meghan is going to be Ilsa's age in five years. The best way to eliminate other answer choices is to try plugging them into the information given in the problem. For instance, for choice **b**, if Ilsa is 10, then Meghan must be 5. The difference between their ages is five years. The difference between Ed's age, 29, and Meghan's age, 5, is 24. Is 24 two times 5? No. Then choice **b** is wrong. You can eliminate choice **c** in the same way and be left with choice **d**.

2. c. Note the word *not* in the question, and go through the answers one by one. Is the truck driver in choice **a** "operating a commercial vehicle"? Yes, idling counts as "operating," so he needs to have a commercial driver's license. Likewise, the bus operator in choice **b** is operating a commercial vehicle; the question doesn't say the operator has to be on the street. The limo driver in choice **d** is operating a commercial vehicle, even though it doesn't have a passenger in it. However, the driver in choice **c** is not operating a commercial vehicle, but his own private car.

3. a. You can eliminate choice **b** simply because of the presence of the word *all*. Such absolutes hardly ever appear in correct answer choices. Choice **c** looks attractive until you think a little about what you know—aren't fewer people smoking these days, rather than more? So how could smoking be responsible for increasing mortality rates? (If you didn't know that *mortality rate* means the rate at which people die, you might keep this choice as a possibility, but you would still be able to eliminate two answers and have only two to choose from.) And choice **d** is plain silly, so you can eliminate that one, too. You are left with the correct choice, **a**.

4. a. How you use the process of elimination here depends on which words you recognize as being spelled incorrectly. If you know that the correct spellings are *outrageous*, *domesticated*, and *understandable*, then you are home free. You probably know that at least one of those words is spelled wrong in the question.

YOUR GUESSING ABILITY

The following are ten really hard questions. You are not supposed to know the answers. Rather, this is an assessment of your ability to guess when you don't have a clue. Read each question carefully, as if you were expected to answer it. If you have any knowledge of the subject, use that knowledge to help you eliminate wrong answer choices.

1.	ⓐ	ⓑ	ⓒ	ⓓ	**5.**	ⓐ	ⓑ	ⓒ	ⓓ	**9.**	ⓐ	ⓑ	ⓒ	ⓓ
2.	ⓐ	ⓑ	ⓒ	ⓓ	**6.**	ⓐ	ⓑ	ⓒ	ⓓ	**10.**	ⓐ	ⓑ	ⓒ	ⓓ
3.	ⓐ	ⓑ	ⓒ	ⓓ	**7.**	ⓐ	ⓑ	ⓒ	ⓓ				
4.	ⓐ	ⓑ	ⓒ	ⓓ	**8.**	ⓐ	ⓑ	ⓒ	ⓓ				

1. September 7 is Independence Day in
  a. India.
  b. Costa Rica.
  c. Brazil.
  d. Australia.

2. Which of the following is the formula for determining the momentum of an object?
  a. $p = MV$
  b. $F = ma$
  c. $P = IV$
  d. $E = mc^2$

3. Because of the expansion of the universe, the stars and other celestial bodies are all moving away from each other. This phenomenon is known as
  a. Newton's first law.
  b. the big bang.
  c. gravitational collapse.
  d. Hubble flow.

4. American author Gertrude Stein was born in
  a. 1713.
  b. 1830.
  c. 1874.
  d. 1901.

5. Which of the following is NOT one of the Five Classics attributed to Confucius?
  a. *I Ching*
  b. *Book of Holiness*
  c. *Spring and Autumn Annals*
  d. *Book of History*

6. The religious and philosophical doctrine that holds that the universe is constantly in a struggle between good and evil is known as
  a. Pelagianism.
  b. Manichaeanism.
  c. neo-Hegelianism.
  d. Epicureanism.

7. The third Chief Justice of the U.S. Supreme Court was
  a. John Blair.
  b. William Cushing.
  c. James Wilson.
  d. John Jay.

8. Which of the following is the poisonous portion of a daffodil?
  a. the bulb
  b. the leaves
  c. the stem
  d. the flowers

9. The winner of the Masters golf tournament in 1953 was
  a. Sam Snead.
  b. Cary Middlecoff.
  c. Arnold Palmer.
  d. Ben Hogan.

10. The state with the highest per capita personal income in 1980 was
  a. Alaska.
  b. Connecticut.
  c. New York.
  d. Texas.

Answers

Check your answers against the following correct answers.

  1. c
  2. a
  3. d
  4. c
  5. b
  6. b
  7. b
  8. a
  9. d
  10. a

How Did You Do?

You may have simply gotten lucky and actually known the answer to one or two questions. In addition, your guessing was probably more successful if you were able to use the process of elimination on any of the questions. Maybe you didn't know who the third Chief Justice was (question 7), but you knew that John Jay was the first. In that case, you would have eliminated choice **d** and, therefore, improved your odds of guessing right from one in four to one in three.

According to probability, you should get 2.5 answers correct, so getting either two or three right would be average. If you got four or more right, you may be a really terrific guesser. If you got one or none right, you may be a really bad guesser.

Keep in mind, though, that this is only a small sample. You should continue to keep track of your guessing ability as you work through the sample questions in this book. Circle the numbers of questions you guess on as you make your guess; or, if you don't have time while you take the practice tests, go back afterward and try to remember which questions you guessed at.

Remember, on a test with four answer choices, your chance of guessing correctly is one in four. So keep a separate "guessing" score for each exam. How many questions did you guess on? How many did you get right?

If the number you got right is at least one-fourth of the number of questions you guessed on, you are at least an average guesser—maybe better—and you should always go ahead and guess on the real exam.

If the number you got right is significantly lower than one-fourth of the number you guessed on, you would be safe in guessing anyway, but maybe you would feel more comfortable if you guessed only selectively, when you can eliminate a wrong answer or at least have a good feeling about one of the answer choices.

Remember, even if you are a play-it-safe person with lousy intuition, you are still safe guessing every time.

Step 7: Reach Your Peak Performance Zone

Time to complete: 10 minutes to read; weeks to complete!
Activity: Complete the Physical Preparation Checklist.

To get ready for a challenge like a big exam, you have to take control of your physical, as well as your mental, state. Exercise, proper diet, and rest will ensure that your body works with, rather than against, your mind on test day, as well as during your preparation.

Exercise

If you don't already have a regular exercise program going, the time during which you are preparing for an exam is actually an excellent time to start one. And if you are already keeping fit—or trying to get that way—don't let the pressure of preparing for an exam fool you into quitting now. Exercise helps reduce stress by pumping wonderful good-feeling hormones called endorphins into your system. It also increases the oxygen supply throughout your body, including your brain, so you will be at peak performance on test day.

A half hour of vigorous activity—enough to raise a sweat—every day should be your aim. If you are really pressed for time, every other day is okay. Choose an activity you like and get out there and do it. Jogging with a friend always makes the time go faster, or take a radio. But don't overdo it. You don't want to exhaust yourself. Moderation is the key.

Diet

First of all, cut out the junk food. Go easy on caffeine and nicotine, and eliminate alcohol and any other drugs from your system at least two weeks before the exam. Promise yourself a treat the night after the exam, if need be.

What your body needs for peak performance is simply a balanced diet. Eat plenty of fruits and vegetables, along with protein and carbohydrates. Foods that are high in lecithin (an amino acid), such as fish and beans, are especially good brain foods. The night before the exam, you might carbo-load the way athletes do before a contest. Eat a big plate of spaghetti, rice and beans, or whatever your favorite carbohydrate is.

Rest

You probably know how much sleep you need every night to be at your best, even if you don't always get it. Make sure you do get that much sleep, though, for at least a week before the exam. Moderation is important here, too. Extra sleep will just make you groggy.

If you are not a morning person and your exam will be given in the morning, you should reset your internal clock so that your body doesn't think you are taking an exam at 3 A.M. You have to start this process well before the exam. The way it works is to get up half an hour earlier each morning, and then go to bed half an hour earlier that night. Don't try it the other way around; you will just toss and turn if you go to bed early without having gotten up early. The next morning, get up another half an hour earlier, and so on. How long you will have to do this depends on how late you are used to getting up. Use the Physical Preparation Checklist on the next page to make sure you are in tip-top form.

PHYSICAL PREPARATION CHECKLIST

For the week before the exam, write down what physical exercise you engaged in and for how long and what you ate for each meal. Remember, you're trying for at least half an hour of exercise every other day (preferably every day) and a balanced diet that's light on junk food.

Exam minus 7 days

Exercise: _____ for _____ minutes

Breakfast: _____

Lunch: _____

Dinner: _____

Snacks: _____

Exam minus 6 days

Exercise: _____ for _____ minutes

Breakfast: _____

Lunch: _____

Dinner: _____

Snacks: _____

Exam minus 5 days

Exercise: _____ for _____ minutes

Breakfast: _____

Lunch: _____

Dinner: _____

Snacks: _____

Exam minus 4 days

Exercise: _____ for _____ minutes

Breakfast: _____

Lunch: _____

Dinner: _____

Snacks: _____

Exam minus 3 days

Exercise: _____ for _____ minutes

Breakfast: _____

Lunch: _____

Dinner: _____

Snacks: _____

Exam minus 2 days

Exercise: _____ for _____ minutes

Breakfast: _____

Lunch: _____

Dinner: _____

Snacks: _____

Exam minus 1 day

Exercise: _____ for _____ minutes

Breakfast: _____

Lunch: _____

Dinner: _____

Snacks: _____

Step 8: Get Your Act Together

Time to complete: 10 minutes to read; time to complete will vary
Activity: Complete the Final Preparations worksheet.

You are in control of your mind and body; you are in charge of test anxiety, your preparation, and your test-taking strategies. Now it's time to take charge of external factors, like the testing site and the materials you need to take to the exam.

Find Out Where the Exam or Exams Are, and Make a Trial Run

Do you know how to get to the testing site? Do you know how long it will take to get there? If not, make a trial run, preferably on the same day of the week at the same time of day as when you will be taking your test. Note, on the Final Preparations worksheet on the next page, the amount of time it will take you to get to the exam site. Plan on arriving 30 to 45 minutes early so you can get the lay of the land, use the bathroom, and calm down. Then figure out how early you will have to get up that morning, and make sure you get up that early every day for a week before the exam.

Gather Your Materials

The night before the exam, lay out the clothes you will wear and the materials you have to bring with you to the exam. Plan on dressing in layers; you won't have any control over the temperature of the examination room. Have a sweater or jacket that you can take off if it's warm. Use the checklist on the Final Preparations worksheet to help you pull together what you will need.

Don't Skip Breakfast

Even if you don't usually eat breakfast, do so on exam morning. A cup of coffee doesn't count. Don't eat doughnuts or other sweet foods, either; a sugar high will leave you with a sugar low in the middle of the exam. A mix of protein and carbohydrates is best: Cereal with milk and just a little sugar, or eggs with toast, will do your body a world of good.

Step 9: Do It!

Time to complete: 10 minutes, plus test-taking time
Activity: Ace the Praxis® tests!

Fast-forward to exam day. You are ready. You made a study plan and followed through. You practiced your test-taking strategies while working through this book. You are in control of your physical, mental, and emotional state. You know when and where to show up and what to bring with you. In other words, you are better prepared than most of the other people taking the exam. You are psyched.

Just one more thing. When you are finished with the exam, you will have earned a reward. Plan a celebration. Call up your friends and plan a party, or have a nice dinner for two—whatever your heart desires. Give yourself something to look forward to. And then do it. Go into the exam full of confidence and armed with test-taking strategies you have practiced until they're second nature. You are in control of yourself, your environment, and your performance on the exam. You are ready to succeed. So do it. Go in there and ace the exam. And look forward to your future career as a teacher!

FINAL PREPARATIONS

Getting to the Exam Site

Location of exam site: _____

Date: _____

Departure time: _____

Do I know how to get to the exam site?   Yes ___   No ___

If no, make a trial run.

Time it will take to get to the exam site: _____

Things to Lay Out the Night Before

Clothes I will wear   _____

Sweater/jacket   _____

Watch   _____

Calculator   _____

Photo ID   _____

Admission ticket   _____

Four #2 pencils and
blue or black ink pens
(if taking the paper-
based test)   _____

Other Things to Bring/Remember

_____

_____

_____

_____

_____

_____

_____

CHAPTER

3 ▶

PRAXIS II® MATHEMATICS: CONTENT KNOWLEDGE DIAGNOSTIC TEST (5161)

CHAPTER SUMMARY

This is the first of the two full-length exams in this book based on the structure and difficulty level of the Praxis II® Mathematics: Content Knowledge test. Use this test to see how you would do if you were to take the exam today.

This chapter contains a practice test that mirrors the Praxis II® Mathematics: Content Knowledge exam. Though the actual exam you will take might be computer-based, the question types for each exam are replicated here for you in the book.

As you take this first test, do not worry too much about timing. The actual time you will be allotted for each exam is at the beginning of each test, but you should take this Diagnostic Test in as relaxed a manner as you can to find out which areas you are skilled in and in which ones you will need extra work.

After you finish taking your practice test, you should review the answer explanations. See A Note on Scoring after the final answer explanation to find information on how to score your exam.

Good luck!

1.	ⓐ	ⓑ	ⓒ	ⓓ
2.	ⓐ	ⓑ	ⓒ	ⓓ
3.	ⓐ	ⓑ	ⓒ	ⓓ
4.	ⓐ	ⓑ	ⓒ	ⓓ
5.	ⓐ	ⓑ	ⓒ	ⓓ
6.	ⓐ	ⓑ	ⓒ	ⓓ
7.	ⓐ	ⓑ	ⓒ	ⓓ
8.	ⓐ	ⓑ	ⓒ	ⓓ
9.	ⓐ	ⓑ	ⓒ	ⓓ
10.	ⓐ	ⓑ	ⓒ	ⓓ
11.	ⓐ	ⓑ	ⓒ	ⓓ
12.	ⓐ	ⓑ	ⓒ	ⓓ
13.	ⓐ	ⓑ	ⓒ	ⓓ
14.	ⓐ	ⓑ	ⓒ	ⓓ
15.	ⓐ	ⓑ	ⓒ	ⓓ
16.	ⓐ	ⓑ	ⓒ	ⓓ
17.	ⓐ	ⓑ	ⓒ	ⓓ
18.	ⓐ	ⓑ	ⓒ	ⓓ
19.	ⓐ	ⓑ	ⓒ	ⓓ
20.	ⓐ	ⓑ	ⓒ	ⓓ

21.	ⓐ	ⓑ	ⓒ	ⓓ
22.	ⓐ	ⓑ	ⓒ	ⓓ
23.	ⓐ	ⓑ	ⓒ	ⓓ
24.	ⓐ	ⓑ	ⓒ	ⓓ
25.	ⓐ	ⓑ	ⓒ	ⓓ
26.	ⓐ	ⓑ	ⓒ	ⓓ
27.	ⓐ	ⓑ	ⓒ	ⓓ
28.	ⓐ	ⓑ	ⓒ	ⓓ
29.	ⓐ	ⓑ	ⓒ	ⓓ
30.	ⓐ	ⓑ	ⓒ	ⓓ
31.	ⓐ	ⓑ	ⓒ	ⓓ
32.	ⓐ	ⓑ	ⓒ	ⓓ
33.	ⓐ	ⓑ	ⓒ	ⓓ
34.	ⓐ	ⓑ	ⓒ	ⓓ
35.	ⓐ	ⓑ	ⓒ	ⓓ
36.	ⓐ	ⓑ	ⓒ	ⓓ
37.	ⓐ	ⓑ	ⓒ	ⓓ
38.	ⓐ	ⓑ	ⓒ	ⓓ
39.	ⓐ	ⓑ	ⓒ	ⓓ
40.	ⓐ	ⓑ	ⓒ	ⓓ

41.	ⓐ	ⓑ	ⓒ	ⓓ
42.	ⓐ	ⓑ	ⓒ	ⓓ
43.	ⓐ	ⓑ	ⓒ	ⓓ
44.	ⓐ	ⓑ	ⓒ	ⓓ
45.	ⓐ	ⓑ	ⓒ	ⓓ
46.	ⓐ	ⓑ	ⓒ	ⓓ
47.	ⓐ	ⓑ	ⓒ	ⓓ
48.	ⓐ	ⓑ	ⓒ	ⓓ
49.	ⓐ	ⓑ	ⓒ	ⓓ
50.	ⓐ	ⓑ	ⓒ	ⓓ
51.	ⓐ	ⓑ	ⓒ	ⓓ
52.	ⓐ	ⓑ	ⓒ	ⓓ
53.	ⓐ	ⓑ	ⓒ	ⓓ
54.	ⓐ	ⓑ	ⓒ	ⓓ
55.	ⓐ	ⓑ	ⓒ	ⓓ
56.	ⓐ	ⓑ	ⓒ	ⓓ
57.	ⓐ	ⓑ	ⓒ	ⓓ
58.	ⓐ	ⓑ	ⓒ	ⓓ
59.	ⓐ	ⓑ	ⓒ	ⓓ
60.	ⓐ	ⓑ	ⓒ	ⓓ

Recommended Time—150 minutes
60 questions

Directions: Read each item and select the response that best answers the question.

1. Find the number of real solutions to this system of equations:
$$2x^2 + y^2 = 24$$
$$x^2 - y^2 = -12$$
   a. four
   b. three
   c. two
   d. one

2. Find the range of the function
$$f(x) = x^2 - 4x - 6.$$
   a. $[-10,\infty)$
   b. $[2,\infty)$
   c. $[-6,\infty)$
   d. all real numbers

3. Find c so that the function $f(x)$ is continuous on the entire real line.
$$f(x) = \begin{cases} 3cx - 5, & x \le -3 \\ -5cx + 1, & x > -3 \end{cases}$$
   a. $-\frac{3}{8}$
   b. $-\frac{1}{4}$
   c. $\frac{1}{4}$
   d. does not exist

4. Solve $\frac{4x - 1}{x + 2} \le 5$
   a. $[-11,-2]$
   b. $(-\infty,-2]$
   c. $(-\infty,-11]\cup(-2,\infty)$
   d. $(-\infty,-2]\cup(11,\infty)$

5. This table gives values of the differentiable functions $f(x)$ and $g(x)$ and their derivatives at $x = 1$.

x	$f(x)$	$f'(x)$	$g(x)$	$g'(x)$
1	3	−5	−3	4

   If $h(x) = f(x) \cdot g(x)$, then $h'(1) =$
   a. 27
   b. −3
   c. 3
   d. −29

6. Given $f(x) = 2x + 1$ and $g(x) = \frac{1}{\sqrt{1 - 3x}}$, find the domain of $g(f(x))$.
   a. $x > -\frac{1}{3}$
   b. $0 < x < \frac{1}{3}$
   c. $x < -\frac{1}{3}$
   d. all real numbers

7. Which of the following best describes the transformations that can be applied to the graph of $g(x) = x^3$ to obtain the graph of $h(x) = -\frac{1}{3}(x + 5)^3 + 7$?
   a. Shift $g(x)$ 5 units right and then 7 units up; then reflect in the x-axis, and then shrink by a factor of $\frac{1}{3}$.
   b. Shift $g(x)$ 5 units left and then 7 units up; then reflect in the x-axis, and then shrink by a factor of $\frac{1}{3}$.
   c. Shift $g(x)$ 5 units left, then reflect in the x-axis, then shrink by a factor of $\frac{1}{3}$, and then shift up 7 units.
   d. Shift $g(x)$ 5 units right, then reflect in the x-axis, then shrink by a factor of $\frac{1}{3}$, and then shift up 7 units.

8. Given that $\lim_{x \to 4} \frac{2x^2 + bx - 4}{x - 4} = 9$, find b.
   a. $-\frac{19}{4}$
   b. 0
   c. −9
   d. −7

9. An insurance company bought a new truck to use for roadside assistance. The new truck cost $64,000. The company plans to sell the truck at auction in 10 years for $30,000. Assuming the value of the truck decreases linearly over time, find the best estimate for the value of the truck after 6 years of ownership.

a. $50,400
b. $60,600
c. $56,000
d. $43,600

10. Two dice are loaded so that each has the property that a 2 or a 4 is three times as likely to appear on each roll as a 1, 3, 5, or 6, which are all equally likely to appear. What is the probability that a sum of 7 will appear when the two dice are rolled?

a. 0.14
b. 0.07
c. 0.109
d. 0.218

11. Suppose A is a 2-by-2 invertible matrix, with X and B 2-by-1 matrices. Which of the following statements is/are true about the matrix equation $AX = B$?

I. The equation has no solution.
II. The equation has one unique solution.
III. The equation has a solution of the form $X = A^{-1}B$.
IV. The equation has a solution of the form $X = BA^{-1}$.

a. I only
b. II and IV
c. II and III
d. III and IV

12. The number of bacteria present at time t is modeled by $P(t) = P_0 e^{kt}$, where $P(t)$ is the number of bacteria present at time t, P_0 is the number of bacteria present at $t = 0$, and k is the growth constant. If the researcher notices that the number of bacteria triples in 1 hour, approximately how long will it take for the number of bacteria to reach 10 times the number of bacteria initially present in the sample, P_0?

a. 1.2 hours
b. 2.1 hours
c. 1.1 hours
d. 2.3 hours

13. Find the inverse of the function $f(x) = \sqrt[3]{4 - 5x}$.

a. $f^{-1}(x) = \frac{4 - x^3}{5}$
b. $f^{-1}(x) = \frac{x^3}{5} - 4$
c. $f^{-1}(x) = 5x^{\frac{1}{3}} + 4$
d. $f^{-1}(x) = 4 + 5x^3$

14. Solve for x, $\log_3(x - 3) + \log_3(x + 5) = 2$.

a. −6 only
b. −6 and 4
c. 4 only
d. no solution

15. Find the center and the radius of the circle given by $x^2 + y^2 + 12x - 16y + 36 = 0$.

a. center at (−6,8), radius 64
b. center at (6,−8), radius 8
c. center at (−6,8), radius 8
d. center at (6,−8), radius 64

16. Consider the function $f(x)$, whose graph is sketched here. Suppose the area of region A is 14, the area of region C is 40, and $\int_{-5}^{6} f(x)\,dx = 44$. Find the area of region B.

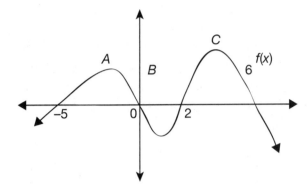

a. 10

b. −10

c. 30

d. 4

17. An oil company charges a flat fee for delivery of heating oil to a residence, and then a certain amount for every gallon (or part of a gallon) that a customer uses. Frank used 90 gallons of oil last month and received a bill from the oil company for $380. Frank's neighbor, Susan, used only 60 gallons of oil last month, and her bill was $260. Determine the oil company's flat fee for delivery of heating oil.

a. $120

b. $4

c. $20

d. $30

18. Convert the polar coordinates $\left(\sqrt{3}, \frac{2\pi}{3}\right)$ to rectangular coordinates (x,y).

a. $\left(\frac{3}{2}, \frac{\sqrt{3}}{2}\right)$

b. $\left(-\frac{3}{2}, \frac{\sqrt{3}}{2}\right)$

c. $\left(-\frac{\sqrt{3}}{2}, \frac{\sqrt{3}}{2}\right)$

d. $\left(-\frac{\sqrt{3}}{2}, \frac{3}{2}\right)$

19. Suppose a particle moves along the x-axis with acceleration given by the function $a(t) = \frac{1}{\sqrt[3]{t}} + t$, for $t > 0$. Find the velocity function for this particle if $v(8) = 24$.

a. $\frac{3}{2}\left(\sqrt[3]{t}\right)^2 - 14$

b. $\frac{3}{2}\left(\sqrt{t}\right)^3 + 24$

c. $\frac{3}{2}\left(\sqrt[3]{t}\right)^2 + 24$

d. $\frac{3}{2}\left(\sqrt[3]{t}\right)^2 + 14$

20. Which of the following is an exponential function that passes through the points $(2,24)$ and $(5,3)$?

a. $f(x) = 96 \cdot \left(\frac{1}{2}\right)^x$

b. $f(x) = 6 \cdot (2)^x$

c. $f(x) = -7x + 38$

d. $f(x) = \frac{3}{8} \cdot (8)^x$

21. Which of the following definite integrals represents the area of the region bounded by the curves $f(x) = 2x$ and $g(x) = -x^2 + 8$?

a. $\int_{-2}^{4} -x^2 - 2x + 8\,dx$

b. $\int_{-4}^{2} x^2 + 2x - 8\,dx$

c. $\int_{-4}^{2} -x^2 - 2x + 8\,dx$

d. $\int_{-2}^{4} x^2 + 2x + 8\,dx$

22. Find the period and phase shift for the function $f(x) = 2\sin[8(x + \frac{\pi}{3})]$.

a. period $= \frac{\pi}{4}$; phase shift $= -\frac{\pi}{3}$

b. period $= \frac{\pi}{4}$; phase shift $= \frac{\pi}{3}$

c. period $= \frac{\pi}{3}$; phase shift $= \frac{\pi}{4}$

d. period $= 2\pi$; phase shift $= \frac{\pi}{3}$

23. Given that 2 is a zero of the function, find the solutions to the equation $f(x) = 0$.

a. $x = 1,-\frac{3}{2},2$

b. $x = -1,\frac{3}{2},2$

c. $x = -1,\frac{2}{3},2$

d. $x = -1,-\frac{2}{3},2$

24. A 20-foot antenna sits on top of a skyscraper. A surveyor on the ground measures the angle of elevation of the bottom of the antenna to be 72°, and measures the angle of elevation to the top of the antenna to be 72.8°. Find the height of the skyscraper to the nearest foot.

a. 403 feet

b. 384 feet

c. 364 feet

d. 423 feet

25. Solve the equation
$$\begin{bmatrix} -1 & 4 \\ 2 & 6 \end{bmatrix} \cdot \begin{bmatrix} x \\ y \end{bmatrix} = \begin{bmatrix} 12 \\ 4 \end{bmatrix}.$$

a. 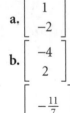 $\begin{bmatrix} 1 \\ -2 \end{bmatrix}$

b. $\begin{bmatrix} -4 \\ 2 \end{bmatrix}$

c. $\begin{bmatrix} -\frac{11}{7} \\ \frac{12}{7} \end{bmatrix}$

d. $\begin{bmatrix} 2 \\ \frac{1}{6} \end{bmatrix}$

26. Find $\lim\limits_{x \to \infty} \frac{15x}{3x^2 + 9}$.

a. 0

b. 5

c. ∞

d. −∞

27. Let $y = f(x)$ be a function whose domain is the open interval $(-2,3)$, and let the derivative of $y = f(x)$ have the graph in the following figure. Using the graph of the derivative of f, find the intervals on which the function is increasing. Each tick mark is one unit.

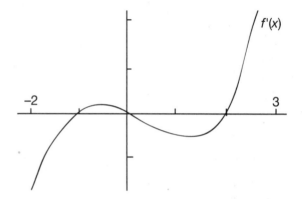

a. $(-2,-0.5) \cup (1,3)$

b. $(-2,-1) \cup (1,2)$

c. $(-1,0) \cup (2,3)$

d. $(-2,-1) \cup (2,3)$

28. Which of the following functions are odd?

I. $f(x) = x^3 + 9x^2 - 7$

II. $g(x) = \frac{2x^2 + 5}{x}$

III. $h(x) = 2\cos3x$ on $[-\pi,\pi]$

IV. $j(x) = 2\sin3x$ on $[-\pi,\pi]$

a. I and III

b. III and IV

c. II and IV

d. II and III

29. The sale prices of homes in a particular region are found to be normally distributed with a mean of $250,000 and standard deviation of $20,000. If 1,000 people bought homes in this region, how many people paid between $230,000 and $270,000?
  a. 840
  b. 680
  c. 950
  d. 815

30. Suppose the position of a particle as a function of time in seconds is given by $x = s(t) = 7t + 24t^2 - t^4$ for $t \geq 0$. Find the time at which the maximum velocity of the particle occurs.
  a. $t = 1$
  b. $t = 2$
  c. $t = 3.5$
  d. no such value

31. A television regularly priced at $600 is on sale for $480. What percentage has the price of the television been discounted?
  a. 2%
  b. 80%
  c. 25%
  d. 20%

32. Find $\int (1 - 5x^2)^9 x\, dx$.
  a. $-\frac{1}{10}(1 - 5x^2)^{10} + C$
  b. $-\frac{1}{100}(1 - 5x^2)^{10} + C$
  c. $-10(1 - 5x^2)^{10} + C$
  d. $-100(1 - 5x^2)^{10} + C$

33. If $\cos\theta = \frac{5}{13}$, for $\frac{3\pi}{2} < \theta < 2\pi$, then $\tan 2\theta =$
  a. $\frac{13}{12}$
  b. $\frac{120}{169}$
  c. $\frac{120}{119}$
  d. $-\frac{120}{169}$

34. Find the coefficient of the x^2y^3 term in the binomial expansion of $(2x - y)^5$.
  a. -40
  b. -20
  c. -240
  d. 20

35. A restaurant offers a $7.50 lunch special that includes a sandwich, a cup of soup, a cookie, and a beverage. The sandwiches available are peanut butter and jelly, ham and cheese, chicken salad, and meatball. The soup choices are tomato, cream of broccoli, and chicken noodle. For cookies, the restaurant offers chocolate chip, oatmeal raisin, sugar, peanut butter, and white chocolate chip. The beverages available are water, iced tea, milk, and soda. How many different lunch specials consisting of a sandwich, a cup of soup, a cookie, and a beverage are there?
  a. $4 \cdot 5!$
  b. $2 \cdot 5!$
  c. $5 \cdot 4!$
  d. $2 \cdot 4!$

36. A concert hall has 30 rows of seats. There are 80 seats in the first row. Each row contains two more seats than the row in front of it. Thus, the second row has 82 seats, the third row 84 seats, and so on. What is the seating capacity of the concert hall?
  a. 2,820
  b. 3,270
  c. 2,100
  d. 2,460

37. Find $\log_7 3$ to the nearest thousandth.
  a. 0.565
  b. 1.771
  c. 0.847
  d. 3.045

38. If $i = \sqrt{-1}$, find $i^{23} \cdot \left(\frac{2 + i}{3 - i}\right)$.

   a. $\frac{1}{2} + \frac{1}{2}i$

   b. $\frac{1}{2} - \frac{1}{2}i$

   c. $-\frac{1}{2} + \frac{1}{2}i$

   d. $-\frac{1}{2} - \frac{1}{2}i$

39. The matrix $A = \begin{bmatrix} -4 & -3 \\ c & 9 \end{bmatrix}$ is invertible for all

values of c EXCEPT

   a. $\frac{27}{4}$

   b. $\frac{4}{3}$

   c. 12

   d. −12

40. Assuming no subsequent deposits or withdrawals, how much money, rounded to the nearest cent, must be deposited in an account today in order to accumulate $22,000 in seven years if the nominal interest rate is 6.7% compounded quarterly?

   a. $13,972.42

   b. $13,763.18

   c. $13,817.38

   d. $13,781.77

41. Given $\triangle ABC$, find the measure of $\angle B$.

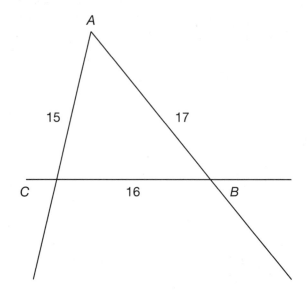

   a. 58.82°

   b. 53.97°

   c. 66.42°

   d. 36.03°

42. Find the equation of the line perpendicular to the line $3x - 4y + 20 = 0$ passing through the point $(-4,12)$.

   a. $y = \frac{3}{4}x + 15$

   b. $y = -\frac{4}{3}x + 5$

   c. $y = -\frac{4}{3}x + \frac{20}{3}$

   d. $y = \frac{3}{4}x - 13$

43. The graph of $f(x) = \frac{3x^2 + 22x - 45}{x + 9}$ consists of a line and a removable discontinuity. Find the equation of the line and the coordinates of the removable discontinuity.

   a. line: $y = 3x - 5$; removable discontinuity: $(-9,-32)$

   b. line: $y = 3x - 5$; removable discontinuity: $(-9,-5)$

   c. line: $y = x + 9$; removable discontinuity: $(3,5)$

   d. line: $y = x + 9$; removable discontinuity: $(9,18)$

44. Given the following scatter plot of a set of data, the correlation coefficient is closest to which value?

    a. 1
    b. −1
    c. 0.05
    d. −0.05

45. The following is a list of the salaries of 12 employees at an advertising firm. Use this data to determine the relationships between the mean salary, median salary, and mode salary at this particular firm.

$32,500, $28,700, $15,000, $68,000, $72,700, $90,000, $84,000, $94,400, $95,500, $68,000, $79,900, $120,000

    a. The median salary is greater than both the mean salary and the mode salary.
    b. The median salary is greater than the mode salary, but less than the mean salary.
    c. The mode salary is greater than both the median salary and the mean salary.
    d. The mean salary is greater than both the mode salary and the median salary.

46. In the diagram of the circle centered at G, chords $\overline{AC}$ and $\overline{BE}$ intersect at F. Secant $\overline{DCA}$ and tangent $\overline{DE}$ are drawn to the circle. The length of $\overline{AF}$ is two more than the length of $\overline{CF}$. The length of $\overline{BF}$ is 2. The length of $\overline{EF}$ is 12, and the length of $\overline{CD}$ is 8. Find the length of $\overline{DE}$.

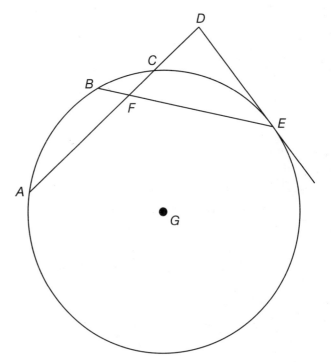

    a. 12
    b. 6
    c. 10
    d. 8

47. After a powerful hurricane hit a small coastal city, residents were told that the city's water could no longer be used for drinking. In order to help its citizens, the city dispatched three trucks—truck 1, truck 2, and truck 3—to deliver large water jugs to every household. Truck 1 could supply every household in 12 hours. Truck 2 could deliver water to all households in 10 hours, and truck 3 could deliver to all households in 14 hours. All three trucks begin delivering water, but truck 2 breaks down two hours later. How many hours in all, to the nearest hour, does it take the three trucks to deliver the water?

a. three
b. four
c. five
d. six

48. A chemist needs 40 liters of 15% solution of hydrochloric acid (HCl). She has a large amount of 5% and 30% HCl solutions and decides to use these solutions to make 40 liters of the 15% solution. How many liters of 30% solution will the chemist need?

a. 16
b. 24
c. 28
d. 12

49. If matrix A is a 3-by-2 matrix, matrix B is a 2-by-3 matrix, and matrix C is a 2-by-4 matrix, then what size is the matrix BAC?

a. 3 by 2
b. 3 by 4
c. 2 by 3
d. 2 by 4

50. Given the equation for an ellipse in standard form $\frac{(x-2)^2}{9} + \frac{(y-1)^2}{5} = 1$, determine the foci of this ellipse.

a. (2,1) and (4,1)
b. (1,0) and (1,4)
c. (0,1) and (2,1)
d. (0,1) and (4,1)

51. Which of the following represents $\cot(\arccos 5x)$ for $0 \le x \le \frac{1}{5}$?

a. $\frac{1}{5x}$
b. $5x$
c. $\frac{5x}{\sqrt{1-25x^2}}$
d. $\frac{\sqrt{1-25x^2}}{5x}$

52. Given the recursive function $a(m,n) =$

$$\begin{cases} n+1, & \text{if } m = 0 \\ a(m-1,1), & \text{if } m > 0 \text{ and } n = 0 \\ a(m-1, a(m,n-1)) & \text{if } m > 0 \text{ and } n > 0 \end{cases}$$

evaluate $a(1,2)$.

a. 8
b. 6
c. 4
d. 2

53. The seventh term of a geometric sequence is 125, and the tenth term is $\frac{125}{64}$. Find the fourteenth term.

a. $\frac{125}{4,096}$
b. $\frac{125}{16,384}$
c. $\frac{125}{1,024}$
d. $\frac{125}{65,536}$

54. If the discriminant of a quadratic function is -32, then

a. the function has two real irrational roots.
b. the function has two real rational roots.
c. the function has one real root.
d. the function has two complex roots.

55. A sphere is inscribed in a cone with radius 6 and height 8. Find the volume of the sphere.
a. $\frac{32}{3}\pi$
b. 36π
c. 12π
d. $2,304\pi$

56. A farmer has 2,000 feet of fencing to enclose three rectangular fields of equal area, as in the figure. Find the maximum total area the farmer can enclose.

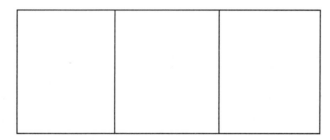

a. 187,500 square feet
b. 750,000 square feet
c. 150,000 square feet
d. 125,000 square feet

57. There is a 40% chance that a doctor visit will result in a subsequent visit to a specialist. There is a 50% chance that a doctor appointment will lead to blood work. There is a 25% chance that a visit to the doctor will result in neither blood work nor a subsequent visit to a specialist. What is the probability that a visit to the doctor will lead to both blood work and a visit to a specialist?
a. 0.10
b. 0.15
c. 0.25
d. 0.90

58. The reduced row echelon form (RREF) that results from the Gauss-Jordan reduction of a system of linear equations in the variables x, y, and z, in that order, is

$$\begin{bmatrix} 1 & 0 & 0 & -4 & 0 \\ 0 & 1 & 3 & 0 \\ 0 & 0 & 0 & 1 \end{bmatrix}$$

Find all solutions to the system of linear equations, if any.
a. $(4,-3,-1,0)$
b. $(z + 4, z - 3, z)$
c. $(-4,3,1)$
d. no solution

59. A student earned a 76% on her first exam in math class. There will be three more exams. What does her average score on these three remaining exams have to be in order to earn an overall average of at least 93%?
a. 99
b. 110
c. 98
d. 96

60. Which of the following is/are true statement(s) about the set of natural numbers
$\cdot = \{1,2,3,\ldots\}$?
   I. The set is closed under addition.
   II. The set has an additive identity element.
   III. The set is closed under subtraction.
   IV. No element in $\cdot$ has a multiplicative inverse.
a. II, III, and IV
b. I and III
c. I only
d. I and IV

Answers and Explanations

1. a. We can use the method of elimination:

$$2x^2 + y^2 = 24$$

$$+\ x^2 - y^2 = -12$$

$$\overline{3x^2 + 0y = 12}$$

So, $3x^2 = 12 \Rightarrow x^2 = 4 \Rightarrow x = \pm 2$. For $x = 2$, we can use either equation to find the corresponding y-values: Using $x^2 - y^2 = -12$ and $x = 2$, we obtain $4 - y^2 = -12 \Rightarrow y^2 = 16 \Rightarrow y = \pm 4$. We do the same thing for $x = -2$. Now we see that the solutions to this system are $(-2,-4)$, $(-2,4)$, $(2,-4)$, $(2,4)$, and so there are *four* real solutions.

2. a. We recognize the graph of this function as a parabola opening up:

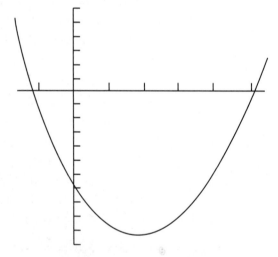

The x-coordinate of the vertex is given by $x = -\frac{b}{2a} = -\frac{-4}{2(1)} = 2$, and the y-coordinate is $f(2) = 2^2 - 4(2) - 6 = -10$. The range of a function is the set of all y-values such that $f(x) = y$. On the parabola this is seen to be all y-values greater than or equal to the y-value of the vertex, -10. Choice **b** uses the x-value instead of the y-value. Choice **c** is the range of a parabola opening down. Choice **d** is the domain of the function.

3. b. Since $f(x)$ is a piecewise defined linear function, both of its pieces are continuous everywhere except possibly at $x = -3$. In order for $f(x)$ to be continuous at $x = -3$, the limit of the function as x approaches -3 from the right, $\lim\limits_{x \to -3^+} f(x)$, must equal the limit of the function as x approaches -3 from the left, $\lim\limits_{x \to -3^-} f(x)$. $\lim\limits_{x \to -3^+} f(x) = \lim\limits_{x \to -3} -5cx + 1 = 15c + 1$. $\lim\limits_{x \to -3} 3cx - 5 = -9c - 5$. Setting $15c + 1 = -9c - 5$ and solving for c gives $c = -\frac{1}{4}$. Choices **a** and **c** result from a sign error in the calculation. Choice **d** is impossible.

4. c. Begin by rewriting the given inequality as $\frac{4x - 1}{x + 2} - 5 \le 0$. We then find the least common denominator (LCD), so that we can combine the two terms:

$$\frac{4x - 1}{x + 2} - \frac{5(x + 2)}{x + 2} \le 0 \Rightarrow \frac{4x - 1 - 5x - 10}{x + 2} \le 0$$

$$\Rightarrow \frac{-x - 11}{x + 2} \le 0.$$

From this we see that at $x = -11$ the left-hand side is equal to 0, while at $x = -2$ the left-hand side is undefined. We can organize this information on the real number line and perform a sign analysis:

In order to find where the left-hand side is strictly less than 0, we test values below -11, between -11 and -2, and above -2 in the expression $\frac{-x - 11}{x + 2}$. For example, using $x = -12$, we see we get $\frac{12 - 11}{-12 + 2} = \frac{1}{-10}$. However, all we care about in this situation is whether or not the number is positive or negative; since $\frac{+}{-}$ is negative, we can say that for all numbers less than $x = -11$ the expression $\frac{-x - 11}{x + 2}$ is less than 0, and satisfies our inequality. We summarize this result as follows:

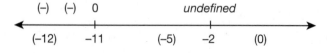

Next we can use, say, $x = -5$ to test between -11 and -2. We get $\frac{(-)}{(-)}$, which tells us that, for all numbers between $x = -11$ and $x = -2$, $\frac{-x - 11}{x + 2}$ is greater than 0, and therefore does *not* satisfy our inequality.

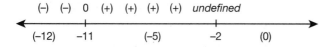

(−)　(−)　0　(+)　(+)　(+)　(+)　*undefined*

(−12)　−11　(−5)　−2　(0)

Finally, choose $x = 0$ to represent all numbers greater than -2. This gives $\frac{(-)}{(+)}$, so for all numbers greater than -2, $\frac{-x - 11}{x + 2} < 0$.

(−)　(−)　0　(+)　(+)　(+)　(+)　*undefined*　(−)　(−)　(−)

(−12)　−11　(−5)　−2　(0)

Since the function is exactly 0 at $x = -11$, we include -11 in the solution set. Because the function is undefined at $x = -2$, we cannot include -2 in the solution set since it is not in the domain of the function. Choices **a**, **b**, and **c** are incorrect, as they involve errors in sign during the calculation, or including $x = -2$.

5. a. Since $h(x) = f(x) \cdot g(x)$ is a product of two functions, we need to use the product rule to compute the derivative of $h(x)$. Thus $h'(1) = f(1)g'(1) + f'(1)g(1)$. The table of values gives values for $f(1)$, $g(1)$, $f'(1)$, $g'(1)$, and $h'(1) = 3 \cdot 4 + -5 \cdot -3 = 27$. Choices **b**, **c**, and **d** are incorrect as they calculate $h'(1)$ incorrectly.

6. c. First we note that the domains of the component functions, $f(x)$ and $g(x)$, are all real numbers and $x < \frac{1}{3}$, respectively. Next we perform the composition $g(f(x)) = \dfrac{1}{\sqrt{1 - 3(2x + 1)}}$ and simplify to get $g(f(x)) = \dfrac{1}{\sqrt{-6x - 2}}$. Then we solve the inequality $-6x - 2 > 0$ since the denominator being 0 results in the function being undefined, and negative values in the radicand result in nonreal numbers. Solving $-6x - 2 > 0$ gives $x < -\frac{1}{3}$. Choice **a** incorrectly changes the direction of the inequality. Choice **b** involves the domain of a component function and the fact that 0 in the denominator must be excluded from the domain. Choice **d** is the domain of the component function $f(x)$.

7. c. Here we need to recognize that the order in which we perform transformations on a function is important. If we start with $g(x) = x^3$ and then shift left 5 units, we have $(x + 5)^3$. Following this with a reflection in the x-axis gives $-(x + 5)^3$. Shrinking by $\frac{1}{3}$ gives $-\frac{1}{3}(x + 5)^3$. Ending with a vertical shift up 7 units gives $h(x) = -\frac{1}{3}(x + 5)^3 + 7$. Choice **a** would give $h(x) = -\frac{1}{3}((x - 5)^3 + 7)$. Choice **b** gives the function $h(x) = -\frac{1}{3}((x - 5)^3 + 7)$, and choice **d** gives the function $h(x) = -\frac{1}{3}((x - 5)^3 + 7)$.

8. c. In order for $\lim\limits_{x \to 4} \dfrac{2x^2 + bx - 4}{x - 4}$ to equal 9, the function $\dfrac{2x^2 + bx - 4}{x - 4}$ must factor as $\dfrac{(2x - c)(x - 4)}{x - 4}$. Thus $\lim\limits_{x \to 4} \dfrac{2x^2 + bx - 4}{x - 4} = \lim\limits_{x \to 4} \dfrac{(2x - c)(x - 4)}{x - 4} = \lim\limits_{x \to 4} \dfrac{(2x - c)(x - 4)}{x - 4} = \lim\limits_{x \to 4} 2x - c = 8 - c$. Solving $8 - c = 9$ for c gives $c = -1$. Substituting this value for c into $\dfrac{(2x - c)(x - 4)}{x - 4}$ gives $\dfrac{(2x + 1)(x - 4)}{x - 4}$, and multiplying gives $\dfrac{2x^2 - 9x - 4}{x - 4}$.

9. d. We can summarize the information given by expressing each of the pairs of time values and dollar values as points: (0, 64,000), (10, 30,000). We can then use the slope formula to determine how much value the truck is losing per year: $\frac{64,000 - 30,000}{0 - 10} =$ −3,400. This means that in 6 years the truck loses 6(3,400) = 20,400 in value. Therefore the value of the truck after 6 years is $64,000 − 20,400 = \$43,600$. Choice **a** is incorrect, a consequence of adding $20,400 to the value of the truck after 10 years. Choice **b** is incorrect and is the value after one year. Choice **c** is incorrect and would be the value after 6 years if the truck lost only $3,000 in value per year.

10. a. In order for this to be a valid probability distribution, the sum of the probabilities must be 1. Thus we have the equation Pr(1) + Pr(2) + Pr(3) + Pr(4) + Pr(5) + Pr(6) = 1. Let Pr(i) = x. Since both 2 and 4 are three times as likely as any other outcome, we have $x + 3x + x + 3x + x + x = 1$. Solving for x, we get $x = 0.1$. Next we consider the experiment of rolling two distinct dice and the possible ways in which to roll a sum of 7. A sum of 7 can be rolled by: rolling a 1 on the first die and a 6 on the second die or vice versa, a 2 on the first and a 5 on the second or vice versa, or a 3 on the first and a 4 on the second or vice versa. This means Pr(sum of 7) = 2Pr(1)Pr(6) + 2Pr(2)Pr(5) + 2Pr(3)Pr(4). Therefore, Pr(sum of 7) = 2(0.1)(0.1) + 2(0.3)(0.1) + 2(0.1)(0.3) = 0.14. Choice **b** is incorrect because it takes into account only half of the ways to roll a sum of 7. Choice **c** is incorrect because it assigns only the 2 or the 4 as three times as likely. Choice **d** is incorrect because it is twice choice **c**.

11. c. Since A is invertible, we can find A^{-1} and use it to solve for X in $AX = B$. In order to do this, we need to multiply AX on the left by A^{-1}, and whatever we do to one side of an equation we must do to the other side. However, matrix multiplication is not commutative, so multiplying AX on the left means we also have to multiply B on the left: $A^{-1}AX = A^{-1}B$. Performing the multiplication gives $X = A^{-1}B$.

12. b. First, we set up the equation $3P_0 = P_0e^{k\cdot 1}$. Dividing both sides by P_0, we get $3 = e^k$. Solving for k by taking the natural logarithm of both sides gives: $\ln 3 = \ln e^k \Rightarrow \ln 3 = k$. This is the decay constant. We now use this decay constant to determine the time it will take for the bacteria to grow to 10 times its initial amount, P_0. Set up the equation: $10P_0 = P_0e^{\ln 3 \cdot t}$ and solve for t: $10P_0 = P_0e^{\ln 3 \cdot t} \Rightarrow 10 = e^{\ln 3 \cdot t} \Rightarrow 10 = (e^{\ln 3})^t$ using rules of exponents. We then recognize $e^{\ln 3} = 3$, so we have $10 = 3^t$. We solve for t by taking the natural logarithm of both sides: $\ln 10 = \ln 3^t$, and applying properties of logarithms: $\ln 10 = t \ln 3$. Therefore, $t = \frac{\ln 10}{\ln 3} \approx 2.1$. Choice **a** is incorrect and results from incorrectly applying rules of logarithms and getting $\ln(\frac{10}{3})$. Choice **c** is incorrect and results from incorrectly concluding that the decay constant is the time we're looking for. Choice **d** is incorrect and would result from thinking that since the decay constant is $\ln 3$, then the time should be $\ln 10$.

13. a. To find the inverse of a function, we need to apply the idea that inverse functions switch the roles of inputs, x, and outputs, y. We represent this by switching x and y in the given function: $x = \sqrt[3]{4 - 5y}$. Next we solve for y: $x^3 = \left(\sqrt[3]{4 - 5y}\right)^3$, $x^3 = 4 - 5y$, $y = \frac{4 - x^3}{5}$. Choice **b** uses incorrect order of operations when solving for y. Choice **c** incorrectly simplifies the original function while inverting only the subtraction. Choice **d** incorrectly uses the inverse function of the cube root function and the inverse of subtraction.

14. c. Apply properties of logarithms to the left-hand side: $\log_3((x - 3)(x + 5)) = 2$; multiplying in the argument of the logarithm gives $\log_3(x^2 + 2x - 15) = 2$. Next we rewrite this logarithmic function in exponential form as $(x^2 + 2x - 15) = 3^2 = 9$. We now have the quadratic equation: $x^2 + 2x - 24 = 0$. We can solve this by factoring: $(x - 4)(x + 6) = 0$. The solutions to the quadratic equation are $x = 4$ and $x = -6$. However, the solution to our original logarithmic equation is $x = 4$ only, since $x = -6$ would give the logarithm of a negative number, which is undefined. Recall that the domain of $y = \log_b(x)$ is $x > 0$. Choice **a** would result from remembering the domain of a log function incorrectly. Choice **b** would result from not checking both solutions in the original equation. Choice **d** would result from incorrect factoring or from not knowing how to isolate the variable in the original equation.

15. c. The standard form of a circle is $(x - h)^2 + (y - k)^2 = r^2$ with center at (h,k) and radius r. We are given a circle in general form. In order to convert a general form quadratic to one in standard form, we use the method of completing the square:
$$x^2 + y^2 + 12x - 16y + 36 = 0$$
$$(x^2 + 12x) + (y^2 - 16y) = -36$$
$$(x^2 + 12x + 36) + (y^2 - 16y + 64)$$
$$= -36 + 36 + 64$$
$$(x + 6)^2 + (y - 8)^2 = 64$$
Choice **a** has the correct center, but fails to take the square root to obtain the radius. Choice **b** gives the incorrect center, using the signs in front of the variables from the standard form. Choice **d** gives the incorrect center and incorrect radius.

16. a. $\int_{-5}^{6} f(x)\,dx = 44$ can be expressed as
$$\int_{-5}^{6} f(x)\,dx = \int_{-5}^{0} f(x)\,dx + \int_{0}^{2} f(x)\,dx$$
$+ \int_{2}^{6} f(x)\,dx$. Since region A is entirely above the x-axis, the area or region $A = \int_{-5}^{0} f(x)\,dx$. Region C is also entirely above the x-axis, so the area of region $C = \int_{2}^{6} f(x)\,dx$. Thus,
$$\int_{0}^{2} f(x)\,dx = \int_{-6}^{5} f(x)\,dx - \int_{-6}^{0} f(x)\,dx$$
$- \int_{2}^{5} f(x)\,dx$, and
$$\int_{0}^{2} f(x)\,dx = 44 - 14 - 40 = -10.$$
Since -10 is the signed area of region B, the area of region B is 10. Choice **b** confuses the definite integral with area. The definite integral gives "signed" area, while area as a measurement is always positive. Choice **c** thinks we can find the desired area by subtracting the area of region A from $\int_{-5}^{6} f(x)\,dx = 44$. Choice **d** subtracts the area of region C from $\int_{-5}^{6} f(x)\,dx = 44$.

17. c. We find the price per gallon charged by the oil company by computing the slope of the line through the points (90,380) and (60,260). $m = \frac{380 - 260}{90 - 60} = \frac{120}{30} = \$4$ per gallon. We can use either Frank's or Susan's usage to find the delivery fee. Using Frank's, we see that since he used 90 gallons, his usage charge is \$360. This is \$20 less than his overall bill. It follows that the flat delivery fee must \$20. Choice **a** confuses the difference between the bills with the flat fee. Choice **b** confuses the price per gallon with the flat fee. Choice **d** mistakes the difference in gallons used for the flat fee.

18. d. $\left(\sqrt{3}, \frac{2\pi}{3}\right)$ is a point of the form (r,θ). In order to convert points of the form (r,θ) to rectangular coordinates (x,y), we use the facts that $x = r\cos\theta$ and $y = r\sin\theta$. For $x = r\cos\theta$, we have $x = \sqrt{3}\cos\left(\frac{2\pi}{3}\right)$.

$\cos\left(\frac{\pi}{3}\right) = \frac{1}{2}$, but $\left(\frac{2\pi}{3}\right)$ is in quadrant II, so $\cos\left(\frac{2\pi}{3}\right) = -\frac{1}{2}$. We conclude that

$x = \sqrt{3} \cdot \left(-\frac{1}{2}\right) = -\frac{\sqrt{3}}{2}$. For $y = r\sin\theta$,

$y = \sqrt{3}\sin\left(\frac{2\pi}{3}\right)$. The sine function is

positive in quadrant II, so $y = \sqrt{3}\frac{\sqrt{3}}{2} = \frac{3}{2}$. Choice **a** mistakes the special angle values of the sine and cosine and does not recognize the angle as one in quadrant II. Choice **b** recognizes that the cosine of a QII angle is negative, but uses the wrong special angle values. Choice **c** does not multiply the y-coordinate by $\sqrt{3} = r$.

19. a. Since $v(t) = \int a(t)\,dt$, it would be beneficial to rewrite $a(t)$ in a way that makes using the simple power rule for integration easier:

$v(t) = \int a(t)\,dt = \int t^{-\frac{1}{3}} + t\,dt.$

$v(t) = \int t^{-\frac{1}{3}} + t\,dt = \frac{3}{2}t^{\frac{2}{3}} + \frac{t^2}{2} + c.$

We now use the condition $v(8) = 24$ to determine c:

$v(8) = \frac{3}{2}(8)^{\frac{2}{3}} + \frac{(8)^2}{2} + c$

$v(8) = \frac{3}{2}(\sqrt[3]{8})^2 + \frac{(8)^2}{2} + c$

$24 = \frac{3}{2}(2)^2 + \frac{64}{2} + c$

$24 = 6 + 32 + c$

Therefore $c = -14$. Choice **b** thinks that the initial condition $v(0) = 24$ is given rather than $v(3)$ and incorrectly rewrites the radical term. Choice **c** only mistakes the initial condition. Choice **d** makes a sign error.

20. a. All answer choices that are exponential functions are of the form $f(x) = ab^x$. Using this form we can write (2,24) as $24 = ab^2$ and (5,3) as $3 = ab^5$. Next we need to remember that an exponential function can be characterized by data that exhibits a constant ratio of y-values for consecutive x-values. Thus we divide: $\frac{24}{3} = \frac{ab^2}{ab^5}$, and this gives $8 = b^{-3}$.

Therefore $b = 8^{-\frac{1}{3}} = \frac{1}{\sqrt[3]{8}} = \frac{1}{2}$. There is only one answer choice with base $\frac{1}{2}$. Choice **b** does not account for the negative exponent and thus has a base of 2. Choice **c** is a linear function whose slope could be found by using the two given points. Choice **d** fails to take the cube root of 8 and account for the negative exponent.

21. c. We can understand the area between two curves as $\int_a^b$ top curve − bottom curve dx, where a and b are the x-values that bound the region and where the two curves intersect. The graph of $f(x)$ is a line with slope 2 and y-intercept 0. The graph of $g(x)$ is a parabola opening down:

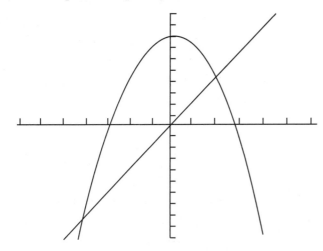

Thus the top curve must be $g(x)$ and $f(x)$ is, therefore, the bottom curve, and we have $\int_a^b (-x^2 + 8) - (2x)\, dx$. All that is left to find are the x-values at which these two functions intersect. We do this by setting the functions equal and solving for x: $-x^2 + 8 = 2x$. We can rewrite this as the quadratic equation $0 = x^2 + 2x - 8$, and this factors as $0 = (x + 4)(x - 2)$. Therefore, the upper limit of integration is $a = 2$, and the lower limit is $b = -4$. Choice **a** factors incorrectly and so has the incorrect limits of integration. Choice **b** has the incorrect top curve. Choice **d** has both incorrect limits of integration and incorrect top curve.

22. a. For a trigonometric function of the form $f(x) = A\sin(Bx - C)$, the amplitude is given by A, the period is given by $\frac{2\pi}{B}$, and the phase shift is given by $\frac{C}{B}$.

$$f(x) = 2\sin\left[8\left(x + \frac{\pi}{3}\right)\right] =$$

$$f(x) = 2\sin\left(8x + 8\frac{\pi}{3}\right).$$ Therefore the

period is $\frac{2\pi}{8} = \frac{\pi}{4}$, and the phase shift is

$\dfrac{8\left(-\frac{\pi}{3}\right)}{8} = -\frac{\pi}{3}$. Choice **b** has the incorrect phase shift, shifting right instead of left. Choice **c** confuses the period and phase shift. Choice **d** gives the standard period for the sine function, and the incorrect phase shift.

23. c. Since we are told that 2 is a zero of the function, it follows by the factor theorem that $(x - 2)$ is a factor of $f(x)$. This means we can divide $f(x)$ by $(x - 2)$ and expect a 0 remainder and a quadratic polynomial as quotient. We now perform the polynomial long division:

$$
\begin{array}{r}
3x^2 + x - 2 \\
(x - 2)\overline{)3x^3 - 5x^2 - 4x + 4} \\
\underline{3x^3 - 6x^2} \\
0 + x^2 - 4x \\
\underline{x^2 - 2x} \\
-2x + 4 \\
\underline{-2x + 4} \\
0
\end{array}
$$

This means we can write $f(x) = (x - 2)(3x^2 + x - 2)$. Next we notice that we can factor $(3x^2 + x - 2)$ as $(3x - 2)(x + 1)$, so, completely factored, $f(x) = (x - 2)(3x - 2)(x + 1)$. Therefore the solutions to $f(x) = 0$ are $x = -1, \frac{2}{3}, 2$. Choices **a**, **b**, and **d** result from incorrect factoring of the quadratic polynomial.

24. a. We can draw the following diagram:

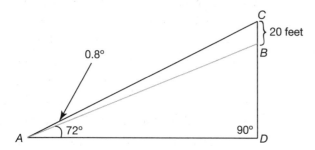

We can see that $m\angle ABD = 180 - 90 - 72 = 18$, so $m\angle ABC = 180 - 18 = 162$. We also see that $m\angle ACB = m\angle ACD = 180 - 90 - 72.8 = 17.2$. Now we use the law of sines to compute the length of $\overline{AB}$: $\frac{20}{\sin 0.8} = \frac{AB}{\sin 17.2}$. Thus $\overline{AB} = 423.584$. Since $\sin\theta = \frac{\text{opposite}}{\text{hypotenuse}}$, we can use $\sin 72° = \frac{BD}{AB} = \frac{\text{height}}{423.584}$, so the height of the tower is $0.951057(423.584) = 402.85$. Choice **b** uses the angle 72.8 instead of 72. Choice **c** tries to correct for the 20-foot tower and uses 72.8 instead of 72. Choice **d** uses the correct angle, but then adds 20 feet.

25. b. Multiplying the matrices, we see that this is the system of linear equations in two unknowns: $\begin{array}{l}-x + 4y = 12 \\ 2x + 6y = 4\end{array}$. We can use the method of elimination to solve this system:

$$2(-x + 4y = 12) \rightarrow -2x + 8y = 24$$
$$\underline{2x + 6y = 4 \quad \rightarrow \quad 2x + 6y = 4}$$
$$0 + 14y = 28$$

Thus $y = 2$. Backsolving gives $x = -4$. Writing this solution in matrix form gives the answer. Choices **a**, **c**, and **d** incorrectly solve the equation.

26. a. To evaluate limits at infinity of rational functions, we focus on the terms of highest degree in both the numerator and the denominator. Thus, as $x \to \infty$, $\frac{15x}{3x^2 + 9} \approx \frac{15x}{3x^2} = \frac{5}{x}$ and as x gets larger and larger $\frac{5}{x}$ gets closer and closer to 0. Choice **b** thinks the numerator and denominator have the same degree. Choice **c** thinks the numerator has higher degree. Choice **d** has the numerator with higher degree than the denominator and also introduces a negative sign.

27. c. The graph we are given is the graph of the *derivative* of the function $f(x)$. The function $f(x)$ is increasing when its derivative is positive. So we need to identify the intervals on which the given graph is positive (i.e., above the x-axis). The graph of the derivative is above the x-axis between -1 and 0, and then again between 2 and 3. Choice **a** thinks we are looking at the graph of the function itself and tries to approximate where the graph is increasing. Choice **b** makes the same mistake as choice **a**, but then does not extend past where the graph is 0. Choice **d** also mistakes the graph of the derivative for the graph of the function.

28. d. An odd function when graphed is symmetric through the origin. We should recognize the graph of the sine function on a symmetric interval, like $[-\pi, \pi]$. An odd function is defined to be a function such that $f(-x) = -f(x)$. Given a polynomial function, one fast way to check if a function is odd is to determine if every exponent on every variable is odd. This is clearly not the case for function I. For II, $g(x)$ can be rewritten as $g(x) = \frac{2x^2 + 5}{x} = \frac{2x^2}{x} + \frac{5}{x} = 2x + 5x^{-1}$. Now it is obvious that each exponent is odd, and so $g(x)$ is an odd function. Choices **a**, **b**, and **c** are incorrect because they contain functions that are *not* odd.

29. d. For a normal distribution we can use the 68–95–99.7 rule. The values we are given are between −1 and 2 standard deviations from the mean. So we have the full 68% of the houses plus $\frac{1}{2}(95 - 68) = 13.5\%$. Thus between −1 and 2 standard deviations from the mean we have 81.5% of houses. Since a total of 1,000 people bought homes, 815 of them paid between \$230,000 and \$290,000. Choices **a**, **b**, and **c** are all incorrect because they use an incorrect variation of the 68–95–99.7 rule.

30. b. Velocity is the derivative of position. Velocity is maximized at t that makes the derivative of velocity 0. We find the velocity function by taking the derivative of the given position function:

$v(t) = x'(t) = 7 + 48t - 4t^3$

In order to find the time at which maximum velocity occurs, we need to find the derivative of the velocity function, set it equal to 0, and solve for x:

$v'(t) = 48 - 12t^2$

$0 = 12(4 - t^2) = 12(2 - t)(2 + t)$

Therefore $t = 2$. Choice **a** is an incorrect calculation. Choice **c** sets velocity to 0 instead of the derivative of velocity. Choice **d** would result if one fails to factor the velocity function instead of the derivative of the velocity function.

31. d. We just need to think about how we compute discounts in everyday life. If the price of an item is \$600 and it is discounted by x, then the new price of the item can be computed by multiplying 600 by x, and then subtracting this result from 600. In this problem we know $600 - 600x = 480$. Solving for x: $x = \frac{600 - 480}{600} = \frac{1}{5} = .2$. Choice **a** is off by a power of 10. Choice **b** divides 480 by 600. Choice **c** divides 600 by 480 and then subtracts 100.

32. b. This is an application of the general power rule for antiderivatives (i.e., the method of u-substitution). It is much easier to think of this roughly as the antiderivative version of the chain rule. In the chain rule for differentiation, we take the derivative of the outside function and then multiply by the derivative of the inside function. In the analogous rule for antiderivatives, we take the antiderivative of the outside function and divide by the derivative of the inside function. In order to apply this rule for antiderivatives, we need to make sure that the integrand is of the appropriate form so that we do not introduce division by a variable expression. In this problem our integrand is of the appropriate form, so we can proceed:

$\int (1 - 5x^2)^9 \, x \, dx = \frac{(1 - 5x^2)^{10}}{10} \cdot \frac{1}{-10x} \, x$
$+ C = -\frac{1}{100}(1 - 5x^2)^{10} + C$

Note: If there was not a factor of x in the original integrand, then we could not use this method to evaluate the integral. Choices **a**, **c**, and **d** are incorrect applications of the general power rule for antiderivatives.

33. c. $\tan 2\theta = \frac{\sin 2\theta}{\cos 2\theta}$. So in order to find $\tan 2\theta$, we need to find $2 \sin \theta$ and $\cos \theta$. This means we will need to use the double-angle identities for both of these trigonometric functions: $\sin 2\theta = 2 \sin \theta \cos \theta$ and $\cos 2\theta = 2 \cos^2 \theta - 1$. But before we do, we need to complete the right triangle corresponding to $\cos \theta = \frac{5}{13}$ in quadrant IV:

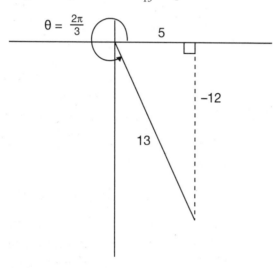

Using the diagram, we see that $\sin \theta = \frac{-12}{13}$. Thus $\sin 2\theta = 2\left(\frac{-12}{13}\right)\left(\frac{5}{13}\right) = -\frac{120}{169}$ and

$\cos 2\theta = 2\left(\frac{5}{13}\right)^2 - 1 = -\frac{119}{169}$. Therefore,

$\tan 2\theta = \frac{-\frac{120}{169}}{-\frac{119}{169}} = \frac{120}{119}$. Choice **a** gives $\tan \theta$.

Choice **b** gives $\sin 2\theta$, for an angle that is not in quadrant IV. Choice **d** gives the $\sin 2\theta$.

34. a. The x^2y^3 term is the fourth term in the binomial expansion of $(2x - y)^5$; as such, it is of the form $\binom{5}{3}(2x)^{5-3}(-y)^3 = \frac{5 \cdot 4 \cdot 3}{3 \cdot 2 \cdot 1}(4x^2)(-y^3) = -40x^2y^3$. Choice **b** is off by a factor of 2, which could result from incorrectly applying properties of exponents. Choice **c** results from using 5 permute 3 instead of 5 choose 3. Choice **d** incorrectly applies rules of exponents to both variable factors.

35. b. Since there are four choices for sandwiches, three choices for soups, five choices for cookies, and four choices for beverages, we use the multiplication principle to see that there are a total of $4 \cdot 3 \cdot 5 \cdot 4$ ways to choose a lunch special. This product can also be written as $2 \cdot 5 \cdot 4 \cdot 3 \cdot 2 \cdot 1$. Choices **a**, **c**, and **d** are incorrect.

36. b. We recognize this as an arithmetic sequence with first term $a_1 = 80$, common difference $d = 2$. To find the seating capacity of the concert hall with 30 rows, we find the sum of the first 30 terms of this arithmetic sequence, S_{30}. We use the fact that the sum of the first n terms of an arithmetic sequence can be computed using the formula $S_n = \frac{n(a_1 + a_n)}{2}$. In order to use this formula, we need to find a_{30}, the 30th term of our concert hall arithmetic sequence. This can be done by noting that for an arithmetic sequence the nth term can be found by $a_n = nd + c$, where $c = a_1 - d$. For us, $c = 80 - 2 = 78$, so $a_{30} = 2 \cdot 30 + 78 = 138$. This means that the number of seats in row 30 is 138. We can now find the seating capacity. It is $S_{30} = \frac{30(80 + 138)}{2} = 3{,}270$. Choice **a** uses a common difference of 1 instead of 2. Choice **c** neglects to find $c = a_1 - d$. Choice **d** simply multiplies 80 by 30 and then adds 60 to account for the additional two seats in each row.

37. a. Since there is no $\log_7(x)$ button on the calculator, we must change the base of this logarithm to a base that is available on a calculator (either base 10 or base e). We choose base e. First let's recognize that $\log_7(x)$ stands for "the exponent on 7 that gives x." If we let $y = \log_7(x)$, then we have the exponential equation $7^y = x$. This means that we can write $\log_7 3$ as $7^y = 3$ and solve this equation for y. When we do this, in general we obtain the change-of-base formula: $\log_g x = \frac{\log_w(x)}{\log_w(g)}$, where g is the base we are given, and w is the base we want. In this problem the base we are given is 7 and the base we want is e, so $\log_7 3 = \frac{\ln(3)}{\ln(7)}$. Typing this into a calculator gives 0.564575. Choice **b** thinks that the change-of-base formula is the reciprocal of the true formula. Choice **c** is $\ln 3 - \ln 7$. Choice **d** is $\ln 3 + \ln 7$.

38. b. To compute this product we can first determine i^{23} using the fact that powers of i are cyclical; that is, $i^0 = 1$, $i^1 = \sqrt{-1}$, $i^2 = -1$, $i^3 = -i$, $i^4 = 1$. This gives us the facts that $i^{4k+0} = 1$, $i^{4k+1} = i$, $i^{4k+2} = -1$, and $i^{4k+3} = -i$. We then note that $23 = 4 \cdot 5 + 3$. Thus $i^{23} = i^{4 \cdot 5 + 3} = -i$. Next we compute the quotient $\left(\frac{2+i}{3-i}\right)$. Division of complex numbers is defined to be multiplication by the conjugate over itself, so $\frac{2+i}{3-i} = \frac{2+i}{3-i} \cdot \frac{3+i}{3+i} = \frac{6 + 2i + 3i - 1}{9 + 1} = \frac{1}{2} + \frac{1}{2}i$. Next we complete the calculation by multiplying by $-i$: $-i\left(\frac{1}{2} + \frac{1}{2}i\right) = -\frac{1}{2}i + \frac{1}{2}$. Choices **a**, **c**, and **d** are all incorrect, as they incorrectly calculate the powers of i.

39. c. A matrix is invertible if and only if it has a nonzero determinant. Recall the determinant of a 2-by-2 matrix is defined as
$$\det\left(\begin{bmatrix} a & b \\ c & d \end{bmatrix}\right) = ad - bc.$$ Thus
$$A = \begin{bmatrix} -4 & -3 \\ c & 9 \end{bmatrix}$$ is invertible if
$$\det\left(\begin{bmatrix} -4 & -3 \\ c & 9 \end{bmatrix}\right) = -36 - (-3c) \neq 0.$$
Therefore, $3c \neq 36 \Rightarrow c \neq 12$. Choices **a**, **b**, and **d** are all incorrect because the matrix is invertible for these values of c.

40. c. Using the formula for discrete compound interest, we set up the equation:
$$22{,}000 = x \cdot \left(1 + \frac{.067}{4}\right)^{4 \cdot 7}$$
Therefore $x = \frac{22{,}000}{(1.01675)^{28}} = 13{,}817.38$. Choice **a** is incorrect because it uses annual compounding. Choice **b** is incorrect because it uses the formula for continuous compound interest, $P = P_0 e^{rt}$. Choice **d** is incorrect because it uses monthly compounding.

41. b. To find $m\angle B$, we us the law of cosines: $b^2 = a^2 + c^2 - 2ac\cos B$. Solving for B:
$$B = \arccos\left(\frac{a^2 + c^2 - b^2}{2ac}\right)$$
$$= \arccos\left(\frac{16^2 + 17^2 - 15^2}{2(16)(17)}\right) = \arccos\left(\frac{10}{17}\right).$$
Therefore $m\angle B \approx 53.97°$. Choice **a** comes from mistaking $\cos B$ as an angle measurement. Choice **c** gives the measure of angle C. Choice **d** gives the angle measure obtained using the sine instead of the cosine.

42. c. We begin by rewriting the given equation in slope-intercept form, so that the slope of the given line is obvious from the formula: $3x - 4y + 20 = 0 \Rightarrow 3x + 20 = 4y \Rightarrow y = \frac{3}{4}x + 5$ Since we are asked for the line perpendicular to this line, we need to use the fact that perpendicular lines have negative reciprocal slopes. In other words, when we multiply these slopes together we should get -1. Since the slope of the given line is $m = \frac{3}{4}$, the slope of the line perpendicular to this line must have slope $m = -\frac{4}{3}$. We now use this slope and the given point to write a linear function in slope-intercept form: $y - 12 = -\frac{4}{3}(x + 4)$, $y = -\frac{4}{3}x - \frac{16}{3} + \frac{36}{3}$, so $y = -\frac{4}{3}x + \frac{20}{3}$. Choice **a** finds the equation on the line parallel to the given line passing through the given point. Choice **b** finds the slope of the perpendicular line, but keeps the y-intercept of the given line. Choice **d** finds the equation of a parallel line and switches the x and y coordinates of the given point.

43. a. We see that $f(x)$ factors as $f(x) = \frac{(3x - 5)(x + 9)}{x + 9}$. This means that away from $x = -9$, $f(x)$ looks like the line $y = -3x - 5$. Since $f(-9) = \frac{0}{0}$, an indeterminate form, $f(x)$ is undefined at $x = -9$. However, we can find $\lim\limits_{x \to -9} \frac{3x^2 + 22x - 45}{x + 9}$:

$$\lim_{x \to -9} \frac{3x^2 + 22x - 45}{x + 9} = \lim_{x \to -9} \frac{(3x - 5)(x + 9)}{x + 9}$$

$$= \lim_{x \to -9} \frac{(3x - 5)(x + 9)}{x + 9} = -32$$

Thus the removable discontinuity occurs at the point $(-9, -32)$. Choice **b** is incorrect because while the equation of the line is correct, the coordinates of the removable discontinuity are incorrect. Choices **c** and **d** are incorrect because in each case both the equation of the line and the coordinate of the removable discontinuity are incorrect.

44. b. This scatter plot has data points that seem to lie along a line with negative slope. This would result in a correlation coefficient that is close to -1. Choice **a** corresponds to a scatter plot that shows the data points lying along a line with positive slope. Choices **c** and **d** correspond to scatter plots that show data that has no apparent linear quality.

45. a. We compute the mean salary by adding up all the salaries and dividing by 12. This gives a mean salary of $70,725. We compute the median salary by rewriting the list of salaries in numerical order from least to greatest. Since there is an even number of salaries, the median is found by taking the average of the middle two salaries: $\frac{72,700 + 79,900}{2} = 76,300$. The mode is the most frequently occurring salary, which is $68,000. Choices **b**, **c**, and **d** are incorrect because they do not identify the correct relationships between the mean salary, median salary, and mode salary.

46. a. Since we are asked to find the length of a tangent segment drawn to a circle and we are given information about a secant segment, we need to recall a theorem that says: *When a secant segment and a tangent segment are drawn to a circle from a point outside the circle, the product of the length of the total secant segment and the length of its external portion is equal to the length of the tangent segment squared.*

Notice that we are given the length of the external portion of the secant; it is $\overline{CD} = 4$. We do not know, however, the length of the internal portion, and this prevents us from knowing the length of the entire secant segment.

In order to find the length of the entire secant segment, we will use the theorem that says: *Given two chords intersecting inside a circle, the product of the lengths of the segments of one chord is equal to the product of the lengths of the segments of the other chord.* Using the latter theorem, first we have that:

$AF \cdot CF = BF \cdot EF$

$(x + 2)(x) = 2 \cdot 12 = 24$

This gives: $x^2 + 2x = 24$. We now find x by solving the quadratic equation $x^2 + 2x - 24 = 0$. The quadratic expression factors: $(x - 4)(x + 6) = 0$; therefore, $x = 4$. Now we see that the product of the entire secant segment and its external segment is $18 \cdot 8 = 144$. By the first theorem, 144 is equal to the length of the tangent segment squared. Therefore, $DE = 12$. Choices **b**, **c**, and **d** are incorrect because they do not identify the correct length of $\overline{DE}$.

47. c. For the first two hours of the job all three trucks are working together. We can determine the rate at which these trucks work together by adding together their per hour rates. Truck 1 completes the job alone in 12 hours. This means truck 1's per hour rate is $\frac{1}{12}$. Similarly, truck 2's rate is $\frac{1}{10}$, and truck 3's is $\frac{1}{14}$. Together their combined rate is $\frac{1}{12} + \frac{1}{10} + \frac{1}{14} = \frac{35 + 42 + 30}{420} = \frac{107}{420}$ job per hour. At the time truck 2 breaks down, the three trucks have completed $2\left(\frac{107}{420}\right) = \frac{214}{420}$ of the job. Notice how the units work out: $2 \text{ hours}\left(\frac{107 \text{ job}}{420 \text{ hours}}\right) = \frac{214}{420}$ of the job completed. After two hours there is still $1 - \frac{214}{420} = \frac{206}{420}$ of the job left. Of course, with truck 2 out of commission, only truck 1 and truck 3 are left to complete the job. Working together, truck 1 and truck 3 can work at a rate of $\frac{1}{12} + \frac{1}{14} = \frac{13}{84}$ job per hour. To find how much time it will take for truck 1 and 3 to complete the remaining $\frac{206}{420}$ of the job, we solve the equation $\frac{13}{84}t = \frac{206}{420}$ for t. This gives $t = \frac{84}{13} \cdot \frac{206}{420} = \frac{206}{65} = 3.16 \approx 3$. Therefore the total time it takes for all three of the trucks to complete the job is the two hours spent working as three trucks plus the 3.16 hours working as two trucks. This gives a total of approximately five hours. Choices **a**, **b**, and **d** are incorrect because they do not correctly answer how many hours it takes the three trucks to deliver the water.

48. a. First, let x be the number of liters of 5% solution and y be the number of liters of the 30% solution. It follows that $x + y = 40$. Taking into account the concentrations of our three solutions, we have that $.05x + .30y = .15(40)$. Now $x + y = 40$ means $y = 40 - x$. We substitute this into our concentration equation: $.05x + .30(40 - x) = .15(40)$. Next we solve for x:

$.05x + .30(40 - x) = .15(40)$

$.05x + 12 - 0.3x = 6$

$-.25x = -6$

$x = 24$

Therefore, $y = 40 - 24 = 16$. Choices **b**, **c**, and **d** do not correctly solve how many liters of 30% solution the chemist will need.

49. d. In order to multiply two matrices A and B, the number of columns in A must equal the number of rows in B. The size of the product matrix AB is then the number of rows in A by the number of columns in B. We apply this idea to the current situation:

$\underset{(2\times3)}{B} \cdot \underset{(3\times2)}{A} \cdot \underset{(2\times4)}{C}$

$\underset{(2\times2)}{BA} \cdot \underset{(2\times4)}{C}$

$\underset{(2\times4)}{BAC}$

Choices **a**, **b**, and **c** are incorrect sizes for matrix ABC.

50. d. An ellipse in standard form $\frac{(x - 2)^2}{9} + \frac{(y - 1)^2}{5} = 1$ indicates that the major axis is horizontal since $a > b$, where $a = \sqrt{9} = 3$ and $b = \sqrt{5}$. The foci of an ellipse lie on the major axis c units away from the center where $c^2 = a^2 - b^2 = 9 - 5 = 4$. Thus, $c = 2$. The center of this ellipse is the point $(2,1)$. Therefore the foci are the points $(0,1)$ and $(4,1)$. Choices **a**, **b**, and **c** are incorrect foci of the ellipse.

51. c. We are given that arccos $5x$. This means that for some angle θ, $\cos \theta = 5x$, so we can use $\theta = $ arccos $5x$. Since $\cos \theta = \frac{\text{adjacent}}{\text{hypotenuse}}$, we can draw this right triangle to calculate $\cot(\text{arccos } 5x)$:

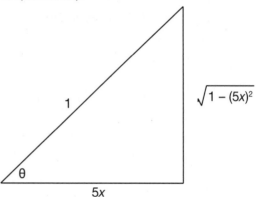

And now we can calculate $\cot \theta = \frac{\text{adjacent}}{\text{opposite}}$ $= \frac{5x}{\sqrt{1-(5x)^2}}$. Choices **a**, **b**, and **d** are incorrect calculations.

52. c. To compute the value of this recursive function, we apply the definition until the process terminates as follows:

$a(1,2) = a(0,a(1,1))$; $a(1,1) = a(0,a(1,0))$

Using part 2 of the definition $a(1,0) = a(0,1)$ and using part 1, $a(0,1) = 1 + 1 = 2$, we substitute this back into the first equation:

$a(1,2) = a(0,a(1,1)) = a(0,a(0,2))$

And $a(0,2) = 3$, so $a(1,2) = a(0,a(1,1)) = a(0,3) = 4$. Choices **a**, **b**, and **d** are incorrect evaluations of the recursive function.

53. b. In order to find any term in a geometric sequence, we need to find the common ratio, r. We are given the tenth term of the sequence, $a_{10} = \frac{125}{64}$, and that the seventh term is $a_7 = 125$. We use these to find r, but first we note that we can move from the first term of a geometric sequence to any other term by multiplying by an appropriate power of the common ratio. For example, $a_2 = a_1 r$ and $a_3 = a_1 r^2$. This example is enough, for now, to establish the general pattern that $a_n = a_1 r^{n-1}$. Now we write our given $a_{10} = \frac{125}{64}$ and $a_7 = 125$ in terms of a_1.

$$a_{10} = \frac{125}{64} = a_1 r^9; \, a_7 = 125 = a_1 r^6$$

Next we divide: $\frac{a_{10}}{a_7} = \frac{\frac{125}{64}}{125} = \frac{a_1 r^9}{a_1 r^6}$

This gives us that $\frac{1}{64} = r^3$, and so our common ratio is $r = \frac{1}{64}$.

Next we notice that $a_{10} = a_7 r^3$, and we use this idea to compute a_{14}: $a_{14} = a_{10} r^4 = \frac{125}{64} \cdot \frac{1}{4^4} = \frac{125}{16,384}$. Choice **a** uses the wrong power of the common ratio. Choice **c** thinks the common ratio is 2. Choice **d** uses 5 as the power on the common ratio.

54. d. The discriminant is $b^2 - 4ac$. It appears in the quadratic formula, $x = \frac{-b \pm \sqrt{b^2 - 4ac}}{2a}$, which calculates the roots of a quadratic function. In other words, the quadratic formula gives us the x-values at which $f(x) = 0$. When $b^2 - 4ac = -32$, then $\sqrt{b^2 - 4ac} = \sqrt{-32} = 4\sqrt{-2} = 4i\sqrt{2}$, and since complex roots occur in conjugate pairs, this means we have two complex roots. Choice **a** occurs when the discriminant is a positive number that is not a perfect square, like 7. Choice **b** occurs when the discriminant is a positive number that is a perfect square, like 36. Choice **c** occurs when the discriminant is 0.

55. b. Begin by drawing a diagram:

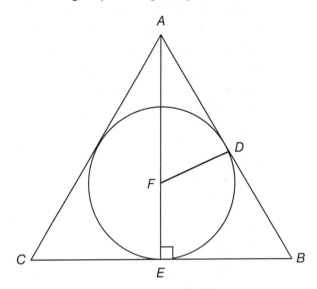

The triangle represents a cross section of the cone. The circle with center F is the cross section of the sphere. Since the sphere is inscribed in the cone, $\overline{AB}$ is tangent to the circle at point D. $\overline{FD}$ is a radius of the circle drawn to a tangent, which means that $\angle ADF$ is a right angle. It follows that $\angle ADF$ is similar to $\angle AEB$. Using similar triangles, we have $\frac{BE}{DF} = \frac{AE}{AD}$. Let $DF = EF = r$, since both segments are radii of the circle. Given $BE = 6$, we have $\frac{6}{r} = \frac{AE}{AD}$. We notice that $(AD)^2 = (AF)^2 - r^2$, and that $AF = AE - r = 8 - r$. Thus, we have $\frac{6}{r} = \frac{8}{\sqrt{(8-r)^2 - r^2}}$. Simplifying gives:

$$\frac{6}{r} = \frac{8}{\sqrt{64 - 16r + r^2 - r^2}}$$

$$\frac{6}{r} = \frac{8}{\sqrt{64 - 16r}}$$

$$\frac{6}{r} = \frac{8}{\sqrt{16(4 - r)}} = \frac{8}{4\sqrt{4 - r}}$$

Now, we can solve for r by cross-multiplying: $6 \cdot 4\sqrt{4 - r} = 8r$. Then

$$24\sqrt{4 - r} = 8r$$

$$3\sqrt{4 - r} = r$$

and squaring both sides gives $9(4 - r) = r^2$.

This is the quadratic equation $r^2 + r - 36 = 0$, which we can factor: $(r + 12)(r - 3) = 0$. Therfore, the radius of the sphere is $r = 3$, and the volume is $V = \frac{4}{3}\pi(3)^3 = 36\pi$. Choices **a**, **c**, and **d** incorrectly calculate the volume of the sphere.

56. d. First, we can label the diagram as follows:

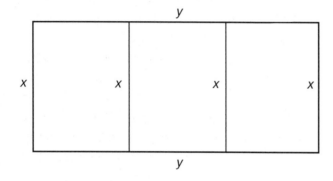

Then, we see that $4x + 2y = 2,000$. The area of our rectangle is given by $A = xy$. Using $4x + 2y = 2,000$, we can write $y = 1,000 - 2x$, so $A = x(1,000 - 2x) = -2x^2 + 1,000$. This is a quadratic function whose maximum occurs at $x = -\frac{b}{2a} = -\frac{1,000}{2(-2)} = 250$. It follows that $y = 500$, so the maximum area is $A = 250 \cdot 500 = 125,000$. Choice **a** uses only $x = 250$ and assumes each field is a square. Choice **b** uses only $y = 500$ and assumes each field is a square. Choice **c** rounds the x side length to 300.

57. b. Let S be the event that a patient must visit a specialist. Let B be the event that a patient must get blood work. We are given that $\Pr(S^c \cap B^c) = 0.25$. By De Morgan's Law, $\Pr(S^c \cap B^c) = \Pr(S \cup B)^c = 0.25$, and by the negation rule $\Pr(S \cup B) = 1 - \Pr(S \cup B)^c = 1 - 0.25 = 0.75$. We are given $\Pr(S) = 0.4$ and $\Pr(B) = 0.5$. Since S and B are not mutually exclusive, $\Pr(S \cup B) = \Pr(S) + \Pr(B) - \Pr(S \cap B)$, and the event $S \cap B$ is the event that a patient must visit a specialist and get blood work. Therefore, $\Pr(S \cap B) = 0.4 + 0.5 - 0.75 = 0.15$. Choice **a** simply subtracts the sum of probability of S and the probability of B from 1. Choice **c** subtracts the probability of the union of S and B from 1. Choice **d** adds the probability of S to the probability of B.

58. d.
$$\begin{bmatrix} 1 & 0 & -4 & 0 \\ 0 & 1 & 3 & 0 \\ 0 & 0 & 0 & 1 \end{bmatrix}$$ represents the system of

linear equations: $\begin{aligned} x - 4z &= 0 \\ y + 3z &= 0. \\ 0 &= 1 \end{aligned}$

However, the statement "$0 = 1$" is a contradiction. Therefore we conclude that there is no solution to this system of linear equations. Geometrically speaking, we are given three planes in 3-D space, and having no solution to this system means that these three planes do not simultaneously intersect each other in a point or along a line. The remaining choices misread the information in the given *RREF* matrix. Choice **a** has this as being a system of four equations in four unknowns. Choice **b** has z as being a free variable, and the system as having infinitely many solutions. This would correspond geometrically to the three planes intersecting along a line. Choice **c** has the three planes intersecting at a single point with the system having one unique solution.

59. a. In order to find the student's average on the remaining three exams, we can assume that she gets the same score on these three exams. This assumption allows us to use the fact that her average on the final three exams is exactly equal to her score on one of these exams. Thus, we solve the equation $\frac{76 + 3x}{4} = 93$ for x and get $x = 98.67$. Choice **b** assumes that there is only one exam remaining. Choice **c** rounds down. Choice **d** results in an overall average of 91.

60. c. We can consider the statements one at a time: Statement I means that if we take any two elements in the natural numbers and add them, the sum is another element in the natural numbers. This is clearly the case. For statement II to be true, there must be an element that acts like 0. This means in · we would need an element, say a, so that $a + n = n + a = n$ for every n a natural number. There is no such element in this set as defined. For statement III, we can consider any number of examples like $2 - 5 = -3$. We see that it is possible to take two natural numbers, subtract them, and have a difference, like −3 that is not a natural number. Therefore, · is not closed under subtraction. For statement IV, a multiplicative inverse is a number, say m, such that $m \cdot n = 1$. While most numbers in · have no multiplicative inverse, 1 is in the set and $1 \cdot 1 = 1$. Thus 1 is its own multiplicative inverse. Choices **a, b,** and **d** are incorrect because they are not true statements about the set of natural numbers.

A Note on Scoring

Your score on this exam is based on the number of questions you answered correctly; there is no guessing penalty for incorrect answers and no penalty for unanswered questions. The Educational Testing Service does not set passing scores for these tests, leaving this up to the institutions, state agencies, and associations that use the tests.

First find the total number of questions you got right on the entire test. As noted earlier, questions you skipped or got wrong don't count; just add up how many questions you got right. Then, divide the number of questions you got right by the total number of questions (60) to arrive at a percentage. You can check your score against the passing scores in the state or organization that requires you to take the exam. If you are unsure of the passing score you will need, you can set yourself a goal of at least 70% of the answers right on the exam.

Use your percentage score in conjunction with the LearningExpress Test Preparation System guide in Chapter 2 of this book to help you devise a study plan. Then, turn to your study materials to work more on those subjects that gave you the most trouble. You should plan to spend more time on the lessons that correspond to the questions you found hardest and less time on the lessons that correspond to areas in which you did well.

NUMBER AND QUANTITY REVIEW

CHAPTER SUMMARY

Numbers are mathematical objects used to measure quantities of some kind. The ideas of quantity and number are fundamental to mathematics as well as the human experience itself. Without these ideas, civilization would not have advanced as it did. In this chapter, without going too much into their history or their importance—which cannot be overstated—we discuss these two ideas and how they are used to solve various mathematical problems relevant to the real world.

Properties of Exponents

The following is a brief review of the properties of exponents and some basic applications of these properties.

Rules of Exponents

Product Rule: $a^m \cdot a^n = a^{n+m}$

Quotient Rule: $\dfrac{a^m}{a^n} = a^{m-n}$

Power Rule: $(a^m)^n = a^{mn}$

Zero Exponent: $a^0 = 1$

Negative Exponent: $a^{-n} = \dfrac{1}{a^n}$

Rational Exponent: $a^{\frac{m}{n}} = \sqrt[n]{a^m}$

For these rules to work in general, it must be assumed that $a \neq 0$.

Before we turn to some examples, we need some vocabulary.

Definition: In the expression $C \cdot b^n$, C is called the *coefficient* (and gives the number of times we add b^n to itself), b is the *base*, and n is the *exponent*. The entire expression, $C \cdot b^n$, is called the *power*.

Here are some examples using the properties just mentioned.

Example

Compute $2^3 \cdot 2^4$.

Solution: $2^3 \cdot 2^4 = (2 \cdot 2 \cdot 2) \cdot (2 \cdot 2 \cdot 2 \cdot 2) = 2^{3+4} = 2^7$

Note that, by the product rule, we could have omitted the expression between the first and second equal signs.

Example

Compute $\frac{3^5}{3^3}$.

Solution: $\frac{3^5}{3^3} = \frac{3 \cdot 3 \cdot 3 \cdot 3 \cdot 3}{3 \cdot 3 \cdot 3} = \frac{3 \cdot 3 \cdot \cancel{3} \cdot \cancel{3} \cdot \cancel{3}}{\cancel{3} \cdot \cancel{3} \cdot \cancel{3}}$

$= 3^{5-3} = 3^2$

Again, the expressions after the first and second equal signs could have been omitted.

Example

Compute $(5^2)^3$.

Solution: $(5^2)^3 = 5^2 \cdot 5^2 \cdot 5^2 = (5 \cdot 5)(5 \cdot 5)(5 \cdot 5)$

$= 5^6$

Notice that we can combine the power rule and the product rule, to get a more general power rule:

$$(C \cdot b^n \cdot b^m)^q = C^q b^{q(n+m)}$$

Combining the power rule and the quotient rule gives another general rule:

$$\left(\frac{C b^n}{D b^m} \right)^q = \frac{C^q}{D^q} b^{q(n-m)}$$

Example

Simplify $\left(\frac{3x^2 y^3}{4xy} \right)^3$.

Solution: $\left(\frac{3x^2 y^3}{4xy} \right)^3 = \left(\frac{3}{4} xy^2 \right)^3 = \frac{27}{64} x^3 y^6$

Rules for rational exponents and negative exponents follow from the product and quotient rules.

Negative Exponents

Without using the quotient rule:

$\frac{5^3}{5^7} = \frac{\cancel{5} \cdot \cancel{5} \cdot \cancel{5}}{\cancel{5} \cdot \cancel{5} \cdot \cancel{5} \cdot 5 \cdot 5 \cdot 5 \cdot 5} = \frac{1}{5^4}$. Applying the quotient rule to this same expression gives $\frac{5^3}{5^7} = 5^{3-7} = 5^{-4}$. So we see that $5^{-4} = \frac{1}{5^4}$, which matches our rule for negative exponents: $b^{-n} = \frac{1}{b^n}$.

Rational Exponents

Rational exponents are exponents of the form $\frac{q}{r}$ such that $r \neq 0$ and q,r are integers with no common factors. *Note:* The integer exponents we have considered thus far are just a special case of rational exponents with $r = 1$.

As stated on the previous page, the general rule for rational exponents is $\sqrt[n]{b^m} = b^{\frac{m}{n}}$, and it is often convenient that we can decide whether to apply the radical first or the power. As long as $b > 0$, we have

$$b^{\frac{m}{n}} = \left(b^{\frac{1}{n}} \right)^m = \left(b^m \right)^{\frac{1}{n}} = \sqrt[n]{b^m} = \left(\sqrt[n]{b} \right)^m$$

This commutativity in the exponent is useful for evaluating expressions.

Example

Simplify $27^{\frac{2}{3}}$.

Solution: $27^{\frac{2}{3}} = \sqrt[3]{27^2} = \left(\sqrt[3]{27} \right)^2 = 3^2 = 9 = 81$

Notice that it is easier to find $\sqrt[3]{27}$ and then square it than it is to find $\sqrt[3]{729}$. This emphasizes the difference in computing $\left(\sqrt[3]{27} \right)^2$ versus $\sqrt[3]{27^2}$.

Before talking more about numbers and the kinds of operations we can do with them, such as exponentiation, it would be beneficial to talk about the kinds of numbers there are.

Real and Complex Number Systems

In this section, we review the evolutions and the construction of the number systems we use to solve equations and measure certain quantities. First, there are the *counting numbers* (which are called the *natural numbers*, and denoted by $\mathbb{N}$). The natural numbers are defined to be the set $\mathbb{N} = \{1, 2, 3, \ldots\}$. If we throw in the number 0 and the negatives of the natural numbers, we end up with the set of *integers*, $\mathbb{Z} = \{\ldots, -3, -2, -1, 0, 1, 2, 3, \ldots\}$. However, the integers do not give us a way to express fractions or parts of a whole; so we need to define the rational numbers, which are defined by the set $\mathbb{Q} = \{\frac{a}{b}$ such that $a, b \in \mathbb{Z}$ and $b \neq 0\}$.

After all this, we quickly discover that there are *irrational numbers*, which are numbers that cannot be expressed as fractions, like π and $\sqrt{2}$. We can think of the real numbers, $\mathbb{R}$, as the set of numbers that contains all rational and irrational numbers. Finally, we are confronted with the fact that there is no real number that is $\sqrt{-1}$ (why we care about this particular radical number will be discussed in a later section). We define $\sqrt{-1} = i$, called the *imaginary unit*, and we define the complex numbers, $\mathbb{C}$, to be the set that contains all real numbers, a, and all imaginary numbers, bi (here b is a real number and i is the imaginary unit), and all combinations of real and imaginary numbers, $a + bi$. As sets, our number systems exhibit the following relationship: $\mathbb{N} \subset \mathbb{Z} \subset \mathbb{Q} \subset \mathbb{R} \subset \mathbb{C}$. The irrational numbers are also a subset of the real numbers, and thus a subset of the complex numbers. However, it is clear that the irrational numbers are not a subset of the rational numbers. The following diagram more clearly shows all the relationships between our number systems.

The Number Systems

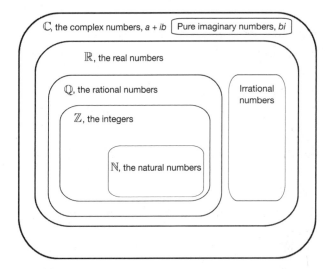

Properties of the Counting Numbers

The simplest real numbers are the *natural numbers* or *counting numbers*. Remember, they are the set $\mathbb{N} = \{1, 2, 3, \ldots\}$. We obtain the (nonnegative) whole numbers by adding 0 to $\mathbb{N}$. Within the whole numbers we have two disjoint sets: the even numbers, $E = \{0, 2, 4, 6, \ldots\}$ and the odd numbers, $O = \{1, 3, 5, 7, \ldots\}$. E and O are disjoint sets (recall that two sets are *disjoint* if they have no elements in common). With these two sets in front of us, it is easy to recall some facts about operations within and between these sets.

ADDITION PROPERTIES OF EVEN AND ODD NUMBERS	MULTIPLICATION PROPERTIES OF EVEN AND ODD NUMBERS
1. *even + odd = odd*	1. *even · odd = even*
2. *even + even = even*	2. *even · even = even*
3. *odd + odd = even*	3. *odd · odd = odd*

In the whole numbers, we recall that some numbers are prime and some are composite. We'll define these in a bit, but let's ease ourselves into the definitions by considering an example.

Definition: A *factor*, *a*, of a number *n* is number that can be multiplied by another number, say *b*, so that $a \cdot b = n$. We also say that *n* is a *multiple* of *a*. (*Note:* We could just as easily say that *n* is a multiple of *b*.)

Example

Factor the number 36.

Solution: First we must admit that we can factor 36 in a number of ways, so a factorization of a number is not unique. We can factor 36 as: $36 = 12 \cdot 3$ or $36 = 9 \cdot 4$ or $36 = 6 \cdot 6$. But in each case we can go further, and each case would end up in the following way. We can fully factor 36 as $36 = 2 \cdot 2 \cdot 3 \cdot 3$. We say that 36 is now *factored completely* (or *fully*). This is called the *prime factorization* of 36. And as long as the factor 1 is not used, this factorization is unique up to the order of the factors.

The "prime" in prime factorization leads us to another discussion.

Prime and Composite Numbers

Definition: A *prime number n* is a number that can be factored as $n \cdot 1$ only. In other words, its factors consist of 1 and itself. Any number that is not prime is called a *composite* number.

Example

Determine which of the following numbers are prime and which are composite: 7, 31, 57, 92.

Solution: 7 and 31 are prime since the factors of 7 are 7 and 1, and similarly for 31. The number 57 can be factored as $57 = 3 \cdot 19$, so 57 is composite. The number 92 is also composite, since $92 = 2 \cdot 46$. Notice we can find other factorizations of 92, and we certainly could factor 96 completely, but finding just one other number besides 1 and 92 that divides 92 is enough to show that 92 is indeed composite.

In this last example we saw that 92 is a composite number. It is also clear that 92 is an even number. *All even numbers except for 2 (and 0) are composite numbers.* This is because every even number has 2 as a factor.

Note: 0 and 1 are neither prime nor composite, by convention.

Finding a prime factorization helps us in other ways, like helping us to find the *greatest common factor* (GCF) and *least common multiple* (LCM) of a set of numbers.

Example

Find the prime factorizations of 42 and 56.

Solution: The prime factorization of 42 is $42 = 2 \cdot 3 \cdot 7$, while the prime factorization of 56 is $56 = 2 \cdot 2 \cdot 2 \cdot 7$.

Least Common Multiple and Greatest Common Factor

Definition: The *greatest common factor* (GCF) of two or more given numbers (or terms) is the largest number that divides all the given numbers.

Example

Find the GCF of 42 and 56.

Solution: First we write down the prime factorizations of both numbers, by simply copying the work we did in the previous example: $42 = 2 \cdot 3 \cdot 7$ and $56 = 2 \cdot 2 \cdot 2 \cdot 7$. We see that both 42 and 56 have a 2 and a 7 in their prime factorizations; therefore we can conclude that the greatest number that divides both numbers is $2 \cdot 7 = 14$.

Definition: The *least common multiple* (LCM) of two or more numbers (or terms) is the smallest number that is a multiple of the given numbers.

Example

Find the least common multiple of 42 and 56.

Solution: Just as in the previous example, we begin with the prime factorizations of our given numbers: $42 = 2 \cdot 3 \cdot 7$ and $56 = 2 \cdot 2 \cdot 2 \cdot 7$. We see in these factorizations the factors and the number of factors we need in the LCM: We need three factors of 2, one of 3, and one of 7. Therefore, the LCM of 42 and 56 is $8 \cdot 3 \cdot 7 = 168$.

Although the natural numbers are useful and have properties that extend to the integers and to the entire real number system, we need much more than just the natural numbers if we want to solve realistic problems. The need for more than just the natural numbers can be seen in the following example.

Example
Solve $x + 3 = 0$ using only natural numbers.

Solution: This linear equation is asking us to determine the x-intercept of the line $y = x + 3$, with slope 1 and y-intercept 3. The solution to this equation is $x = -3$. However, -3 is *not* a natural number, so this equation has *no solution* using only natural numbers.

Definition: A set is said to be *closed* under a given operation or have a *closure property* with respect to a given operation whenever the operation is performed on any two members of the set, and the result of the operation is again in the set.

Example
$2 + 3 = 5$

This example indicates (but does not prove) that the set $\mathbb{N}$ is closed under the operation of addition (+). We added two natural numbers and the result is a natural number. We also note that the natural numbers are closed under the operation of multiplication.

Example
$2 \cdot 3 = 6$

It is natural to point out here that the operations of addition and multiplication of natural numbers (and of all real numbers, for that matter) are *commutative*.

Definition: An operation is said to be *commutative* if changing the order of the numbers involved in the operation does *not* change the result.

Example
$2 + 3 = 5$ and $3 + 2 = 5$

Example
$2 \cdot 3 = 6$ and $3 \cdot 2 = 6$

Nonetheless, the natural numbers are not closed under every operation, and not every operation is commutative.

Example
$2 - 3 = -1$

This example indicates that the set $\mathbb{N}$ is *not* closed under the operation of subtraction (−), since the number -1 is not in the set of natural numbers.

Also notice that $2 - 3 = -1$ while $3 - 2 = 1$, which shows that the operation of subtraction on natural numbers is *not* commutative. The operation of division is also not commutative.

However, the natural numbers under the operations of addition and multiplication do exhibit properties that *extend to the entire set of real numbers and complex numbers.*

Associative Property of Addition and Multiplication: For real numbers a, b, and c, $(a + b) + c = a + (b + c)$, and $(ab)c = a(bc)$. Thus we say the operations of addition and multiplication are *associative*. This means no matter how we associate (or group) the summands or factors in our sums or products, the result is the same. Associativity also holds for the complex numbers.

Example

$(2 + 3) + 4 = 9 = 2 + (3 + 4)$ and $(2 \cdot 3) \cdot 4 = 24 = 2 \cdot (3 \cdot 4)$

We emphasize here that the presence of parentheses indicates which sum or product we should evaluate first.

In light of the last example, we consider the order of operations. What order *should* we perform operations in?

Order of Operations

The operations of $+$, $-$, $\times$, and $\div$ can be ordered using the grouping symbols "(" and ")" (the opening and closing parentheses, respectively), and calculations are then performed in the conventional order: **P**arentheses, **E**xponents, **M**ultiplication, **D**ivision, **A**ddition, and **S**ubtraction. This is commonly abbreviated as **PEMDAS** and can also be remembered by reciting the phrase "Please Excuse My Dear Aunt Sally." Note that we can consider exponents as carrying parentheses with them. For example, $3 \cdot 2^2 = 3(2)^2$. This makes it clear that we square 2 first and then multiply by 3. This is not the same as $(3 \cdot 2)^2 = (6)^2$. We recall that by properties of exponents $(3 \cdot 2)^2 = 3^2 \cdot 2^2$.

Example

(In the natural numbers) calculate $(2 + 3)^2 + 5 \cdot 2 + 3 \cdot 2^2$.

Solution: Following the order of operations:

We first perform the operation in parentheses:
$(5)^2 + 5 \cdot 2 + 3 \cdot 2^2$

Next, we evaluate the exponential expressions:
$25 + 5 \cdot 2 + 3 \cdot 4$

Next, we perform the multiplications:
$25 + 10 + 12$

Finally, we add:
$25 + 10 + 12 = 47$

The order of operations applies to the real numbers, the complex numbers, and all the subsets of these number systems in the number systems diagram shown earlier.

In addition to the associative property, the natural numbers (as well as all our other sets of numbers) exhibit the *distributive property of multiplication over addition*, which we will refer to as simply the *distributive property*.

The Distributive Property: For real numbers a, b, and c, $c(a + b) = ca + cb$. This means that if we distribute the number c to each summand in parentheses, we will get the same result as if we were to follow the order of operations, summing a and b first, and then multiplying by c. We emphasize again that this property holds for real numbers, complex numbers, and their subsets listed at the beginning of this section.

The distributive property will be used heavily in algebra.

While the set of natural numbers does exhibit some nice properties under addition and multiplication that extend to all the sets of numbers that contain the natural numbers, its failure to be closed under division and subtraction is a concern. Also a concern, and a consequence of this closure failure, is the lack of an *additive identity element*, 0. A further consequence is that no natural number has an *additive inverse*.

Definition: An *additive identity element* of a set is a number o such that for any number in the set, n, we have that $o + n = n + o = n$.

Definition: An *additive inverse* is a number j such that for a particular number n, we have that $j + n = n + j = 0$.

Example

Since -2 is not in the set of natural numbers, the number 2 does not have an additive inverse when considered as a part of the natural numbers.

However, since the number 1 is an element of the natural numbers, the natural numbers do contain a *multiplicative identity*, 1.

Definition: A *multiplicative identity* element is a number l such that for any number in the set, n, we have $l \cdot n = n \cdot l = n$.

There is only one element in $\mathbb{N}$, however, that has a *multiplicative inverse*.

Definition: A *multiplicative inverse* is a number m such that for a particular number n, we have that $mn = nm = l$.

Example
The only number in the natural numbers that has a multiplicative inverse is the number 1, since $1 \cdot 1 = 1$. Thus, 1 in the natural numbers is its own inverse. No other number in $\mathbb{N}$ has such an inverse—or any inverse at all for that matter.

The Integers

The previous examples show the need for at least a set of numbers that contains 0 and negative numbers, so that we can solve more sophisticated equations. As we've seen, the set containing all the natural numbers, zero, and all negative whole numbers is called the *integers*, and is denoted by $\mathbb{Z}$.

Closure Properties of the Integers
We can easily see that the integers are closed under the operations of addition, subtraction, and multiplication. The integers are not closed under division (the simplest set of numbers closed under division is the set of rational numbers).

We also can easily check that the *associative* properties of addition and multiplication hold, as well as the *distributive* property. We also have guaranteed the existence of the *additive identity*, 0, and have

made sure that every element has an *additive inverse*; for example, 3 has –3 as its additive inverse since $3 + (-3) = 0$. Furthermore, since 1 is still in the set of integers, $\mathbb{Z}$ has a *multiplicative identity*.

Nevertheless, we can't help but notice that again only the number 1 has a multiplicative inverse, itself. In order to obtain a set of numbers that has all the previously listed properties of the integers *and* also has the property that each element has a multiplicative inverse, we need to define the rational numbers, $\mathbb{Q}$.

Example
Solve $2x = 1$ so that x is an integer.

Solution: This is impossible since the solution to this equation is $x = \frac{1}{2}$, which is *not* an integer.

We will define the rational numbers (and the irrational numbers) in the next section. For now we'll consider only the integers, and recall some facts about multiplying and dividing signed numbers that will be very useful when solving equations and inequalities and when determining the type of relative extrema of a function in calculus.

Multiplying and Dividing Signed Numbers
1. The product or quotient of two numbers with the *same sign* is *positive*.

Example
$5 \cdot 2 = 10$ and $\frac{-18}{-2} = 9$.

In summary:
$(+) \cdot (+) = (+), \frac{(+)}{(+)} = (+)$ and
$(-) \cdot (-) = (+), \frac{(-)}{(-)} = (+)$

2. The product or quotient of two numbers with *opposite sign* is *negative*.

Example
$5 \cdot -2 = -10$ and $\frac{-18}{2} = -9$

In summary:
$(+) \cdot (-) = (-), \frac{(+)}{(-)} = (-)$ and

$(-) \cdot (+) = (-), \frac{(-)}{(+)} = (-)$

3. When multiplying more than two numbers, the sign of the product depends on the number of negative factors.

Example
$5 \cdot -2 = -10; 5 \cdot -2 \cdot -3 = 30; 5 \cdot -2 \cdot -3 \cdot -1$
$= -30$

In summary, we see that if a product contains an *odd number of negative factors*, then it is *negative*. If a product contains and *even number of negative factors*, then the product is a *positive* number.

Properties of Rational and Irrational Numbers

We are now ready to build on the integers to define a number system in which each element has a multiplicative inverse. The rational numbers have this property. Rational numbers are those numbers that can be expressed as repeating or terminating decimals. This is equivalent to the more formal definition of rational numbers.

The *rational numbers*, $\mathbb{Q}$, can be thought of as any number that can be written as the ratio of two integers, $\frac{p}{q}$, where $q \neq 0$. We also require $\frac{p_1}{q_1} = \frac{p_2}{q_2}$ if $p_1 q_2 - p_2 q_1 = 0$; that is, we consider, for example, $\frac{1}{2} = \frac{2}{4} = \frac{3}{6} = \cdots$

(You should also note that every integer is a rational number with denominator 1.)

For this review, we will define the *irrational numbers* as those real numbers that *cannot* be expressed as rational numbers. For instance, $\sqrt{2}, \frac{\sqrt{3}}{4}, \pi$, and e are examples of irrational numbers.

Properties of the Rational Numbers
The *rational numbers* are closed under addition and multiplication. The set is also closed under division and subtraction. Since 0 and 1 are elements of the rational numbers, the rationals contain both an additive identity and a multiplicative identity, respectively. The rational numbers, just like the integers, have an associative addition and multiplication. The distributive property holds. Each rational number has an additive inverse: $\frac{p}{q}$ has $-\frac{p}{q}$ and each rational number, except 0, has a multiplicative inverse: $\frac{p}{q}$ has $\frac{q}{p}$ since $\frac{q}{p} \cdot \frac{p}{q} = 1$ (provided $p \neq 0$).

Notice that we can now solve any equation of the form $qx = p$, where p and $q \neq 0$ and are integers.

Example
Solve $2x = 1$.

Solution: $x = \frac{1}{2}$

Properties of the Irrational Numbers
The *irrational numbers* are *not* closed under addition, since, for example, $1 + \sqrt{2}$ and $1 - \sqrt{2}$ are irrational numbers, but their sum is 2, which is rational. The irrationals are also *not* closed under multiplication, since for example $\sqrt{2} \cdot \sqrt{2} = 2$, which is a rational number. This means, by consequence, that the set is *not* closed under subtraction, nor division. Since 0 and 1 are elements of the rational numbers, the irrationals do not contain an additive identity, nor a multiplicative one. Nonetheless, just like the rational numbers and the integers, the irrationals have an associative addition and multiplication. The distributive property also holds for irrationals. Each irrational number has an additive inverse: An irrational number j has $-j$ as its additive inverse. Every irrational also has a multiplicative inverse: Each irrational number j has $\frac{1}{j}$ as its multiplicative inverse.

Notice that the irrational numbers now give us the power to solve any equation of the form $x^2 - c = 0$. Previously, limited to only the rational numbers, we could solve such an equation only if c was a perfect square, or a ratio of perfect squares. Now we can solve this for any positive real number c.

Example
Solve $x^2 - 5 = 0$.

Solution: $x = \pm\sqrt{5}$

We will now use some examples to consider how the rationals and irrationals behave when added, subtracted, multiplied, and divided.

Adding and Subtracting Rationals and Irrationals

We can add or subtract fractions if both have the same denominator. Thus, in adding and subtracting rationals, we first need to make sure each rational number in the sum and/or difference has a common denominator, or, even better, a least common denominator (LCD).

Example
Compute $\frac{5}{7} + \frac{1}{2} - \frac{3}{4}$.

Solution: $\frac{5}{7} + \frac{1}{2} - \frac{3}{4} = \frac{5}{7} \cdot \frac{4}{4} + \frac{1}{2} \cdot \frac{14}{14} - \frac{3}{4} \cdot \frac{7}{7}$
$$= \frac{20}{28} + \frac{14}{28} - \frac{21}{28} = \frac{13}{28}$$

The LCD here is 28.

Addition and Subtraction among the Irrationals

Before we talk about combining irrational numbers, let's review some terminology. Given an irrational number in radical form like $\sqrt[n]{r}$, we call n the *index* and r the *radicand*. Two irrational numbers can be combined via addition or subtraction if they both have exactly the same index and radicand. And, as we've shown before when stating that the irrationals are not closed under addition, combining two irrationals by addition or subtraction can result in a sum or difference that either is still irrational or is rational. With this in mind, let's jump into some examples.

Example
Compute $\sqrt{2} + 5\sqrt{2}$.

Solution: $\sqrt{2} + 5\sqrt{2} = 6\sqrt{2}$

Note that this is exactly the same principle you applied to variable expressions in algebra: $5xy^2 + 7xy^2 = 12xy^2$. In both cases, we refer to this procedure as *combining like terms*.

Now recall that we saw that radical expressions can be rewritten using rational exponents, for example,

$$\sqrt{2} = 2^{\frac{1}{2}}$$

We can thus use the rules of exponents to our advantage to rewrite certain sums or differences of irrational numbers so that radicals with the same index might also have the same radicand, and thus be combined:

Example
Compute the difference $7\sqrt[3]{24} - 11\sqrt[3]{81}$ and write in simplest form.

Solution:
$$7\sqrt[3]{24} - 11\sqrt[3]{81} = 7\sqrt[3]{8 \cdot 3} - 11\sqrt[3]{27 \cdot 3}$$
$$= 7\sqrt[3]{8} \cdot \sqrt[3]{3} - 11\sqrt[3]{27} \cdot \sqrt[3]{3}$$
$$= 14\sqrt[3]{3} - 33\sqrt[3]{3}$$
$$= -19\sqrt[3]{3}$$

Here we are using a version of the product rule for exponents.

If rewriting radical expressions in a sum and/or difference does not lead to radicals with the same index and same radicand, then these two numbers can, of course, still be added and/or subtracted. It's just that we cannot express the sum and/or difference in a simpler form.

Example

Compute $5\sqrt{2} + 9\sqrt{3}$ and write in simplest form.

Solution: $5\sqrt{2} + 9\sqrt{3} = 5\sqrt{2} + 9\sqrt{3}$

(Very anticlimactic, but we actually can't do anything further.)

Now let's look at the case where combining two irrationals results in a rational number. This happens when we add two *conjugates*. We will see conjugates again when we discuss complex numbers, but in the context of irrational/rational numbers we make the following definition.

Definition: The *conjugate* of the irrational number $a + \sqrt{b}$ is the number $a - \sqrt{b}$. (Here b is not a perfect square.) Taken together, these two numbers are referred to as a *conjugate pair*. The reason we like conjugate pairs is that when we add or multiply them we get a rational number. This often helps us to simplify expressions.

There is a limit to how much we can simplify the sum or difference of a rational and an irrational.

Example

We can't do anything with $5 + \sqrt{3}$, while we can simplify, $2 + (1 + \sqrt{2}) = 3 + \sqrt{2}$, but not much.

At this point the following should be clear:

- The sum (or difference) of two rational numbers is rational.
- The sum (or difference) of two irrational numbers may be either irrational or rational.
- The sum (or difference) of a rational and an irrational is irrational.

Multiplication and Division among the Rationals and Irrationals

Recall that we multiply fractions in the following way:

$$\frac{a}{b} \cdot \frac{c}{d} = \frac{ac}{bd}$$

We can then write our product in simplest form by dividing out any common factors of ac and bd. In practice, however, it often easier to simplify first, and then multiply. We can simplify by canceling factors in the numerator with factors in the denominator.

Example

Multiply $\frac{6}{7} \cdot \frac{28}{9}$.

Solution: $\frac{6}{7} \cdot \frac{28}{9} = \frac{\cancel{6}^2}{\cancel{7}_1} \cdot \frac{\cancel{28}^4}{\cancel{9}_3} = \frac{2}{1} \cdot \frac{4}{3} = \frac{8}{3}$

When dividing fractions, we can recite the mantra: "copy, change, flip." This refers to the following procedure in which we divide rational numbers by multiplying by the reciprocal of the denominator.

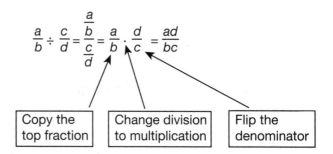

| Copy the top fraction | Change division to multiplication | Flip the denominator |

Example

Compute $\frac{\frac{2}{3}}{5}$.

Solution: $\frac{\frac{2}{3}}{5} = \frac{\frac{2}{3}}{\frac{5}{1}} = \frac{2}{3} \cdot \frac{1}{5} = \frac{2}{15}$

We use the product rule and the quotient rule for exponents when we multiply and divide irrational numbers. Just as when we reviewed rules of exponents, irrationals that can be written using radicands can be combined by multiplication and/or division in a simpler form as long as the factors have the same base.

Example

$\sqrt[3]{7} \cdot \sqrt{7}$

Solution:

$$\sqrt[3]{7} \cdot \sqrt{7} = \underbrace{7^{\frac{1}{3}} \cdot 7^{\frac{1}{2}} = 7^{\frac{1}{3} + \frac{1}{2}} = 7^{\frac{5}{6}}}_{\text{product rule for exponents}} = \sqrt[6]{7^5}$$

If the radicands (bases) are different, but the indexes (exponents) are the same, we can write a product or quotient of two irrational numbers in a simpler form. Again we use a rule of exponents.

Example

Divide $\dfrac{\sqrt[5]{2}}{\sqrt[5]{3}}$.

Solution: $\dfrac{\sqrt[5]{2}}{\sqrt[5]{3}} = \dfrac{2^{\frac{1}{5}}}{3^{\frac{1}{5}}} = \left(\dfrac{2}{3}\right)^{\frac{1}{5}} = \sqrt[5]{\dfrac{2}{3}}$

Note that we are using the quotient rule for radicals (as it is sometimes called) here.

The Quotient Rule for Radicals:
$$\frac{\sqrt[n]{b}}{\sqrt[n]{c}} = \sqrt[n]{\frac{b}{c}}$$

The analogous rule for products is:

The Product Rule for Radicals:
$$\sqrt[n]{b} \cdot \sqrt[n]{c} = \sqrt[n]{bc}$$

The following examples not only show us how to simplify some radical expressions when multiplying or dividing, but also remind us that the irrationals are not closed under multiplication or division.

Example

Multiply $\sqrt{2} \cdot \sqrt{2}$.

Solution: $\sqrt{2} \cdot \sqrt{2} = \sqrt{2 \cdot 2} = \sqrt{4} = 2$

Example

Multiply $\sqrt[5]{7^2} \cdot \sqrt[5]{7^3}$.

Solution:

$$\underbrace{\sqrt[5]{7^2} \cdot \sqrt[5]{7^3} = \sqrt[5]{7^2 \cdot 7^3}}_{\text{product rule for radicals}} = \sqrt[5]{7^5} = 7^{\frac{5}{5}} = 7^1 = 7$$

We may also look at these in a way to emphasize the rules of exponents instead of radicals.

Example

Multiply $\sqrt{2} \cdot \sqrt{2}$.

Solution: $\sqrt{2} \cdot \sqrt{2} = 2^{\frac{1}{2}} \cdot 2^{\frac{1}{2}} = 2^{\frac{1}{2} + \frac{1}{2}} = 2^1 = 2$

Example

Multiply $\sqrt[5]{7^2} \cdot \sqrt[5]{7^3}$.

Solution: $\sqrt[5]{7^2} \cdot \sqrt[5]{7^3} = 7^{\frac{2}{5}} \cdot 7^{\frac{3}{5}} = 7^{\frac{2}{5} + \frac{3}{5}} = 7^1 = 7$

We see that the product or quotient of two irrational numbers will be rational if they each have the same radicand (base) and their exponents when written in exponential form sum to 1.

Rational numbers and irrational numbers can always be combined by multiplication and division since multiplication is just the abbreviation of the operation of repeated addition, and division is simply multiplication by a reciprocal.

Example

Multiplying a rational and an irrational and of the "repeated addition" quality of multiplication:

$$5 \cdot \sqrt{7} = 5\sqrt{7} = \sqrt{7} + \sqrt{7} + \sqrt{7} + \sqrt{7} + \sqrt{7}$$
$$= 5\sqrt{7}$$

The expression after the second equal sign is written for emphasis. In practice, one would not need to show that.

Example

Dividing a rational and an irrational and of division as multiplication by a reciprocal:

$$\sqrt[3]{5} \div \frac{2}{7} = \frac{\sqrt[3]{5}}{\frac{2}{7}} = \sqrt[3]{5} \cdot \frac{7}{2} = \frac{7\sqrt[3]{5}}{2} = \frac{7}{2}\sqrt[3]{5}$$

Sometimes when dividing by irrational numbers we wind up with an irrational number as the denominator of a fraction. In some contexts, this is unfavorable. We can remedy the situation by *rationalizing the denominator*.

Rationalizing Denominators

It is a common exercise to rationalize a fraction when that fraction has an irrational expression in the numerator or denominator. When we do this, we are using the idea that the product of two irrational numbers is rational precisely when those two numbers have the same radicand and their exponents sum to 1.

Example

Rationalize the denominator in $\frac{7}{\sqrt[3]{5}}$.

Solution: $\frac{7}{\sqrt[3]{5}} = \frac{7}{5^{\frac{1}{3}}} = \frac{7}{5^{\frac{1}{3}}} \cdot \frac{5^{\frac{2}{3}}}{5^{\frac{2}{3}}} = \frac{7 \cdot 5^{\frac{2}{3}}}{5} = \frac{7\sqrt[3]{25}}{5}$

Notice that here we multiply the numerator and denominator by $5^{\frac{2}{3}}$, since that would make the exponent of the denominator become 1. Also recall that we have to multiply both the numerator and denominator, since doing so does not change the value of the original expression (because we're essentially multiplying by 1, written in a convenient way).

It is often the case that we want to rationalize expressions of the form $a \pm \sqrt{b}$. To do this we simply need to multiply the numerator and denominator by its conjugate. This takes advantage of the difference of two squares formula, since $(a \pm \sqrt{b})(a \mp \sqrt{b}) = a^2 - b$, by the difference of two squares. (You could also do this the long way by expanding using the distributive property.)

Example

Multiply $(2 + \sqrt{3})(2 - \sqrt{3})$.

Solution: Using the distributive property and simplifying,

$$(2 + \sqrt{3})(2 - \sqrt{3}) = 2(2 - \sqrt{3}) + \sqrt{3}(2 - \sqrt{3})$$
$$= 4 - 2\sqrt{3} + 2\sqrt{3} - 3 = 1$$

Let's apply this to a rationalizing the numerator problem.

Example

Rationalize the numerator in $\frac{4 - \sqrt{5}}{10}$.

Solution:

$$\frac{4 - \sqrt{5}}{10} \cdot \frac{4 + \sqrt{5}}{4 + \sqrt{5}} = \frac{16 - 5}{10(4 + \sqrt{5})} = \frac{11}{10(4 + \sqrt{5})}$$

A WORD OF CAUTION

Conjugates might look very different if square roots are not involved. For example, the conjugate of $a + \sqrt[3]{b}$ is *not* $a - \sqrt[3]{b}$. Rather, its conjugate is actually $a^2 - ab^{\frac{1}{3}} + b^{\frac{2}{3}}$. Multiplying by this takes advantage of the sum of two cubes formula, and gets rid of the radical expression.

The Real Numbers

The precise definition of the real numbers is beyond the scope of this review. We will define the real numbers roughly as the set of numbers containing both the rationals and irrationals. This set is denoted by the symbol $\mathbb{R}$. We can picture the real numbers as the real number line that we call the *x*-axis, pictured here.

The Real Number Line (x-Axis)

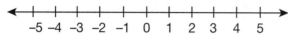

We notice that in our picture of the real numbers only the integers are labeled, but we understand that the lines between each integer represent all possible real numbers in that interval. This means that, although numbers like $\sqrt{2}$, e, and π are not usually labeled on the number line, they are indeed present.

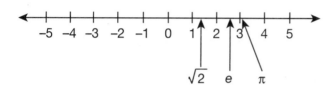

Properties of the Real Numbers

The real numbers consist of the rational numbers and the irrational numbers. The real numbers are *closed* under the operations of addition, subtraction, multiplication, and division (with the exception that we cannot divide by zero). Furthermore, the operations of addition and multiplication of real numbers are both *commutative* and *associative*, and the *distributive property* still holds. Just as in the rational numbers, the real numbers contain the *additive identity*, 0, and the *multiplicative identity*, 1. In the real numbers, each element has an *additive inverse* and each non-zero element has a *multiplicative inverse*.

We will accept the fact that under the real numbers we can solve every polynomial equation that has real solutions. Although we will study solving polynomial equations in a later chapter, an example is presented here.

Example
Solve $x^3 - 3x = 0$.

Solution: We can solve this equation by factoring:

$$x^3 - 3x = 0$$

First, we factor out the greatest common monomial factor, x:

$$x(x^2 - 3) = 0$$

Next, we recall how to factor the difference of two squares: $x^2 - a^2 = (x + a)(x - a)$, and we apply this idea to the factor $x^2 - 3$. We can think of 3 as $\left(\sqrt{3}\right)^2$, so

$$x^2 - 3 = x^2 - \left(\sqrt{3}\right)^2 = \left(x + \sqrt{3}\right)\left(x - \sqrt{3}\right)$$

Thus, we have completely factored our algebraic expression, and our equation can now be written as

$$x\left(x + \sqrt{3}\right)\left(x - \sqrt{3}\right) = 0$$

We can now see the x-values that make this equation true, by setting each factor equal to 0:

$$x = 0; \ \left(x - \sqrt{3}\right) = 0; \ \left(x + \sqrt{3}\right) = 0$$

Therefore, the solutions to this polynomial equation are $x = 0$, $x = \sqrt{3}$, and $x = -\sqrt{3}$, where $x = 0$ is a rational number, and $x = \sqrt{3}, -\sqrt{3}$ are conjugate irrational numbers.

While it is fantastic that we have enough numbers to solve equations like this one, and infinitely more, there are still some polynomial equations that cannot be solved using the real numbers.

Example
Solve $x^2 + 1 = 0$ under the real numbers.

Solution: $x^2 + 1 = 0$
$$x^2 = -1$$
$$x = \sqrt{-1} \ \text{ and } \ x = -\sqrt{-1}$$

No solution!

There is no such real number n such that $n^2 = n \cdot n = -1$, since one factor would have to be negative and the other factor positive; n would have to be both positive and negative, and a positive nonzero number is never equal to a negative nonzero number! Therefore, we cannot solve this equation using real numbers.

The Complex Numbers

In order to address the fact that we cannot solve a seemingly simple equation like $x^2 + 1 = 0$ using real numbers, we define the *imaginary unit*.

Definition: Let $i = \sqrt{-1}$ be called the *imaginary unit*.

This number i is *not* a real number. We call it a *pure imaginary* number. The definition of this number gives rise to a new system of numbers, which contains all the number systems we have reviewed so far.

Definition: The *complex numbers* is the set $\mathbb{C} = \{a + ib \mid a$ and b are real numbers$\}$. We notice that if $b = 0$, then the complex number is actually a real number, so the complex numbers contain the real numbers. If $a = 0$, then the complex number is a pure imaginary number. Thus, the complex numbers contain the pure imaginary numbers.

Properties of the Complex Numbers

Since i is the number that separates the complex numbers from the real numbers, we begin with a look at the properties of the imaginary unit.

The Cycle of i

By definition $i = \sqrt{-1}$; this means that $i^2 = (\sqrt{-1})^2 = -1$. Multiplying by i again, we find that $i^3 = i \cdot i^2 = -i$. Continuing this process, we see that $i^4 = i^2 \cdot i^2 = 1$, and then, $i^5 = i \cdot i^4 = i$. So we are back to where we started. This shows that repeatedly multiplying by i creates a cycle. This "cycle of i" is illustrated by the following diagram.

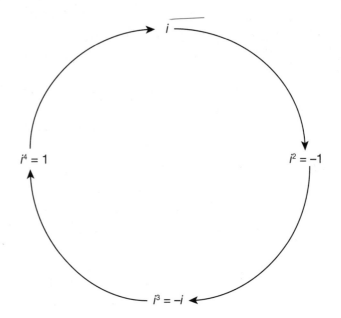

Consequently, we have two facts:

1. There are only four possibilities for any i^k, where k is a positive integer: $i, -1, -i$, or 1.
2. We can determine which of the four possibilities it is by dividing k by 4 and looking at the remainder.

Example
Simplify i^{39}.

Solution: If we divide 39 by 4, the result is 9 with remainder of 3, so $39 = 4(9) + 3$, and hence it follows that

$$i^{39} = i^{4(9)+3} = i^{4(9)} \cdot i^3 = 1^9 \cdot i^3 = i^3 = -i$$

So we get that $i^{39} = -i$.

Addition and Subtraction of Complex Numbers

The procedure for adding and subtracting complex numbers is exactly analogous to the procedure for adding and subtracting numbers of the form $a + \sqrt{b}$, which we looked at previously. Essentially, you add or subtract like terms.

Example

Combine $(3 + 2i) - (4 - 5i) + (1 + i)$.

Solution: We follow the correct order of operations and first clear the parentheses:

$$(3 + 2i) - (4 - 5i) + (1 + i) = 3 + 2i - 4 + 5i + 1 + i$$

We finish by combining the real numbers with the real numbers, and the pure imaginary numbers with the pure imaginary numbers. Simply put, we combine like terms:

$$3 + 2i - 4 + 5i + 1 + i = 0 + 8i$$

Multiplication of Complex Numbers

We multiply complex numbers by applying the distributive property. Again, this way of multiplying is analogous to what we did when multiplying irrational numbers. However, when multiplying complex numbers, we will be able to take advantage of the fact that $i^2 = -1$, and our other results for powers of i, if applicable.

Example

Multiply $(-2 + 3i)(1 + 5i)$.

Solution: Using the distributive property, we distribute the 2 to each term in the second factor, and distribute the 3 to each term in the second factor. We are careful about the sign of the numbers in our product, and we make sure to use the fact that $i^2 = -1$.

$$(-2 + 3i)(1 + 5i)$$

So we get:

$$
\begin{aligned}
(-2 + 3i)(1 + 5i) &= -2(1) - 2 \cdot (5i) + 3i(1) + 3i(5i) \\
&= -2 - 10i + 3i + 15i^2 \\
&= -2 - 10i + 3i - 15 \\
&= -17 - 7i
\end{aligned}
$$

Division of Complex Numbers

Before we can define the quotient of two complex numbers, we need to make the following definition.

Definition: The *conjugate* of the complex number $a + bi$ is the complex number $a - bi$. The complex numbers $a + bi$ and $a - bi$ are called *conjugate pairs*.

Now, in order to divide one complex number by another, we simply multiply the numerator and denominator by the conjugate of the denominator.

Example

Divide $\frac{3 - 7i}{4 + i}$ and express the quotient in $a + bi$ form.

Solution:

$$
\begin{aligned}
\frac{3 - 7i}{4 + i} &= \frac{3 - 7i}{4 + i} \cdot \frac{4 - i}{4 - i} \\[2mm]
&= \frac{12 - 3i - 28i + 7i^2}{16 - i^2} \\[2mm]
&= \frac{12 - 3i - 28i - 7}{16 + 1} = \frac{5 - 31i}{17} = \frac{5}{17} - \frac{31}{17}i
\end{aligned}
$$

A First Look at Complex Solutions to Polynomial Equations

Equipped with the complex numbers we can now find solutions to every nonconstant single variable polynomial equation, and state the *fundamental theorem of algebra for quadratic polynomials*.

The Fundamental Theorem of Algebra (for Quadratic Polynomials)

Every quadratic polynomial of the form $ax^2 + bx + c$ with $a \neq 0$ and a, b, and c complex numbers has at least one complex root.

Furthermore, the solutions are given by the quadratic formula. That is, if $ax^2 + bx + c = 0$ with

$a \neq 0$, then $x = \frac{-b \pm \sqrt{b^2 - 4ac}}{2a}$. We get two complex solutions (up to multiplicity) precisely when $b^2 - 4ac < 0$.

We note that the fundamental theorem of algebra applies in general to any nonconstant polynomial. The complex numbers give us the power to find n roots (up to multiplicity) of *any* nonconstant polynomial of degree n. This power is one of the reasons why the complex numbers are so important, and it is the reason why, as far as solving polynomials is concerned, we need no other larger number system. The complex numbers are all that we need.

It is also important to note that the fundamental theorem holds for a, b, c real number coefficients, since real numbers are just complex numbers $m + ni$ with $n = 0$. Solving polynomial equations will be discussed in more detail in the next chapter. For now, we look again at the following seemingly simple quadratic equation.

Example

In the complex numbers, solve $x^2 + 1 = 0$.

Solution: $x^2 + 1 = 0$
$$x^2 = -1$$
$$x = \pm\sqrt{-1}$$
$$x = \pm i$$

This example also indicates a fact we will see in the Algebra Review chapter (Chapter 5): If a polynomial equation has a complex solution $a + bi$, then the conjugate $a - bi$ is also a solution to the equation. Hence we have the catchphrase: "Complex solutions come in conjugate pairs."

Example

Factor $x^2 + a^2$.

Solution: Recall that we can factor the difference of two squares $x^2 - a^2$ as $x^2 - a^2 = (x - a)(x + a)$. We now apply this idea to expressions of the form $x^2 + a^2$, recognizing that the "+" indicates the presence of i^2. Since $i^2 = -1$, we can rewrite the equation $x^2 + 1 = 0$ as $x^2 - i^2 = 0$. This now is clearly a difference of two squares, which we can factor!

$$x^2 + 1 = x^2 - i^2 = (x + i)(x - i)$$

Thus our equation becomes $(x + i)(x - i) = 0$ and we see that the solutions of this equation are $x = i$ and $x = -i$, as we saw previously.

We can generalize this example by saying that $x^2 + a^2 = (x + ai)(x - ai)$.

Matrices

In this we section we consider another type of mathematical object: arrays of numbers called matrices. (Matrices is the plural of matrix.) Matrices have many uses, not the least of which is their application in solving systems of equations by arranging information about the system in rows and columns.

Definition: A *matrix* is an array of numbers in rows and columns, usually denoted with a capital letter, like A.

Here is an example.

$$A = \begin{bmatrix} 1 & 2 & 3 \\ 7 & -1 & 4 \end{bmatrix}$$

The numbers in a matrix are called *entries*.

Every matrix can be characterized by its *size* or *dimension*.

Definition: The *size* of a matrix is the number of rows by the number of columns. That is, a matrix with n rows and m columns is said to have size $n \times m$, and is called an $n \times m$ matrix.

Example
Given the matrix $A = \begin{bmatrix} 1 & 2 & 3 \\ 7 & -1 & 4 \end{bmatrix}$,

state its size (dimension).

Solution: Matrix A has two rows and three columns, so we say A is a 2×3 (read "two by three") matrix. We denote the *entries* in matrix A with the same letter but lowercase, a_{ij}. The subscript ij gives the location of the entry in the matrix, where i = row number and j = column number.

Example
In the matrix $A = \begin{bmatrix} 1 & 2 & 3 \\ 7 & -1 & 4 \end{bmatrix}$,

state the entry a_{23}.

Solution: The notation a_{23} stands for the entry in row 2, column 3 of matrix A. Therefore $a_{23} = 4$.

Since matrices are made up of numbers, it is reasonable to ask if we can add, subtract, multiply, and divide matrices, just as we do real numbers. The answer is yes, provided certain conditions hold. While we can add, subtract, and multiply matrices, we *cannot* divide matrices.

Addition and Subtraction of Matrices

Two or more matrices can be added or subtracted as long as they are all exactly the *same size*. If they are not the same size, the operation cannot be performed. We add or subtract matrices by adding or subtracting corresponding entries.

Example
Given the matrices $A = \begin{bmatrix} 1 & 2 & 3 \\ 7 & -1 & 4 \end{bmatrix}$,

$B = \begin{bmatrix} 0 & -3 & 5 \\ -1 & -9 & 2 \end{bmatrix}$, and $C = \begin{bmatrix} 6 & 8 \\ -7 & 1 \end{bmatrix}$,

compute $A + B$, $B - A$, and $A + C$.

Solution:

$$A + B = \begin{bmatrix} 1+0 & 2-3 & 3+5 \\ 7-1 & -1-9 & 4+2 \end{bmatrix} = \begin{bmatrix} 1 & -1 & 8 \\ 6 & -10 & 6 \end{bmatrix}$$

$$B - A = \begin{bmatrix} 0-1 & -3-2 & 5-3 \\ -1-7 & -9+1 & 2-4 \end{bmatrix} = \begin{bmatrix} -1 & -5 & 2 \\ -8 & -8 & -2 \end{bmatrix}$$

$A + C$ cannot be computed since A and C are *not* the same size.

When talking about the operation of addition, we are necessarily led to a discussion of additive inverses and additive identities.

Definition: The additive identity for a matrix of any size is called the *zero matrix*. It is the matrix Z such that for a matrix A, $Z + A = A + Z = A$.

Example

For $A = \begin{bmatrix} 1 & 2 & 3 \\ 7 & -1 & 4 \end{bmatrix}$, the zero matrix is

$Z = \begin{bmatrix} 0 & 0 & 0 \\ 0 & 0 & 0 \end{bmatrix}$, as it is for

$B = \begin{bmatrix} 0 & -3 & 5 \\ -1 & -9 & 2 \end{bmatrix}$. For $C = \begin{bmatrix} 6 & 8 \\ -7 & 1 \end{bmatrix}$,

the zero matrix is $Z = \begin{bmatrix} 0 & 0 \\ 0 & 0 \end{bmatrix}$.

Now that we have the zero matrix, it is easy to see that every matrix, regardless of size, has an *additive inverse*.

Definition: The additive inverse of a matrix M is the matrix $-M$, in which all entries are the negation of the entries in M, so that $M + (-M) = Z$.

Example
The additive inverse of $A = \begin{bmatrix} 1 & 2 & 3 \\ 7 & -1 & 4 \end{bmatrix}$ is

the matrix $-A = \begin{bmatrix} -1 & -2 & -3 \\ -7 & 1 & -4 \end{bmatrix}$.

The notation we used for the additive inverse, $-M$, leads to the next topic.

Scalar Multiplication

Definition: A matrix that consists of one row is called a *row vector*. A matrix that consists of one column is called a *column vector*.

A column vector $\begin{bmatrix} x \\ y \end{bmatrix}$ can be viewed as an arrow in the xy plane whose tail is at the origin, whose tip is at the point (x,y), and whose length (magnitude), l, is given by the Pythagorean theorem, $l = \sqrt{x^2 + y^2}$.

Example
Sketch the vector $\begin{bmatrix} 1 \\ 2 \end{bmatrix}$ on the x- and y-axes and state its magnitude.

Solution:

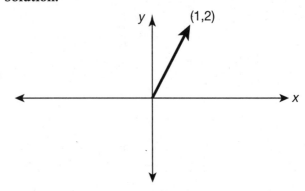

The magnitude of $\begin{bmatrix} 1 \\ 2 \end{bmatrix}$ is $\sqrt{1^2 + 2^2} = \sqrt{5}$.

Multiplying a vector, or any matrix for that matter, by a constant is called *scalar multiplication*. We perform scalar multiplication by multiplying each entry in a matrix by the same constant.

Example
Multiply $2\begin{bmatrix} 1 \\ 2 \end{bmatrix}$, sketch the resulting vector along with the vector $\begin{bmatrix} 1 \\ 2 \end{bmatrix}$, and compute its magnitude.

Solution:

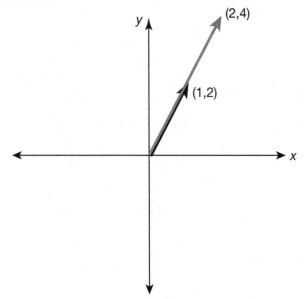

$$2 \begin{bmatrix} 1 \\ 2 \end{bmatrix} = \begin{bmatrix} 2 \cdot 1 \\ 2 \cdot 2 \end{bmatrix} = \begin{bmatrix} 2 \\ 4 \end{bmatrix}$$

The magnitude of $\begin{bmatrix} 2 \\ 4 \end{bmatrix}$ is $\sqrt{2^2 + 4^2} = \sqrt{20} =$

$\sqrt{4 \cdot 5} = 2\sqrt{5}$.

The previous example shows that scalar multiplication is so called because multiplying a matrix by a constant does not change the direction of the vector, but rather scales it up or down. The constant being multiplied is therefore aptly called a *scalar*.

Next we see the geometric meaning of the additive inverse of a vector.

Example

Let $M = \begin{bmatrix} 1 \\ 2 \end{bmatrix}$. Sketch $M = \begin{bmatrix} 1 \\ 2 \end{bmatrix}$ and

$-M = \begin{bmatrix} -1 \\ -2 \end{bmatrix}$ on the same coordinates' axes.

Solution:

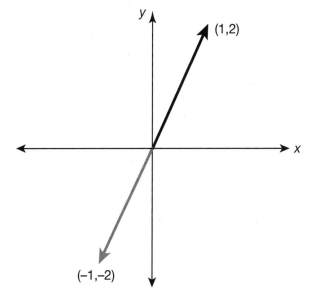

We see that multiplying a vector by −1 results in a reflection through the origin, or a 180° rotation about the origin (0,0).

Matrix Multiplication

Multiplying two matrices is not as straightforward as multiplying a matrix by a scalar, or adding and subtracting matrices. We multiply two matrices, A and B, by multiplying the row entries in A and the column entries in B. This is best seen by trying a few examples.

Example

Let $A = [-2\ 3]$ and $B = \begin{bmatrix} 4 \\ 5 \end{bmatrix}$, and multiply AB.

Solution: In order to compute AB, we multiply the entry in row 1, column 1, in A by the entry in row 1, column 1, in B.

$$[-2 \quad 3] \begin{bmatrix} 4 \\ 5 \end{bmatrix}$$

At the same time we multiply the entry in row 1, column 2, of A by the entry in row 2, column 1, of B.

$$[-2 \quad 3] \begin{bmatrix} 4 \\ 5 \end{bmatrix}$$

After multiplying the corresponding entries as shown, we must add them. So we have $[-2 \cdot 4 + 3 \cdot 5]$. There is no second row, so that's it. This results in $[-8 + 15]$ $= [7]$.

Notice that we multiplied a 1×2 matrix by a 2×1 matrix and wound up with a 1×1 matrix.

This one example shows us what must be true about the two matrices in order for them to be multiplied by each other. It also shows us the size of the product when matrices are multiplied.

In order to multiply two matrices, *the number of columns in the left-hand matrix must equal the number of rows in the right-hand matrix.*

When two matrices can be multiplied, *the size of the product is the number of rows in the left-hand matrix by the number of columns in the right-hand matrix.*

That is:

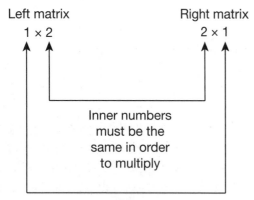

Left matrix
1 × 2

Right matrix
2 × 1

Inner numbers
must be the
same in order
to multiply

Outer numbers
give the dimension
of the result.

Example

Given $A = \begin{bmatrix} 1 & 2 & 3 \\ 7 & -1 & 4 \end{bmatrix}$,

$B = \begin{bmatrix} 0 & -3 & 5 \\ -1 & -9 & 2 \end{bmatrix}$, and

$D = \begin{bmatrix} -1 & 3 \\ 5 & -4 \\ -7 & 1 \end{bmatrix}$, find the products AB and

AD, if possible.

Solution: For AB, we see that A is a 2 × 3 matrix and B is a 2 × 3 matrix as well. The number of columns in A is not equal to the number of rows in B, so AB cannot be found.

AD is a different story. We see that each entry in a row of A has a corresponding entry in a column of D. Thus, we can indeed multiply these two matrices. This is done by multiplying each entry in row 1 of matrix A to the corresponding entry in column 1 of D and then adding these products. The first row of A populates the first row of the result, while the second row of A will populate the second row of the result. When we multiply the entries in row 1 of A by the entries in column 1 of D and add, we get the entry in row 1, column 1, of resulting matrix AD. After multiplying each entry in row 1 of A to column 1 of D and adding, we multiply row 1 of A by column 2 of D, and add. This gives the entry in row 1, column 2, of the result. Then we move to row 2 of matrix A and multiply row 2 by column 1 of D (and add), and finally multiply row 2 of A by column 2 of D. The calculation is:

$$\begin{bmatrix} 1 & 2 & 3 \\ 7 & -1 & 4 \end{bmatrix} \begin{bmatrix} -1 & 3 \\ 5 & -4 \\ -7 & 1 \end{bmatrix} = \begin{bmatrix} (1 \cdot -1) + (2 \cdot 5) + (3 \cdot -7) & (1 \cdot 3) + (2 \cdot -4) + (3 \cdot 1) \\ (7 \cdot -1) + (-1 \cdot 5) + (4 \cdot -7) & (7 \cdot 3) + (-1 \cdot -4) + (4 \cdot 1) \end{bmatrix}$$

$$= \begin{bmatrix} (-1) + (10) + (-21) & (3) + (-8) + (3) \\ (-7) + (-5) + (-28) & (21) + (4) + (4) \end{bmatrix}$$

$$= \begin{bmatrix} -12 & -2 \\ -40 & 29 \end{bmatrix}$$

Note that the size of the result AD is the number of rows in A by the number of columns in D, 2×2.

When we speak of multiplication, we naturally want to discuss the possibility of a multiplicative identity, and multiplicative inverses. In the case of matrices, these two things exist for only a special kind of matrices.

Square Matrices

Definition: A matrix that has the same number of rows and columns is called a *square matrix.*

Example

$C = \begin{bmatrix} 6 & 8 \\ -7 & 1 \end{bmatrix}$ is a 2×2 square matrix.

Notice that if we consider only square $n \times n$ matrices for a specific n, then these matrices are *closed under addition, scalar multiplication,* and *matrix multiplication.* Furthermore, matrix multiplication for square matrices is *distributive* and *associative.* However, matrix multiplication is *not commutative,* as the following example shows.

Example

Letting $M = \begin{bmatrix} -1 & 3 \\ 2 & -4 \end{bmatrix}$ and

$C = \begin{bmatrix} 6 & 8 \\ -7 & 1 \end{bmatrix}$,

find MC and CM to show $MC \neq CM$.

Solution:

$$MC = \begin{bmatrix} -1 & 3 \\ 2 & -4 \end{bmatrix}\begin{bmatrix} 6 & 8 \\ -7 & 1 \end{bmatrix} = \begin{bmatrix} -1(6) + 3(-7) & -1(8) + 3(1) \\ 2(6) + -4(-7) & 2(8) + -4(1) \end{bmatrix} = \begin{bmatrix} -27 & -5 \\ 40 & 12 \end{bmatrix}$$

$$CM = \begin{bmatrix} 6 & 8 \\ -7 & 1 \end{bmatrix}\begin{bmatrix} -1 & 3 \\ 2 & -4 \end{bmatrix} = \begin{bmatrix} 6(-1) + 8(2) & 6(3) + 8(4) \\ -7(-1) + 1(2) & -7(3) + 1(4) \end{bmatrix} = \begin{bmatrix} 10 & 50 \\ 9 & -17 \end{bmatrix}$$

Thus, $MC \neq CM$, and matrix multiplication is *not* commutative.

This is not a peculiarity of square matrices; rather, matrix multiplication is *not* commutative in general.

Definition: The multiplicative identity for matrices, called the *identity matrix* and denoted I, is an $n \times n$ matrix such that for any other $n \times n$ matrix A we have $IA = AI = A$.

Example

Show that $I = \begin{bmatrix} 1 & 0 \\ 0 & 1 \end{bmatrix}$ is the 2×2 identity matrix.

Solution: Let $A = \begin{bmatrix} a & b \\ c & d \end{bmatrix}$ be an arbitrary 2×2 matrix. We will multiply AI and IA, and see that either way our result is A:

$$AI = \begin{bmatrix} a & b \\ c & d \end{bmatrix}\begin{bmatrix} 1 & 0 \\ 0 & 1 \end{bmatrix} = \begin{bmatrix} a \cdot 1 + b \cdot 0 & a \cdot 0 + b \cdot 1 \\ c \cdot 1 + d \cdot 0 & c \cdot 0 + d \cdot 1 \end{bmatrix} = \begin{bmatrix} a & b \\ c & d \end{bmatrix}$$

$$IA = \begin{bmatrix} 1 & 0 \\ 0 & 1 \end{bmatrix}\begin{bmatrix} a & b \\ c & d \end{bmatrix} = \begin{bmatrix} 1 \cdot a + 0 \cdot c & 1 \cdot b + 0 \cdot d \\ 0 \cdot a + 1 \cdot c & 0 \cdot b + 1 \cdot d \end{bmatrix} = \begin{bmatrix} a & b \\ c & d \end{bmatrix}$$

All identity matrices are of the form $\begin{bmatrix} 1 & 0 & \cdots & 0 \\ 0 & 1 & 0 & M \\ M & 0 & 0 & 0 \\ 0 & L & 0 & 1 \end{bmatrix}$. So the 3×3 identity is $\begin{bmatrix} 1 & 0 & 0 \\ 0 & 1 & 0 \\ 0 & 0 & 1 \end{bmatrix}$, and the 4×4 identity is $\begin{bmatrix} 1 & 0 & 0 & 0 \\ 0 & 1 & 0 & 0 \\ 0 & 0 & 1 & 0 \\ 0 & 0 & 0 & 1 \end{bmatrix}$, and so on.

Sometimes we may use subscripts to specify which size identity matrix we are considering. So a 3×3 identity matrix may be referred to as I_3.

Now that we have a good idea of the multiplicative identity for matrices, we can consider if and when a square matrix has a multiplicative inverse.

Definition: The *inverse* of an $n \times n$ matrix, A, if it exists, is the $n \times n$ matrix A^{-1} such that $AA^{-1} = A^{-1}A = I$.

We will discuss methods for finding the inverse of a square matrix, if it exists, in the next chapter. Here we simply emphasize that not every square matrix has a multiplicative inverse. So, the question is: How do we know if a matrix has a multiplicative inverse? There is a function called the *determinant*, which assigns a number to each matrix. We can use this function to determine when a matrix has an inverse. There is a formula for 2×2 matrices that gives us the determinant quickly, and enables us to determine if the matrix has an inverse. Defining the determinant for larger matrices is a bit more complicated.

Definition: The *determinant* of a square 2×2 matrix, $A = \begin{bmatrix} a & b \\ c & d \end{bmatrix}$ is given by $\det(A) = |A| = ad - cb$

Example
Find the determinant of the matrix.

Solution:

$$\det(A) = \begin{vmatrix} -1 & 3 \\ 4 & -5 \end{vmatrix} = (-1)(-5) - (3)(4) = -7$$

We now state a fact that we will justify in the Algebra Review chapter:

Theorem: A square matrix A has a multiplicative inverse A^{-1} if and only if $\det(A) \neq 0$.

Problem Solving Using Numbers and Units

Units help us to put numbers in context and determine what they are measuring in a way that is widely understood. The first instances in which we encounter units are in measuring certain quantities: The dimensions of a room are measured in feet, the time it takes to travel to the beach may be measured in hours, the distance a car can drive on a single tank of gas can be measured in miles or kilometers, the weight of a bag of coffee may be measured in ounces, the amount of vitamin C contained in a glass of orange juice may be measured in milligrams, and so on.

All of the examples mentioned are examples of what are called *base* units. There are two common systems of measurement: the English system and the metric system. The metric system is used in the International System of Units (SI), which gives *SI base units*.

Base units, as our example suggests, measure the quantities of length, mass, and time. The International System of Units gives four more base units for measuring electric current (ampere), thermodynamic temperature (kelvin), amount of substance (mole), and luminous intensity (candela). Our focus in this review will be on the base units for the first three quantities mentioned: length, mass, and time.

The SI base unit for *length* is the *meter*, denoted m. The SI base unit for *mass* is the *kilogram*, kg, and the base unit for *time* is the *second*, sec. While kelvin is the SI base unit for thermodynamic temperature, we usually measure metric *temperature* in degrees *Celsius*, °C. The metric base unit for *volume* is the *liter*, L. We will talk more about volume soon, since it is also measured using *derived units*, for example, cubic centimeters, denoted cm³.

The English base unit for *length* is the *foot*, ft.; for *mass* is the *pound*, lb.; for *time*, the *second*; for *temperature*, degrees *Fahrenheit*, °F. A base unit for *volume* could be the *gallon*, but again, volume is a derived unit that can be expressed in terms of feet as cubic feet, denoted ft.³, or as the cube of some other measure of length.

Many problems arise simply from converting from one system of measurement to another, or from converting units within a single system. In order to do this type of conversion, we need to make use of the following equivalences.

Converting within the Metric System (SI Units)

The reason the metric system is convenient is that conversion between base units usually requires multiplication by a power of 10. To know which power of 10 is needed, we need to review the metric system in a little more detail. In particular, we need to review the meaning of some standard prefixes.

Some Common Metric Prefixes (listed from least to greatest):

PREFIX	NOTATION	NUMERICAL MEANING
micro	μ	$\frac{1}{1,000,000} = 10^{-6}$
milli	m	$\frac{1}{1,000} = 10^{-3}$
centi	cm	$\frac{1}{100} = 10^{-2}$
deci	d	$\frac{1}{10} = 10^{-1}$
—	—	1
deca	da	$10 = 10^{1}$
hecto	h	$100 = 10^{2}$
kilo	k	$1,000 = 10^{3}$

We will use the SI unit of length as our primary example; all other metric base units behave similarly:

The SI base unit of length is the meter:

$$1 \text{ meter} = 1,000 \text{ millimeters}$$
$$1 \text{ meter} = 100 \text{ centimeters}$$
$$1 \text{ meter} = \tfrac{1}{1,000} \text{ kilometer}$$

In order to help us make conversions easier and more systematic, we can use *conversion factors*. Conversion factors are numbers associated with units that can be multiplied to convert units. Conversion factors are constructed from unit equivalences like the ones listed earlier. This means that the conversion factor is a multiplicative identity.

Example

Create a conversion factor from the equivalence 1 meter = 100 centimeters.

Solution: $1 = \frac{100 \text{ cm}}{1 \text{ m}}$ and $1 = \frac{1 \text{ m}}{100 \text{ cm}}$

Conversion factors for SI Units

Based on the equivalences we have, we can write conversion factors.

To convert *from meters to millimeters*, we can use the factor $\frac{1,000 \text{ mm}}{1 \text{ m}}$.

To convert *from millimeters to meters*, however, we use the factor $\frac{1 \text{ m}}{1,000 \text{ mm}}$.

In general, a conversion factor should be a fraction. Which unit goes in the numerator or denominator is determined by which unit we want to eliminate or keep.

Example

Determine the number of centigrams in a 50-gram sample of a particular substance.

Solution: Since we want centigrams, but we're given grams, we can use the conversion factor $\frac{100 \text{ cg}}{1 \text{ g}}$, and now we multiply:

$$50 \ \cancel{g} \cdot \frac{100 \text{ cg}}{1 \ \cancel{g}} = 5,000 \text{ cg}$$

Notice how we can divide units in the same way we can divide numbers, and that common units cancel just like common factors.

Converting Units within the English System

In the English system we can take advantage of the following equivalences:

LENGTH	MASS (WEIGHT)	VOLUME	TIME
1 foot = 12 inches 1 yard = 3 feet 1 mile = 5,280 feet	1 pound = 16 ounces 1 ton = 2,000 pounds	1 gallon = 4 quarts 1 quart = 2 pints 1 pint = 2 cups	1 minute = 60 seconds 1 hour = 60 minutes 1 day = 24 hours 1 year = 365 days

Example

An inchworm crawled 25 yards; determine how many inches the worm traveled.

Solution: We need to convert from yards to inches. Looking at our equivalences table, we have one that will allow us to convert from yards to feet: 1 yard = 3 feet; and one that allows us to convert from feet to inches: 1 foot = 12 inches. Since we are given yards, our first conversion factor must be $\frac{3 \text{ ft.}}{1 \text{ yd.}}$. Since we want inches, our second conversion factor must be $\frac{12 \text{ in.}}{1 \text{ ft.}}$. The conversion is as follows:

$$25 \text{ yd.} \cdot \frac{3 \text{ ft.}}{1 \text{ yd.}} \cdot \frac{12 \text{ in.}}{1 \text{ ft.}} = 900 \text{ inches}$$

Converting between English and Metric

For converting from English units to metric units and vice versa, we do not have equivalences, but we can use the following approximations.

1 inch ≈ 2.54 cm	1 mile ≈ 1.6093 km
1 foot ≈ 0.305 m	1 pound ≈ 0.4536 kg
1 yard ≈ 0.9144 m	1 gallon ≈ 3.785 L

Derived Units

Many of the quantities that are important to us cannot be measured using base units, but rather must be measured using units derived from base units. *Derived units are units that result from multiplying or dividing quantities that are measured in base units.*

There are many examples of quantities measured in derived units. Perhaps the most basic examples are the units for measuring *area* in either the English system or the metric system. In order to measure the area of a rectangular room, we would measure the length of the room and then measure the width of the room. Both of these measurements would be measurements of length in the same unit of length, say feet. Using the fact that the area of a rectangle is given by multiplying its length and width gives us a measurement in ft. × ft. = ft.^{2} (square feet) for the unit of area. Similarly, using the fact that the volume of a cube is given by multiplying its length by its width and its height, we derive that the unit of volume would be ft. × ft. × ft. = ft.^{3} (cubic feet).

Example

The length of a room is measured to be 108 inches, and the width of the room is measured to be 10 feet. Find the area of the room in square feet.

Solution: First we need to convert our length measurement to feet.

$$108 \text{ inches} \cdot \frac{1 \text{ foot}}{12 \text{ inches}} = 9 \text{ feet}$$

Therefore the area of the room in square feet is

$$9 \text{ ft.} \cdot 10 \text{ ft.} = 90 \text{ ft.}^2$$

We may also have occasion to use derived units to solve problems.

Example
Mike's car gets an average of 30 miles per gallon (mpg). The price of gas at Mike's local gasoline station is \$3.45 for one gallon of unleaded gas. Mike needs to drive 105 miles for work. How much money (in dollars) will Mike spend on gasoline for this trip?

Solution: We need to organize the given information to set up conversion factors so that the units of the product of the factors are in dollars. We use the units to help us.

Ultimately we want dollars. We are given $\frac{miles}{gallon}$, $\frac{dollars}{gallon}$, and miles. So we see that if we multiply $\frac{\$}{gal.} \cdot \frac{gal.}{miles} \cdot miles = \$$, we obtain the units we require. Therefore, for this trip, gasoline will cost Mike

$$\frac{\$3.45}{gal.} \cdot \frac{gal.}{30\ miles} \cdot 105\ miles = \$12.08$$

Ratio and Proportion

Our discussion of derived units leads us to consider *ratios* and *proportion*.

Definition: A *ratio* is a comparison between two quantities.

For example, Mike's car gets 30 miles per gallon of gas. This is a ratio of number of miles to number of gallons. Ratios are usually expressed as rational numbers, but they can also be expressed in words or using different notation.

Example
From our last example we see that it costs Mike approximately \$12 in gasoline to drive 105 miles. From this information we can say that the ratio of dollars to miles is 12 to 105, or we can write the ratio of dollars to miles as 12:105, or we can express this ratio as a fraction, $\frac{12}{105}$.

(It is important to notice that we are expressing the ratio of number of dollars to number of miles. If we were to express the ratio of number of miles to number of dollars, the notation would be switched: $\frac{105}{12}$ and 105:12.)

Once we have a ratio, we can set up a proportion to solve certain problems.

Definition: A *proportion* is an equation involving ratios, $\frac{a}{b} = \frac{c}{d}$.

Notice that if we have the proportion $\frac{a}{b} = \frac{c}{d}$, we can cross multiply and write $ad = bc$.

Example
Mike pays \$12 to drive 105 miles. How much does it cost Mike to drive 147 miles?

Solution: We can solve this problem by setting up a proportion:

$$\frac{12}{105} = \frac{?}{147}$$

By cross multiplying, we obtain ? = 16.80, so a drive of 147 miles costs Mike \$16.80.

Definition: A *unit rate* is the ratio of one quantity to a single unit of another quantity.

For example, if we are given that gas costs \$3.45 per gallon, we are given a unit rate since the ratio we are given is 3.45 dollars to one gallon.

Example
Compute the unit rate of dollars to miles, if it costs \$12 to drive 105 miles.

Solution: In order to compute this unit rate, we simply divide 12 by 105:

$$\frac{\$12}{105 \text{ miles}} = \frac{\$0.114}{1 \text{ mile}} = 0.114 \text{ dollars per mile}$$

Example
Compute the unit rate of miles to dollars, if it costs $12 to drive 105 miles.

Solution: Since the ratio is written as miles to dollars, we divide 105 by 12:

$$\frac{105 \text{ miles}}{\$12} = \frac{8.75 \text{ miles}}{\$1} = 8.75 \text{ miles per dollar}$$

We can also view the ratios of like quantities as *scale factors*.

Definition: A *scale factor* is a number that multiplies like quantities.

Example
If it costs $12 to drive 105 miles, determine the cost of driving 420 miles.

Solution: Here we see that 420 is 4 times 105; that is to say, 4 is the *scale factor*. Therefore a trip of 420 miles will cost $4 \times \$12 = \$48$.

We also use *proportions to convert ratios to percent* (per 100).

Example
Mike earned 74 points out of 90 total points on his most recent math exam. The class average on this exam was 79%. Determine if Mike's score was above or below the class average.

Solution: We can set up a proportion to determine Mike's grade as a percent:

$$\frac{74}{90} = \frac{x}{100}$$

Next we solve for x: $x = 100 \cdot \frac{74}{90} = 82.22\%$. Mike's score of 82.22% was above the class average of 79%.

Directly and Inversely Proportional

Definition: Two quantities x and y are *directly proportional* if as x increases, y increases by the same proportion.

For example, the cost in dollars for gasoline is directly proportional to the number of miles driven.

We can express this relationship algebraically as $y = Cx$. The constant C is called the *constant of proportionality*.

For instance, the unit rates we determined earlier can be considered constants of proportionality.

Example
For $C = 0.114$ dollars per mile, find the cost in dollars of driving 5,000 miles.

Solution: Since cost in dollars is directly proportional to number of miles driven, we have that $d = C \cdot m$, where d represents number of dollars spent on gas, and m represents the number of miles driven. Thus we see that the cost in dollars is given by

$$d = 0.114 \cdot 5,000 = 570$$

It is both useful and important to see how the units work out in this calculation. We display the previous calculation with units:

$$d \text{ dollars} = \frac{\$0.114}{1 \text{ mile}} \cdot 5,000 \text{ mile} = \$570$$

Definition: Two quantities x and y are *inversely proportional* if they are related by $y = \frac{C}{x}$ where $C > 0$. Put another way, two quantities are inversely proportional if as one quantity increases the other decreases at the same rate.

For example, the lower the price of a one-pound bag of coffee, the more bags of coffee a customer is likely to purchase. Price and items purchased may be inversely proportional.

Example
Stella's budget allows her to spend $16 for coffee. When the price of a one-pound bag of coffee is $8.00, she buys two pounds of coffee. What price would a pound of coffee have to sell for in order for Stella to buy three pounds of coffee?

Solution: We know that Stella can buy more coffee if the price is less. Using the inverse relationship $y = \frac{C}{x}$ with x pounds of coffee and y price, we have the equation

$$8 = \frac{C}{2}$$

Thus, $C = 16$. We now use this constant and $x = 3$ to determine the price at which Stella could purchase three pounds of coffee:

$$y = \frac{16}{3} = \$5.33$$

Therefore, if a one-pound bag of coffee sells for $5.33, Stella can buy three one-pound bags.

Error in Measurement

Another consequence of derived units is the propagation of error. If a measurement of length is off by a little bit, then this error will be carried over into any measurement using this length measurement. More generally, any quantity that is computed using base units that have inherent errors will naturally inherit this error.

Absolute Error

Definition: The *absolute error* in measurement is the absolute value of the difference between the measured value and the value of maximum error (the value that differs by the greatest amount from the measured value).

Example
The length of the side of a cube is measured to be 5.253 inches. The gradations on the ruler that was used to measure the side length of the cube are at every $\frac{1}{8}$ inch. Thus, the length measurement is accurate to 0.125 inches. This means the true length of the side of the cube is between 5.128 and 5.378. Determine the absolute error in the measurement of length.

Solution: Since our measured valued is 5.253 inches and the difference between the measured value and the other two values is 0.125, the absolute error of our measurement is 0.125.

Example
Again, the length of the side of a cube is measured to be 5.253 inches, and the gradations on the ruler that was used to measure the side length of the cube are at every $\frac{1}{8}$ inch; thus, the length measurement is accurate to 0.125 inches. Determine the absolute error in the measurement of volume of this cube.

Solution: The volume of a cube is given by $V = s^3$, where s denotes the side of the cube. Since the length of the side of the cube is between 5.128 and 5.378 inches, we cube both of these values to determine the values between which the true volume measurement resides. We see that the volume of the cube is between 134.848 cubic inches and 155.547 cubic inches. The measured value of the volume is $(5.253)^3 = 144.951$. The absolute differences between the measured value and the two error values are $|144.951 - 134.848| = 10.103$ and $|155.547 - 144.951| = 10.596$. Therefore, the absolute error in our volume measurement is 10.596 cubic inches.

Relative and Percent Error

We now need to determine if and when an error in measurement is significant. We do this by computing the relative error and/or the percent error.

Definition: The *relative error* of a measurement is given by

$$\text{Relative error} = \frac{\text{Absolute error}}{\text{Measured value}}$$

Definition: The *percent error* of a measurement is given by

$$\text{Percent error} = \text{Relative error} \cdot 100\%$$

Example

Determine the relative error and the percent error of our measurement of the length of the side of a cube as 5.253 inches accurate to $\frac{1}{8}$ of an inch.

Solution: The absolute error of this length measurement is 0.125 inches. Our measured value for the length is 5.250 inches. Thus the relative error is

$$\text{Relative error} = \frac{0.125}{5.253} = 0.0238$$

The percent error is $0.0238 \cdot 100\% = 2.38\%$.

Example

Determine the relative error and the percent error of our volume measurement in the previous examples.

Solution: The absolute error of our volume measurement is 10.596 cubic inches and our measured value for volume is 144.951 cubic inches. Thus the relative error is $\frac{10.596}{144.951} = 0.0731$, and the percent error is $0.0731 \cdot 100\% = 7.31\%$.

Dealing with Very Large and Very Small Numbers

Sometimes the quantities we measure turn out to be very large or very small. For example, the distance from the earth to the sun is 92,960,000 miles, while the width of a pixel on a tablet computer can be as small as 0.0078 cm.

Dealing with very large or very small numbers can be cumbersome. One way to make working with these numbers more manageable is the use of scientific notation.

Scientific Notation

Definition: A positive number, S, is written in *scientific notation* if it is expressed as the product of a number n such that $1 \le n < 10$, and 10^m, where m is an integer. That is,

$$S = n \times 10^m$$

Example

Write 900 in scientific notation.

Solution: $900 = 9 \times 100 = 9 \times 10^2$.

Example

Write 0.09 in scientific notation.

Solution: $0.09 = \frac{9}{100} = 9 \times 10^{-2}$

From these two examples we can see that there is an easy way to write a number in scientific notation that essentially only requires us to move the decimal point of the original number either right or left a certain number of places, and keep track of the number of places we move the decimal point.

More precisely, if the number in standard form is *greater than 10*, we move the decimal point to the *left* the number places needed to make a new number that is greater than or equal to 1 and less than 10. If the number in standard form is *less than 1*, we move the decimal point to the *right* the number of places needed to make a new number that that is greater than or equal to 1 and less than 10. The number of places we need to move the decimal point is the exponent on 10. This exponent is negative, if the number in standard form is less than 1. The exponent is positive, if the number in standard form is greater than 10.

Example

For 0.09 we move the decimal point *two* places to the right to get 9.0, and since the number 0.09 is less than 1 we have $0.09 = 9 \times 10^{-2}$.

Example

Write 0.0000000485 and 92,960,000 in scientific notation.

Solution: For 0.0000000485 we need to move the decimal point *eight* places to the right to get 4.85 (a number between 1 and 10). And since the number in standard form is clearly less than 1, we see that $0.0000000485 = 4.85 \times 10^{-8}$ in scientific notation.

For 92,960,000 we need to move the unwritten decimal point sitting at the far right *seven* places to the left to obtain 9.296×10^7.

It is also sometimes useful to write a given number in scientific notation in standard form. To do this, we simply reverse the procedure we employed above.

Example

Write 8.7345×10^{-5} in standard form.

Solution: We follow the instructions given to us by the exponent on 10 and move the decimal point *five* places to the *left*: $8.7345 \times 10^{-5} = 0.000087345$.

Addition and Subtraction in Scientific Notation

We can add and subtract numbers in scientific notation as long as they each have the same exponent on 10. We must be careful, however; if the sum or difference in the first factor becomes a number larger than 10 or less than 1, we will have to adjust our final answer so that it will remain in proper scientific notation.

Example

Compute $(7.8 \times 10^9) + (9.5 \times 10^9)$.

Solution: $(7.8 \times 10^9) + (9.5 \times 10^9) = 17.3 \times 10^9 = 1.73 \times 10^{10}$

Multiplication and Division in Scientific Notation

We can multiply and divide two numbers in scientific notation without concern for the exponents being exactly the same. We simply multiply the first factors and the second factors separately. When multiplying the second factors we can use rules of exponents. Nonetheless, we still may need to adjust our product or quotient so that our final expression is in proper scientific notation.

Example

Compute $(3.2 \times 10^{-7})(4.1 \times 10^{-5})$

Solution: $(3.2 \times 10^{-7})(4.1 \times 10^{-5}) = (3.2 \cdot 4.1) \times (10^{-7} \cdot 10^{-5}) = 13.12 \times 10^{-12} = 1.312 \times 10^{-11}$

Example

Compute $\dfrac{8.2 \times 10^{-7}}{2.1 \times 10^{-5}}$

Solution: $\dfrac{8.2 \times 10^{-7}}{2.1 \times 10^{-5}} = \left(\dfrac{8.2}{2.1}\right) \times \left(\dfrac{10^{-7}}{10^{-5}}\right) = 3.9 \times 10^{-2}$

Another way to deal with very large or very small numbers is estimating them by powers of 10. One way to estimate numbers in this fashion is to consider their *orders of magnitude*.

Orders of Magnitude

Definition: A number's *order of magnitude* is the nearest power of 10 when the number is rounded up from 3 (instead of from 5).

Example
Determine the order of magnitude of the numbers 99 and 4 and 2.

Solution: First we round 99 to 100 and see that $100 = 10^2$. Therefore, 99 has order of magnitude 2. Next we consider the number 4. We round 4 up to 10, and so 4 has order of magnitude 1. We would round 2 down to 1 (not up to 10), so 2's order of magnitude is 0.

Example
Use orders of magnitude to approximate the width of a pixel (in cm) on a tablet computer display, and to approximate the distance from the earth to the sun (in miles).

Solution: We will accept as given that the width of a pixel is 0.0078 cm. We could reasonably round this number to 0.0100 cm. And since,

$$0.0100 \text{ cm} = \tfrac{1}{100} \text{cm} = 10^{-2} \text{ cm}$$

the order of magnitude of the width of a pixel is –2.

The distance from the earth to the sun is 92,960,000 miles. We can round this number to 100,000,000 and $100,000,000 = 10^8$, so the order of magnitude of this distance is 8.

We can also compare two numbers based on their orders of magnitude. When doing this, we consider two numbers the same if they have the same order or magnitude. If two numbers are not of the same order of magnitude, then we say they differ by the absolute difference between their respective orders of magnitude.

Example
Compare the width of a pixel on a tablet screen with the distance from the earth to the sun using order or magnitude.

Solution: We first convert to the same unit of length in order to do the comparison. Let's work in miles.

$$0.00078 \text{ cm} \cdot \tfrac{1 \text{ m}}{100 \text{ cm}} \cdot \tfrac{1 \text{ km}}{1,000 \text{ m}} \cdot \tfrac{1 \text{ mile}}{1.609 \text{ km}}$$
$$= 0.0000000485 \text{ miles}$$

We round 0.0000000485 miles up to $0.0000001000 = \tfrac{1}{10,000,000} = 10^{-7}$. Thus, in miles, the order of magnitude is –7. We recall from our previous example that the order of magnitude of the distance from the earth to the sun is 8. Therefore, the distance from the earth to the sun and the width of a pixel differ by $|8 - (-7)| = 15$ orders of magnitude!

5 ▶ ALGEBRA REVIEW

CHAPTER SUMMARY

When most people think of mathematics, it is algebra that is conjured in the mind's eye—and this is no coincidence. As far as elementary mathematics goes, algebra is one of the most widely studied areas of mathematics, and it is one of the first kinds of rigorous, abstract study undertaken by any student. From basic algebra through multivariable calculus and beyond, algebra remains one of the most basic yet invaluable tools of abstraction in mathematics. From the study of equations to solving abstract problems by using symbols to represent quantities, algebra helps us to make sense of the quantitative problems we face in everyday life—though it often does not seem that way when looking at equations. In this chapter, we review the basic topics in algebra, beginning with algebraic expressions.

Algebraic Expressions

Algebraic expressions are expressions that are built from constants, variables, and a finite number of the operations of addition, subtraction, multiplication, division, and/or exponentiation. The following are examples of algebraic expressions:

1. x
2. $3t$
3. $3x^2y$

4. $3x^2y + 9y^2 - 10\sqrt{x}$

5. $\frac{3}{8x^2} - 7y + \sqrt{\frac{2x}{5}}$

6. $\frac{3x^2 - 5x + 1}{2x - 7}$

The two main examples of algebraic expressions that we will look at in this chapter are polynomial expressions and rational expressions, which are built from polynomial expressions. Algebra gives us an often-effective way to model and hence solve real-world problems. In order to use algebra to solve problems, we first must translate our given problem into an algebraic expression or an equation. Once we have made this translation, successfully solving the problem is then reduced to manipulating and rewriting algebraic expressions in such a way as to make the solution obvious. We begin by reviewing common algebraic expressions and methods we use to simplify these expressions.

Polynomial Expressions

Definition: A *polynomial expression* in a single variable is of the form $a_nx^n + a_{n-1}x^{n-1} + \ldots + a_1x + a_0$ where the a's are constants, called *coefficients*, and the x's are called *indeterminates* or *variables*. Each summand in a polynomial expression is called a *term*.

Examples of *polynomial* expressions are x, $3x^2 + x$, $-y^2 + x^2 + 9$, $5xy^3 + 2xy - 7$.

Note the difference between polynomial expressions and more general algebraic expressions. Polynomial expressions can have only nonnegative integer exponents. As discussed in the previous chapter, negative exponents will give us rational expressions; rational exponents will give us radical expressions. General real number exponents give us something different entirely.

We will mostly concern ourselves with single-variable polynomials, like x and $3x^2 + x$, but multi-variable polynomials, like $-y^2 + x^2 + 9$ and $5xy^3 + 2xy - 7$, do exist.

Example
$3x^2 + x$ is an example of a polynomial expression. It is obvious that $3x^2 + x$ has two terms (two summands), $3x^2$ and x.

Definition: The largest exponent on any variable in a polynomial expression is called the *degree* of the polynomial. We see that $3x^2 + x$ is a degree 2 polynomial.

Definition: The term of highest degree in a polynomial is called the *leading term*, and the coefficient of the leading term is, not surprisingly, called the *leading coefficient*. For $3x^2 + x$, the leading term is $3x^2$, and the leading coefficient is 3.

Polynomial expressions that have only one term, like x, are called *monomials*. Some other examples of monomials are $-7x^5$, $4xy^3$, $\frac{1}{2}xyz$. Polynomial expressions that have exactly two terms, such as $3x^2 + x$, are called *binomials*, while polynomial expressions that have exactly three terms, like $ax^2 + bx + c$, are called *trinomials*.

Simplifying Polynomial Expressions: Combining Like Terms
We will encounter, derive, evaluate, or create algebraic expressions when we attempt to solve problems. It is in our best interest to make sure the expressions are in as simple a form as possible.

Example
Evaluate $3x^2 + x^2 + 7x - 2x + 11$ at $x = -1$.

Solution: This is of course asking us to substitute -1 in for x and perform the operations indicated following the familiar order of operations. Substituting, we obtain

$$3(-1)^2 + (-1)^2 + 7(-1) - 2(-1) + 11$$
$$= 3 + 1 - 7 + 2 + 11 = 10$$

This could have been computationally easier, however, had we noticed that we could have combined the terms $3x^2$ and x^2, and the terms $7x$ and $-2x$. (These terms are called *like terms* since they have the exact same variable expression.) Only like terms may be added or subtracted. The activity of adding or subtracting like terms is commonly referred to as *combining like terms*. Combining like terms results in a simpler expression and reduces the number of times we need to substitute the number -1 into the expression.

Example

Simplify $3x^2 + x^2 + 7x - 2x + 11$ and then evaluate at $x = -1$.

Solution: First we combine the like terms:

$$\underbrace{3x^2 + x^2}_{4x^2} + \underbrace{7x - 2x}_{5x} + 11 = 4x^2 + 5x + 11$$

Next we substitute in -1 for x:

$$4(-1)^2 + 5(-1) + 11$$

And, essentially, we combine like terms one more time to obtain our numeric result:

$$4(-1)^2 + 5(-1) + 11 = 4 - 5 + 11 = 10$$

Here is another example. This time we simplify a multivariable polynomial expression.

Example

Simplify $3xy^2 - x^2y + 9x^2 - 7xy^2 + x^2$.

Solution: We scan the polynomial expression and see that there are two pairs of like terms: $3xy^2$ and $-7xy^2$, and $9x^2$ and x^2. Combining like terms (i.e., adding these polynomials) gives

$$3xy^2 - x^2y + 9x^2 - 7xy^2 + x^2 = -4xy^2 + 10x^2 - 7x^2y$$

Combining like terms is a phrase that describes the procedure used to *add and subtract polynomial expressions*.

Example

Suppose we are given two polynomial expressions, $P = -5x^2 + 9x$ and $Q = -3x^2 + 7$, and asked to find $P - Q$.

Solution: We set up the expression $-5x^2 + 9x - (-3x^2 + 7)$, and note that the parentheses around the second expression are needed so that we know to use the distributive property to distribute the subtraction to both terms in the second expression:

$$-5x^2 + 9x - (-3x^2 + 7) = -5x^2 + 9x + 3x^2 - 7$$

Finally, we combine like terms:

$$-5x^2 + 9x + 3x^2 - 7 = -2x^2 + 9x - 7$$

Solving Polynomial Equations: Linear Equations

The goal of solving any equation is to find a numeric value or a precise expression for the variable (or variables) featured in the algebraic expression that makes up the equation. The simplest type of polynomial equations are called *linear equations*. Linear equations involve polynomial expressions of degree 1. The following is a simple example of solving a linear equation. The solution highlights the procedures that can be used to isolate the variable on one side of the equal sign. That is, "solving for x" means to end up with "$x =$ something."

Example

Solve $7x + 2 = 3x - 5$ for x.

Solution: Our goal here is to find a specific value for the indeterminate, x, that makes this sentence true. This means we want x on one side of the equation, and everything else on the other side of the equation.

$$7x + 2 = 3x - 5$$
$$4x + 2 = -5 \quad \text{Subtracted } 3x \text{ from both sides.}$$
$$4x = -7 \quad \text{Subtracted 2 from both sides.}$$
$$x = -\frac{7}{4} \quad \text{Divided both sides by 4.}$$

Sometimes linear equations may appear at first glance to be nonlinear, and our answer, as mentioned previously, may not be a specific number, but an algebraic expression.

Example

Solve $\frac{ax - b}{2a} = \frac{c - x}{b}$ for x, where a, b, and c are real numbers.

Solution: We begin by "clearing the fractions." We do this by finding the least common multiple (LCM) of the two fractions, namely $2a$ and b. The LCM here is $2ab$ and we multiply both sides of the equation by this number to clear the fractions:

$$2ab \cdot \frac{ax - b}{2a} = \frac{c - x}{b} \cdot 2ab \Rightarrow b(ax - b) = 2a(c - x)$$

Next we use the distributive property of real numbers:

$$b(ax - b) = 2a(c - x) \Rightarrow abx - b^2 = 2ac - 2ax$$

We now proceed to isolate the variable as we did in the previous example.

$$abx + 2ax - b^2 = 2ac \quad \text{Added } 2ax \text{ to both sides.}$$
$$abx + 2ax = 2ac + b^2 \quad \text{Added } b^2 \text{ to both sides.}$$

$$x(ab + 2a) = 2ac + b^2 \quad \text{Factored out the common } x \text{ on the left. (distributive property)}$$
$$x = \frac{2ac + b^2}{ab + 2a} \quad \text{Divided both sides by } ab + 2a, \text{ assuming it's not zero.}$$

But what about word problems describing linear expressions and equations?

Example

Twelve less than three times a number is the same as twice the sum of the number and 2. Find this number.

Solution: Let n represent this unknown number. The phrase *Twelve less than three times a number* can be translated as $3n - 12$, while the phrase *twice the sum of the number and 2* can be represented as $2(n + 2)$. The phrase *the same as* tells us to set these two expressions equal to one another and thus write the equation:

$$3n - 12 = 2(n + 2)$$

We now solve the equation for n:

$$3n - 12 = 2(n + 2)$$
$$3n - 12 = 2n + 4 \quad \text{Distribute the 2 on the right side.}$$
$$n - 12 = 4 \quad \text{Subtract } 2n \text{ from both sides.}$$
$$n = 16 \quad \text{Add 12 to both sides.}$$

Therefore, we find that $n = 16$.

Example

A chemist needs 12 L of a 40% acid solution. She has only 10 L of 20% solution and 5 L of 70% solution in stock. Does the chemist have enough 70% solution to make the desired 40% solution?

Solution: First we note that the amount of acid in the solution is the product of the volume of the solution and the concentration of the acid. This means that the chemist's desired amount of acid is $12 \cdot (0.4) = 4.8$. The 12 L of 40% solution is to be made from the 20% solution and the 70% solution. We do not yet know how many liters of either solution the chemist will need. Let x represent the number of liters of the 70% solution required. This means that $12 - x$ must represent the number of liters of 20% solution required. The amount of acid obtained from the 70% solution is $.7x$, and the amount obtained from the 20% solution is $.2(12 - x)$. We use these amounts to set up the linear equation:

$$.7x + .2(12 - x) = 4.8$$

We solve for x:

$$.7x + .2(12 - x) = 4.8$$
$$.7x + 2.4 - .2x = 4.8$$
$$.5x = 2.4$$
$$x = 4.8 \text{ L of 70\% solution}$$

Therefore, we see that since the chemist has 5 L of 70% solution, she does indeed have enough to make her 40% solution. Notice that she also has enough 20% solution to make the desired 40% solution.

Example

The sum of three consecutive even integers is 972. Find the largest of the three consecutive even integers.

Solution: We can represent three consecutive even integers as x, $x + 2$, and $x + 4$. Notice that if the problem had instead required three consecutive odd integers, we would represent them in exactly the same way. With our three consecutive even integers in hand, we can now express their sum:

$$x + (x + 2) + (x + 4) = 972$$

The parentheses in the equation are unnecessary since we are using addition exclusively, but we include them here to highlight the three integers we are working with. This equation can be simplified by combining like terms:

$$x + (x + 2) + (x + 4) = 972$$
$$3x + 6 = 972$$

Solving for x, we have $x = 322$. Therefore the largest of these three consecutive even integers is $x + 4 = 326$.

Linear Inequalities

Rather than finding a specific x-value, we may be interested in finding a set of x-values. For instance, when looking for an apartment you are asked to specify the least number of bedrooms you need. If your answer is two, and we let b denote number of bedrooms, then we have just set up the inequality $b \geq 2$; the number of bedrooms needed is greater than or equal to 2. We graph this inequality on the real number line (x-axis) as shown:

This inequality can also be written in *interval notation* as $[2, \infty)$.

Solving inequalities is much like solving equations except that our solutions will be intervals of real numbers instead of specific real numbers. Additionally, we need to be diligent about the ordering of positive real numbers in contrast to the ordering of negative real numbers. For example, $2 < 3$ (2 is less than 3), but $-2 \not< -3$; rather, $-2 > -3$.

Example

Solve the inequality $7 - 3x < -5$.

Solution: In order to avoid making a mistake involving the direction of the inequality symbol, let's add $3x$

to both sides. To be more efficient, let's, at the same time, add 5 to both sides:

$$
\begin{array}{cccc}
7 & -3x < -5 & & \\
+5 & +3x & +5 & +3x \\
\hline
12 & & < & 3x
\end{array}
$$

Dividing both sides by 3 solves the equality:

$$\tfrac{12}{3} < \tfrac{3x}{3} \Rightarrow 4 < x$$

This solution can graphed as

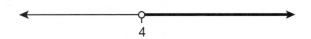

4

Since we have that x must be strictly greater than 4, we draw an open circle at 4, meaning that 4 is *not* included in the solution set. This is expressed in interval notation as $[4,\infty)$.

Quadratic Expressions and Equations

Quadratic expressions are polynomial expressions of the form $ax^2 + bx + c$ (degree 2 polynomial). The form $ax^2 + bx + c$ is called the *general form*. We will also find it very useful in this chapter and the next to write our quadratic expressions in *standard form*, $a(x-h)^2 + k$. A factored form $(rx-n)(jx-m)$ is useful for solving equations; for example, we may recall that $(rx-n)(jx-m) = 0 \Rightarrow x = \frac{n}{r}$ or $x = \frac{m}{j}$.

Quadratic expressions can be built by multiplying together two linear expressions. The next example shows how a quadratic expression is the product of two linear expressions and also shows how to *multiply polynomials*. Multiplication of polynomials is an application of the *distributive property* of the real numbers. We will display the distribution in the solution to the example. In the special case when we are multiplying two binomials, it is common to use the first, outer, inner, last (FOIL) method. We use the distribution method since it works when multiplying any two polynomials, not just binomials.

> **Example**
> Let $P = 2x + 3$ and $Q = x - 7$. Calculate $P \times Q$.

Solution:
$$
\begin{aligned}
PQ &= (2x+3)(x-7) = 2x \cdot x + 2x(-7) + 3x + 3(-7) \\
&= 2x^2 - 14x + 3x - 21 \\
&= 2x^2 - 11x - 21
\end{aligned}
$$

Now that we have introduced quadratic expressions, it is time to move to methods of solving quadratic *equations*.

Quadratic equations are equations that can be written as $ax^2 + bx + c = 0$. These are special cases of the more general problem of finding zeros of a polynomial function. There are several standard methods we can use to solve for x in quadratic equations. Our options depend on the coefficients in the quadratic equation itself.

Method 1 for Solving Quadratic Equations: Factoring

Factoring is the most desirable method to use whenever possible (sometimes it is way too difficult, and we would try the other methods), so it is the first one we will look into. Factoring to solve a quadratic equation relies on the fact that quadratic expressions are the product of two linear expressions; factoring is a way to figure out what these linear expressions are and then use them to solve the equation. Our ability to solve in this case is because of the zero factor property: for real (or complex) numbers a and b:

If $a \cdot b = 0$, then either $a = 0$ or $b = 0$.

> **Example**
> Solve $2x^2 - 11x - 21 = 0$.

Solution: If we recognize that $2x^2 - 11x - 21 = (2x + 3)(x - 7)$, then our equation becomes

$$(2x + 3)(x - 7) = 0$$

By the zero factor property,

$$2x + 3 = 0 \text{ or } x - 7 = 0$$

Thus we obtain

$$x = -\frac{3}{2} \text{ or } x = 7$$

We now review two procedures that allow us to start with a quadratic expression in general form and obtain a quadratic expression in factored form.

Greatest Common Factor

When thinking of factoring a single-variable quadratic (or any other single-variable polynomial) the first thing to look for is the GCF. We've already discussed this notion for numbers in the preceding chapter, but it also applies to algebraic expressions in general. To extract the GCF of a polynomial equation, one must first locate the GCF of the coefficients and the GCF of the variable terms (the single variable raised to the smallest power that appears). The product of these is the GCF of the polynomial.

Example
Factor the GCF from the expression $8x^5 + 20x^4 - 48x^3$.

Solution: The greatest monomial expression that divides (i.e., goes into) each term equally is $4x^3$. We divide each term by this expression to obtain the rewritten and partially factored expression, $8x^5 + 20x^4 - 48x^3 = 4x^3(2x^2 + 5x - 12)$.

Now, $2x^2 + 5x - 12 = (2x - 3)(x + 4)$, so we have that

$$8x^5 + 20x^4 - 48x^3 = 4x^3(2x - 3)(x + 4)$$

But how did we factor the quadratic at the end? We will discuss two methods.

Factoring Method 1: Trial and Error

Factoring a quadratic expression using the method of trial and error sounds like this procedure depends on the luck of the person doing the factoring; however, this method is more procedural than its name implies, and it is very quick if one gets good at doing it.

Let's look back at $2x^2 + 5x - 12$. We want to write it as $2x^2 + 5x - 12 = (rx - n)(jx - m)$.

We begin the process by *factoring* both the *leading term* and the *constant term* in the expression, $2x^2$ and -12, respectively:

$$2x^2 = 2x \cdot x$$

At this stage, we have $(2x\ \ )(x\ \ )$. This guarantees that our first term must be $2x^2$. In order to guarantee that our last (constant) term is -12, we have to use factors of -12.

$$-12 = -12 \cdot 1 \text{ or } 12 \cdot -1, \text{ or}$$
$$-6 \cdot 2 \text{ or } 6 \cdot -2, \text{ or}$$
$$-4 \cdot 3 \text{ or } 4 \cdot -3$$

The factors of -12 that will work are those that cause the sum of the products of the outer and inner terms to add up to the middle term.

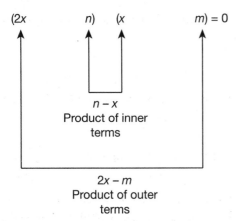

$n - x$
Product of inner
terms

$2x - m$
Product of outer
terms

We need $2x \cdot m + n \cdot x = +5x$, the original middle term.

Choosing $n = -3$ and $m = 4$ accomplishes this. For then the product of the outer terms is $8x$ and the product of the inner terms is $-3x$, and $8x - 3x = 5x$, which is our middle term! Note that the n and m were factors of the constant, -12. We just had to pick the right pair to get the needed middle term. The more practice one has with this, the better and faster the process will be. So practice! (The "trial and error" comes with choosing the right pair. But experience will help you to see the appropriate pair to choose a lot quicker.)

Thus, we end up with $2x^2 + 5x - 12 = (2x - 3)(x + 4)$, and the previous example works out beautifully.

The following is an example of how we use factoring to help us solve quadratic equations.

Example

An object is launched with an initial velocity of 40 feet per second from a height of 200 feet. Find the time at which the object hits the ground.

Solution: First we must translate this problem into an algebraic one. For basic projectile motion problems such as this, we use a quadratic expression to represent the motion of the object for time $t > 0$. (A basic calculus course or physics course would explain why we can model this using a quadratic; we won't go

into that here.) The expression that represents the position of a projectile, in general, is given by $at^2 + v_0 t + h_0$ where a is half the acceleration due to gravity, v_0 is the initial velocity of the object, and h_0 is the initial height of the object. This means that our expression for position where distance is measured in feet and time is measured in seconds is $-16t^2 + 40t + 200$. The phrase *hits the ground* indicates that we need to find the time, t, at which the height $-16t^2 + 40t + 200$ is 0; that is, we need to solve the equation

$$-16t^2 + 40t + 200 = 0$$

One way to solve this equation is to rewrite the algebraic expression using factoring:

$$-16t^2 + 40t + 200 = -8(2t^2 - 5t - 25)$$
$$= -8(2t + 5)(t - 5)$$

Using this form, it is now easy to solve the equation $-16t^2 + 40t + 200 = 0$. We just need to solve the equivalent equation $-8(2t + 5)(t - 5) = 0$ and see that $t = -\frac{5}{2}$ or $t = 5$ seconds. The only reasonable answer is $t = 5$, and we are done. It will take 5 seconds for the object to hit the ground.

Factoring Method 2: Decomposing the Middle Term/ac Method

An alternative and slightly more systematic method of factoring that does not rely so much on trial and error is the method of *decomposing the middle term*, or the *ac method*. The *ac* comes from the fact that we will be looking at the product *ac* for a given quadratic $ax^2 + bx + c$. This method involves exactly what it says, "decomposing the middle term," which means that we will break the middle (linear) term into two linear summands. The next example illustrates this method.

Example

Factor $2x^2 + 5x - 12$ by decomposing the middle term.

Solution: We will proceed step-by-step.

Step 1: Find *ac*. Multiply the first term and the last term: $2x^2 \cdot -12 = -24x^2$

Step 2: "List" the factorizations of this product. The word *list* is in quotation marks because the hope is that we will not have to physically write down all the factors after we read what step 3 requires.

Step 3: Choose the factorization of the product that contains the factors that add to give the middle term. We see that, for example, $-24x^2 = 8x \cdot -3x$, and we have that $8x + (-3x) = 5x$, which is the middle term. (Since our middle term is *positive* $5x$, the sign of the larger number, 8, must also be positive. So we would *not* consider, for example, $-8x$ and $+3x$.)

Step 4: Decompose the middle term using the factors from step 3:

$$2x^2 + 5x - 12 = 2x^2 + 8x - 3x - 12$$

Step 5: Group the first two terms and the last two terms (be careful!):

$$2x^2 + 5x - 12 = (2x^2 + 8x) + (-3x - 12)$$

We need to be careful to preserve the signs of all the terms in our four-term polynomial. This will sometimes require us to insert an addition symbol in between the two groupings, as here.

Step 6: Factor the GCF from the two groups of terms (this is called "factor by grouping"); if done right, a common factor will appear:

$$2x^2 + 5x - 12 = (2x^2 + 8x) + (-3x - 12)$$
$$= 2x(x + 4) + (-3)(x + 4)$$
$$= 2x(x + 4) - 3(x + 4)$$

Step 7: Factor the GCF from the two remaining terms.

We see that $2x(x + 4)$ and $3(x + 4)$ have $(x + 4)$ as a common factor, so we can factor $2x(x + 4) - 3(x + 4)$ as

$$2x(x + 4) - 3(x + 4) = (x + 4)(2x - 3)$$

Pretty cool how that works. We're done!

You may be wondering if the order of the terms matters. If we wrote $-3x + 8x$ instead of $8x - 3x$, would things factor differently? The answer is no. The order does not matter, and as long as you have the right factors, you will end up with the right factorization.

Method 2 for Solving Quadratic Equations: Completing the Square

By far the simplest quadratic expression is x^2, and the simplest quadratic equations are equations using only this simplest of all quadratic expressions and a constant: $x^2 = c$ or $x^2 - c = 0$.

If we write this type of equation as $x^2 - c = 0$ (with $c > 0$), we can use the method of *factoring the difference of two squares* as discussed in Chapter 4.

Example
Solve $x^2 - 5 = 0$ by factoring the difference of squares.

Solution: We can factor $x^2 - 5$ as $\left(x - \sqrt{5}\right)\left(x + \sqrt{5}\right)$. Thus, our equation becomes

$$\left(x - \sqrt{5}\right)\left(x + \sqrt{5}\right) = 0$$

The zero factor property gives $x = \sqrt{5}$ or $x = -\sqrt{5}$ as the solution.

This is, of course, the same solution we would have obtained if we were simply to solve the equation $x^2 = 5$ using the *square root property*. The square root property is the fact that to solve an equation of the form $x^2 = c$ for some real number c, we simply take the positive and negative square roots of both sides of the equation.

Example

Solve $x^2 = 5$ using the square root property.

Solution: $\quad x^2 = 5$

$$\sqrt{x^2} = \pm\sqrt{5}$$

$$x = \pm\sqrt{5}$$

We can also use this property to solve quadratic equations of the form $(x - h)^2 + k = 0$. It is important to recognize that the left-hand side of this equation is a quadratic expression in *standard form* (not general form).

Example

Solve $(x + 7)^2 - 9 = 0$ using the square root property.

Solution: $(x + 7)^2 - 9 = 0$

$$(x + 7)^2 = 9$$

$$\sqrt{(x + 7)^2} = \pm\sqrt{9}$$

$$(x + 7) = \pm 3$$

Therefore, $x = 3 - 7 = -4$ or $x = -3 - 7 = -10$.

We see, with just this one example, that if we have a quadratic expression in *standard form*, then it is super easy to use the square root property to solve the corresponding quadratic equation. Thus, the problem now becomes: How can we transform a quadratic expression in general form to an equivalent expression in standard form? The method for doing this is called *completing the square*.

Recipe for Completing the Square

Starting with $ax^2 + bx + c$,

1. Group $ax^2 + bx$: $(ax^2 + bx) + c$.
2. Factor out the leading coefficient:
$$a\left(x^2 + \frac{b}{a}x \right) + c.$$

3. Add and subtract the square of half the coefficient of the middle term:
$$a\left(x^2 + \frac{b}{a}x + \left(\frac{b}{2a} \right)^2 - \left(\frac{b}{2a} \right)^2 \right) + c.$$

4. Free the $-\left(\frac{b}{2a} \right)^2$ by multiplying it by a:
$$a\left(x^2 + \frac{b}{a}x + \left(\frac{b}{2a} \right)^2 \right) - a\left(\frac{b}{2a} \right)^2 + c.$$

Notice that the $a\left(\frac{b}{2a} \right)^2$ can be simplified:
$$a\left(\frac{b}{2a} \right)^2 = a \cdot \frac{b^2}{4a^2} = \frac{b^2}{4a},$$
so at this point we have
$$a\left(x^2 + \frac{b}{a}x + \left(\frac{b}{2a} \right)^2 \right) - \frac{b^2}{4a} + c.$$

5. The final step is to factor the perfect square trinomial: $a\left(x + \left(\frac{b}{2a} \right) \right)^2 - \frac{b^2}{4a} + c$

The formulas might look complicated, but in practice, it will be easier when the constants a, b, and c are replaced with numbers.

Example

Rewrite $x^2 - 10x + 17$ in standard form.

Solution:

$x^2 - 10x + 17 = (x^2 - 10x) + 17 \quad$ Step 1 and 2 of our recipe ($a = 1$, so no need to factor it out).

$$= (x^2 - 10x + (-5)^2 - (-5)^2) + 17 \qquad \text{Step 3 of our recipe } ((-\tfrac{10}{2})^2 = 25).$$

$$= (x^2 - 10x + (-5)^2) - (-5)^2 + 17 \qquad \text{Step 4 of our recipe.}$$

$$= (x-5)^2 - 25 + 17 \qquad \text{Step 5 of our recipe.}$$

$$= (x-5)^2 - 8 \qquad \text{Simplify.}$$

A shortcut to seeing this: You might be familiar with the fact that $(x - 5)^2 = x^2 - 10x + 25$, so the thought would be: If only we had +25 instead of +17. To remedy this, we would just add and subtract 25 from the expression (we subtract what we add so as not to change the value of our expression). The first three terms would then be perfect square trinomials that we can factor as was shown. Also, writing $(-5)^2$ instead of 25 was a tactic to know what number to put in the trinomial: $(x - 5)^2$.

Example

Complete the square on $x^2 + 14x$ and write the expression in standard form.

Solution: There is no c, but that should not stop us. We proceed as planned.

$$x^2 + 14x + 49 - 49$$

At this point, the first three terms will factor as a perfect square.

$$(x^2 + 14x + 49) - 49 = (x + 7)(x + 7) - 49$$
$$= (x + 7)^2 - 49$$

Example

Complete the square on $2x^2 - 12x + 5$ to write the expression in standard form.

Solution:
$$2x^2 - 12x + 5 = (2x^2 - 12x) + 5$$
$$= 2(x^2 - 6x) + 5$$
$$= 2(x^2 - 6x + (-3)^2 - (-3)^2) + 5$$
$$= 2(x^2 - 6x + (-3)^2) - 2 \cdot (-3)^2 + 5$$
$$= 2(x - 3)^2 - 18 + 5$$
$$= 2(x - 3)^2 - 13$$

We now apply the method of completing the square to solving quadratic equations of the form $ax^2 + bx + c = 0$.

Example

Solve $3x^2 - 12x + 7 = 0$ by completing the square.

Solution: We will simply complete the square on the left side of the equation, and then solve for x using the square root property.

$$3x^2 - 12x + 7 = 0$$
$$3(x^2 - 4x) + 7 = 0$$
$$3(x^2 - 4x + (-2)^2 - (-2)^2) + 7 = 0$$
$$3(x^2 - 4x + (-2)^2) - 3 \cdot (-2)^2 + 7 = 0$$
$$3(x - 2)^2 - 12 + 7 = 0$$
$$3(x - 2)^2 - 5 = 0$$

We have completed the square; now we solve for x:

$$3(x - 2)^2 = 5$$
$$(x - 2)^2 = \frac{5}{3}$$
$$x - 2 = \pm\sqrt{\frac{5}{3}}$$

And finally, we have that

$$x = 2 \pm\sqrt{\frac{5}{3}}$$

Method 3 for Solving Quadratic Equations: The Quadratic Formula

There is a third method to solve quadratics that actually follows from completing the square. As it turns out, if we complete the square in a quadratic equation to obtain

$$a\left(x + \frac{b}{2a}\right)^2 - \frac{b^2}{4a} + c = 0$$

we can solve for by the square root property to obtain (and you can verify this by hand):

$$x = \frac{-b \pm \sqrt{b^2 - 4ac}}{2a}$$

This is called the *quadratic formula*, and it can be used to solve *any* quadratic equation.

Example
Use the quadratic formula to solve $2x^2 - 5x + 7 = 0$.

Solution: Since our quadratic expression is in general form, we can readily see that $a = 2$, $b = -5$, and $c = 7$. We put these parameters into our formula to obtain

$$x = \frac{-(-5) \pm \sqrt{(-5)^2 - 4(2)(7)}}{2(2)}$$

Simplifying gives the solutions:

$$x = \frac{5 \pm \sqrt{25 - 56}}{4}$$

$$x = \frac{5 \pm \sqrt{-31}}{4}$$

$$x = \frac{5}{4} - \frac{\sqrt{31}}{4}i \text{ and } x = \frac{5}{4} + \frac{\sqrt{31}}{4}i$$

Notice that we get complex solutions here. This happens in the case where the quadratic has no real solutions. It will, in that case, have two complex ones. We could have known beforehand that this would happen by looking at the *discriminant*.

The Discriminant: A Helpful Part of the Quadratic Formula

The *discriminant* is the part of the quadratic formula that is under the square root, namely, $b^2 - 4ac$. It can tell us what kind of solutions a quadratic equation will have.

VALUE OF $b^2 - 4ac$	NUMBER OF, AND TYPE OF, SOLUTIONS TO $ax^2 + bx + c = 0$
If it is equal to 0	One solution of multiplicity 2, rational
Greater than 0 *and* a perfect square	Two distinct solutions, rational
Greater than 0, but *not* a perfect square	Two distinct solutions, irrational
Less than 0	Two distinct solutions, complex

Note: In the case of complex solutions, the solutions will always come in conjugate pairs. So if one solution is $a + ib$, then the other will be $a - ib$, and vice versa.

Example
Use the discriminant to determine the number and type of solutions to the quadratic equation $4x^2 - 9x + 10 = 0$.

Solution: Since $b^2 - 4ac = 81 - 160$, we see that the discriminant is less than 0. This means that we will have *two* distinct complex solutions.

Higher-Degree Polynomials

We will now look at higher-degree polynomials. The simplest polynomial expression of higher degree than a quadratic polynomial is the expression x^3. This expression is called *cubic* since it gives the volume of a cube of side length x.

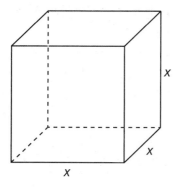

$$V = x \cdot x \cdot x = x^3$$

Our primary concern will be solving higher-degree polynomial equations of the form

$$a_n x^n + a_{n-1} x^{n-1} + \ldots + a_1 x + a_0 = 0$$

The solutions to this type of equation (i.e., the x-values that make the equation exactly 0) are called *zeros* or *roots* of the polynomial.

Note that quadratic equations are just a special case of polynomial equations. We saw that quadratic equations can have at most *two* roots (real or complex). In certain cases, we are concerned only with real number solutions to equations with real coefficients. However, if we allow both our solutions and our coefficients to be complex numbers (of which real numbers are a special case), then we have the following theorem.

The Fundamental Theorem of Algebra

Definition: Every polynomial equation $a_n x^n + a_{n-1} x^{n-1} + \ldots + a_1 x + a_0 = 0$ with complex coefficients such that $a_n \neq 0$ has exactly n many solutions when we count roots with multiplicity.

The simplest example of a higher-degree polynomial equation is $x^3 = 0$. Clearly, the solution is $x = 0$. The next simplest is $x^3 - 1 = 0$. Again, this equation is easy to solve by using a method analogous to the square root property.

Example
Solve $x^3 - 1 = 0$ for x.

Solution: $x^3 - 1 = 0 \Rightarrow x^3 = 1$

$$\sqrt[3]{x^3} = \sqrt[3]{1} = 1$$

This means that $x^3 - 1 = 0$ has one real root, $x = 1$. The Fundamental Theorem of Algebra says that this polynomial must have exactly three roots. This means that the other two zeros must be complex numbers of the form $a + bi$ where $b \neq 0$. But how do we find these? Taking our cues from factoring is of some help.

Factoring's effectiveness relies on a general result known as the *Factor Theorem*. We will invoke the Factor Theorem whenever we solve any polynomial equation

$$a_n x^n + a_{n-1} x^{n-1} + \ldots + a_1 x + a_0 = 0$$

by factoring.

Factor Theorem
Definition: Let $P = a_n x^n + a_{n-1} x^{n-1} + \ldots + a_1 x + a_0$ then $(x - k)$ is a factor of P if and only if P evaluated at $x = k$ is 0; that is, $a_n k^n + a_{n-1} k^{n-1} + \ldots + a_1 k + a_0 = 0$.

We saw this theorem at work when we solved quadratic equations by factoring. The *if and only if* in the statement of the theorem means we can use the theorem in two ways.

The first way we are already familiar with from solving quadratic equations by factoring.

Example
Solve the equation $x^2 - 6x + 9 = 0$.

Solution: By the Fundamental Theorem of Algebra, this equation has exactly two solutions, counting multiplicity. We can factor to get

$$(x - 3)(x - 3) = 0$$

At this point, we can invoke the Factor Theorem. Since $x - 3$ is a factor of polynomial $x^2 - 6x + 9$, the Factor Theorem says that $x = 3$ is the solution to the equation. However, since $x^2 - 6x + 9$ is the product of *two* factors of $x - 3$, we say $x = 3$ has *multiplicity 2*.

We will now apply the Factor Theorem and polynomial long division to find the *three* solutions to the equation $x^3 - 1 = 0$.

Example

Find all solutions to the equation $x^3 - 1 = 0$ over the complex numbers.

Solution: We showed earlier that $x = 1$ is a solution to the equation $x^3 - 1 = 0$. By the Factor Theorem this means that $x - 1$ is a factor of $x^3 - 1$, which really means that we can write

$$x^3 - 1 = (x - 1)(ax^2 + bx + c)$$

Since $x - 1$ is a factor of $x^3 - 1$, we know that if we divide $x^3 - 1$ by $x - 1$, we will have no remainder. This is exactly what it means to be a factor. We can divide a polynomial of higher degree by a polynomial of lower degree using the method of *polynomial long division*. We begin by dividing $x^3 - 1$ by $x - 1$. However, $x^3 - 1$ does not have a term of every degree less than 3 represented as written. In order to perform this division, we need to have a term of every degree less than the degree of the polynomial represented in the polynomial expression, and we need to write this polynomial in descending powers of x. This is easily done. We simply write $x^3 - 1 = x^3 + 0x^2 + 0x - 1$. Now we can perform the division.

$$
\begin{array}{r}
x^2 + x + 1 \\
x - 1 \overline{\smash{)}\ x^3 + 0x^2 + 0x - 1} \\
\underline{-\ x^3 - x^2} \\
x^2 + 0x \\
\underline{-\ x^2 - x} \\
x - 1 \\
\underline{-\ x - 1} \\
0
\end{array}
$$

We see that $x^3 - 1 = (x - 1)(x^2 + x + 1)$, and now we can use the quadratic formula on the expression $x^2 + x + 1$ to find the remaining solutions.

$$x = \frac{-(1) \pm \sqrt{(1)^2 - 4(1)(1)}}{2(1)} = \frac{-1 \pm i\sqrt{3}}{2}$$

$$x = -\frac{1}{2} \pm \frac{\sqrt{3}}{2}i$$

Therefore, the equation $x^3 - 1 = 0$ has exactly *three* solutions over the complex numbers,

$$x = 1, x = -\frac{1}{2} - \frac{\sqrt{3}}{2}i, \text{ and } x = -\frac{1}{2} + \frac{\sqrt{3}}{2}i$$

We see here that the complex solutions came in conjugate pairs. We could also have noted that there is a *difference of two cubes* formula:

$$a^3 - b^3 = (a - b)(a^2 + ab + b^2)$$

Taking and $a = x$ and $b = 1$, we would see that $x^3 - 1 = (x - 1)(x^2 + x + 1)$ and proceed from there. There is also a *sum of two cubes* formula:

$$a^3 + b^3 = (a + b)(a^2 + ab + b^2)$$

So far, we have used the Factor Theorem to help us find solutions to polynomial equations. We can also use it to help us write polynomial expressions given the solutions to the corresponding polynomial equations.

Example

If the only solutions to a third-degree polynomial equation are $x = -1$, $x = 0$, and $x = 3$, find the polynomial expression in general form given by these three solutions.

Solution: Since $x = -1$, $x = 0$, and $x = 3$ are the only solutions to a polynomial equation of degree three, we know by the Factor Theorem that the polynomial expression is the product of the three factors, $x - (-1) = x + 1$, $x - 0 = x$, and $x - 3$. In other words,

$$a_3x^3 + a_2x^2 + a_1x + a_0 = (x + 1)(x)(x - 3)$$

$(x + 1)(x)(x - 3)$ is the factored form of our desired polynomial expression. In order to obtain a polynomial expression in general form, we simply use the distributive and associative properties of multiplication to multiply these factors together. The general form polynomial expression will be the product of these three factors:

$$\begin{aligned}(x + 1)(x)(x - 3) &= (x^2 + x)(x - 3)\\ &= x^3 - 3x^2 + x^2 - 3x\\ &= x^3 - 2x^2 - 3x\end{aligned}$$

The degree three (cubic) polynomial we obtained in the previous example is an instance of a higher-degree polynomial that is easily factored.

Example

Factor $x^3 - 2x^2 - 3x$ completely.

Solution: $\begin{aligned}x^3 - 2x^2 - 3x &= x(x^2 - 2x - 3)\\ &= x(x - 3)(x + 1)\end{aligned}$

It is not as easy, however, to see that the expression $2x^3 - 5x^2 - 22x - 15$ factors as

$$2x^3 - 5x^2 - 22x - 15 = (x + 1)(2x + 3)(x - 5)$$

In order to factor these types of expressions (if possible) we will need to take advantage of another important theorem.

The Rational Zero Theorem or Rational Roots Theorem

Definition: If $a_nx^n + a_{n-1}x^{n-1} + \ldots + a_1x + a_0 = 0$, such that each coefficient a_i is an integer, with $a_n \neq 0$ and $a_0 \neq 0$, then each rational solution to the equation, r, will be of the form $r = \frac{p}{q}$, where p is an integer factor of a_0 (the constant term) and q is an integer factor of a_n (the leading coefficient).

Example

Find all possible solutions to
$0 = 3x^4 - 2x^3 - 17x^2 + 8x + 20$.

Solution: The first thing to be done is to list *all* possible rational roots. By the Rational Roots Theorem, the possible candidates for rational roots would be:

$$r = \pm\frac{2}{3}, \pm1, \pm\frac{4}{3}, \pm\frac{5}{3}, \pm2, \pm\frac{10}{3}, \pm10, \pm\frac{20}{3}, \pm20$$

We could now begin to check each and every possibility by evaluating each one in the polynomials and seeing if we get 0. This process, however, could prove tedious; so let's start with the possibilities that are the easiest to check: ±1 and ±2.

Let's check $x = 1$ first.

$$\begin{aligned}p(1) &= 3(1)^4 - 2(1)^3 - 17(1)^2 + 8(1) + 20\\ &= 3 - 2 - 17 + 8 + 20 = 12 \neq 0\end{aligned}$$

Does not work! Let's continue and try $x = -1$.

$$\begin{aligned}p(-1) &= 3(-1)^4 - 2(-1)^3 - 17(-1)^2 + 8(-1) + 20\\ &= 3 + 2 - 17 - 8 + 20 = 0\end{aligned}$$

Aha! This means $x = -1$ is a root of our polynomial, which is the same thing as saying that $x = -1$ is a solution to the equation $0 = 3x^4 - 2x^3 - 17x^2 + 8x + 20$. By the Factor Theorem, we know that $x - (-1) = x + 1$ is a factor of this polynomial. We would now factor this polynomial, in other words, *divide* this polynomial by this factor. To do this we will use the method of *polynomial long division*.

$$
\begin{array}{r}
3x^3 - 5x^2 - 12x + 20 \\
x + 1 \overline{\smash{)}3x^4 - 2x^3 - 17x^2 + 8x + 20} \\
\underline{-3x^4 + 3x^3} \qquad \downarrow \qquad \downarrow \qquad \downarrow \\
-5x^3 - 17x^2 \\
\underline{--5x^3 - 5x^2} \\
-12x^2 + 8x \\
\underline{--12x^2 - 12x} \\
20x + 20 \\
\underline{20x + 20} \\
0
\end{array}
$$

(Be careful! The remainder should be 0; if not, you made a mistake somewhere.) This means that we can write the dividend, $3x^4 - 2x^3 - 17x^2 + 8x + 20$, as the product of the divisor, $x + 1$, and the quotient, $3x^3 - 5x^2 - 12x + 20$; that is,

$$
3x^4 - 2x^3 - 17x^2 + 8x + 20
$$
$$
= (x + 1)(3x^3 - 5x^2 - 12x + 20)
$$

Now, all we have to do is determine a rational root/ factor of the polynomial $3x^3 - 5x^2 - 12x + 20$ and then we will be left with a quadratic factor, which will allow us to use methods from the previous section to determine the remaining two roots of the polynomial.

We again apply the Rational Zero Theorem to the quotient $3x^3 - 5x^2 - 12x + 20$; this time let's try $x = 2$. It works! We get 0 when we plug it in. By the Factor Theorem, if $x = 2$ is a root, then $x - 2$ is a factor. We divide again.

$$
\begin{array}{r}
3x^2 + x - 10 \\
x - 2 \overline{\smash{)}3x^3 - 5x^2 - 12x + 20} \\
\underline{-3x^3 - 6x^2} \\
x^2 - 12x \\
\underline{-x^2 - 2x} \\
-10x + 20 \\
\underline{--10x + 20} \\
0
\end{array}
$$

Now we get that our polynomial can be written as

$$
3x^4 - 2x^3 - 17x^2 + 8x + 20
$$
$$
= (x + 1)(x - 2)(3x^2 + x - 10)
$$

We can now determine the remaining roots, rational or not, from the quadratic. If they are rational, we should be able to factor the quadratic without much difficulty. If they are irrational or complex, the quadratic formula will help us out. As it turns out here, we can factor.

$$
3x^2 + x - 10 = (3x - 5)(x + 2)
$$

And so, ultimately, our original equation can be written as

$$
(x + 1)(x - 2)(3x - 5)(x + 2) = 0
$$

And so, by the Factor Theorem, all solutions are: $x = -2, -1, \frac{5}{3}$, and 2.

Synthetic Division

In the previous example, we did polynomial long division. There is an alternative method one can use to divide a polynomial by a linear factor, and it is called *synthetic division*. We illustrate this method with an example.

Example

Divide $p(x) = 3x^3 - 5x^2 - 12x + 20$ by $x - 2$ using synthetic division.

Solution:

1. Start with the higher-degree polynomial written in descending powers of x with a term of every degree less than the degree of the polynomial represented. If a term of a certain degree is not represented, say x^i, write $0x^i$.

   Write the linear factor as $x - k$ (note that this means that k is a solution to the corresponding polynomial equation).

   Notice that in our example we have a term of every degree, and our linear factor is also written in the desired form, so step 1 is complete.

2. Write down only the coefficients of the polynomial, and the value of k from the linear factor as follows:

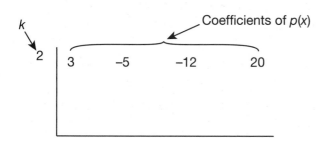

3. Bring down the leading coefficient, multiply it by k, and place the result under the second coefficient.

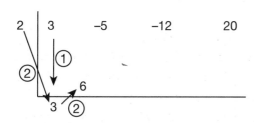

① Bring down leading coefficient.

② Multiply k by leading coefficient.

4. Add the second coefficient to the result of the last step, and bring that result down. Then repeat this process.

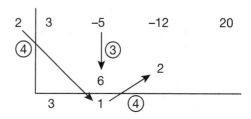

③ Add.

④ Multiply.

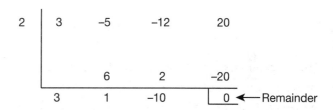

⑤ Repeat.

$$(x - 2)(3x^2 + x - 10)$$

Notice in the bottom line, the first number is the leading coefficient in the quotient, which will be one degree lower than the original polynomial.

Note that synthetic division works only when dividing a polynomial by a linear factor, and quite often even when we can apply synthetic division we will wind up with a nonzero remainder. Polynomial long division is much more versatile, and can be used to divide a polynomial by a nonlinear polynomial. Nonetheless, we will still many times wind up with a nonzero remainder. When this occurs we will have a bona fide rational expression/function.

Example

Divide $x^3 + 6x^2 - 7$ by $x^2 + 1$.

Solution:

$$
\begin{array}{r}
x + 6 \\
x^2 + 0x + 1{\overline{\smash{\big)}\,x^3 + 6x^2 + 0x - 7}} \\
\underline{-x^3 + 0x^2 + x} \\
6x^2 - x - 7 \\
\underline{-6x^2 + 0x + 6} \\
-x - 13
\end{array}
$$

Thus, we have that

$$
\frac{x^3 + 6x^2 - 7}{x^2 + 1} = x + 6 + \left(\frac{-x - 13}{x^2 + 1}\right)
$$

This is just an example of the Euclidean division algorithm, which says that $\frac{\text{dividend}}{\text{divisor}} = \text{quotient} + \frac{\text{remainder}}{\text{divisor}}$.

Rational Expressions

Whenever we divide polynomials, we form rational expressions.

Definition: A *rational expression (function)* is an expression of the form $r(x) = \frac{p(x)}{q(x)}$, where $p(x)$ and $q(x)$ are polynomial expressions (functions).

In our last example from the previous section we encountered the expression $\frac{x^3 + 6x^2 - 7}{x^2 + 1}$. This is a perfect example of a rational expression, where $p(x) = x^3 + 6x^2 - 7$ and $q(x) = x^2 + 1$.

Since rational expressions are made up of polynomial expressions, we can ask and answer the same questions about rational expressions as we did with polynomial expressions. Namely, we can find the zeros of rational equations—that is, solutions to equations of the form $r(x) = \frac{p(x)}{q(x)} = 0$.

However, we must be aware that rational expressions are not defined for x-values that make $q(x) = 0$. As a matter of fact, any time we have to deal with rational expressions (or functions) we will need to be

mindful of all the values of x that would make the denominator of the expression equal to zero. In the next chapter when we review functions, we will say that the *domain* of a rational function is the set of all x-values such that $q(x) \neq 0$.

Example

Find all the x-values that make the expression $\frac{x^2 - 3x - 10}{x^2 - 6x + 1}$ undefined or indeterminate.

Solution: An expression/function is *undefined* at a particular x-value if, upon evaluating the expression at that x-value, we end up with an expression of the form $\frac{N}{0}$ for $N \neq 0$. If $N = 0$, on the other hand, giving $\frac{0}{0}$, this is called an *indeterminate form*, and is so called because it has no meaningful mathematical value. But, strangely, this case carries with it some hope; for example, we would be able to evaluate limits in such a case when we get to calculus. The x-values that lead to an indeterminate form in a rational function indicate the presence of a *removable discontinuity* (hole) in the graph of the function. A value of x that makes a rational function undefined indicates the presence of a *vertical asymptote* in the graph of the function. These x-values are usually considered to be bad because of the lack of mathematical value when they occur.

With these definitions in mind, we see that we can find the desired x-values by simply setting the expression in the denominator equal to zero and solving for x.

$$x^2 - 6x + 1 = 0$$

$$(x - 5)(x - 1) = 0 \quad \text{only if it had been } x^2 - 6x + 5 = 0!$$

This means that $x = 5$ and $x = 1$ make the expression either undefined or indeterminate.

Now let's look at an example where the process of finding zeros is affected by bad values of x.

Example
Find all the zeros of the expression $\frac{x^2 - 3x - 10}{x^2 - 6x + 1}$.

Solution: Here we are asked to find all the values of x that make the equation

$$\frac{x^2 - 3x - 10}{x^2 - 6x + 1} = 0$$

A natural thing to want to do is multiply both sides by the expression in the denominator, but this is a bad idea, since it would eliminate important information, namely the x-values that make the function undefined or indeterminate. Instead, set the numerator and denominator to 0.

$$x^2 - 3x - 10 = 0$$

and

$$x^2 - 6x + 1 = 0$$

Luckily, both of these quadratic expressions factor, and give us

$$(x - 5)(x + 2) = 0$$

and

$$(x - 5)(x - 1) = 0$$

Let's put this back into the context of our rational equation.

$$\frac{x^2 - 3x - 10}{x^2 - 6x + 1} = \frac{(x - 5)(x + 2)}{(x - 5)(x - 1)} = 0$$

We see that $x = 5$ makes both the numerator and the denominator equal to zero. Since $x = 5$ makes the denominator equal to zero, it makes the overall rational expression *indeterminate*. Thus, $x = 5$ is not allowed to be used in the expression. It is not in the *domain* of the rational function, $r(x) = \frac{x^2 - 3x - 10}{x^2 - 6x + 1}$. In particular, $x = 5$ is *not* a solution to the equation

$$\frac{x^2 - 3x - 10}{x^2 - 6x + 1} = 0$$

Therefore, the only zero of the rational expression is $x = -2$, the zero that corresponds to the $x + 2$ factor in the numerator.

We are also interested in solving rational inequalities. In order to do this correctly, we will always need to pay attention to the x-values that make $q(x) = 0$. Oftentimes it will be helpful to write our inequality in the form $\frac{p(x)}{q(x)}$? 0, where ? is $\leq$ or $\geq$ or $<$ or $>$.

Example *needs to be* ✗
Solve $\frac{(x - 7)}{(x + 1)} \leq 3$.

Solution: Let's write this in a more convenient form as indicated previously.

$$\frac{(x + 7)}{(x + 1)} - 3 \leq 0$$

$$\frac{(x + 7)}{(x + 1)} - \frac{3(x + 1)}{x + 1} \leq 0$$

$$\frac{x + 7 - 3x - 3}{x + 1} \leq 0$$

$$\frac{4 - 2x}{x + 1} \leq 0$$

As before, set the numerator and denominator equal to 0. This gives $x = 2$ for the numerator to be 0, and $x = -1$ for the denominator to be 0.

Of course, $x = -1$ is bad, so it cannot be a part of our solution. But, $x = 2$ gives a zero of the function, and we want the zeros (since we have a ≤ 0 inequality, in particular, we want the $= 0$ part to be solved). With this in mind, we can plot these two numbers on a number line.

The −1 is unshaded since we cannot touch it. The 2 is shaded since it is okay for x to be 2; in fact, it is in our range of solutions. Now we plug in values in each of the three intervals that we created. These values should be easy to evaluate in our original function.

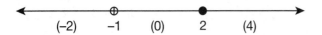

Each test value represents an entire interval of real numbers; $x = -2$ represents the interval of all real numbers less than −1, denoted $(-\infty, 0)$.

Testing $x = -2$:

$$\frac{4 - 2(-2)}{-2 + 1} = \frac{(+)}{(-)} = (-) < 0$$

Testing $x = 0$:

$$\frac{4 - 2(0)}{0 + 1} = \frac{(+)}{(+)} = (+) > 0$$

Testing $x = 4$:

$$\frac{4 - 2(4)}{2 + 1} = \frac{(-)}{(+)} = (-) < 0$$

This means the intervals represented by $x = -2$ and $x = 4$ are a part of our solution.

This can be represented as $x < -1$ or $x \geq 2$, or in interval notation as $(-\infty, -1) \cup (2, \infty)$.

We conclude this chapter with two typical problems that involve rational expressions.

Example

Marci can do a job in 20 hours. If Frank helps Marci, they can complete the same job in 15 hours. How long would it take Frank to complete the same job by himself?

Solution: Let $x =$ the number of hours it takes Frank to complete the job by himself. Then in 1 hour Frank can complete $\frac{1}{x}$ of the job. Since it takes Marci 20 hours to complete the job by herself, in 1 hour Marci can complete $\frac{1}{20}$ of the job. We know that together Marci and Frank can complete the job in 15 hours. This means that in 15 hours Marci can complete $\frac{15}{20}$ of the job, Frank can complete $\frac{15}{x}$ of the job, and together they complete the entire job. Thus, we have the equation

$$\frac{15}{20} + \frac{15}{x} = 1$$

Solving for x:

First we see that x cannot be zero for two reasons—it does not make sense in the context of the problem, and it would make the second term in the equation undefined.

$$\frac{15}{x} = 1 - \frac{15}{20}$$

$$\frac{15}{x} = \frac{5}{20}$$

$$\frac{15}{x} = \frac{1}{4}$$

$$60 = x$$

Therefore, it would take Frank 60 hours to complete the job by himself.

Example

A train travels 816 miles between Albany, New York, and Chicago, Illinois. From Albany to Chicago, the train encounters some bad weather and must travel 25 mph slower, which adds 1 hour to the trip. On the trip back from Chicago to Albany, the train arrives on time with no delays. Find the average speed of the train both coming and going.

Solution: Let $r =$ speed of the train, $t =$ travel time in hours, and $d =$ distance traveled in miles. The crucial relationship among the variables here is that the distance is the product of rate and time, $d = rt$. From this equation we have $r = \frac{d}{t}$ and $t = \frac{d}{r}$. We can arrange the information in a table.

	r	t	d
Albany to Chicago	$\frac{816}{t+1}$	$t+1$	816
Chicago to Albany	$\frac{816}{t}$	t	816

From the statement of the problem, we see that if the speed the train had traveled was 25 mph faster from Albany to Chicago, then the speeds (and travel time) both coming and going would be equal. Thus, we have the equation:

$$\frac{816}{t+1} + 25 = \frac{816}{t}$$

We now solve this equation for t. Notice that $t \neq 0$ and $t \neq -1$, since these two values not only would make the expression undefined, but also would not make sense in the context of the problem.

Solving for t: $\frac{816}{t+1} + 25 = \frac{816}{t}$

$$\frac{t}{t} \cdot \frac{816}{t+1} + \frac{t(t+1)}{t(t+1)} 25 = \frac{(t+1)}{(t+1)} \frac{816}{t}$$

$$\frac{816t + 25t(t+1)}{t(t+1)} = \frac{816(t+1)}{t(t+1)}$$

Since we already dispensed with the possibility of $t = 0$ and $t = -1$, we focus on the value(s) for t that make(s) the numerators equal:

$$816t + 25t(t+1) = 816(t+1)$$
$$816t + 25t^2 + 25t = 816t + 816$$
$$0 = 25t^2 + 25t - 816$$

We have reduced our rational equation to a quadratic equation, and now we can use the quadratic formula to find values for t.

$$t = \frac{-25 \pm \sqrt{25^2 - 4(25)(-816)}}{2(25)}$$

$$t \approx 5.23498 \text{ and } t \approx -6.23498$$

A negative value for time does not make sense, however, so we reject $t \approx -6.23498$ and conclude that unimpeded it took the train $t \approx 5.23498$ hours to travel from Chicago to Albany. Evaluating our expressions for speed at this time value gives that the average speed from Albany to Chicago was $\frac{816}{6.23498} = 130.87$ mph and the speed from Chicago to Albany was $\frac{816}{5.23498} = 155.87$ mph.

CHAPTER 6

FUCTIONS REVIEW

CHAPTER SUMMARY

The topic of relations is a very important topic in mathematics. Relations will be dealt with in detail in Chapter 10, but here we study a special class of relations, a class that is perhaps the most widely studied and important kind of relation in elementary mathematics, and certainly the most studied topic in algebra, precalculus, and calculus—the function. While a relation is a set of ordered pairs with little restriction, a function is a set of ordered pairs that must abide by a rigid standard. In this chapter, we explore what functions are, how they are used, and the kinds of problems you will encounter involving them, and regain an appreciation for why the study of functions is a supremely important part of studying mathematics.

The Function Concept and the Use of Function Notation

A function may be thought of in two equivalent ways. The first is the way a math student would typically be taught when first encountering functions.

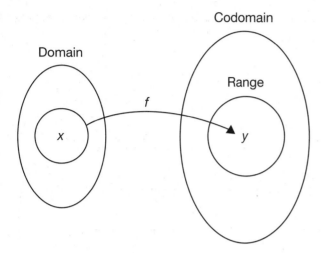

Domain

Codomain

Range

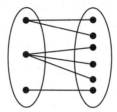

A "one-to-many" mapping (not a function)

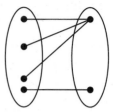

A "many-to-one" mapping (a function)

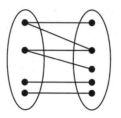

A "many-to-many" mapping (not a function)

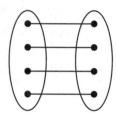

A one-to-one" mapping (a function)

Definition: A function is a rule that assigns to *every* member in one set (called the *domain* of the function) *exactly one* member in another set (called a *range* of the function). Sometimes, the range is thought of as a subset of a larger set. In this case, the larger set is called the *codomain* of the function.

The first illustration is a typical kind of diagram used to explain a function. Another is the following:

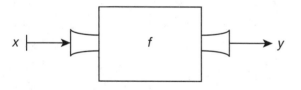

These illustrations showcase the notion that a function will take, as input, a value x in the domain and will perform some special rule to assign it a single element y in the range. The name of the function here is called f. This is a typical letter to use for the name of a function. Functions are often named using lowercase letters (including non-English ones).

Mappings are also commonly used to represent functions when learning about them for the first time. The following are various types of mapping diagrams. The ones that are functions are indicated. You should be able to recognize if a rule is a function by looking at mapping diagrams (if they are given).

Note: "One-to-many" means you have one input or several inputs, where each input maps to many outputs but the outputs for each input are unique to the outputs for the other inputs. "Many-to-many" means there are many inputs where each maps to many outputs that may not be unique. Neither of these rules forms a function. "Many-to-one" means you have a situation where many inputs can map to the same output, but each input still has only one output. "One-to-one" means each input maps to only one output, and this output is unique to that input. (We will talk more about many-to-one and one-to-one functions later. You may recall that $f(x) = x^2$ is an example of a many-to-one function, while $f(x) = x$ is an example of a one-to-one function.)

Another definition for a function is the following:

Definition: Let A and B be nonempty sets. A function from A to B is a set of ordered pairs where the first coordinate comes from A and the second coordinate comes from B such that *every* element of A appears as the first coordinate of exactly one ordered pair.

If the function is given the name f, then a function from A to B may be denoted $f: A \rightarrow B$. Moreover, A is the *domain* of f and B is the *codomain* of f. The set of elements of B that appear as second coordinates in the function is called the *range* of f. (In case you haven't made this connection, we can think of the domain as the set of first coordinates, which is in fact all of A.)

These definitions are equivalent. If the pair (a,b) $\in f$, then we would say b is "assigned" to a, and since each $a \in A$ appears in exactly one coordinate in f, it follows that each element in A is assigned exactly one element in B. One should also think on the definitions: *the domain is the set of possible inputs; the range is the set of corresponding outputs.*

More notation: If the name of a function is f and this function assigns a value y to a domain value x, then we may write $f(x) = y$. Notice that on the left side, the brackets do *not* indicate multiplication. The notation $f(x) = y$ means "f takes x as input and outputs y."

Definition: If x is used as a generic variable to represent an arbitrary input value, it is called the *independent variable*; if y is used to represent an arbitrary output, it is called the *dependent variable*, since its value depends on x.

Example

Consider the function $f: \mathbb{R} \rightarrow \mathbb{R}$, defined by $f(x) = 2x + 3$. Here we recognize the rule as "Whatever input you're given, multiply it by 2, and then add 3." This gives a unique value to any number that is put into the function. So, for instance, $f(1) = 5$ (if you take 1, double it, and then add 3, the result is 5). To write it out, we would write $f(1) = 2 \cdot 1 + 3 = 5$. So the independent variable is replaced by a value, and a new value is computed.

This could also be illustrated by using a mapping diagram:

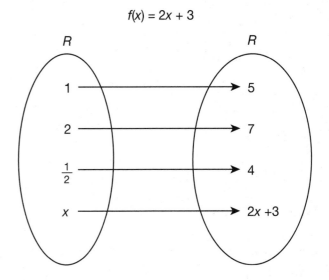

$$f(x) = 2x + 3$$

or a table of values:

x	y
1	5
2	7
$\frac{1}{2}$	4
...	...

or a set of ordered pairs:

$$f = \{(1,5),(2,7),(\tfrac{1}{2},4),\ldots,(x,2x + 3),\ldots\}$$

We can also create a graph of the function—a very useful pictorial representation. The graph is drawn on a pair of axes called the *Cartesian axes* or the *xy*-plane. The values of the independent variable are plotted as on a number line on the horizontal axes, while the values of the dependent variable are plotted similarly, but on the vertical axis.

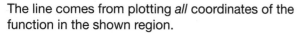

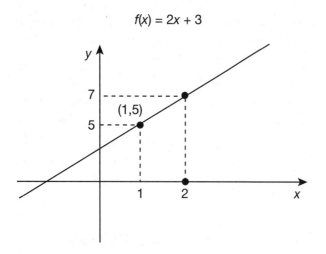

The line comes from plotting *all* coordinates of the function in the shown region.

Analyzing Function Behavior: Finding the Domain, Range, Maximum, Minimum, and Other Features

It is also very important that you can recognize important features on a graph. These include (local) maximums, (local) minimums, when and where a graph is increasing (moving up as you move from left to right) or decreasing (moving down as you move from left to right), the graph's domain and range, and whether the graph is periodic (repeats a certain pattern).

Example

For the given graph of a function $f: \mathbb{R} \to \mathbb{R}$, identify the domain, the range, the intervals where the function is increasing or decreasing, and the maximums and minimums of the function.

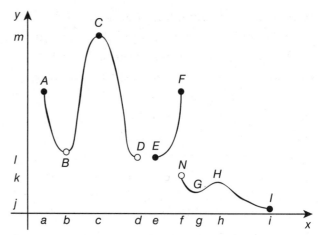

Solution:

Domain: The domain of this graph is the set of all $x \in \mathbb{R}$ such that $x \in [a,b) \cup (b,d) \cup [e,i]$. (That is, the x-value b is *not* in the domain of the function; neither are the intervals $[d,e),(-\infty,a)$, or (i,∞).)

Range: The range of the function is the set of all $y \in \mathbb{R}$ such that $y \in [j,k) \cup [l,m]$. (That is, the intervals $[k,l),(-\infty,j)$, and (m,∞) are *not* in the range.)

Increasing: The function is increasing for the interval $(b,c) \cup (e,f) \cup (g,h)$.

Decreasing: The function is decreasing on the interval $(a,b) \cup (c,d) \cup (f,g) \cup (h,i)$.

Maximum(s): The function has (local) maximums at points C, F, and H; point C is also the global maximum. Local maximum refers to the maximum point, if any, in a local region; global maximum, if any, refers to the point(s) that attains the maximum value over the entire domain of the function. Note that point N is not a local maximum. It is not in the domain of the function.

Minimum(s): The function has (local) minimums at points E, G, and I. The function also has a global minimum at the point *I*. Note that the point *B* is *not* a minimum point, since it is not in the domain of the function. In the local region around *B*, there is no minimum *y*-value. A similar reasoning yields that *D* is also *not* a local minimum.

One should be able to identify these features on a graph. (Identifying all these features without the use of a graph falls under the umbrella of calculus. See Chapter 7 for a review of calculus; in calculus you will also learn how to identify other important features of graphs, such as concavity and inflections.)

There are many kinds of functions you should be aware of and be able to readily identify their key features. Some of these have already been covered in the algebra section. Such functions include polynomials, exponential functions, radical functions, piecewise functions, absolute value functions, rational functions, and logarithmic and trigonometric functions.

Properties You Should Be Familiar with (the Largest Domain and Range Possible Is Assumed)

TYPE OF FUNCTION	FORMULA	DOMAIN	RANGE	ASYMPTOTES?
Polynomials (*n*th degree)	$f(x) = a_n x^n + a_{n-1} x^{n-1} + \ldots + a_1 x + a_0$ where the a_i's are real numbers, $a_n \neq 0$	$(-\infty, \infty)$	If *n* is odd: $(-\infty, \infty)$ If *n* is even: $[\min, \infty)$ if $a_n > 0$ $(-\infty, \max]$ if $a_n < 0$	None
Exponentials	$f(x) = C \cdot a^x + k$ where $C, a, k \in \mathbb{R}, C \neq 0, a > 0$	$(-\infty, \infty)$	(k, ∞) if $C > 0$ $(-\infty, k)$ if $C < 0$	$y = k$ (horizontal)

Radicals	$f(x) = \sqrt[n]{g(x)}$ where $n \in \mathbb{Z}, n \geq 2$	The domain of $g(x)$ must be satisfied, intersected with:
		if *n* is odd:
		$(-\infty, \infty)$
		if *n* is even:
		$\{x : g(x) \geq 0\}$
			Depends on $g(x)$	None

Piecewise	Varies greatly, example $f(x) = \begin{cases} g(x), a \leq x \leq b \\ h(x), b < x \leq c \end{cases}$	Depends on $f(x)$	Depends on $f(x)$	Depends on $f(x)$
Absolute value	$f(x) = \lvert g(x) \rvert$	Has the same domain as $g(x)$	Depends on $g(x)$; just keep in mind this function keeps things nonnegative	Depends on $g(x)$. In general, the vertical asymptotes will be preserved.
Rational	$f(x) = \frac{p(x)}{q(x)}$ where $p(x), q(x)$ are polynomials	$\{x : q(x) \neq 0\}$	Depends on $f(x)$	Vertical asymptotes occur at the *x*-values where $q(x) = 0$. Nonvertical asymptotes can occur, depending on the degrees of $p(x)$ and $q(x)$.
Logarithmic	$f(x) = C \cdot \log_a g(x)$	$\{x : g(x) > 0\}$	Depends on $g(x)$, but typically at this level it will be $(-\infty, \infty)$	Vertical asymptote where $g(x) = 0$
Trigonometric	Varies: e.g., $f(x) = \sin x$, $\cos x$, $\sec x$, etc.	Varies; but for $\sin x$ and $\cos x$, the domain is $(-\infty, \infty)$	Varies; but for $\sin x$ and $\cos x$ the range is $[-1,1]$	Varies; but $\sin x$ and $\cos x$ have none, $\tan x$ has vertical asymptotes at, $x = \frac{n\pi}{2}$ where *n* is odd.

Some Graphs You Should Be Familiar With

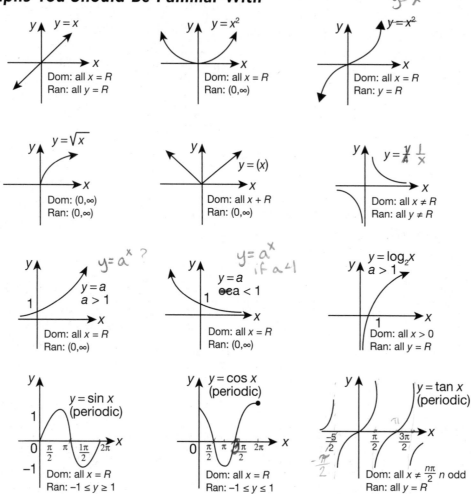

You should also remember how to use transformations to create more complicated versions of these graphs; we will cover that a bit later.

Now let's talk about using algebraic manipulation to rewrite functions in convenient forms. This might be necessary to elicit various properties and features of the graph. Some features we might care about are zeros, extreme values, and symmetry.

It is perhaps best to remind ourselves of what these things are before we learn how to find them.

Definition: The *zeros* of a function are the input values that make the function zero, that is, give a zero output. For example, the zeros of $f(x) = x^2 - x - 2$ are $x = -1$ and $x = 2$, since $f(-1) = 0$ and $f(2) = 0$.

Definition: The *extreme values* of a function are the outputs of its local maximum and minimum points, if any. If a specified closed interval for the function is given, global max and min points are also considered—these may occur at the end points of the closed interval.

Definition: For a graph in the Cartesian plane, an *axis of symmetry* is a line that cuts the graph into two sections so that the sections are exactly the same, in the sense that the graph on one side of the line is the mirror image of the other side. A graph with an axis of symmetry is said to *exhibit symmetry*.

Now we can talk about rewriting a function using algebraic manipulation to identify the mentioned properties. Perhaps the best kind of function to showcase this with is a quadratic.

Example

Let $f(x) = -x^2 + x + 2$. By rewriting the function in a convenient form, identify its zeros, extreme values, and symmetry, if any.

Solution: To figure out zeros, the best way is to factor (if possible); otherwise, you can use the quadratic formula (but in this case, using the quadratic formula would not be following the instructions). This function can be factored, so let's do that:

$$f(x) = -(x + 1)(x - 2)$$

To find the zeros, we set $f(x) = 0$ and solve for x.

$$-(x + 1)(x - 2) = 0$$

$\Rightarrow \boxed{x = -1}$ or $\boxed{x = 2}$, by the zero factor property.

To find the extreme points and symmetry, writing the function as close to a complete square as possible is best. We can accomplish this by completing the square.

$$f(x) = -x^2 + x + 2$$

$$\Rightarrow f(x) = -(x^2 - x - 2)$$

$$\Rightarrow f(x) = -(x^2 - x + (-\tfrac{1}{2})^2 - (-\tfrac{1}{2})^2 - 2)$$

$$\Rightarrow f(x) = -((x - \tfrac{1}{2})^2 - \tfrac{9}{4})$$

$$\Rightarrow f(x) = -(x - \tfrac{1}{2})^2 + \tfrac{9}{4}$$

Since $-(x - \tfrac{1}{2})^2 \leq 0$ for all x, we know that this function has a maximum value of $\tfrac{9}{4}$. It has no minimum value. In this form, we can also tell that the *vertex* (another feature we could easily find in this form if

we were required to) occurs at the point $(\tfrac{1}{2}, \tfrac{9}{4})$, so we know the axis of symmetry is $x = \tfrac{1}{2}$.

Many times, formulas will have a quadratic form though they are not strictly quadratic (for example, $f(x) = -x^6 + x^3 + 2$ can be thought of as $f(x) = -(x^3)^2 + (x^3) + 2$, which is a quadratic in x^3), and in such cases, similar techniques as described previously can be used. In any case, the ability to factor and do other manipulations like completing the square is invaluable in rewriting formulas to elicit certain features of the function you are considering. Reviewing the algebra chapter will help you with this.

Even and Odd Functions

Another approach to determining symmetry and function behavior is categorizing functions in terms of being even or odd.

Definition: A function $f(x)$ is called *even* if $f(-x) = f(x)$. That is, if all x's in the function are replaced by $-x$, it will make no difference.

Even functions are precisely those functions that are symmetric about the y-axis. That is, the part of the graph of the function on the right side of the y-axis is the mirror image of the part of the graph on the left side. For the sake of putting an image to this, the standard examples given for even functions are and $y = x^2$ and $y = \cos x$.

Definition: A function $f(x)$ is called *odd* if $f(-x) = -f(x)$. That is, if all x's in the function are replaced by $-x$, the result will be the negative of the original function.

Odd functions are precisely those functions that are symmetric about the origin. That is, if you rotate the part of the graph on the right of the y-axis about the origin by 180°, it will fit exactly over the part of the graph on the left side of the y-axis. This means the first quadrant will rotate to become the third quadrant, and so on. Another way to look at this kind of symmetry is taking two reflections, once across each coordinate axis. That is, take the part of the graph on the right side of the y-axis, reflect it in the y-axis, and then reflect the resulting graph over the x-axis.

A bit of a tangent here (pardon the pun), but even and odd functions come up in calculus; and knowing which one you're dealing with can cut down the amount of computation one has to do, for integrals, for instance. You should recall that

$$\int_a^b f(x)\,dx = \begin{cases} 2\int_0^b f(x)\,dx, \text{ if } f \text{ is even} \\ 0, \text{ if } f \text{ is odd} \end{cases}$$

But that is a discussion best left for the calculus chapter.

Example

Determine whether the given functions are even, odd, or neither.
a. $f(x) = x^2 + 1$
b. $f(x) = x^3 + 1$
c. $f(x) = \cos x + x^4$
d. $f(x) = \sin x + x^3$

Solution:
a. Since $f(-x) = (-x)^2 + 1 = x^2 + 1 = f(x)$, the function is even.
b. Since $f(-x) = (-x)^3 + 1 = -x^3 + 1 \neq f(x)$ or $-f(x)$, the function is neither even nor odd.
c. Since $f(-x) = \cos(-x) + (-x)^4 = \cos x + x^4 = f(x)$, the function is even.
d. Since $f(-x) = \sin(-x) + (-x)^3 = -\sin x - x^3 = -(\sin x + x^3) = -f(x)$, the function is odd.

Modeling Relationships between Quantities with Functions

One reason the study of functions is so important is that functions can be used as models of the relationships between quantities. By using these models, we can use mathematics to solve problems in the real world. Later, we will go over growth models with functions, but in this section, we want to give a general feel for the concept of using functions as models.

The challenge here is the following: In and out of math class, many problems are presented verbally, as word problems—as opposed to being given as an equation to solve or an operation to compute. And, of course, because life is not easy, sometimes a problem is not phrased for you at all; one must analyze a situation and phrase the problem in words in a way that would lend itself to being modeled mathematically. Some general steps to take would be the following.

Five Steps to Use Functions as a Model to Solve Problems, Where Applicable

Step 1: *Read and understand the problem. If the problem is not stated in a way that lends itself to being modeled, reword it.* (There are words that lend themselves to mathematical modeling well; for instance, *is* can usually be translated to "=", *of* translates to *multiply*, *per* translates to *divide* or *for every*, and so on. If a problem does not use many of these key words, it would be a good idea to reword the problem using such key words, if only in your head.)

Step 2: *If possible, draw a diagram.* Geometry can often help us figure out how to construct functions. For example, if your diagram is a rectangle, formulas like area = length × width should come to mind, or perimeter = sum of the lengths of all sides.

Step 3: *Use variables to label what you want to find, and also label any quantities that change over time.* This should be done on the diagram if you drew one, but you can make a list of variables and their meanings if a diagram was not drawn.

Step 4: Based on the wording of the problem, *come up with an equation (or equations) that relate all the variables you made in step 3.* Solve these equations to find what you need to give a solution to the problem.

Step 5: *Give the solution to the problem—that is, exactly what is asked for!* This sounds obvious, but many times students neglect to do this. If, for example, you had to determine the dimensions of a rectangle that would be optimal in some sense, it is not good enough to find the area, or the length of one side, or the perimeter; the problem was to find the dimensions—be sure to do just that and state them as the solution!

Now let's try some examples.

Example
A car rental company charges a flat fee of $50 to rent a compact car, plus $3 per mile driven.
a. How much would it cost to rent a compact car and drive 150 miles?
b. How many miles could you drive if you rented a compact car from this company and you had only $215 in your budget for car travel expenses (neglecting fuel)?

Solution: This problem is worded conveniently enough and does not lend itself to a diagram, so we can skip to step 3 in our process.

Let C be the total cost to rent the car and let m be the number of miles driven during the car's rental. (Notice that in part (a) we want to solve for C while in part (b) we want to solve for m.) Here $3 per mile means $3 for every mile, so the mileage cost is $3m$.

Since there is a flat fee of $50, this must be added to the mileage cost to get the total cost. This yields

$$C = 3m + 50$$

So this situation can be modeled using a linear function. Now we can solve the problems:

a. $C = 3m + 50$
$\Rightarrow$ if $m = 150$ miles are driven,
$C = 3(150) + 50 = 500$

Therefore, it would cost $500 to rent a car and drive 150 miles.

b. $C = 3m + 50$
$\Rightarrow$ if the total cost is $C = \$215$, then
$215 = 3m + 50$
$\Rightarrow = \frac{215 - 50}{3} = 55$

Therefore, you could drive 55 miles if you had only $215 to spend on the car rental.

Example
A cruise ship that can hold a maximum of 300 passengers sets its prices in the following way for its Ultimate Island Cruise: The cost is $3,500 per person up to 200 passengers. For every passenger above 200, the price will drop by $10 per passenger for all passengers on board. The ship must have a minimum of 200 passengers in order to embark on the cruise.
a. Develop a formula to model the ship's revenue.
b. How much revenue would the ship make if it takes on only 200 passengers?
c. How much revenue would the ship make if it takes on the maximum number of passengers?
d. If the ship wants to make $714,000 in revenue on a single cruise, how many passengers should it take on?

e. How many passengers should the ship take on if it wants to maximize its revenue? What is the maximum revenue?

f. Suppose the ship incurs a cost of $300 per passenger. How many passengers should the ship take on to maximize profits? What is the maximum profit in this case?

Solution:

a. Let x be the number of passengers above 200. Then the number of passengers on the ship would be $200 + x$, where $0 \leq x \leq 100$. Since the cost starts at \$3,500 and is reduced by \$10 for each person above 200, the cost is reduced by $10x$, for x additional passengers above 200. Thus, the price per passenger is $3,500 - 10x$. The revenue (the amount of money the ship will make) will be given by the number of passengers times the price per passenger. This means, if $R(x)$ is the revenue function, we get
$$R(x) = (200 + x)(3,500 - 10x)$$
$$\Rightarrow \boxed{R(x) = -10x^2 + 1,500x + 700,000}$$

b. In this case, $x = 0$. Thus, if it takes on only 200 passengers, it would make $R(0) = 700,000$. Thus, the revenue would be $\boxed{\$700,000}$.

c. We have the maximum number of passengers when $x = 100$. This means the ship would make $R(100) = 750,000$; that is, $\boxed{\$750,000}$.

d. Here we want the revenue to be \$714,000. So set $R(x) = 714,000$ and solve for x.
$$\Rightarrow 714,000 = -10x^2 + 1,500x + 700,000$$
$$\Rightarrow -10^2 + 1,500x - 14,000 = 0$$
$$\Rightarrow x = 10$$
where the answer was obtained using the quadratic formula, or by factoring the quadratic as $-10(x - 140)(x - 10)$. This would give solutions $x = 140$ and $x = 10$, but of course, $x = 140$ is rejected since the maximum value for x is 100. This means, to obtain the desired revenue, the ship must take on $200 + 10 = \boxed{210 \text{ passengers}}$.

e. Note that the revenue is modeled using a quadratic whose graph is a parabola that opens downward. This means the maximum revenue occurs at the vertex of the parabola. Recall that the x-coordinate of the parabola $y = ax^2 + bx + c$ is given by $x = -\frac{b}{2a}$. Thus, here, the vertex is given by $x = -\frac{1,500}{2 \cdot -10} = 75$. This means, to earn the maximum revenue, the ship must take on $200 + 75 = \boxed{275 \text{ passengers}}$. The maximum revenue would be $R(75) = 756,250$, so $\boxed{\$756,250}$.

f. Let $C(x)$ be the cost function. Since there are $200 + x$ passengers, the cost insured by the ship would be $300(200 + x)$. Thus, the actual profit made by the ship would be given by
$$P(x) = R(x) - C(x) = (200 + x)(3,500 - 10x)$$
$$- 300(200 + x)$$
$$\Rightarrow P(x) = -10x^2 + 1,200x + 640,000$$
The vertex for $P(x)$ occurs at $x = -\frac{1,200}{2 \cdot -10} = 60$. So to maximize profits, the ship needs to take on $\boxed{260 \text{ passengers}}$ and it would make \$$P(60)$ $= \boxed{\$676,000}$ in profits.

Sometimes, recursion might be needed, and we can build up a function by going through a process. Recursion is dealt with in more detail in Chapter 10, but we can do a simple and typical kind of example here.

Example
You take out a \$1,000 loan at 5% interest compounded annually. Suppose you make no payments for three years:

a. Follow a recursive process to find the amount you would owe at the end of three years.

b. Develop a formula to compute the amount you would owe after t years of nonpayment.

Solution: Let $A(t)$ be the amount owed after t years of nonpayment.

Note that a recursive formula would look like $A(t) = $ old amount + interest $= A(t-1) + 0.05A(t-1)$ $= 1.05A(t-1)$. That is, to get the amount owed the tth year, you would take 5% (= 0.05) of the amount owed the previous year, and add it to the amount owed the previous year. For (a), we would go through this process three times.

a. At the end of the 1st year, you owe:
$A(1) = 1.05A(0) = 1.05 \cdot 1,000 = 1,050$.
At the end of the 2nd year, you owe:
$A(2) = 1.05A(1) = 1.05 \cdot 1,050 = 1,102.50$.
At the end of the 3rd year, you owe:
$A(3) = 1.05A(2) = 1.05 \cdot 1,102.50 \approx 1,157.63$.
Thus, after three years of nonpayment, you would owe $\boxed{\$1,157.63}$.

b. Notice that you repeatedly multiplied by 1.05. So in this situation, a formula for the process can be given as an exponential function, which models repeated multiplication. We can use
$$A(t) = A_0 \cdot (1.05)^t$$
where $A(t)$ is the amount owed at the end of t years of nonpayment, A_0 (= 1,000 in this example) is the initial amount owed at 0 years, and t is the number of years. So here we could write:
$$\boxed{A(t)=1,000 \cdot (1.05)^t}$$
To check our answer to part (a),
$$A(3)=1,000 \cdot (1.05)^3 \approx 1,157.63$$

Creating New Functions from Existing Ones (Compositions, Inverses, Transformations, and More!)

Given functions, we can create new ones from them. Often this is beneficial since the new functions will not only describe variations within a given situation modeled by the original function, but they will often preserve some convenient properties of their ancestor function, and thus, knowing about the previous function can help us analyze the new function. There are many ways to get new functions from old ones. One way is via compositions.

Compositions

In layperson's terms, we compose two functions by plugging one function into the other; the result is called a *composite function*. This notion can be described in other words as well. For example, if we have two functions $f(x)$ and $g(x)$, and we take the $g(x)$ and plug it into the $f(x)$, the result is the composite function "f composed with g." It is denoted by $f \circ g(x)$ or $(f \circ g)(x)$ or $f(g(x))$. The latter notation really describes what is happening—the $g(x)$ is literally taken as the input for the $f(x)$. Informally, we may call the $f(x)$ the *outside* function and the $g(x)$ the *inside* function in this case.

Example
Suppose that $f(x) = x^2 + 2x + 3$ and $g(x) = 3x + 1$. Find the indicated composite functions:
a. $f(g(x))$
b. $f \circ f(x)$
c. $g(f(x))$
d. $f(\smiley)$

Solution:
a. So, $f(x) = x^2 + 2x + 3$ and $g(x) = 3x + 1$. The trick is to think of the x's of the outside function as being placeholders for potential inputs. So we can look at the $f(x)$ as if it were $f(\ ) = (\ )^2 + 2(\ ) + 3$, where we can put anything in the parentheses: 1, 3, π, $\smiley$ ... well, maybe not $\smiley$, but whatever is theoretically in the domain of the function may be placed in the parentheses; in this case we want to place $g(x)$ in the parentheses. So,
$f(g(x)) = (g(x))^2 + 2(g(x)) + 3$
Replace every instance of x with $g(x)$.
$= (3x + 1)^2 + 2(3x + 1) + 3$
This may be simplified to:
$= \boxed{9x^2 + 12x + 6}$

b. Similarly, we now want to replace each x in $f(x)$ with $f(x)$.

Rewriting the notation.

$f \circ f(x) = f(f(x))$

An optional step to help visualize what to change.

$= (f(x))^2 + 2(f(x)) + 3$

Plugging in.

$= (x^2 + 2x + 3)^2 + 2(x^2 + 2x + 3) + 3$

Simplify.

$= \boxed{x^4 + 4x^3 + 12x^2 + 16x + 18}$

c. It is hoped that we're getting the hang of this by now:

$g(f(x)) = 3(f(x)) + 1$

$\qquad = 3(x^2 + 2x + 3) + 1$

$\qquad = \boxed{3x^2 + 6x + 10}$

d. Okay, so this was done mostly as a joke; but it's a good one, and you can learn from it. The idea is, as always, that whatever shows up in the parentheses on the left replaces *every* instance of x in the definition of the function rule on the right.

$$f(\copyright) = (\copyright)^2 + 2(\copyright) + 3$$

(We are, humorously and theoretically, considering $\copyright$ to be in the domain of $f(x)$.)

Example

In calculus, there is a formula to create a special composite function called the *difference quotient*. This composite function is used to model the slope of a secant line. One way in which it may be defined for a function $f(x)$ is by $\frac{f(x + h) - f(x)}{h}$. Compute and simplify the difference quotient for the function $f(x) = x^2$.

Solution: Nothing new here. We will replace each x in $f(x)$ with $x + h$ to get the first function in the numerator, and continue from there.

$$\frac{f(x + h) - f(x)}{h} = \frac{(x + h)^2 - (x)^2}{h}$$

$$= \frac{x^2 + 2xh + h^2 - x^2}{h}$$

$$= \frac{2xh + h^2}{h}$$

$$= \boxed{2x + h}$$

Warning: A very common mistake among students here is to use $f(x) + h$ instead of $f(x + h)$. That is, a student might mistakenly do something like

$$\frac{f(x + h) - f(x)}{h} = \frac{x^2 + h - x^2}{h} = \ldots Don't\ do\ this!$$

This is very incorrect, and in fact, by doing something like this, you will always end up with 1 as the answer, which makes no sense (it's possible for the slope of a secant line to be something other than 1). You must remember that "$+h$" is not something separate; it is a part of the expression that *every* x in $f(x)$ must be replaced by.

Inverse Functions

The word *inverse* brings with it the connotation of being *opposite* or *contrary* and, in the case of *inverse functions*, we mean the former. A bit more precisely:

Definition: (If it exists—we'll come back to this.) The *inverse* of a function $f(x)$ is a function that does the opposite or reverse of $f(x)$. It is denoted by $f^{-1}(x)$. If f^{-1} exists, then f is said to be *invertible*.

The inverse function does the opposite in the sense that the input of f^{-1} is the output of f and the output of f^{-1} is the input of f (it takes the output of f and brings it back to the original input—reversing the function). Of course, the same relationship would exist in the other direction, so that f could be called the inverse of f^{-1}, or we could say that f and f^{-1} are *inverses of each other.* The following diagram illustrates that if $f(x) = y$, then (provided f^{-1} exists) we would have $f^{-1}(y) = x$.

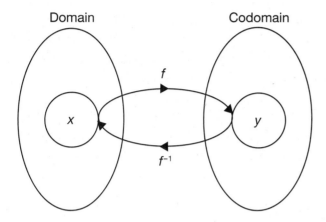

Domain ⟶ Codomain

(*Warning:* Do *not* confuse $f^{-1}(x)$ with $\frac{1}{f(x)}$! That's a rookie mistake. The "−1" is a notational thing; it is not thought of as a conventional exponent.)

The diagram and the sentence preceding it give us two important facts: (1) The output of f^{-1} is the input of f and vice versa; (2) for f and f^{-1}, we have the following:

> If the inverse of f^{-1} a function f exists, then the following equations hold simultaneously:
> i. $f \circ f^{-1}(x) = x$, and
> ii. $f^{-1} \circ f(x) = x$

These two equations provide an algebraic way to (1) find the inverse of a function, provided it exists, and (2) verify that two functions are indeed the inverses of each other.

Example
Verify that the given functions are inverses of each other: $f(x) = x^3 + 1$ and $g(x) = \sqrt[3]{x - 1}$.

Solution: We need to verify that $f(g(x)) = x$ and $g(f(x)) = x$.

$$f(g(x)) = (\sqrt[3]{x - 1})^3 + 1$$
$$= (x - 1) + 1$$
$$= x$$

and

$$g(f(x)) = \sqrt[3]{(x^3 + 1) - 1}$$
$$= \sqrt[3]{x^3}$$
$$= x$$

Therefore, f and g are inverses of each other.

Example
Find the inverse of the function $f(x) = \frac{5x + 2}{3}$.

Solution: We know that the input for f is the output for f^{-1} and vice versa. So let's run with that concept. We can do this by letting $y = f(x)$, switching x and y, and then solving for y. (This means we switch the output to the input, and then solve for the output variable.)

$$y = \frac{5x + 2}{3}$$

For the inverse, we switch the output to the input:

$$\Rightarrow x = \frac{5y + 2}{3}$$

Now we solve for the new output:

$$\Rightarrow 3x = 5y + 2$$
$$\Rightarrow \frac{3x - 2}{5} = y$$

So we have that

$$\boxed{f^{-1}(x) = \frac{3x - 2}{5}}$$

Now, let's go back to the "if it exists" part. For this we need a couple more definitions.

Definition 1: A function is called *one-to-one* or *1–1* or *injective* if $f(x) = f(y)$ implies that $x = y$, for every x and y in the domain of f. That is, if the outputs are the same, then the inputs must be the same.

What this means is that each input value is assigned exactly one output value that is unique from the output values of all other input values (no two inputs can be assigned to the same output; if the outputs match, then the inputs must match as well).

At this point it would be nice to mention some graphical properties. We can recognize that a graph is a function if it passes the *vertical line test*; that is, *any vertical line will touch the graph of a function at most once.* We can recognize that a function is one-to-one if, in addition to passing the vertical line test, it also passes the *horizontal line test*; that is, *any horizontal line will touch the graph at most once.* This is illustrated by the diagram.

Function or not?

Yes	Yes	No
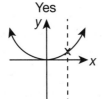	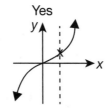	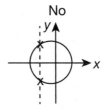
Passed the vertical line test	Passed the vertical line test	Failed the vertical line test

One-to-one function or not?

No	Yes
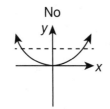	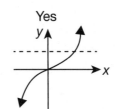
Failed the horizontal line test	Passed the horizontal line test

Example

Which of the following functions are one-to-one?

a. $f(x) = x^2$

b. $f(x) = x^3$

c. $f(x) = 2x + 3$

Solution:

a. Set $f(x) = f(y)$

$\Rightarrow x^2 = y^2$

$\Rightarrow \sqrt{x^2} = \sqrt{y^2}$

$\Rightarrow x = \pm y$

$\Rightarrow f(x)$ is *not* one-to-one.

Another way to see this is to observe that $f(1) = f(-1) = 1$, so that we have two different inputs giving the same output. (An example could be created for any positive $k \in \mathbb{R}$; you will notice that $f(k) = f(-k) = k^2$, and thus f is not one-to-one.)

b. Set $f(x) = f(y)$

$\Rightarrow x^3 = y^3$

$\Rightarrow \sqrt[3]{x^3} = \sqrt[3]{y^3}$

$\Rightarrow x = y$

$\Rightarrow f(x)$ is one-to-one.

c. Set $f(x) = f(y)$

$\Rightarrow 2x + 3 = 2y + 3$

$\Rightarrow 2x = 2y$

$\Rightarrow x = y$

$\Rightarrow f(x)$ is one-to-one.

For these functions, one could also sketch the graphs and argue that the first function fails the horizontal line test, while the last two pass it.

Definition: A function is called *onto* or *surjective* if its codomain is equal to its range. That is, a function f is onto if for every element y in the range of f, there exists an element x in the domain of f such that $f(x) = y$.

> **Example**
> Determine, with justification, whether the following functions are onto.
> a. $f: \mathbb{R} \to \mathbb{R}$, defined by $f(x) = x^2$
> b. $f: \mathbb{R} \to [0, \infty)$, defined by $f(x) = x^2$
> c. $f: \mathbb{R} \to \mathbb{R}$, defined by $f(x) = \frac{5x + 2}{3}$

Solution:
a. Note that $-1 \in \mathbb{R}$, but there is no $x \in \mathbb{R}$ such that $f(x) = x^2 = -1$. Therefore, there is an element in the codomain that is not in the range, so we have that $f(x)$ is *not* onto.
b. Let $y \in [0, \infty)$. Then $x = \sqrt{y} \in \mathbb{R}$, and $f(x) = f\left(\sqrt{y}\right) = \sqrt{y^2} = y$. Thus, for any y in the range of f, we can find an element in the domain $\mathbb{R}$, such that f sends that element to y. (In fact, we can find two: $-\sqrt{y}$ would also work.)
c. Let $y = \mathbb{R}$. Then if we take $x = \frac{3y - 2}{5}$, which is also in $\mathbb{R}$, we have

$$f(x) = f\left(\frac{3y - 2}{5}\right)$$

$$= \frac{5\left(\frac{3y - 2}{5}\right) + 2}{3}$$

$$= y$$

Since $\frac{3y - 2}{5}$ is in the domain, we have that f is onto.

Now, on to the important result; we will not prove it, but the proof can easily be found in many math texts and all over the Internet, and the odds are pretty good that you've come across it in your undergraduate career.

Result: A function f is invertible if and only if it is one-to-one and onto.

This means, if we know a function is one-to-one and onto, then we know its inverse exists. Finding it might be a pain, but it's out there. And the opposite is true—if we know the function has an inverse, then it means it is one-to-one and onto.

Definition: A function that is both one-to-one and onto is called a *bijective function*.

One more thing one should remember about functions and their inverses: Graphically, you can obtain the graph of the inverse of a function by mirroring the graph of the original function over the line $y = x$. This comes from the concept of the output becoming the input, and so on, and is illustrated here:

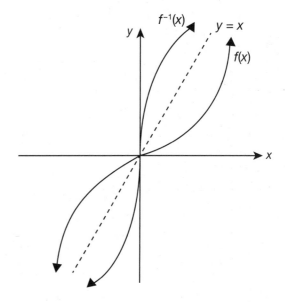

So, at the end of the day, one can *determine whether a function has an inverse* by checking whether it is one-to-one and onto. One can also *verify if two given functions are inverses of each other* by checking their composition with each other in both directions. If the result is x in both directions, they are inverses of each other. Graphically, we can *know two graphs are of a*

function and its inverse if, when we mirror one graph in the line $y = x$, we get the other graph.

Some Quick but Important Comments

1. There are times when we know an inverse exists but we don't need to find it; rather, we just need to find the value of the inverse function at a certain point. The reader should be able to do this even if given the original function in a variety of different ways.

If the function is given as a table or a set of ordered pairs: This means you know the corresponding y-values for each x-value, and so, by what we've discussed before, if you need to find a table or a set of ordered pairs for the inverse function, simply switch the x- and y-values. That is, if $(a,b) \in f$, then we know that $(b,a) \in f^{-1}$. So as far as ordered pairs or table values are concerned, f and its inverse have a symmetric relationship. (See Chapter 10 for more on symmetry. Also, think about how you would prove result 1 in light of the previous discussion.)

If the function formula is given: So let's say you're given a formula for a function, and you want to find the value of its inverse function at some point. One way is to find the inverse function and plug in the point that you care about. If that is doable and convenient, then, by all means, do that. But it is not always doable or convenient. Take, for example, the function $f(x) = x^5 + 14x^3 + 2$. Suppose we wanted to find $f^{-1}(2)$ (that is, we want to find the x-value that gives an output of 2 when plugged into $f(x)$). By inspection, one can notice that $f(0) = 2$, so we would know that $f^{-1}(2) = 0$ without really doing any work other than seeing it. Finding the formula for the inverse function wasn't necessary!

If the function is given graphically: We can again just find coordinates on the original graph, and then

switch the x- and y-coordinates to find coordinates on the inverse function's graph.

2. You should also be aware of how to determine the largest possible interval where a noninvertible function would be invertible. This can be done in a variety of ways, based on what you're given. Take the function $f: \mathbb{R} \to [0, \infty)$, defined by $f(x) = x^2$, for example. We know this is not invertible (it is not one-to-one). Let's determine the largest interval in its domain where it is invertible.

By the formula: Example (b) $f: \mathbb{R} \to [0, \infty)$, defined by $f(x) = x^2$, provided earlier, shows that this function is onto, so one-to-one is the problem. In trying to see if it was one-to-one, we noticed that $f(x) = f(y) \Rightarrow x = \pm y$. The $\pm$ gives a hint. We notice that the negative inputs will give the same outputs as the positive inputs of the same magnitude. That is, get rid of either the positives or the negatives, and we would have an invertible function! That is, take the domain to be either $(-\infty, 0]$ or $[0, \infty)$, and the resulting function would be invertible. In addition to this, this is the largest domain for which this can happen (because making either of those domains any larger would intersect the other domain, thereby creating the $\pm$ issue).

By the graph: Given the graph of $f(x) = x^2$ for the previous domain and range, one simply needs to eliminate a part of the graph so that the resulting graph has as large a domain as possible and passes the horizontal line test. Again, the domains $(-\infty, 0]$ or $[0, \infty)$ should stand out as the optimal choices here.

By coordinate pairs of table values: This is a bit tricky to explain, but the idea would be to eliminate the coordinates where y-values are repeated in such a way that the corresponding x-values remain in the same interval. Doing this in a way that keeps the most *x*-values would be the goal. Then, one would simply let the domain and codomain be defined by the remaining pairs.

Exponential and Logarithm Functions

We've touched on the exponential function already in this chapter. Now let's quickly review logarithms before discussing the connection between them.

Definition: Logarithms (or simply logs) are exponents in a special context. The logarithm to a base, *a*, of a number, *b*, is the power to which the base must be raised to give the number. This is denoted by $\log_a b$, and read "log to the base *a* of *b*." The definition tells us that

$$\log_a b = c \text{ means } a^c = b$$

where $a, b > 0$, $a \neq 1$.

Become well-acquainted with the following chart. The first rule is the definition. All other rules can be derived from this. To derive the next four rules is a slight challenge. The last five rules follow very easily from the first five, but it is good to have them memorized so that they can be used off the top of your head at a moment's notice. Knowing these ten rules, and knowing them well, is the key to being a master of logarithms—until you get to calculus, where you will need to know an additional five rules or so. But even at the level of calculus, what follows now is invaluable. Rule 5 is called the "change of base formula (for logarithms)." We will see how that comes in handy soon.

The Ten Invaluable Rules of Logarithms

#	RULE	#	RULE
Rule 1	$\log_a b = c \Leftrightarrow$ $a^c = b$	Rule 6	$\log_a 1 = 0$
Rule 2	$\log_a(x^n) =$ $n \log_a x$	Rule 7	$\log_a 0$ is undefined. In fact, $\log_a b$ is undefined for $b \leq 0$.
Rule 3	$\log_a(xy) =$ $\log_a x + \log_a y$	Rule 8	$\log_a a^x = x$
Rule 4	$\log_a(\frac{x}{y}) =$ $\log_a x - \log_a y$	Rule 9	$a^{\log_a x} = x$
Rule 5	$\log_a b = \frac{\log_c b}{\log_c a}$	Rule 10	$\ln y = x \Leftrightarrow e^x = y$ That is, $\ln x$ means $\log_e x$. The other nine rules still hold if "$\log_a$" is replaced by "ln."

Note: There are times when the base is omitted. This is when the logarithm is the standard logarithm that is used. Essentially, there are only two standard logarithms, and the one that is used depends on the level of math you're doing. In elementary mathematics (everything before advanced calculus), $\log x$ would mean $\log_{10} x$, whereas in higher mathematics, $\log x$ would be taken to mean $\ln x$. So be aware of the source you're reading from. For the purposes of this review, we will follow the convention that $\log x = \log_{10} x$.

Rule 1 tells us things like $\log_2 8 = 3$, because $2^3 = 8$.

Rules 2, 3, and 4 are some of the rules that show why logs can be so convenient. They can turn powers into multiples, products into sums, and quotients into subtractions. The latter operations tend to be easier to compute than the former ones. These rules also make it easier to do calculus in a variety of scenarios where powers and/or products and/or quotients run rampant.

Rule 5 is also important in doing calculus with general bases. In this rule, c can be thought of as any convenient base. The number e is very often a convenient base to use. For instance, "ln" is the most convenient log to use when doing calculus, and rule 5 makes it easy to convert any other log to "ln" by simply doing the operation $\log_a b = \frac{\ln b}{\ln a}$.

Rule 5 also makes it easy to use your calculator to evaluate logs. Most calculators have only $\log_{10} x$ and $\ln x$ programmed in their software. The change of base formula allows you to compute "strange" logs, like $\log_{3.5} 7.11 = \frac{\log_{10} 7.11}{\log_{10} 3.5} = \frac{\ln 7.11}{\ln 3.5} \approx 1.56574 \ldots$.

Rule 5 helps out algebraically, too. Say you wanted to compute $\log_4 8$. You know the answer is between 1 and 2 since $4^1 = 4$ and $4^2 = 16$. But what exactly is the number? Well, using rule 5 we can compute that

$$\log_4 8 = \frac{\log_2 8}{\log_2 4} = \frac{3}{2}$$

Rules 6 and 7 are straightforward observations. Since for any positive number a we have $a^0 = 1$, we get that $\log_a 1 = 0$. And since there is no power that you could raise a positive number a to in order to get zero, the log of 0 does not exist. In fact, $x = 0$ is a vertical asymptote of the graph of $y = \log_a x$.

Rule 10 simply defines what we mean when we write "ln" instead of "log" to some base.

Rules 8 and 9 tie in very nicely to what we were doing immediately preceding this section. Notice that these rules show that if you compose a log function with an exponential function, and vice versa, the result is the original input.

Result: Exponential functions and logarithmic functions are inverses of each other! Specifically, $y = a^x$ and $y = \log_a x$ are inverses of each other.

Rules 8 and 9 illustrate this algebraically, but this can be seen graphically as well.

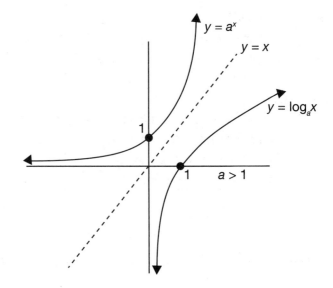

Knowing that the exponential and logarithmic functions are inverses allows us to solve equations involving them.

Taking advantage of this relationship isn't always necessary. Take the following example:

Example

Solve the equation $4^{x+1} = \frac{1}{32}$.

Solution: Here something as sophisticated as logarithms isn't necessary. Simply rewrite both sides in terms of the same base. We can write both sides using 2 as a base; this yields:

$$(2^2)^{x+1} = \frac{1}{2^5}$$
$$\Rightarrow 2^{2x+2} = 2^{-5}$$
$$\Rightarrow 2x + 2 = -5$$
$$\Rightarrow \boxed{x = -\frac{7}{2}}$$

But what if we wanted to solve any of these?

Example

Solve the equations:

a. $10^x = 5$

b. $2 \cdot e^x = 34$

c. $3 \cdot 2^x = 51$

d. $\log_2(5x) = 7$

e. $2\log x - \log 4 = 2$

f. $\ln(x-3) + \ln(x+6) = \ln 2 + \ln(x-8)$

Solution:

a. Here, writing both sides in the same base is not straightforward at all. However, we can get rid of the exponential by taking the logarithm (to the base 10) of both sides.

$10^x = 5$

$\Rightarrow \log 10^x = \log 5$ Take the log of both sides.

$\Rightarrow x = \log 5$ The left side simplifies according to rule 8.

$\Rightarrow \boxed{x \approx 0.699}$ A calculator can be used to get an approximation for the right side.

b. The same idea can be used; the base is e, so using "ln" seems to be the way to go.
$2 \cdot e^x = 34$
$\Rightarrow e^x = 17$
$\Rightarrow \ln e^x = \ln 17$
$\Rightarrow x = \ln 17$
$\Rightarrow \boxed{x \approx 2.833}$

c. Here, we want to apply the previous concept. The base is 2, so we can take log to the base 2.
$3 \cdot 2^x = 51$
$\Rightarrow 2^x = 17$
$\Rightarrow \log_2 2^x = \log_2 17$
$\Rightarrow x = \log_2 17$
$\Rightarrow \boxed{x \approx 4.087}$

Here the approximation was obtained using rule 5, the change of base formula. The base 2 logarithm is unlikely to appear as a standard function on your calculator, but the base 10 and base logarithms would. Using either, you could find that $\log_2 17 = \frac{\log 17}{\log 2} = \frac{\ln 17}{\ln 2}$, which gives the approximation shown.

However, we could avoid using rule 5 altogether. Let's say we want to solve the problem with the base 10 logarithm (the same principle would work with the base e logarithm); we could simply use rule 2 to our advantage.

$2^x = 17$
$\Rightarrow \log 2^x = \log 17$
$\Rightarrow x \log 2 = \log 17$
$\Rightarrow x = \frac{\log 17}{\log 2}$
$\Rightarrow \boxed{x \approx 4.087}$

Note that we technically applied rule 5 on the second-to-last line. But we just never thought of it as such! This solution might give you some hints as to how to prove rule 5 if you didn't remember the proof.

Now let's get through the remaining examples quickly.

d. $\log_2(5x) = 7$
$\Rightarrow 2^7 = 5x$ By rule 1
$\Rightarrow \boxed{x = \frac{128}{5}}$

e. $2\log x - \log 4 = 2$
$\Rightarrow \log x^2 - \log 4 = 2$ By rule 2
$\Rightarrow \log \frac{x^2}{4} = 2$ By rule 4
$\Rightarrow 10^2 = \frac{x^2}{4}$
$\Rightarrow x = \pm 20$
However, -20 does not work in the original equation; hence
$\boxed{x = 20}$

f. $\ln(x-3) + \ln(x+6) = \ln 2 + \ln(x-8)$

$\Rightarrow \ln[(x-3)(x+6)] = \ln[2(x-8)]$ — By rule 3.

$\Rightarrow e^{\ln[(x-3)(x+6)]} = e^{\ln[2(x-8)]}$ — Using the fact that the exponential is the inverse. This step can be omitted. If you have log(something) = log(something else), then something = something else.

$\Rightarrow (x-3)(x+6) = 2(x-8)$ — By rule 9.

$\Rightarrow x^2 + x - 2 = 0$

$\Rightarrow x = 1 \text{ or } x = -2$

Because of the ln(x – 3) and the ln(x – 8) in the original problem, this equation has no real solutions for x. These values will make what's in the logs negative—which is outside of their domains!

Please take note of how the solutions to parts (a), (b), and (c) were first written as logarithms before writing the answer as an approximation using a calculator. There may be times you're required to leave the answer in logarithm form. Simply stop when you get to that form and don't go further to find the approximation via a calculator.

Now let's go back to the business of creating new functions. We can use compositions and create inverses, but, as you can see, those can be tricky. We look at a simpler way to get new functions—arithmetic!

Combinations from Arithmetical Operations

We can also create new functions by using arithmetic to combine existing functions. You should recall the following:

Let $f(x)$ and $g(x)$ be functions. We define the following:

(i) $(f \pm g)(x) = f(x) \pm g(x)$
(ii) $(f \cdot g)(x) = (fg)(x) = f(x) \cdot g(x)$ (this is multiplication; do not confuse it with composition)
(iii) $\left(\dfrac{f}{g}\right)(x) = \dfrac{f(x)}{g(x)}$ for $g(x) \neq 0$

Example

This process is as straightforward as it seems. The tricky part comes in domain analysis, which we will cover shortly.

Suppose $f(x) = 2x + 3$ and $g(x) = 5x + \sqrt{x}$; then:

i. $f + g = 7x + 3 + \sqrt{x}$
ii. $f \cdot g = 10x^2 + 2x\sqrt{x} + 15x + 3\sqrt{x}$
iii. $\dfrac{f}{g} = \dfrac{2x+3}{5x+\sqrt{x}}$, provided $5x + \sqrt{x} \neq 0$ and $x \geq 0$ per the third row of the function properties table (already doing some domain analysis here)

Now we will discuss a super-important way of getting new functions from old ones—transformations.

Transformations

The study of transformations can get quite deep and the precise mathematical definition can be quite esoteric, to put it mildly, but we will keep it simple and easily digestible.

Definition: A *transformation* of a function is a *translation* (a shift so that all points move in the same direction by the same distance), *reflection* (all points are mirrored over some axis), *rotation* (all points are rotated about the origin by some angle), or *dilation* (scaling: stretching or compressing in the vertical or the horizontal direction or both the vertical and horizontal directions) of the function.

Note that we can also *compose* transformations—that is, perform one after another after another to end up with a new function. For example, we can get a new function by first reflecting, then translating a given function. Also note that transformations themselves, at least the ones that we'll be looking at, can be thought of as special *compositions*. The common transformations we see in elementary mathematics are those that can be described as composing with linear functions and then combining with linear functions arithmetically, and hence, these transformations are called *linear transformations*.

Recall the common linear transformations of a function $f(x)$ in the following table. Note that a, b, c, d, k are constants.

TYPE OF TRANS-FORMA-TION	TRANSFORMATION	FORMULA	COMMENTS	GRAPH EXAMPLE (OLD FUNCTION IS THE SOLID LINE)
Translation	Vertical shift	$f(x) + k$	$k > 0$ shift up by k units, $k < 0$ shift down by k units	
	Horizontal shift	$f(x + k)$	$k > 0$ shift left by k units, $k < 0$ shift right by k units	
Dilation in one direction	Vertical stretch/compress	$kf(x)$	$k > 1$ stretch by a factor of k, $0 < k < 1$ compress by a factor of k	
	Horizontal stretch/compress	$f(kx)$	$k > 1$ compress by a factor of k, $0 < k < 1$ stretch by a factor of k	

(continues)

TYPE OF TRANS-FORMA-TION	TRANSFORMATION	FORMULA	COMMENTS	GRAPH EXAMPLE (OLD FUNCTION IS THE SOLID LINE)
Reflection	Vertical	$-f(x)$	Reflects about x-axis	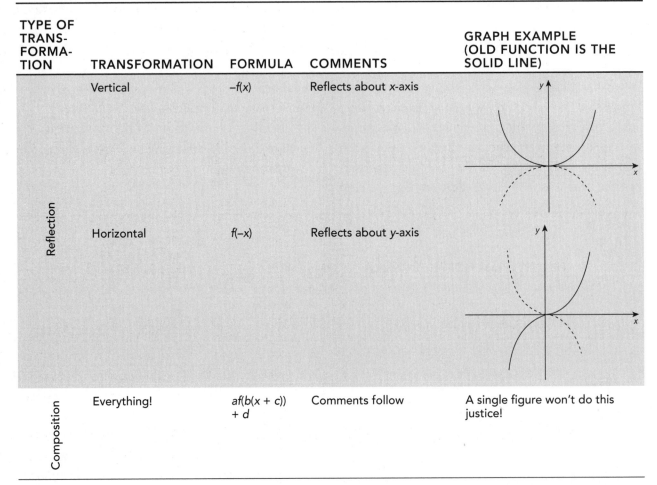
	Horizontal	$f(-x)$	Reflects about y-axis	
Composition	Everything!	$af(b(x + c)) + d$	Comments follow	A single figure won't do this justice!

We will see this again when we cover trigonometric functions, but for now you should be aware that the function $g(x) = a \cdot f(b(x + c)) + d$ that is obtained from $f(x)$ has the following properties:

- a is the vertical scaling factor. If $|a| > 1$, the graph stretches vertically; if $|a| < 1$, the graph compresses vertically; if $a < 0$, you have a reflection upon the x-axis (the graph turns upside down).
- b is the horizontal scaling factor. If $|b| > 1$, the graph compresses horizontally; if $|b| < 1$, the graph stretches horizontally; if $b < 0$, you have a reflection in the y-axis (the graph flips over in a left-right way).
- c is the horizontal shift constant (this is called a phase shift if $f(x)$ is a trigonometric function). If $c > 0$, the graph shifts to the left; if $c < 0$ the graph shifts to the right.

- d is the vertical shift constant. If $d > 0$, the graph shifts up; if $d < 0$, the graph shifts down.

Example
Use your knowledge of transformations to sketch the graph of $y = -2(x - 1)^2 + 3$.

Solution: We begin with the well-known graph of $y = x^2$. The vertex is at $(0,0)$. Since a parabola opens up forever in one direction, we won't notice a stretch very much unless we plot a coordinate on the graph, so let's skip that. The fact that $a = -2$ means the x^2 graph is flipped upside down. Since $b = 1$, there is no horizontal scaling. As $c = -1$, the graph is shifted to the right by one unit (now the vertex is at $(1,0)$). Then, since $d = 3$, the graph is shifted up by 3 units. The vertex is now at $(1,3)$, and the following graph is obtained.

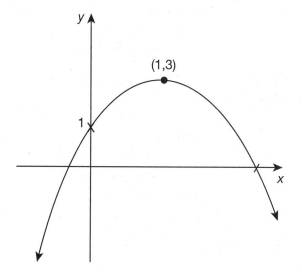

(1,3)

1

Note that the y-intercept was found the old-fashioned way, by setting the x-coordinate equal to 0. We could also have found the x-intercept. That would be $x = 1 \pm \sqrt{\frac{3}{2}}$, which we decided to leave off the graph because it was too bulky.

Domain Analysis

Now you may recall that creating new functions in any of the ways described (compositions, transformations, arithmetic, etc.) may make the properties of the new function significantly different from those of the old ones. One thing that may change drastically is the domain.

REMINDER

It is very important that you remember that the domain of a new function must satisfy the domain of the *inside* function(s) when functions are composed, all the old functions if functions are combined arithmetically, and the domain restrictions of the created function based on the category in the function properties table that the new function falls under.

Now that might be a bit confusing, so let's make this more precise with some examples.

Example

State the domains of the given functions.
a. (i) $f(x) = 2x + 14$, (ii) $g(x) = x + 7$,
   (iii) $h(x) = \sqrt{x}$, (iv) $j(x) = x^2$
b. $r(x) = \left(\frac{f}{g}\right)(x)$
c. $q(x) = h(g(x))$
d. $s(x) = j(h(x))$
e. $t(x) = \frac{g}{h}$
f. $a(x) = fg$
g. $p(x) = fh$
h. $n(x) = g + h$

Solution:

a. We can answer this part directly from the function properties table. For parts (i), (ii), and (iv) the domain is $(-\infty, \infty)$ because f, g, and j are polynomials. Part (iii) has domain $[0, \infty)$ since h is a radical.

b. Here, $r = \frac{f}{g} = \frac{2x + 14}{x + 7} = 2$. Now, if you said the domain is $(-\infty, \infty)$ because 2 is a constant polynomial, you'd unfortunately be incorrect. The function r is actually a rational function, which means it is undefined where $g(x) = 0$ (the fact that we simplified to cancel g does not change this). Thus, the domain of r is $(-\infty, -7) \cup (-7, \infty)$ (since $g(x) = 0$ when $x = -7$).

c. $q(x) = h(g(x)) = \sqrt{x + 7}$. The domain of g is all real numbers, so no restriction there, but $h \circ g$ is a radical. The domain must therefore be given by $x + 7 \geq 0$, which is $x \geq -7$. Or in interval notation, the domain of $q = h \circ g$ is $(-7, \infty)$.

d. $s(x) = j(h(x)) = (\sqrt{x})^2 = x$. Now, if we learned anything from part (b) of this example, we would answer correctly that the domain of $s = j \circ h$ is $(0, \infty)$, because the square root works only for such values, and it is the inside function here. The reminder box warned us of this. The newly created function is a polynomial, so we need not inquire about further restrictions to the domain.

e. $t(x) = \frac{g}{h} = \frac{x+7}{\sqrt{x}}$. Now, the domain of h is $[0,\infty)$ but we cannot take the 0 here, because that would make the denominator of t zero—which is very bad. Thus, the domain of $t = \frac{g}{h}$ is $(0,\infty)$.

f. The domain of $a(x) = fg$ is $(-\infty,\infty)$. f and g are polynomials, so they have no restrictions on their domain, and the product of two polynomials is a polynomial, so the new function has no restriction on its domain, either.

g. $p(x) = fh = \sqrt{x}(2x + 14)$. The only restriction here comes from h, so the domain of $p(x) = fh$ is $[0,\infty)$.

(h) $n(x) = g + h = x + 7 + \sqrt{x}$. Similar to part (g), the domain of $n = g + h$ is $[0,\infty)$.

Differences between Linear, Quadratic, and Exponential Models

We have touched on quadratic models before; they usually arise from the product of linear polynomials, so we will cover them by doing linear models. Other quadratic models arise in situations like distance-velocity-acceleration problems, where the acceleration is constant. Those are best dealt with when we have calculus at our disposal. Therefore, we will mainly look at linear and exponential models in this section.

It is often the case that we wish to model some sort of growth or decay of a quantity, such as the size of a population, or an hourly wage, or the cost or profit in production, or the balance of a bank account, or the amount of a radioactive substance over time. And many times we can model these quantities using linear or exponential functions.

How do we know if a linear model or an exponential model (or neither) should be used?

- A linear model is used if the quantity is changing by a fixed/constant value amount over some unit interval (such as per unit time).
- An exponential model is used if the quantity is changing by a fixed percentage (or proportion, or factor) of its current size per unit interval (such as per unit time).

The governing formulas are in the following table.

TYPE OF MODEL	COMMON SITUATIONS	FORMULA	MEANING OF VARIABLES	NOTES
Linear	*Modeling quantities that change by a fixed amount *Linear growth, wage problems, payment problems with flat fees	$y = mx + b$	m = slope = rate of change. This is the fixed amount the quantity grows by. b = y-intercept. This can be thought of as the initial amount. x is the independent variable. y is the dependent variable.	m can be given but it can also be computed. This can be done in the familiar way of using the $m = \frac{rise}{run}$ or the $m = \frac{y_2 - y_1}{x_2 - x_1}$ formula if you know the situation at two instances (x_1,y_1) and (x_2,y_2).
Exponential	*Modeling quantities that change by a fixed relative (percentage; proportion) amount per unit time *Especially used in population problems and money problems where the current balance is being compounded	$P(t) = P_0 e^{rt}$ for growth $P(t) = P_0 e^{-rt}$ for decay $P = P_0 \cdot 2^{t/T_d}$ for growth $P = P_0 (\frac{1}{2})^{t/T_h}$ for decay $P = P_0(1 \pm r)^t$ for either growth (use the +) or decay (use the –)	$P = P(t)$ is the current amount at time t. P_0 is the initial amount at time 0 (beginning). r is the growth constant; it is the absolute value of percentage change written as a decimal. T_d is the doubling time, the time taken for the growing quantity to double. T_h is the half-life, the time taken for a decaying quantity to be halved.	$T_h = T_d = \frac{\ln 2}{r}$. Note that there are slightly different ways to express the formula. Here we manually put in the negative signs when we want decay. This is not always done. And the equation $T_h = \frac{\ln 2}{r}$ would be different if the negative sign is not manually put in. The first two formulas (the PERT formulas) are the usual ones used.

You may recall that calculus could be thrown into the mix here. For instance, there may be cases where one is asked about the rate of growth or the rate of decay of an exponentially changing quantity; this is referring to the equations $P' = rP$ and $P' = -rP$, respectively. The quantity P' is the rate of growth (or decay) and it is actually a derivative, so one could better tackle that after reviewing calculus. We should look at some more exponential growth and decay problems using the PERT formula, though.

Example

A radioactive substance has a half-life of 512 days. Suppose you start with 25 grams of this substance.

a. What is the decay constant for the substance?

b. Write down a formula for the current amount of the substance after days.

c. How much will be left after a year?

Solution:

a. We know that $T_h = \frac{\ln 2}{r} \Rightarrow 512 = \frac{\ln 2}{r} \Rightarrow$ $\boxed{r \approx 0.0014}$

b. Since we know r and P_0, we simply plug this into the decay formula to obtain $\boxed{P(t) = 25e^{-0.0014t}}$
Note the negative sign in the power! We put it there because it's decay.

c. After a year, $t = 365$, and so we have that $P(365) = 25e^{-0.0014(365)} \approx \boxed{15 \text{ grams}}$

Example

A population of bacteria is increasing at a rate of 7.8% per day. Suppose the population originally has 3 million cells.

a. What is the doubling time of this population?

b. Write down a formula for the current size of the population after days.

c. When will the population reach 5.7 million cells?

Solution:

(a) Here $r = 0.078$ so that the doubling time is given by $T_d = \frac{\ln 2}{r} \approx \boxed{8.89 \text{ days}}$.

(b) Since $r = 0.078$ and $P_0 = 3$ (in millions), we have $\boxed{P(t) = 3e^{0.078t}}$ (in millions).

(c) Here we want to find the time when $P = 5.7$. That is, we want to solve for t in days.
$$5.7 = 3e^{0.078t}$$
$$\Rightarrow 1.9 = e^{0.078t}$$
$$\Rightarrow \ln 1.9 = 0.0078t$$
$$\Rightarrow t = \frac{\ln 1.9}{0.078}$$
$$\Rightarrow \boxed{t \approx 8.23 \text{ days}}$$

Example

A radioactive substance decreases by 5.6% per year.

a. What is the half-life of the substance?

b. If you start with 32.4 grams of the substance, how long will it take for you to have 16.2 grams remaining?

c. Write down a formula for the amount of the substance remaining after t years, if the initial amount is P_0.

d. What percentage of the substance will decay over a period of 17 months?

Solution:

a. Since $r = 0.056$, we have that the half-life is $T_h = \frac{\ln 2}{r} \approx \boxed{12.38 \text{ years}}$.

b. Note that 16.2 is half of 32.4, so the time taken is the half-life. So it would take about $\boxed{12.38 \text{ years}}$.

c. We simply use the value $r = 0.056$ in the radioactive decay formula. We get $\boxed{P(t) = P_0 e^{-0.056t}}$

d. There are 12 months in a year, so 17 months = $\frac{17}{12}$ years. Plugging this into the equation from part (c) we get
$$P\left(\frac{17}{12}\right) = P_0 e^{-0.056\left(\frac{17}{12}\right)}$$
$$\Rightarrow P\left(\frac{17}{12}\right) \approx 0.9237 P_0$$

This means that, after 17 months, roughly 92.37% of the original sample will remain.

This means that roughly
$\boxed{\text{7.63\% of the substance has decayed}}$.

You should also be able to construct linear and exponential functions if you're given a graph or a pair of coordinates or a table of coordinates. The idea behind this is the same.

Example

A hot dog stand vendor notices that if he sells his hot dogs for \$2.50, he sells 42 hot dogs per day. If he drops his price to \$1.75, he is able to sell 65 hot dogs per day. Assume that the demand curve for hot dogs is linear (we could also phrase this as "assume that price and the number of hot dogs sold share a linear relationship").

a. Write a function to describe the number of hot dogs sold, H, in terms of price, p.
b. How many hot dogs would the vendor sell if he changed his price to \$1.50?
c. What is the optimal price at which he should sell his hot dogs?

Solution:

a. We are told to assume that the graph of the number of hot dogs versus price is a straight line. This means that we want to find a straight line that passes through the points (2.50,42) and (1.75,65). (Since the number of hot dogs sold is the dependent variable, its values go in the second coordinate.) Now to find the line, we must first find the slope. Using $(x_1,y_1) = $ (2.50,42) and $(x_2,y_2) = $ (1.75,65), we get
$$m = \frac{y_2 - y_1}{x_2 - x_1} = \frac{65 - 42}{1.75 - 2.50} = -\frac{92}{3}$$
And so the point-slope formula (recall that this is $y - y_1 = m(x - x_1)$) gives us
$$H - 42 = -\frac{92}{3}(p - 2.5)$$

So that $\boxed{H = -\frac{92}{3}p + \frac{356}{3}}$

b. Here we want to find H if $p = 1.50$. So we just plug it in:

$$H = -\frac{92}{3}(1.50) + \frac{356}{3} \boxed{\approx 73 \text{ hot dogs will be sold}}$$

c. The optimal price will be the price that maximizes the vendor's revenue. Revenue is the price times the number of units sold. The price is p and the number of units sold in terms of the price p is $-\frac{92}{3}p + \frac{356}{3}$. Thus, if we let R be the revenue, we would have
$$R = p\left(-\frac{92}{3}p + \frac{356}{3}\right)$$
And so enters a quadratic model. Since the revenue is modeled by a downward opening parabola, the maximum revenue occurs at the vertex, which is $p = \frac{89}{46} \approx 1.93$.
So following this model, roughly
$\boxed{\$1.93 \text{ is the optimal selling price for the hot dogs}}$.

Example

A quantity grows exponentially. Three hours after you started watching it, its size is 24. After an additional two hours, its size is 96.

a. Write an equation to find the size of the quantity, Q, after time t.
b. What was the size of the quantity when you started watching it?
c. What will the size of the quantity be seven hours after you start watching it?
d. After how long will the size of the quantity be 189?

Solution:

a. We are told the quantity is growing exponentially, so we expect it to look like $Q = C \cdot a^t$. We are further given two points on the graph of this function, (3,24) and (5,96). Thus we can say,
$$24 = C \cdot a^3$$
and
$$96 = C \cdot a^5$$

We can divide the second equation by the first to get $4 = a^2 \Rightarrow a = \pm 2$. We reject $a = -2$ because we're talking about the size of a physical quantity.

Since $a = 2$, we can plug that into the first equation to get

$$24 = C \cdot 2^3 \Rightarrow C = 3$$

Thus we get

$$\boxed{Q = 3 \cdot 2^t}$$

b. This model of course assumes we started watching at time zero, that is, when $t = 0$. Plugging this in, we find,

$$Q = 3 \cdot 2^0 = \boxed{3}$$

c. Here we just want $t = 7$. Then,

$$Q = 3 \cdot 2^7 = \boxed{384}$$

d. Here $Q = 189$, and we want to find t.

$$189 = 3 \cdot 2^t$$
$$\Rightarrow 63 = 2^t$$
$$\Rightarrow \log_2 63 = t$$
$$\Rightarrow \boxed{t \approx 5.98 \text{ hours}}$$

There is one thing that is conceptually important as far as linear functions versus exponential functions go—especially in calculus when dealing with things like limits—and that is the rate of growth and the size of these different functions in relation to each other. The reader should recall that exponential functions will eventually outgrow polynomials overwhelmingly as the input variable gets large. So much so, that even though a polynomial is growing, it will eventually appear as a constant in relation to an exponential function.

We could capture this notion by writing something like $a^x \gg p(x)$, where a^x is an exponential function with $a > 1$, and $p(x)$ is a polynomial in the variable x of *any* degree. So, for instance, 2^x will, for *every* x after some point, be larger and grow faster than *any* polynomial you can come up with. Whether the polynomial is the first degree (linear), second

degree (quadratic), third degree (cubic), or 1000th degree, it does not matter; 2^x will eventually be so big and grow so fast that its size and rate of growth will overwhelm that of the polynomial. For completeness, let's end this section by throwing in how some other kinds of functions relate in this sense. Provided $a > 1$, we have the following as x gets larger:

$$\boxed{\log_a x \ll p(x) \ll a^x \ll x! \ll x^x}$$

It is an interesting note that the logarithm function will actually grow at a slower rate the larger the input variable is. It keeps growing, but how fast it will grow slows down. All the other functions in the list will either grow at the same pace or grow quicker as x gets larger. The study of the growth rate of functions is in the realm of calculus, so we won't say more about it here. Let's move on to another important class of functions called the trigonometric functions.

The Unit Circle and Trigonometric Functions

First, let us recall that trigonometric functions are often affectionately called "trig" functions to cut down on writing and syllables when speaking. We will call them trig functions from here on. Now the question is, what are trig functions? The story of trig functions starts with the two main trig functions, cosine and sine (of an angle θ), denoted by $\cos \theta$ and $\sin \theta$, which give the x- and y-coordinates, respectively, of a point on the unit circle that is subtended by an angle θ. (Recall that the angle θ is measured from the positive x-axis, and the unit circle is the circle centered at the origin with radius 1.) This is depicted in the figure.

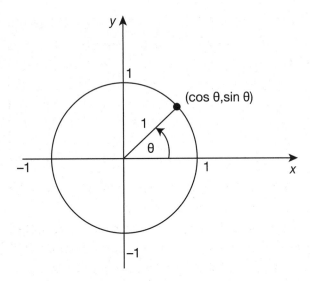

The tangent of θ or tangent θ is denoted tan θ and is defined by $\tan\theta = \frac{\sin\theta}{\cos\theta}$

The secant of θ or secant θ is denoted sec θ and is defined by $\sec\theta = \frac{1}{\cos\theta}$

The cosecant of θ or cosecant θ is denoted csc θ and is defined by $\csc\theta = \frac{1}{\sin\theta}$

The cotangent of θ or cotangent θ is denoted cot θ and is defined by $\cot\theta = \frac{1}{\tan\theta} = \frac{\cos\theta}{\sin\theta}$

The word *trigonometric* comes from the fact that we can use *triangles* to describe these functions. If we draw horizontal and vertical lines to represent the *x*- and *y*-components, respectively, of the point on the unit circle, we get a diagram like this:

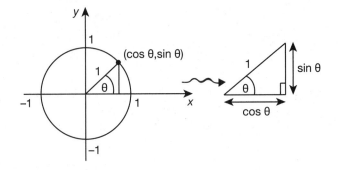

We can use similar triangles, as shown,

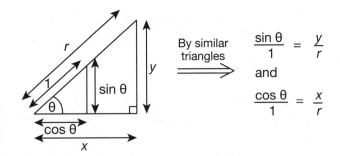

By similar triangles

$$\frac{\sin\theta}{1} = \frac{y}{r}$$

and

$$\frac{\cos\theta}{1} = \frac{x}{r}$$

to obtain some very important equations:

- $\cos\theta = \frac{x}{r}$
- $\sin\theta = \frac{y}{r}$
- $\tan\theta = \frac{y}{x}$ (where it is defined, since we know $\tan\theta = \frac{\sin\theta}{\cos\theta}$)

Now we can reformulate this into more mnemonic-oriented terminology by making use of the definitions illustrated next. For an angle θ in a right triangle, the *opposite side* and the *adjacent side* are those indicated. The *hypotenuse* of the right triangle is the longest side, which is the side opposite the 90° angle.

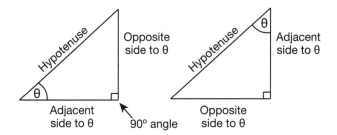

Armed with this terminology, we can employ the mnemonic SOHCAHTOA. This mnemonic stands for:

$$\text{Sine} = \frac{\text{Opposite}}{\text{Hypotenuse}}, \; \text{Cosine} = \frac{\text{Adjacent}}{\text{Hypotenuse}},$$
$$\text{Tangent} = \frac{\text{Opposite}}{\text{Adjacent}}$$

Because we can write the trig functions as ratios in this way (and secant, cosecant, tangent, and cotangent are defined as ratios of sine and cosine), sometimes they are referred to as *trig ratios*.

The domain of sine and cosine are all real numbers, since we can plug in any angle and get a coordinate on the circle. However, the other trig functions are defined in terms of ratios, so any angle that makes their denominator 0 is not in their domain. However, a very important concept to take away here is that knowing about sine and cosine is the same as knowing about the other trig functions. (For example, if you know what the sine and cosine of an angle are, you can just divide the first by the second to find the value of the tangent of that angle. And you can figure out where the tangent is undefined by figuring out where the cosine function is 0.)

Another thing that should pop out at you is that right triangles are the triangles that typically show up (sure, trig can be used with other kinds of triangles, but the basic definition of SOHCAHTOA uses right triangles). And there is one theorem that should always come to mind when thinking about right triangles—the Pythagorean theorem, of course!

The Pythagorean Theorem

Suppose a right triangle has sides of lengths *a*, *b*, and *c*, where *c* is the length of the hypotenuse. Then, the following equation holds:

$$\boxed{a^2 + b^2 = c^2}$$

That is, the square of the hypotenuse is equal to the sum of the squares of the other two sides.

However, looking back at the unit circle, notice that the height of the right triangle is given by $\sin \theta$ and the base of the right triangle is given by $\cos \theta$. Since the hypotenuse is 1, we have by the Pythagorean theorem that $\boxed{\cos^2 \theta + \sin^2 \theta = 1}$. This is called the *Pythagorean identity*, since it is derived from the Pythagorean theorem. It can be written in several forms. If you divide through by $\cos^2 \theta$, you would get $\boxed{1 + \tan^2 \theta = \sec^2 \theta}$. If you divide through by $\sin^2 \theta$, you get $\boxed{1 + \cot^2 \theta = \csc^2 \theta}$. So we have:

The Pythagorean Identities

$$\cos^2 \theta + \sin^2 \theta = 1$$
$$1 + \tan^2 \theta = \sec^2 \theta$$
$$1 + \cot^2 \theta = \csc^2 \theta$$

The Radian Measure of an Angle

Most people are familiar with degrees as a measure of angles, but there is another way to measure angles that turns out to be very convenient—especially for mathematics at the level of calculus and beyond, but also for elementary trigonometry. This is called the radian measure.

The constant π: We cannot do this constant justice here. There is more to be said about π than could be written in this whole book, much less in one chapter. Let's keep it simple, though.

Definition: The *radius* (*r*) of a circle is the distance from the center of the circle to the edge. The *diameter* (*D* = 2*r*) of a circle is twice its radius. The *circumference* (*C* = 2π*r*) of a circle is its perimeter. The ratio of circumference to diameter is a constant. *This constant is denoted π.*

Definition: One *radian* is the measure of an angle that subtends an arc of a circle, where the length of the arc is equal to the radius. By definition, we can obtain that in a circle there are 2π radians.

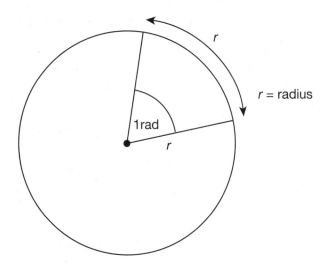

r = radius

We also recall that there are 360 degrees in a circle. So that 2π radians = 360 degrees, or better yet,

$$1 \text{ degree } = \tfrac{\pi}{180} \text{ radians}$$

This formula allows us to convert between degrees and radians. But once you get used to radians, you won't want to go back.

The Special Angles

There are special angles for which we know the values of sine and cosine. First, there are the angles that end up on the axes in the unit circle picture. As measured from the positive *x*-axis, the *x*-axis is at 0 degrees = 0 radians = 2*n*π radians. On the unit circle, this angle is associated with the coordinate (1,0). Hence we obtain

that sin 0 = sin 2*n*π = 0 and cos 0 = cos 2*n*π = 1. Similarly, the coordinate (0,1) tells us that $\sin \tfrac{\pi}{2} = 1$, $\cos \tfrac{\pi}{2}$ = cos $\tfrac{n\pi}{2}$ = 0 (provided *n* is odd). The coordinate (−1,0) tells us that sin π = sin *n*π = 0 and cos π = cos *n*π = −1 (provided *n* is odd). The coordinate (0,−1) tells us that $\sin \tfrac{3\pi}{2} = 0$ and $\cos \tfrac{3\pi}{2} = 0$. (If you're still stuck in degree mode, note that you can figure out these radian angles using the formula box, so you would know 90° = $\tfrac{\pi}{2}$ rad., 180° = π rad., 270° = $\tfrac{3\pi}{2}$ rad., and 360° = 2π rad.

There are other angles that we can figure out as well, and these angles are called the *special angles*. These angles are 30°, 45°, 60° = $\tfrac{\pi}{6}$ rad., $\tfrac{\pi}{4}$ rad., $\tfrac{\pi}{3}$ rad. The sine and cosine values at these angles are usually derived by using triangles.

Take an equilateral triangle of side length 2 and cut it in two perpendicularly to its base. You obtain a 30–60–90 triangle, depicted on the right. Note that the height is found using the Pythagorean theorem.

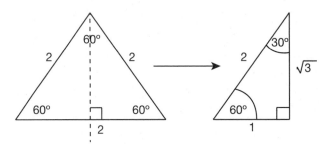

In the triangle on the right, you can see that using SOHCAHTOA we can obtain that sin 30° = $\tfrac{1}{2}$, sin 60° = $\tfrac{\sqrt{3}}{2}$, cos 30° = $\tfrac{\sqrt{3}}{2}$, and cos 60° = $\tfrac{1}{2}$. Using radian angles, this is the same as sin $\tfrac{\pi}{6}$ = $\tfrac{1}{2}$, sin $\tfrac{\pi}{3}$ = $\tfrac{\sqrt{3}}{2}$, cos $\tfrac{\pi}{6}$ = $\tfrac{\sqrt{3}}{2}$, and cos $\tfrac{\pi}{3}$ = $\tfrac{1}{2}$.

Now, if we take an isosceles triangle, where the equal sides have length 1 and the equal angles have measure 45° (see the figure), we get a right triangle, and using SOHCAHTOA we can figure out that sin 45° = cos 45° = $\tfrac{1}{\sqrt{2}}$ = $\tfrac{\sqrt{2}}{2}$.

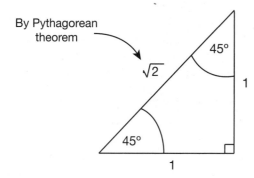

By Pythagorean theorem

Step 4: Divide all the numbers you just square rooted by 2.

θ	30°	45°	60°
$\sin \theta$	$\frac{1}{2}$	$\frac{\sqrt{2}}{2}$	$\frac{\sqrt{3}}{2}$
$\cos \theta$	$\frac{\sqrt{3}}{2}$	$\frac{\sqrt{2}}{2}$	$\frac{1}{2}$

Knowing what a radian is, this means that $\sin \frac{\pi}{4} = \cos \frac{\pi}{4} = \frac{\sqrt{2}}{2}$. These two triangles we've drawn provide a mnemonic for remembering the values of the trig functions at these special angles. There is another way, though—filling out a table.

Step 1: Label the top columns and leftmost rows of a 3×4 table as shown. Count up with the angles from left to right.

θ	30°	45°	60°
$\sin \theta$			
$\cos \theta$			

Step 2: In the sine row, count up from 1 to 3 and go backward for cosine.

θ	30°	45°	60°
$\sin \theta$	1	2	3
$\cos \theta$	3	2	1

Step 3: Take the square root of the numbers you just filled in ($\sqrt{1} = 1$, of course, so it will seem like we did nothing with the 1).

θ	30°	45°	60°
$\sin \theta$	1	$\sqrt{2}$	$\sqrt{3}$
$\cos \theta$	$\sqrt{3}$	$\sqrt{2}$	1

And voilà! The table obtained in step 4 gives you the values of sine and cosine at the special angles. For example, the value for $\sin 45° = \sin \frac{\pi}{4}$ can be found in the second row and third column of the table; the value is $\frac{\sqrt{2}}{2}$.

With the same method, except counting from 0 to 4, one can obtain an even larger table:

θ	0	30°	45°	60°	90°
$\sin \theta$	0	$\frac{1}{2}$	$\frac{\sqrt{2}}{2}$	$\frac{\sqrt{3}}{2}$	1
$\cos \theta$	1	$\frac{\sqrt{3}}{2}$	$\frac{\sqrt{2}}{2}$	$\frac{1}{2}$	0

This table gives the values of sine and cosine that we know for all special angles between 0° and 90°, inclusive. *Note that this means we can find the values of all the other trig ratios at these angles (provided they exist).* At this point, it is useful to cover some more terminology.

Definition: The Cartesian axes (the *x*- and *y*-axes) split the plane into four parts. These parts are called *quadrants*. The quadrants are numbered from 1 to 4 (typically using Roman numerals) in a counterclockwise fashion beginning at the top right (that is, the region where the *x*- and *y*-values are both positive).

This means that the range of angles from 0° to 90° covers the *first quadrant,*

The range of angles from 90° to 180° covers the *second quadrant,*

The range of angles from 180° to 270° covers the *third quadrant*, and

The range of angles from 270° to 360° covers the *fourth quadrant*.

Now, the question is, how do we find the values of the trig functions outside the first quadrant? Three important concepts come into play here.

One is the concept that *trig functions are periodic*. This means that their values and graphs repeat a pattern over and over forever. The standard region to look at for sine and cosine is the region of angles between 0 and 2π radians. This pattern is repeated forever both to the right and to the left. The way trig functions are defined should make it clear why this is so. The trig functions sine and cosine were defined to give coordinates on the unit circle, clearly if you travel around the circle once, but if you keep going, these values will repeat themselves—because you're still on the same circle! With this concept we can see that, as far as angles are concerned, a range of length 2π is one complete revolution around the circle. Trig function values will start to repeat after this. This also means that, given any angle, if you add or subtract any integer multiple of 2π, you will get an angle that brings you back to exactly the same position. These angles are called *coterminal angles*. For example, 0, 2π, and 4π are all coterminal angles. They all take you to the positive *x*-axis. Similarly, $\frac{\pi}{2}$ and $\frac{5\pi}{2}$ are coterminal; they are both on the positive *y*-axis.

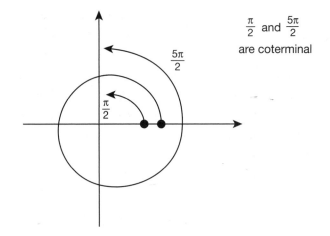

$\frac{\pi}{2}$ and $\frac{5\pi}{2}$ are coterminal

The second important concept is that of *reference angles*. These angles allow us to see that there is an important part of an angle when it comes to evaluating trig functions—and we can largely ignore the other part. In light of the concept explained in the previous paragraph, if an angle is outside of the range $[0,2\pi]$, we can add or subtract as many multiples of 2π as we need to in order to get it in that range. Within this new range, the concept of a reference angle takes effect.

The third concept is that of *signs*. Again, this comes from the definition of our trig functions. Since cosine models the *x*-value on the unit circle, the values of cosine are positive in the first and fourth quadrants and negative in the second and third quadrants. Similarly, the values of sine are positive in the first and second quadrants, and negative in the third and fourth quadrants. Remembering how the other trig functions are defined, we can know how their signs change in the different quadrants. For instance, since tangent is the ratio of sine and cosine, it is positive when ~~sign~~ sine and cosine have the same sign (a tongue, and potentially brain, twister!) and it is negative when they have different signs. So for tangent, its values are positive in the first quadrant (both sine and cosine are positive) and in the third quadrant (both sine and cosine are negative), and its values are negative in the second quadrant (because sine is positive but cosine is negative) and the fourth quadrant (because sine is negative but cosine is positive). A mnemonic to remember this is "**All Students Take Calculus**," (ASTC). This means **A**ll trig ratios are positive in the first quadrant, **S**ine is positive in the second quadrant (and hence cosecant is also), **T**angent is positive in the third quadrant (and hence cotangent is also), and **C**osine is positive in the fourth quadrant (and hence secant is also).

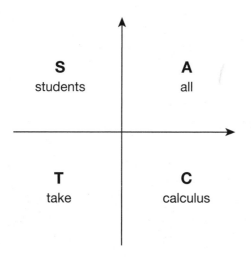

Now with these concepts, we simply need to define what a reference angle is, and then we can figure everything else out from there. The preceding three paragraphs can be summarized in the following conceptual equation.

> The following applies to sine and cosine, and hence to all other trig functions.
>
> sin(*random angle*) = ±sin(*reference angle*)
> cos(*random angle*) = ±cos(*reference angle*)
>
> Whether you apply a + or a – sign will depend on what quadrant the original random angle falls into.

The preceding is especially useful when the reference angle is one of our special angles, of course, because we know what the values of the trig functions are for those angles. But this theory is useless if we don't

know what reference angles are or how to find them. So let's remedy that.

First, be aware that *any angle is coterminal with some angle θ for which* $0 \le \theta \le 2\pi$. All you have to do is keep adding or subtracting multiples of 2π until you get into that range. So, it suffices to define reference angles in terms of angles in the interval $[0, 2\pi]$.

Definition: Let θ be an angle such that $0 \le \theta \le 2\pi$. The *reference angle for* θ is denoted by $\bar{\theta}$ and it is defined to be the smallest angle made by θ with the *x*-axis.

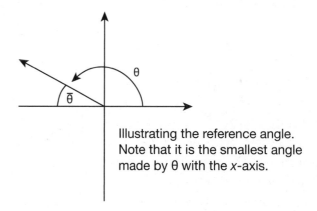

Illustrating the reference angle. Note that it is the smallest angle made by θ with the *x*-axis.

Assuming $0 \le \theta \le 2\pi$, we can use simple arithmetic to figure out the reference angle of θ, depending on the quadrant θ is in. The following figure shows how this is done.

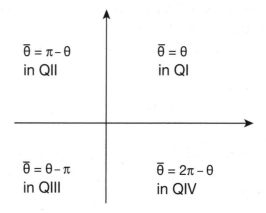

Now, with this knowledge, we can find the values of sine and cosine (and hence, any other trig ratio) for any angle, provided we know the value of the trig function at the reference angle.

Example

Compute the following:

a. $\sin 225°$

b. $\cos 855°$

c. $\cos \frac{5\pi}{6}$

d. $\tan \frac{7\pi}{6}$

e. $\cos \frac{4\pi}{3}$

f. $\sin \frac{9\pi}{4}$

Solution:

a. First note that $\theta = 225°$ is in the third quadrant. Thus, $\overline{\theta} = \theta - 180° = 45°$. So we know that
$$\sin 225° = \pm\sin 45°$$
Since the original angle is in the third quadrant, and sine is negative there (ASTC), we know that
$$\sin 225° = -\sin 45° = \boxed{-\frac{\sqrt{2}}{2}}$$

b. Here $\theta = 855°$, which is outside the $0°$ to $360°$ range. Subtracting $360°$ twice gives us $135°$. This is in the second quadrant. Moreover, $\overline{\theta} = 180° - 135° = 45°$. This means
$$\cos 855° = -\cos 45° = \boxed{-\frac{\sqrt{2}}{2}}$$
where the minus sign comes from the fact we're in the second quadrant (ASTC).

c. Here $\theta = \frac{5\pi}{6}$ is in the second quadrant (it's less than 1π, but bigger than $\frac{\pi}{2} = \frac{3\pi}{6}$). Thus, $\overline{\theta} = \pi - \frac{5\pi}{6} = \frac{\pi}{6}$. Since we're in the second quadrant (ASTC), we have
$$\cos \frac{5\pi}{6} = -\cos \frac{\pi}{6} = \boxed{-\frac{\sqrt{3}}{2}}$$

By now you're hopefully getting the idea. We will run quickly through the remaining problems.

d. $\theta = \frac{7\pi}{6} \Rightarrow \overline{\theta} = \frac{7\pi}{6} - \pi = \frac{\pi}{6}$. Since θ is in the third quadrant, we have
$$\tan \frac{7\pi}{6} = +\tan \frac{\pi}{6} = \frac{\sin \frac{\pi}{6}}{\cos \frac{\pi}{6}} = \frac{\frac{1}{2}}{\frac{\sqrt{3}}{2}} = \frac{1}{\sqrt{3}} = \boxed{\frac{\sqrt{3}}{3}}$$

e. $\theta = \frac{4\pi}{3} \Rightarrow \overline{\theta} = \frac{4\pi}{3} - \pi = \frac{\pi}{3}$, and since θ is in the third quadrant, we get
$$\cos \frac{4\pi}{3} = -\cos \frac{\pi}{3} = \boxed{-\frac{1}{2}}$$

f. $\theta = \frac{9\pi}{4} \Rightarrow \overline{\theta} = \frac{\pi}{4}$, and since this is in the first quadrant, we have
$$\sin \frac{9\pi}{4} = \sin \frac{\pi}{4} = \frac{\sqrt{2}}{2}$$
(Note that the original angle was outside the range of $[0, 2\pi]$, so we first subtracted $2\pi = \frac{8\pi}{4}$. The result was a special angle, so we used that.)

Here is one place where radians pull ahead of degrees: Evaluating trig functions at nice angles becomes easier. It will take longer to explain so it might seem longer, but once this method is mastered, it will help you to evaluate trig functions a lot more quickly.

We will redo the $\sin \frac{9\pi}{4}$ example, but this applies to the others as well.

As long as your angle is not on one of the axes, if you notice that a special angle is just sitting there as a factor, then that's the reference angle. You may have noticed that when doing the examples.

$$\overline{\theta} = \frac{\pi}{5} \qquad \overline{\theta} = \frac{\pi}{6} \qquad \overline{\theta} = \frac{\pi}{3} \qquad \overline{\theta} = \frac{\pi}{4}$$

So for $\theta = \frac{9\pi}{4}$, the reference angle is $\overline{\theta} = \frac{\pi}{4}$. Now think of this as "$\pi$ divided into four equal pieces." So we can do that—divide into four pieces. Quadrants I and II cover the range 0 to π; divide that into four equal pieces, so each piece will have a central angle of $\frac{\pi}{4}$. Continue this pattern and divide up quadrants III and IV in the same way. Your diagram will look like this:

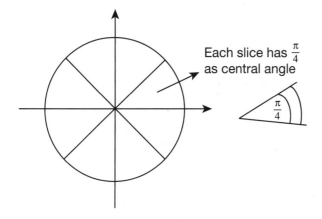

Each slice has $\frac{\pi}{4}$ as central angle

Now, let's start counting the angles up to θ. We have that $\theta = 9 \cdot \frac{\pi}{4}$, that is, nine pieces of $\frac{\pi}{4}$, or nine of the pizza slices in the figure. We start at an angle of 0 on the positive x-axis, and count off nine pieces in the counterclockwise direction. We stop when we get to the ninth piece.

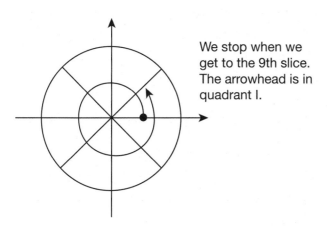

We stop when we get to the 9th slice. The arrowhead is in quadrant I.

Now, we see that $9\frac{\pi}{4}$ is in the first quadrant (without doing any arithmetic, simply by drawing our pizza with eight slices). This tells us that the answer to sin $\frac{9\pi}{4}$ is the same as the answer to $+\sin \frac{\pi}{4} = \boxed{\frac{\sqrt{2}}{2}}$.

Other angles are done similarly. If you know the reference angle is $\frac{\pi}{4}$, you divide each π-range into four pieces, obtaining a pizza with eight slices, and count the number of slices you need. If the reference angle is $\frac{\pi}{3}$, you would get a pizza with six slices; $\frac{\pi}{6}$ will yield a pizza with 12 slices, and so on. Counting the

number of slices you need will tell you what quadrant you're in, and hence what sign you need to use for the particular trig function under consideration.

This method also works if the given angle is negative. You simply have to move in the clockwise direction instead of the counterclockwise one.

Example

Compute $\sin\left(-\frac{9\pi}{4}\right)$.

Solution: Here, the diagram looks like this:

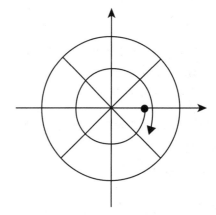

We see that we end up in the fourth quadrant. Hence, $\sin\left(-\frac{9\pi}{4}\right) = -\sin \frac{\pi}{4} = \boxed{-\frac{\sqrt{2}}{2}}$.

It is not a coincidence that we got the negative of the answer to the previous example. In fact, such a phenomenon will always occur with sine, since sine is an *odd function*. Remember we spoke about that in a definition? You may also recall that another definition talked about even functions. The cosine function is an even function. Hence, we have that

$$\sin(-\theta) = -\sin\theta$$
$$\cos(-\theta) = \cos\theta$$

We could also figure this out by looking at the symmetry of their graphs.

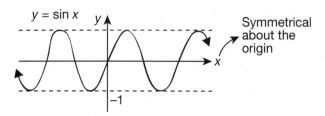

$y = \sin x$ — Symmetrical about the origin

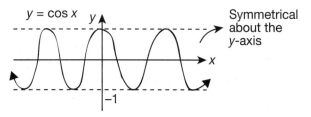

$y = \cos x$ — Symmetrical about the y-axis

Again, once we know this fact about sine and cosine, we can figure out similar facts for the other trig ratios. For example, the fact that tangent is odd follows directly by,

$$\tan(-\theta) = \frac{\sin(-\theta)}{\cos(-\theta)} = \frac{-\sin\theta}{\cos\theta} = -\frac{\sin\theta}{\cos\theta} = -\tan\theta$$

Here is one more example before moving on to the next section.

Example
Compute $\sec\frac{7\pi}{6}$.

Solution: Here the diagram is:

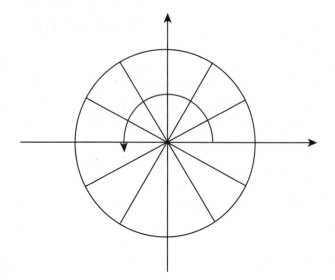

So that $\sec\frac{7\pi}{6} = -\sec\frac{\pi}{6} = -\frac{1}{\cos\frac{\pi}{6}} = -\frac{2}{\sqrt{3}}$

$$= \boxed{-\frac{2\sqrt{3}}{3}}$$

Solving Trig Equations

Now that we know the basics of attaining different trig values, let's look at how to solve equations involving trig functions.

Say we have a function $y = \sin x$. By the preceding section, we know we can find y if we're given, say, $x = \frac{\pi}{2}$. In that case, $y = \sin\frac{\pi}{2} = 1$. That is, given an angle t (a value for the input variable) we are able to compute y (the output variable). However, many times it is the case that we wish to solve for the input variable. This should not be surprising. In dealing with functions $y = f(x)$, we often spend a lot of time solving for x, right?

Thus, one of the first questions we'd like to answer is: "Given a trig function $y = f(\theta)$, how can we switch between solving for the independent variable and the dependent variable?" What if we're given the y and want to solve for the θ? We have to somehow undo our rule of applying the trig function, to figure out what the original input was. If you're thinking along the right lines, you'll recognize that what we're talking about is getting our hands on the *inverse trig functions*. Do such functions even exist? The answer is "yes . . . sort of." By "sort of" we mean there are functions that are good enough to be called inverse trig functions that will allow us to do what we need the inverse trig functions for. Let's expand on this.

Inverse Trig Functions

At first glance, one might say such functions do not exist, because one fundamental problem immediately arises: None of our trig functions pass the horizontal line test! This means that none of them are one-to-one. This is a problem, since a function *needs* to be one-to-one (as well as onto) in order to have an inverse. Not to fret, though: We will simply work around this by restricting the domains of our trig functions. (Remember when we spoke about restricting the domain of a function in order to make it one-to-one? Yes, we will do a similar trick here.)

The restriction of the domains is done in the following way: Take the graph of $y = \sin x$, and take the part of the graph on the interval $-\frac{\pi}{2}$ to $\frac{\pi}{2}$ inclusive (and throw everything else away). This part of the function passes the horizontal line test. We can then find the graph of the inverse function for sine by reflecting over the line $y = x$.

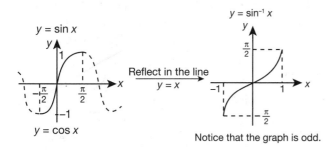

Notice that the graph is odd.

For $y = \cos x$, take the part of the graph between 0 and π inclusive (and throw everything else away). This part of the function will pass the horizontal line test, and we can find the cosine-inverse graph by reflecting over the line $y = x$.

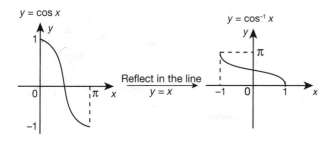

We obtain the inverse for the tangent function in a similar way, this time restricting the domain to the interval $\left(-\frac{\pi}{2}, \frac{\pi}{2}\right)$.

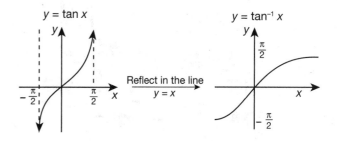

Now that we know what the graphs of the inverse functions of sine and cosine look like, let's talk about notation and some important values.

Notation: In the figures you might have noticed that the graph of the sine inverse function was called $y = \sin^{-1}x$, and the graph of the cosine inverse function was called $y = \cos^{-1}x$. The notation follows notation that was introduced earlier, that the inverse of a function $f(x)$ is denoted by $f^{-1}(x)$. As before, *it is very important* to remember that $\sin^{-1}x \neq \frac{1}{\sin x}$. The right side of that is $\csc x$, which is the reciprocal of sine, not its inverse function. Similarly, $\cos^{-1}x \neq \frac{1}{\cos x}$. These are simply notations for the inverse functions. If someone meant to write $\frac{1}{\sin x}$ or $\frac{1}{\cos x}$, the person would simply write that, or write $\csc x$ or $\sec x$, respectively (or write $(\sin x)^{-1}$ or $(\cos x)^{-1}$). An alternative notation is the *arc* notation, perhaps developed to eliminate the possibility of students confusing the inverse function with the reciprocal functions. The arc notation says that $\sin^{-1}x = \arcsin x$ and $\cos^{-1}x = \arccos x$. Thus we have the following.

The inverse function of sin x
Denoted by: $\sin^{-1}x = \arcsin x$
Definition: $y = \sin^{-1}x$ is equivalent to saying $\sin y = x$.
Domain: $[-1,1]$

Range: $\left[-\frac{\pi}{2}, \frac{\pi}{2}\right]$

Inverse properties: $\sin(\sin^{-1}x)$ for $x \in [-1,1]$ and $\sin^{-1}(\sin x) = x$ for $x \in \left[-\frac{\pi}{2}, \frac{\pi}{2}\right]$

The inverse function of cos x

Denoted by: $\cos^{-1}x = \arccos x$

Definition: $y = \cos^{-1}x$ is equivalent to saying $\cos y = x$.

Domain: $[-1,1]$

Range: $[0,\pi]$

Inverse properties: $\cos(\cos^{-1}x) = x$ for $x \in [-1,1]$ and $\cos^{-1}(\cos x) = x$ for $x \in [0,\pi]$

The inverse function of tan x

Denoted by: $\tan^{-1}x = \arctan x$

Definition: $y = \tan^{-1}x$ is equivalent to saying $\tan y = x$.

Domain: $(-\infty,\infty)$

Range: $\left(-\frac{\pi}{2},\frac{\pi}{2}\right)$

Inverse properties: $\tan(\tan^{-1}x) = x$ for $x \in (-\infty,\infty)$ and $\tan^{-1}(\tan x) = x$ for $x \in \left(-\frac{\pi}{2},\frac{\pi}{2}\right)$

There are several other sets of equations that are invaluable when solving trig equations. These are usually proven geometrically, but they can also be proved using other techniques, such as Euler's equation from complex analysis. We skip the proofs here. But you *must* know the equations!

The addition formulas

$\sin(A \pm B) = \sin A \cos B \pm \sin B \cos A$

$\cos(A \pm B) = \cos A \cos B \mp \sin A \sin B$

$\tan(A \pm B) = \frac{\tan A \pm \tan B}{1 \mp \tan A \tan B}$

The double-angle formulas (derived from the addition formulas)

$\sin 2A = 2\sin A \cos A$

$\cos 2A = \cos^2 A - \sin^2 A$

$\qquad = 2\cos^2 A - 1$

$\qquad = 1 - 2\sin^2 A$

The half-angle formulas (the sign you take follows ASTC and depends on the quadrant $\frac{\theta}{2}$ is in; these formulas can be derived from the double-angle formulas)

$\sin\frac{\theta}{2} = \pm\sqrt{\frac{1 - \cos\theta}{2}}$

$\cos\frac{\theta}{2} = \pm\sqrt{\frac{1 + \cos\theta}{2}}$

You may have also noticed from the graphs of sine and cosine that the graphs seem to be the same, only shifted horizontally. Using the preceding formula, we can show that if you shift a cosine graph by $\frac{\pi}{2}$, the result is a sine graph (and vice versa); this is the smallest angle you would have to shift to turn one graph into the other. We can see this by

$\cos\left(\frac{\pi}{2} - x\right) = \cos\left(x - \frac{\pi}{2}\right)$ Since cosine is an even function

$= \cos x \cos\frac{\pi}{2} + \sin x \sin\frac{\pi}{2}$ By the subtraction formula for cosine

$= \cos x \cdot 0 + \sin x \cdot 1$ By using the known values of sine and cosine at $\frac{\pi}{2}$

$= \sin x$

This sort of calculation shows how we get one of the so-called *cofunction formulas*.

> ### The Confunction Formulas
> $\sin(\frac{\pi}{2} - x) = \cos x$
> $\cos(\frac{\pi}{2} - x) = \sin x$
> $\tan(\frac{\pi}{2} - x) = \cot x$

And again, it is beneficial here to think of these (and the other equations we've mentioned so far) as relationships between the *graphs* of the functions in the equations, rather than just algebraic identities.

That is, the graph of $y = \sin(\frac{\pi}{2} - x)$ would be exactly the same as the graph of $y = \cos x$, for instance.

Now we've covered a lot of ground here with trigonometry. Let's see what we can do with all the concepts we've learned and all the formulas we've memorized.

Example

Evaluate the following:

a. $\sin\frac{7\pi}{12}$

b. $\cos\frac{3\pi}{8}$

c. $1 - 2\sin^2\frac{\pi}{8}$

d. $\cos(\sin^{-1}\frac{3}{5})$

e. If $\cos x = \frac{5}{13}$ and $\tan x < 0$, find the value of all other trig ratios.

Solution:

a. Using the addition formula for sine, we see that

$$\sin\frac{7\pi}{12} = \sin\left(\frac{4\pi}{12} + \frac{3\pi}{12}\right)$$

$$= \sin\left(\frac{\pi}{3} + \frac{\pi}{4}\right)$$

$$= \sin\frac{\pi}{3}\cos\frac{\pi}{4} + \sin\frac{\pi}{4}\cos\frac{\pi}{3}$$

$$= \frac{\sqrt{3}}{2} \cdot \frac{\sqrt{2}}{2} + \frac{\sqrt{2}}{2} \cdot \frac{1}{2}$$

$$= \boxed{\frac{\sqrt{2}}{4}(\sqrt{3} + 1)}$$

b. Using the half-angle formula we see that

$$\cos\frac{3\pi}{8} = \cos\left(\frac{\left(\frac{3\pi}{4}\right)}{2}\right)$$

$$= \sqrt{\frac{1 + \cos\frac{3\pi}{4}}{2}}$$

We take the positive square root since $\frac{3\pi}{8}$ is in the first quadrant.

$$= \sqrt{\frac{1 - \frac{\sqrt{2}}{2}}{2}}$$

$$= \sqrt{\frac{2 - \sqrt{2}}{4}}$$

$$= \boxed{\sqrt{\frac{2 - \sqrt{2}}{2}}}$$

c. By the double-angle formula for cosine,

$$1 - 2\sin^2\frac{\pi}{8} = \cos\left[2 \cdot \left(\frac{\pi}{8}\right)\right]$$

$$= \cos\frac{\pi}{4}$$

$$= \boxed{\frac{\sqrt{2}}{2}}$$

d. We want to compute $\cos(\sin^{-1}\frac{3}{5})$. Let $\theta = \sin^{-1}\frac{3}{5}$; therefore, we wish to compute $\cos\theta$.

Since $\theta = \sin^{-1}\frac{3}{5}$, we have that $\sin\theta = \frac{3}{5}$. By SOHCAHTOA, we can set up a right triangle with acute angle θ, and with 3 as the length of the side opposite and 5 as the hypotenuse.

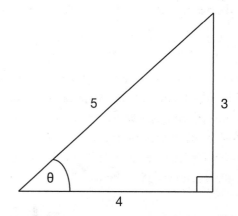

By Pythagoras, or recognizing this is a 3-4-5 triangle

From the triangle we see that

$$\cos\left(\sin^{-1}\frac{3}{5}\right) = \cos\theta$$

$$= \boxed{\frac{4}{5}} \text{ by SOHCAHTOA}$$

e. If $\cos x = \frac{5}{13}$ (which is positive) and $\tan x < 0$, we know by ASTC that we are in the fourth quadrant. This will tell us what signs to use for the other trig ratios. Also, by SOHCAHTOA, we can set up the following right triangle.

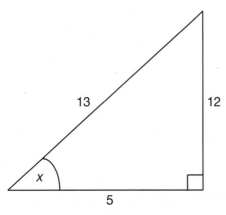

By Pythagoras, or recognizing this is a
5-12-13 triangle.

Again, using SOHCAHTOA, we can figure out
the value for sin x, and hence the other trig
ratios using the following formula box.

$\sin x = -\frac{12}{13}$ Negative since we are in
quadrant 4.

$\tan x = -\frac{12}{5}$

$\sec x = \frac{13}{5}$

$\csc x = -\frac{13}{12}$

Example

Solve the following trig equations. First find the
solutions falling between 0 and 2π radians, then
write down the general solutions:

a. $\tan x = 1$

b. $2\sin\theta + 1 = 0$

c. $2\cos^2 x = 1$

d. $2\cos^2 x + \cos x - 1 = 0$

e. $\cos 2x = \sin x$

f. $\sin x = \cos x$

g. $\sin 2x - \cos x = 0$

Solution:

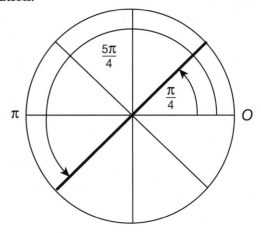

a. $\tan x = 1$

$\Rightarrow x = \tan^{-1}(1)$

$\Rightarrow x = \frac{\pi}{4}$ (reference angle)

$\Rightarrow \boxed{x = \frac{\pi}{4}, \frac{5\pi}{4}}$ for $0 \leq x \leq 2\pi$

$\Rightarrow \boxed{x = \frac{\pi}{4} + n\pi}$ in general, where n is an
integer

b. $2\sin\theta + 1 = 0$

$\Rightarrow \sin\theta = -\frac{1}{2}$ This means our solutions are in
quadrants III and IV.

$\Rightarrow \theta = \frac{7\pi}{6}, \frac{11\pi}{6}$ for $0 \leq \theta \leq 2\pi$

$\Rightarrow \boxed{\theta = \frac{7\pi}{6} + 2n\pi}$ or $\boxed{\frac{11\pi}{6} + 2n\pi}$ in general,
where n is
an integer

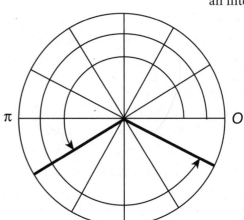

c. $2 \cos^2 x = 1$

$\Rightarrow \cos x = \pm \frac{1}{\sqrt{2}} = \pm \frac{\sqrt{2}}{2}$ This means we want solutions in all quadrants.

$\Rightarrow x = \frac{\pi}{4}, \frac{3\pi}{4}, \frac{5\pi}{4}, \frac{7\pi}{4}$, for $0 \le x \le 2\pi$

$\Rightarrow \boxed{x = \frac{\pi}{4} + n\pi}$ or $\boxed{\frac{3\pi}{4} + n\pi}$ in general, where n is an integer

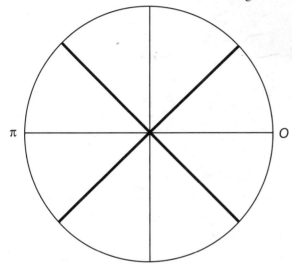

π .... O

d. $2 \cos^2 x + \cos x - 1 = 0$ We can treat this as a quadratic, like $2y^2 + y - 1 = 0$. Factor!

$\Rightarrow (2 \cos x - 1)(\cos x + 1) = 0$

$\Rightarrow \cos x = \frac{1}{2}$ or $\cos x = -1$

If $\cos x = \frac{1}{2}$, then $\boxed{x = \frac{\pi}{3}, \frac{5\pi}{3}}$ for $0 \le x \le 2\pi$

and $\boxed{x = \frac{\pi}{3} + 2n\pi}$ or $\boxed{\frac{5\pi}{3} + 2n\pi}$ for n an integer, in general.

If $\cos x = -1$, then $\boxed{x = \pi}$ for $0 \le x \le 2\pi$, and $\boxed{x = n\pi}$ where n is an *odd* integer, in general.

e. $\cos 2x = \sin x$ Having the double angle is a problem, so use a formula to write it as a single angle. It's best to use the one involving sine only.

$\Rightarrow 1 - 2 \sin^2 x = \sin x$

$\Rightarrow 2 \sin^2 x + \sin x - 1 = 0$ Now we can use the same trick as in the previous problem.

$\Rightarrow (2 \sin x - 1)(\sin x + 1) = 0$

$\Rightarrow \sin x = \frac{1}{2}$ or $\sin x = -1$

If $\sin x = \frac{1}{2}$, then $\boxed{x = \frac{\pi}{6}, \frac{5\pi}{6}}$ for $0 \le x \le 2\pi$

and $\boxed{x = \frac{\pi}{6} + 2n\pi}$ or $\boxed{\frac{5\pi}{6} + 2n\pi}$ for n an integer, in general.

If $\sin x = -1$, then $\boxed{x = \frac{3\pi}{2}}$ for $0 \le x \le 2\pi$ and

$\boxed{x = \frac{3\pi}{2} + 2n\pi}$ for n an integer, in general.

f. $\sin x = \cos x$

$\Rightarrow \frac{\sin x}{\cos x} = 1$ We can divide by cosine since there is no angle that makes both functions zero at the same time. So no angle that would make cosine zero is a solution. Thus we are not dividing by 0.

$\Rightarrow \tan x = 1$

$\Rightarrow \boxed{x = \frac{\pi}{4}, \frac{5\pi}{4}}$ for $0 \le x \le 2\pi$ and

$\boxed{x = \frac{\pi}{4} + n\pi}$ for n an integer, in general.

g. $\sin 2x - \cos x = 0$

$\Rightarrow 2 \sin x \cos x - \cos x = 1$

$\Rightarrow \cos x (2 \sin x - 1) = 0$

$\Rightarrow \cos x = 0$ or $\sin x = \frac{1}{2}$

If $\cos x = 0$, then $\boxed{x = \frac{\pi}{2}, \frac{3\pi}{2}}$ for $0 \le x \le 2\pi$

and $\boxed{x = \frac{n\pi}{2}}$ where n is an *odd* integer, in general.

If $\sin x = \frac{1}{2}$, then $\boxed{x = \frac{\pi}{6}, \frac{5\pi}{6}}$ for $0 \le x \le 2\pi$

and $\boxed{x = \frac{\pi}{6} + 2n\pi}$ or $\boxed{\frac{5\pi}{6} + 2n\pi}$ for n an integer, in general.

Transformations of Trig Graphs

Trig functions are functions at the end of the day, so anything we spoke about before can be discussed in terms of trig functions. Transformations are no different. Among other things, we can shift, stretch, and compress trig graphs. The rules for doing this follow the transformation rules covered in the table. Given one of these transformed graphs, you should be able to ascertain certain details from it—whether you're given the graph itself or the formula for the graph. Some essential information we can take away from a transformed sine or cosine graph can be summarized by the following.

Given a function of the form $y = a\sin k(x - b) + c$ or $y = a\cos k(x - b) + c$, the following hold:
- The amplitude of the graph is $|a|$. This is how much the graph goes up and down from the midline (defined later). It is the vertical stretch factor.
- The phase shift (horizontal shift) is b.
- The vertical shift (the location of the midline, essentially, the new x-axis) is c.
- The period is given by Period $= \frac{2\pi}{|k|}$.
- The subinterval is given by $\frac{period}{4}$.
- The appropriate graphing interval is $[b, b + \frac{2\pi}{|k|}]$ (unless you're asked to graph somewhere else).

The box tells you how to determine some of the important features of the graphs mentioned. Let's expound on this by going through an example.

Example
Let's look at the graph of $y = 2 \sin\left(2x - \frac{\pi}{2}\right) + 3$.

One important thing to know about sine and cosine is that one period of their graphs (the principal period) can be dissected into four sections (which we call *subintervals* here).

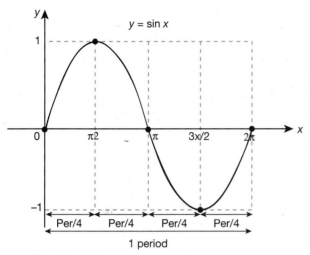

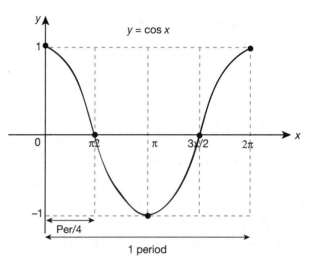

Sine: First subinterval: middle to top
Second subinterval: top to middle
Third subinterval: middle to bottom
Fourth subinterval: bottom to middle

Cosine: First subinterval: top to middle
Second subinterval: middle to bottom
Third subinterval: bottom to middle
Fourth subinterval: middle to top

If we know where the sections are, we will know what the graphs are doing there. If the coefficient *a* is negative, then the graphs simply flip upside down; top becomes bottom and vice versa. We find these sections by finding the period and dividing it by 4. Of course we need to know where to start the dissections. That's where the *b* comes in. The *c* tells us where our new midline is. This will all be made clear in a bit.

First, write the given function in the proper form. We have

$$y = 2 \sin 2\left(x - \frac{\pi}{4}\right) + 3$$

Now we see that $a = 2$, $b = \frac{\pi}{4}$, $c = 3$, $k = 2$. This tells us that the amplitude is 2, the phase shift is $\frac{\pi}{4}$ (to the right), the vertical shift is 3 (upward), the period is $\frac{2\pi}{2} = \pi$, the subintervals have length of $\frac{\pi}{4}$, and we'd probably want to graph it on the interval $\left[\frac{\pi}{4}, \frac{5\pi}{4}\right]$.

We use the *c* to get the new midline.

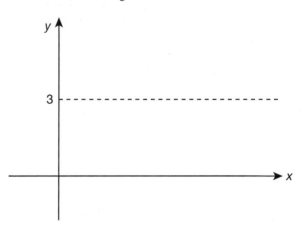

Next, the amplitude tells us how high we go up from the midline, and how low we go down. In this case, we go up two units to the level $y = 5$, and down two units to the level $y = 1$.

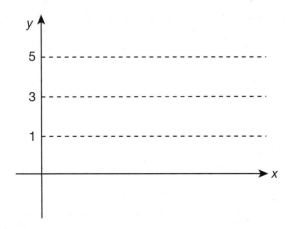

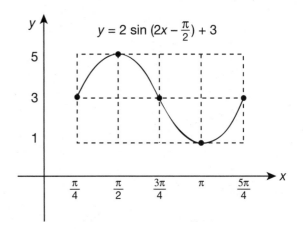

$$y = 2 \sin\left(2x - \frac{\pi}{2}\right) + 3$$

We draw where our period will begin, at the phase shift $b = \frac{\pi}{4}$, and then from there draw a rectangle of length π, which we will cut into four pieces for the subintervals. We can also label the endpoints of the subintervals, because we know each is of length $\frac{\pi}{4}$.

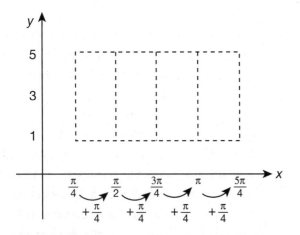

Now we have our familiar grid—the four sections our sine graph will be drawn in. Now, going by how sine behaves, we draw the graph (middle to top, then top to middle, then middle to bottom, then bottom to middle).

Note that, given the graph with all these measurements, we can work backward to figure out the formula for the graph (by seeing what the amplitude, period, phase shift, etc., are).

Here is one example to try on your own:

Example
For the graph $y = -3 \cos\left(\frac{1}{2}x + \frac{\pi}{2}\right) + 1$, state the amplitude, period, phase shift, and vertical shift, and sketch the graph of one full period on an interval of your choice.

Solution: First, write the function in standard form. This is $y = -3 \cos\frac{1}{2}(x - (-\pi)) + 1$.
This means:

- The amplitude is $|a| = |-3| = 3$.
- The period is $\frac{2\pi}{|k|} = \frac{2\pi}{\frac{1}{2}} = 4\pi$.
- The phase shift is $b = -\pi$.
- The vertical shift is $c = 1$.

With this we can graph the function on $[-\pi, 3\pi]$.

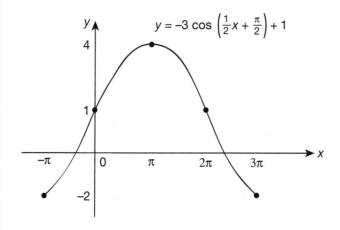

$$y = -3 \cos\left(\tfrac{1}{2}x + \tfrac{\pi}{2}\right) + 1$$

Modeling Periodic Phenomena with Trig Functions

The periodicity of trig functions allows us to use them to model situations where things happen periodically. Knowing how the different trig functions behave will help us choose the right one to get the job done.

Example

A Ferris wheel has a diameter of 26 feet. The lowest point on the Ferris wheel is 5 feet above the ground. When the Ferris wheel is in motion, it takes 2 minutes to make one complete revolution. John gets on the Ferris wheel at the lowest point and then it begins its motion.

a. Find a function to model John's height above the ground after time t minutes has passed.

b. After 3.2 minutes, what will John's height above the ground be?

c. Assuming the ride lasts 6 minutes, when will John be at a height of 15 feet above the ground?

d. Assuming the Ferris wheel ride lasts forever, when will John be at 15 feet above the ground?

Solution: John's height (y) can be described by the following graph.

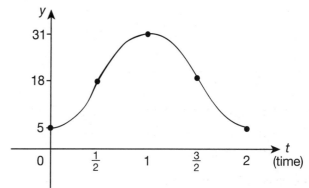

This seems to behave like a (negative) cosine graph, since the initial point is at the lowest point under the midline. We could also look at this like a shifted sine graph, but that would make things more complicated.

a. By using what we learned in the preceding section, we can describe this graph (and hence the height of John, y, at time t) by the function
$y = -13 \cos(\pi t) + 18$

b. Simply plugging in $t = 3.2$, we get
$y = -13 \cos(\pi \cdot 3.2) + 18 \approx \boxed{28.52 \text{ feet}}$

c. One period is 2 minutes long, so 6 minutes will comprise three periods. Thus we want to know when John is at a height of 15 feet within the span of three periods. We know that this will happen six times, since drawing a horizontal line at the level of 15 will cut the graph twice in one period. To find the six solutions, set the height function to 15 and solve for t.
$$\Rightarrow 15 = -13 \cos(\pi t) + 18$$
$$\Rightarrow \tfrac{3}{13} = \cos(\pi t)$$
$$\Rightarrow \cos^{-1}\tfrac{3}{13} = \pi t$$
$$\Rightarrow t = \tfrac{1}{\pi}\cos^{-1}\tfrac{3}{13}$$

The cosine inverse function will give us the solution for the angle in the first quadrant ($0 \le \pi t \le \tfrac{\pi}{2}$), and we can use reference angles and the fact that values repeat every 2π radians to figure out the other values we need. Here, a 2π radian angle is equivalent to a time of 2 minutes, since 2 minutes is the period here. With this idea, three of the solutions are:

$t_1 = \frac{1}{\pi}\cos^{-1} \approx 0.426$ minutes, $t_2 = t_1 + 2 \approx 2.426$ minutes, and $t_3 = t_2 + 2 \approx 4.426$ minutes

For the other solutions, first find the reference angle in the fourth quadrant and then add two periods again.

$t_4 = \frac{1}{\pi}(2\pi - \cos^{-1}\frac{3}{13}) \approx 1.574$ minutes, $t_5 \approx 3.574$ minutes, $t_6 \approx 5.574$ minutes

Thus, John is at a height of 15 feet at the following (approximate) times, in minutes:

0.426, 1.574, 2.426, 3.574, 4.426, 5.574

d. Generalizing what we have done, John will be at 15 feet at the following times (if the ride goes on forever):

0.426 + 2*n* and 1.574 + 2*n*, where *n* is a nonnegative integer

► CALCULUS REVIEW

CHAPTER SUMMARY

Calculus is the mathematics of change. Many quantities in the world do not remain constant. As in calculus we study the mathematics of change, and as functions are used to represent change, we can equivalently describe calculus as the study of functions. In this review chapter we will go over some of the fundamental concepts of calculus.

Consider the speed of a moving car. It starts its 60-mile journey at 12:00 P.M. and comes to rest at 1:00 P.M. We cannot describe the speed of the car by using a number alone. For instance, it would be wrong to say the car is traveling at 60 miles per hour, since on the highway the car may run into traffic that slows it down, or it may speed up above 60 mph if few cars are present on the highway. This example illustrates that the quantity, the speed of the car, cannot be described by a number alone.

So if we cannot use a number to represent the speed of the car, what do we use? The answer is that we use functions. A function is the tool that we use to represent change. This review chapter assumes familiarity with the basic concepts of functions as reviewed in the previous chapter.

Let us see how we can represent the speed of a car with a function.

We create two axes; the horizontal axis we will call t (time) and the vertical axis we will call s (speed). Note that the values of t are confined to all numbers between 0 and 1, as t represents the time past 12:00 P.M. Since the car had a journey from 12:00 P.M. to 1:00 P.M., the values of time t take values between 0 and 1 hour. Thus, $t = 0$ represents time at 12:00 P.M., $t = 1$ represents time at 1:00 P.M., and $t = 0.5$ represents time at 12:30 P.M., as t is measuring the time past noon (in hours). For the vertical axis, s, the speed axis, we associate the corresponding speed at that moment in time. We do that for every moment in time between 0 and 1, and this produces a curve; for example, let us say it looks something like this:

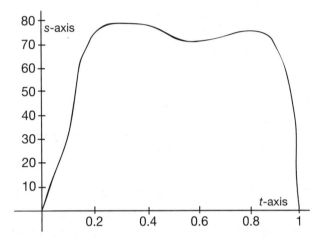

What this means is that when $t = 0.2$, or when the time is 12:12 P.M., the speed of the car was 70 mph. We also see from this curve that the highest speed the car attained was 80 mph, which was attained at time about $t = 0.25$. This is an example of a *function*. As explained in the earlier review chapter in more detail, a function is an association (or a correspondence) of a unique number (output) for each number (input). In this case for every value of t (in the interval between 0 and 1) we associate (correspond) the value of s, the speed of the car, at that particular moment in time. Let us suppose that we have an equation for this function, in which case $s = f(t)$ where $f(t)$ is some formula involving t. Substituting various values of t into $f(t)$ and evaluating the function will produce the value of s that corresponds to the speed at that time.

This simple example shows that functions can be used to represent change of some quantity.

Limits

Let $f(x)$ be a function and a be some number. We will define $\lim_{x \to a^+} f(x)$, what is called the *limit* of $f(x)$ as x approaches a from the right. The idea behind the limit is that we evaluate $f(x)$ as the variable x gets closer to the number a. When we write $x \to a^+$, this indicates that x is approaching a from the right; in other words, x gets closer to a but x is larger than a.

Consider the following example. Let $f(x) = \frac{\sin x}{x}$, and we will determine $\lim_{x \to 0^+} f(x)$. What we need to do is evaluate $f(x)$ as x gets closer to 0 from the right, and see what value the function approaches. Let us form the following table:

$$\begin{bmatrix} x & 1 & 0.5 & 0.2 & 0.1 & 0.05 \\ f(x) & .8414 & .959 & .993 & .998 & .999 \end{bmatrix}$$

On the top row we have the values of x getting closer to but not reaching the value 0 from the right, as they are all larger than 0. On the bottom row we have the values of $f(x)$ evaluated at each particular value of x (recall that in calculus the trigonometric functions are measured in terms of radians). We can see that $f(x)$ is approaching the number 1. It is getting closer to the number 1, but never quite reaching it, as x gets closer to the number 0 from the right.

One may ask the question: Why not simply evaluate $f(0)$? The problem is that $f(x)$ is not defined at $x = 0$, because of the zero denominator! This is an important concept about limits; we can evaluate limits of a function at a point for which it is not defined. Thus, even though $f(x)$ is not defined at $x = 0$, we can still make sense of $\lim_{x \to 0^+} f(x)$.

We can also illustrate this concept of limit using the graph of the function. If we draw the graph of $f(x) = \frac{\sin x}{x}$ for positive values of x, we can see that as $x \to 0^+$ the value of the function fluctuates up and down until we get close to 0, in which case the function becomes nearly stabilized at value of 1:

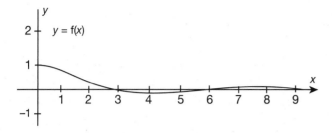

Let us do another example: $g(x) = \frac{1-\cos x}{x^2}$. This time we will compute $\lim_{x \to 0^-} g(x)$; in other words, we will find the limit of $g(x)$ as x gets closer to 0, but *from the left*, as x is less than 0. As before, we form a table of values for the variable x, and for the function $g(x)$, and we consider what happens as x gets closer to 0 from the left:

$$\begin{bmatrix} x & -1 & -0.5 & -0.2 & -0.1 & -0.05 \\ g(x) & +.4597 & +.4897 & +.4983 & +.4996 & +.4999 \end{bmatrix}$$

This shows us that $\lim_{x \to 0^-} g(x) = \frac{1}{2}$. As before, we can draw the graph of the function $g(x)$, say for values of $x < 0$, and we can see from the picture that as x gets closer to 0 the value of the function is approaching the value of $\frac{1}{2}$:

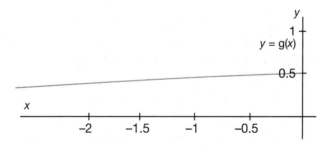

Again, note the danger of saying that $\lim_{x \to 0^-} g(x) = g(0)$, as the function $g(x)$ is not even defined at $x = 0$! But what if the function is defined at the point at which we take the limit? Can we just say that the limit is equal to the value of the function at that point?

Let us consider the following example:

$$F(x) = \begin{cases} x + 1 & \text{if } x > 1 \\ 1 - x & \text{if } x \leq 1 \end{cases}$$

The graph of this function is shown here:

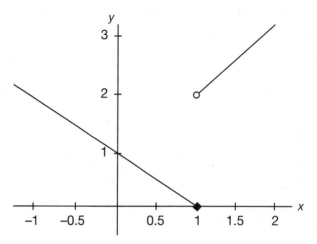

We can see from the picture that $\lim_{x \to 1^+} F(x) = 2$; however, $F(1) = 0$. Thus, even though the function is defined at the limit point, the limit of the function at the point is not the same thing as just evaluating the function at the point. However, note that $\lim_{x \to 1^-} F(x) = 0$, which turns out being equal to $F(0)$. Care needs to be taken before we can simply substitute the limit point into the function.

Some functions $f(x)$ have the property that $\lim_{x \to a^+} f(x)$ and $\lim_{x \to a^-} f(x)$ are both equal to the same limit; let us call that common limit L. In this case we write that $\lim_{x \to a} f(x) = L$. When the limit symbol says $x \to a$ without indicating a^+ or a^-, then it is understood to mean for the limit of $f(x)$ as x approaches a, from both the left and the right. In the example, $\lim_{x \to 1^+} F(x) = 2$ while $\lim_{x \to 1^-} F(x) = 0$, since the left limit at 1 and right limit at 1 are not the same, we say that $\lim_{x \to 1} F(x)$ does not exist. The limit does not exist because it depends on how we approach the number 1; if we approach from the right we get one value, whereas if we approach from the left we get another value. As the values we get can be different, we rather say $\lim_{x \to 1} f(x)$ does not exist (DNE).

Functions that have the property that $\lim_{x \to a} f(x) = f(a)$ are called *continuous*. In order for this equation to make sense it must be that $f(x)$ is defined at $x = a$, that the limit $\lim_{x \to a} f(x)$ exists from both the left and right and gives the same value, and that $\lim_{x \to a} f(x)$, the common limit of both the left and right limits, is equal to $f(a)$. Visually it means that the graph of the function stays in one piece at the point a. In the example, $F(x)$ is not continuous (so we say it is *discontinuous*) at $x = 1$. The easiest way to see this is by looking directly at the graph and noticing that it rips apart at the point $x = 1$. We can also say that $F(x)$ is not continuous at $x = 1$ because $\lim_{x \to 1} F(x)$ does not exist. As we saw, it has different values depending on the left and right limits.

To summarize, a function $f(x)$ is *continuous* at point a if three conditions are satisfied. First, $f(x)$ is defined at $x = a$. Second, $\lim_{x \to a} f(x)$ exists. Third, $\lim_{x \to a} f(x) = f(a)$.

Here is another example. Let us define the function:

$$h(x) = \begin{cases} \frac{\sin x}{x} & \text{if} \quad x \neq 0 \\ 0 & \text{if} \quad x = 0 \end{cases}$$

Here is the graph of this function:

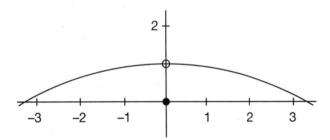

Notice that $\lim_{x \to 0^+} h(x) = 1$, as we see from the picture, and we already did this computation before using a table of limiting values. Similarly, $\lim_{x \to 0^-} h(x) = 1$. Thus, the left limit and right limit both exist and are equal to each other. This means that $\lim_{x \to 0} h(x) = 1$. However, note that $h(0) = 0$, so $\lim_{x \to 0} h(x) \neq h(0)$. This tells us that $h(x)$ is not continuous at $x = 0$; we can see this from the graph as well. Visually the function suddenly jumps down to 0 at $x = 0$, and this creates a break in the graph. As such, it makes $h(x)$ discontinuous at $x = 0$.

Most functions that one encounters in calculus are continuous functions. This includes *polynomial functions*, functions that are just powers of x, such as, for instance, $2 + x^3 - 5x$. *Trigonometric functions*, such as sine, cosine, tangent, and so forth, are continuous at all points at which they are defined, for instance, $\sin(x) + 3 \tan x$. *Rational functions* are quotients of polynomial functions, so, for example, $\frac{2 + x^3 - 5x}{x^2 - 1}$; this is an example of a rational function. *Radical functions* are $\sqrt{x}$, $3\sqrt{x}$, $4\sqrt{x}$, and so forth. Various combinations of these functions are all continuous at every point at which the function is defined.

Computing Limits

The general rule with limit problems is that, if the limit problem involves one of the standard types of functions mentioned in the preceding paragraph, we simply evaluate the function at the limit point. If the function happens to be defined at the point, then that would be the limit of the function.

Example
Compute $\lim_{x \to 1} \frac{1 - x^2}{1 + x^2}$.

Solution: Note that the function $\frac{1 - x^2}{1 + x^2}$ is a rational function. It is continuous at every point at which it is defined. At $x = 1$ the function is defined, so we can evaluate the limit by just substituting $x = 1$ to get the value of 0. This is the limit of the function.

Example
In this problem we will compute $\lim_{x \to 1} \frac{1 + x^2}{1 - x^2}$.

Solution: Contrary to the previous example the function $\frac{1 + x^2}{1 - x^2}$ is not defined at $x = 1$, so we cannot just substitute the value of $x = 1$ into it, as it gives us a zero denominator. To see what the limit is, we can rather create a table of values again. Let us check what happens when $x \to 1^+$; here is a table of values for x approaching 1 from the right and the value of the function right below it:

$$\begin{bmatrix} x & 2 & 1.5 & 1.2 & 1.1 & 1.01 \\ f(x) & -1.66 & -2.66 & -5.55 & -10.52 & -100.50 \end{bmatrix}$$

Notice that $f(x)$ is just getting really negative as we get close to 1. Thus, the limit $\lim_{x \to 1^+} \frac{1-x^2}{1-x^2}$ does not exist, as it is not approaching any value; it is just getting smaller and smaller without any limit approaching. Sometimes we write that $\lim_{x \to 1^+} \frac{1-x^2}{1-x^2} = -\infty$, to symbolize that the function is just getting indefinitely small as x approaches 1. But it does not mean that the limit exists, as $-\infty$ is not a number; it is just a symbolic statement that the function is getting smaller without any bound and so consequently without any limit. Since the limit as $x \to 1^+$ does not exist, it means that the limit $x \to 1$ certainly does not exist, as the limit $x \to 1$ includes the common value of both the left and right limits.

Example

Compute $\lim_{x \to 1} \frac{1-x^2}{1-x}$.

Solution: As before, we cannot simply substitute $x = 1$ into the limit problem as the function $\frac{1-x^2}{1-x}$ is not defined at $x = 1$. We can do the following instead. We can factor and cancel:

$$\lim_{x \to 1} \frac{1-x^2}{1-x} = \lim_{x \to 1} \frac{(1-x)(1+x)}{1-x} = \lim_{x \to 1}(1+x) = 2$$

On the last limit we simply evaluated $1 + x$ at $x = 1$ as the function $1 + x$; a polynomial (and hence continuous) function is defined at $x = 1$, so we may just solve the limit problem by direct evaluation.

Example

Compute $\lim_{x \to 0} \frac{x}{\sqrt{x+1}-1}$.

Solution: As before, direct evaluation does not work. We use an algebra trick known as rationalizing the fraction:

$$\frac{x}{\sqrt{x+1}-1} \cdot \frac{\sqrt{x+1}+1}{\sqrt{x+1}+1} = \frac{x(\sqrt{x+1}-1)}{x+1-1}$$

$$= \frac{x(\sqrt{x+1}+1)}{x} = \sqrt{x+1}+1$$

Thus, the limit problem becomes

$$\lim_{x \to 0}(\sqrt{x+1}+1) = 2$$

Direct valuation works now.

Example

Determine $\lim_{x \to 0} \sin\left(\frac{1}{x}\right)$.

Solution: As direct computation does not work, let us try forming a table of values as $x \to 0^+$. But we will choose this table of values in a clever way, not just randomly chosen points approaching 0 from the right. Instead, we will approach 0 along the following numbers: $\frac{1}{\pi}, \frac{1}{2\pi}, \frac{1}{3\pi}, \frac{1}{4\pi}, \dots$. At each of these points the value of the function is $\sin(\pi), \sin(2\pi), \sin(3\pi), \sin(4\pi), \dots$ all of which equate to zero. Thus, if we form the table we get something like the following:

$$\begin{bmatrix} x & \frac{1}{\pi} & \frac{1}{2\pi} & \frac{1}{3\pi} & \frac{1}{4\pi} \\ f(x) & 0 & 0 & 0 & 0 \end{bmatrix}$$

Along these points the function stays constant at 0. Thus, the limit of this function is 0. However, this is a tricky problem. The reason is that it depends on how else we approach the number 0 from the right. If instead we approach 0 along the points:

$$\begin{bmatrix} x & \frac{1}{\frac{\pi}{2}+\pi} & \frac{1}{\frac{\pi}{2}+2\pi} & \frac{1}{\frac{\pi}{2}+3\pi} & \frac{1}{\frac{\pi}{2}+4\pi} \\ f(x) & 1 & 1 & 1 & 1 \end{bmatrix}$$

In this case the limit along these numbers of the function is 1. Since there is no definitive limit because it depends on how one approaches 0, the limit does not exist.

It is useful to draw the graph of this function to see what happens:

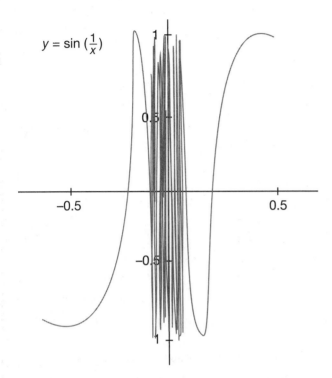

$y = \sin\left(\frac{1}{x}\right)$

The picture should convince that as $x \to 0$ the function fluctuates wildly between -1 and 1 without any limiting value to it. Thus, the limit in this case does not exist.

Just a word of caution: When we did the example with the function we called $F(x)$, everything was defined. But we were unable to conclude that $\lim_{x \to 1} F(x)$ was equal to $F(1)$. The function $f(x)$ is not a polynomial function despite the fact that it is $x + 1$ for $x > 1$ and $1 - x$ for $x \leq 1$. This is because it is a piecewise-defined function. It is two separate functions that happen to be polynomial. As such, we cannot treat it as a continuous function since on the overlap at $x = 1$ the function changes from one type of function to another, so it may become discontinuous, as was the case in that example.

The derivative of a function measures its rate of change. When we graph the function $y = f(x)$ and pick a point $(a, f(a))$ on the graph, the derivative of the function $f(x)$ at the point a, denoted by $f'(a)$, gives the slope of the tangent line at that point. This process of finding the slope of the tangent line is accomplished by using limits. We increase a by a small amount h; this produces the point $(a + h, f(a+h))$:

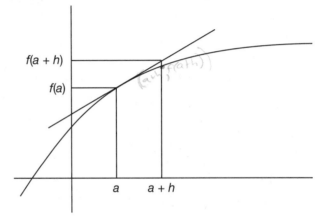

The slope of the line between these two points is then given by:

$$\frac{f(a + h) - f(a)}{(a + h) - a} = \frac{f(a + h) - f(a)}{h}$$

This, however, is not the tangent line. But it is close to the tangent line and the smaller h is, the closer its slope is to the tangent line. Ideally, we would like to let $h = 0$; however, this is not a defined operation as it results in a zero denominator. Instead we consider the limit as $h \to 0$. This is what we call the derivative of $f(x)$ at the point a, and we denote it by $f'(a)$; therefore, we define

$$f'(x) = \lim_{h \to 0} \frac{f(x + h) - f(x)}{h}$$

Note that we use x instead of a, only because the derivative of $f(x)$ is itself a function $f'(x)$, and when evaluated at a particular point a will give the slope at that particular point. Let us see some examples.

Example

Let $f(x) = \sin x$, we will compute $f'(0)$, the derivative at zero.

Solution: We write down the definition:

$$f'(0) = \lim_{h \to 0} \frac{f(0 + h) - f(0)}{h} = \lim_{h \to 0} \frac{\sin h - 0}{h}$$

$$= \lim_{h \to 0} \frac{\sin h}{h} = 1$$

We already computed this limit numerically in the limits section of this chapter.

Example

Let $f(x) = x^2$. Compute $f'(x)$, the derivative of $f(x)$.

Solution:

$$f'(x) = \lim_{h \to 0} \frac{f(x + h) - f(x)}{h} = \lim_{h \to 0} \frac{(x+h)^2 - x^2}{h}$$

$$= \lim_{h \to 0} \frac{x^2 + 2xh + h^2 - x^2}{h} = \lim_{h \to 0} (2x + h) = 2x$$

This produces a formula for $f'(x)$, so if we want to know the derivative of $f(x)$ at $x = 3$ we just substitute $x = 3$ into the derivative formula $f'(x)$ and get $f'(3) = 6$. Geometrically, this means that at $x = 3$ the slope of the tangent line to the curve $y = x^2$ is 6.

Example

Let $f(x) = \sqrt{x}$. Compute $f'(x)$.

Solution:

$$f'(x) = \lim_{h \to 0} \frac{f(x + h) - f(x)}{h} = \lim_{h \to 0} \frac{\sqrt{x+h} - \sqrt{x}}{h}$$

To compute this limit, we rationalize numerator and denominator:

$$\lim_{h \to 0} \frac{\sqrt{x+h} - \sqrt{x}}{h} \cdot \frac{\sqrt{x+h} + \sqrt{x}}{\sqrt{x+h} + \sqrt{x}}$$

$$= \lim_{h \to 0} \frac{h}{h(\sqrt{x+h} + \sqrt{x})}$$

$$= \lim_{h \to 0} \frac{1}{\sqrt{x+h} + \sqrt{x}} = \frac{1}{2\sqrt{x}}$$

Not all functions possess derivatives. Consider for example the function $f(x) = |x|$ with this graph:

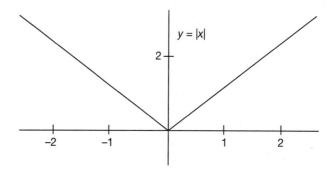

At $x = 0$ the curve has a sharp corner. As such we cannot assign a tangent line to it. Indeed, if we compute the derivative at 0, we find:

$$f'(0) = \lim_{h \to 0} \frac{f(0+h) - f(0)}{h} = \lim_{h \to 0} \frac{|h|}{h}$$

If $h \to 0^+$, then h is positive, so $|h| = h$; then the limit is equal to $\lim_{h \to 0} \frac{h}{h} = 1$. If, however, $h \to 0^-$, then h is negative, so $|h| = -h$; then the limit is equal to $\lim_{h \to 0} \frac{-h}{h} = -1$. We see from here that the limit $\lim_{h \to 0} \frac{|h|}{h}$ does not exist, as it is different along left and right limits.

Functions that possess a derivative at a point (in other words, the limit defining the derivative exists at that point) are called *differentiable*. In the example we just did involving the function $|x|$, we say it was not differentiable at 0, while the example before that with the function x^2 was differentiable at any point x.

Recall that a function $f(x)$ is continuous at a point if it stays in one whole piece, and a function

$f(x)$ is *differentiable* when not only does it stay in one whole piece but it is smooth; in other words, it has no sharp edges, so there is a tangent line existing at that particular point. Thus, we see that $|x|$ is not differentiable at $x = 0$, but it is continuous there. Differentiability is a stronger property than continuity. Differentiability implies continuity, but continuity does not need to imply differentiability.

Example

Consider the following function, $\sqrt[3]{x}$:

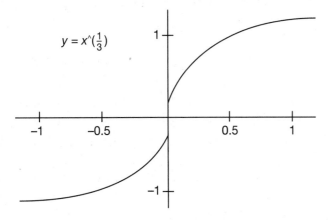

$y = x^{\left(\frac{1}{3}\right)}$

Let us call it $g(x) = \sqrt[3]{x}$ and compute $g'(0)$.

Solution:

$$g'(0) = \lim_{h \to 0}\frac{g(0 + h) - g(0)}{h} = \lim_{h \to 0}\frac{\sqrt[3]{h}}{h} = \lim_{h \to 0}\frac{h^{\frac{1}{3}}}{h}$$

$$= \lim_{h \to 0}\frac{1}{h^{\frac{2}{3}}}$$

The limit of this function does not exist since the numerator stays at 1 and the denominator goes to 0. Note that the curve $y = g(x)$ is not a sharp corner at $x = 0$, but it is still not differentiable at that point, as the derivative limit does not exist. The reason for nondifferentiability can be seen by considering the tangent line at $x = 0$. It is vertical. What slope do vertical lines have? Their slope is not defined. This is the reason why the function fails to be differentiable at $x = 0$.

To summarize, we can inspect if a function is differentiable by looking for sharp corners or vertical tangent lines. Either one of these two will make the function nondifferentiable at that particular point.

Example

Consider the following function $h(x)$ defined on interval $[-5 : 7]$:

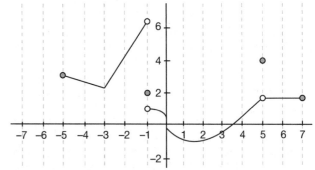

Ignoring the endpoints, we will answer the following four questions:

1. At which points does the function not have a limit?
2. At which points is the function not continuous?
3. At which points is the function not differentiable?
4. What is the derivative at $x = 1$?

Solution:

1. The function has no limit at $x = -1$. This is because the limit from the right and the limit from the left are entirely different. *Note:* The function *does* have a limit at $x = 5$ because the limits from the left and right are equal, even though the function value at that point may be different.

2. The function fails to be continuous at point p when $\lim_{x \to p} f(x) \neq f(p)$; a way to see this is by noticing where the graph of the function breaks apart. This happens at the points $x = -1, 5$.

3. A function that is differentiable at the point p is also continuous there. As the function is not continuous at $x = -1, 5$ it means that it is also not differentiable at those points. A function is also not differentiable when its graph has a sharp corner at a point, and this happens at the point $x = -3$. A function also fails to be differentiable when it has a vertical tangent, and from the picture we see it has a vertical slope at $x = 0$.

4. Notice that the function has a turning point at $x = 1$. We can see that at this point the tangent line to the curve is a horizontal line. As horizontal lines have slope equal to 0, it follows that the derivative at $x = 1$ is equal to zero.

Computing Derivatives

There are various ways to compute the derivative without the need to use the limit to compute it. Here are some basic rules of the derivative:

- Sum rule: $(f(x) + g(x))' = f'(x) + g'(x)$
- Difference rule: $(f(x) - g(x))' = f'(x) - g'(x)$
- Product rule: $(f(x)g(x))' = f'(x)g(x) + f(x)\,g'(x)$
- Quotient rule: $\left(\dfrac{f(x)}{g(x)}\right)' = \dfrac{f'(x)g(x) - f(x)g'(x)}{g(x)^2}$
- Power rule: $(x^n)' = nx^{n-1}$
- $(\sin x)' = \cos x$ and $(\cos x)' = -\sin x$
- Chain rule: $[f(g(x))]' = f'(g(x))g'(x)$

Using these rules, one can compute many derivatives easily. Here are some examples.

Example
Let $f(x) = x^3 - 2x + 1$, and find the derivative $f'(x)$.

Solution: Here we use the sum and difference rules together with the power rule. The derivative of each one separately is $(x^3)' = 3x^2$, $(2x)' = 2$, and $(1)' = 0$.

(Note, $1 = x^0$, so applying the power rule gives $(1)' = 0x^{-1} = 0$. More generally, the derivative of any constant is zero.) Putting this together, we get the answer of $f'(x) = 3x^2 - 2$.

Example
Let $g(x) = x^2 \sin(x)$, and find the derivative $g'(x)$.

Solution: Here we use the product rule. Since $(x^2)' = 2x$ and $(\sin x)' = \cos x$, when we apply the product rule we get $g'(x) = 2x \sin x + x^2 \cos x$.

Example
Let $a(x) = \tan x$, and find the derivative $a'(x)$.

Solution: This one is best solved using the quotient rule by recalling that $\tan x = \dfrac{\sin x}{\cos x}$. Since $(\sin x)' = \cos x$ and $(\cos x)' = -\sin x$, the quotient rule tells us that

$$a'(x) = \frac{(\cos x)\cos x - \sin x(-\sin x)}{\cos^2 x}$$

$$= \frac{\cos^2 x + \sin^2 x}{\cos^2 x} = \frac{1}{\cos^2 x} = \sec^2 x$$

Example
Let $h(x) = \sin\left(\frac{1}{x}\right)$, and find $h'(x)$.

Solution: This one uses the chain rule. We begin by noticing that $h(x)$ can be described as $f(g(x))$ where $g(x) = q(x) = \frac{1}{x}$ and $f(x) = \sin x$. Now $f'(x) = \cos x$ while $g'(x)$ is computed by the power rule by writing $\frac{1}{x} = x^{-1}$ and this gives $g'(x) = -x^{-2}$. Putting this together, we get

$$h'(x) = f'(g(x))g'(x) = \cos(x^{-1}) \cdot (-x^{-2})$$

Rates of Change
Suppose that y is some quantity that depends on time, so $y = f(t)$. The derivative $f'(t)$ at a particular moment in time measures the rate of change of that quantity. It is sometimes convenient to denote the

derivative as $\frac{dy}{dt}$; the numerator dy represents the derivative of the function y, while the denominator dt represents that we are taking the derivative with respect to the t variable of the function.

Example

A spherical balloon is being inflated with a gas at a constant rate of π feet^3 per minute. We will determine how fast the radius is increasing when the radius of the balloon is 2 feet.

Solution: To solve this problem, we recall that $V = \frac{4}{3}\pi r^3$ where V is the volume and r is the radius. Now if we differentiate both sides with respect to t we get

$$\frac{dV}{dt} = 4\pi r^2 \frac{dr}{dt}$$

We know that the volume is increasing at a constant rate of π feet^3 per minute and we want to find $\frac{dr}{dt}$ when $r = 2$. When we substitute all of that, we get $\pi = 4\pi \cdot (2)^2 \frac{dr}{dt}$. Solving for $\frac{dr}{dt}$, we get that the rate at which the radius is increasing is equal to $\frac{1}{16}$ feet per minute.

Example

A computer screen saver displays an inflating rectangle whose width is increasing at a constant rate of 2 pixels per second and height at 3 pixels per second. We will determine the rate at which the area of the rectangle is increasing when the width is 100 pixels and the height is 300 pixels.

Solution: Let x be the width and y be the height. Then $A = xy$ where A is the area of the rectangle. Note that x, y are functions of t, so when we differentiate both sides we apply the product rule:

$$\frac{dA}{dt} = x\frac{dy}{dt} + y\frac{dx}{dt}$$

Now substitute all the information that is given to us in the problem: $A = (100)(3) + (300)(2) = 900$. Thus, the area is increasing at the speed of 900 pixels^2 per second.

Example

Let $y = t^3 + 2t$ be the distance of a particle measured in feet after t seconds. At what rate is the particle accelerating after two seconds?

Solution: If $y = f(t)$ is the distance a particle traveled, then $\frac{dy}{dt}$ will be its speed at time t. In a similar way, if $v = g(t)$ is the speed of a particle at time t, then $\frac{dv}{dt}$ will be its acceleration at time t. After two seconds, its speed can be computed by first finding $\frac{dt}{dt} = 3t^2 + 2$ and then evaluating this quantity at $t = 2$, so we get that the speed at this moment is 14 feet per second. The acceleration function is obtained by differentiating this quantity one more time; since $v = 3t^2 + 2$, if we differentiate once more, we get $\frac{dv}{dt} = 6t$. After two seconds, the particle is accelerating at 12 feet^2 per second.

First Derivative

Given a function $f(x)$, the graph of the function is described by $y = f(x)$. The derivative, $f'(x)$, tells us where the function is increasing and where it is decreasing by the sign of the derivative. Recall that the derivative measures the slope of the tangent line. A function that is increasing has positive slope, so its derivative will be positive. A function that is decreasing has negative slope, so its derivative will be negative. We summarize these results as follows:

- If $f'(x) > 0$ on an interval I, then $f(x)$ is an increasing function on I.
- If $f'(x) < 0$ on an interval I, then $f(x)$ is a decreasing function on I.

Example

Let $f(x) = \sin x$ on the interval $[0,\pi]$, and the curve $y = \sin x$ as given:

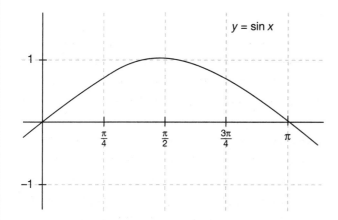

Solution: Note that the function is increasing for $0 < x < \frac{\pi}{2}$ and decreasing for $\frac{\pi}{2} < x < \pi$. Let us check the derivative, $f'(x) = \cos x$. This agrees with the sign of the derivative, as $\cos x$ is positive in the first quadrant, namely for $0 < x < \frac{\pi}{2}$, and negative in the second quadrant, namely for $\frac{\pi}{2} < x < \pi$.

Example

Let $f(x) = \frac{1}{3}x^3 - 4x$. The graph $y = f(x)$ is shown:

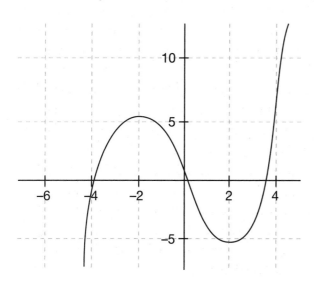

Solution: The function is decreasing on the interval $(-2,2)$. Let us check the derivative sign $f'(x) = x^2 - 4$. Now if $-2 < x < 2$, then $x^2 - 4 < 0$, so $f'(x) < 0$ on this interval, which agrees with the fact that the function is decreasing. On the interval $(2,\infty)$ the function is increasing; indeed, $f'(x) = x^2 - 4 > 0$ if $x > 2$. The same can also be said with the interval $(-\infty,2)$.

Second Derivative

Suppose that I is an interval and $f''(x) > 0$ where $f''(x)$ denotes the second derivative of $f(x)$. This means that $f'(x)$ is increasing on I, because its derivative, $f''(x)$, is positive, and $f'(x)$ is increasing. Geometrically this means the function must have an upward $\cup$ shape, as that is the shape whose slope is increasing. If $f''(x) < 0$, then $f'(x)$ is decreasing on I, so it will have a downward $\cap$ shape, as that is the shape whose slope is decreasing.

We summarize these two results as follows:

- If $f''(x) > 0$ on an interval I, then the curve $y = f(x)$ has an upward shape.
- If $f''(x) < 0$ on an interval I, then the curve $y = f(x)$ has a downward shape.

Here is a picture of the two types of second derivatives:

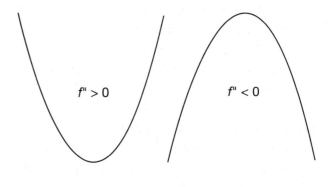

Example

Consider $f(x) = x^3 - x$ and the curve $y = f(x)$, shown here:

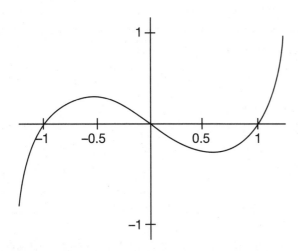

Solution: We can see from the picture that the curve has an upward shape on the interval $(0,\infty)$ and a downward shape on the interval $(-\infty,0)$. Let us check this using the second derivative. We compute $f'(x) = 3x^2 - 1$, so $f''(x) = 6x$. Clearly, if $x > 0$, then $f''(x) = 6x > 0$, so that on the interval $(0,\infty)$ the second derivative is positive; in particular, the curve has an upward shape. If $x < 0$, then $f''(x) = 6x < 0$, so on the interval $(-\infty,0)$ the curve has a downward shape.

Example

Consider $f(x) = \frac{1}{12}x^4 - \frac{1}{2}x^2$ with the curve $y = f(x)$, shown here:

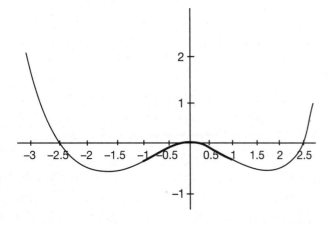

Solution: Part of the curve is darkened to show that on the interval $(-1, 1)$ the curve has a downward shape. Thus, it means the second derivative on this interval will be negative. Let us check this. We compute $f'(x) = \frac{1}{3}x^3 - 2x$ and then $f''(x) = x^2 - 1$. Note that if $-1 < x < 1$, then $f''(x) = x^2 - 1 < 0$, so in particular the curve has a downward shape. However, if $x > 1$ or $x < -1$, then $f''(x) > 0$, which corresponds to the upward shape of the curve in the picture.

Local Extrema

As usual consider the function $f(x)$ and its corresponding graph $y = f(x)$. A point a is called a *local maximum* if $f(x)$ has $x = a$ as its maximum point near to a. A point b is called a *local minimum* if $f(x)$ has $x = b$ as its minimum point near to b. Here is a picture of some generic function $y = f(x)$ with the local maximum points and local minimum points shown.

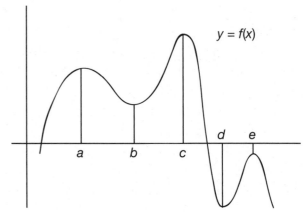

In this picture $x = a$, $x = c$, and $x = e$ are all local maximum points because of those nearby they are the largest in value. Similarly, $x = b$ and $x = d$ are local minimum points because of those nearby they are the smallest in value.

Note, $f(b) > f(e)$ even though b is a local minimum and e is a local maximum.

A point that is either a local minimum or a local maximum is called a *local extrema* point. Note that the local extrema points have horizontal tangent lines, so, in particular, their slopes are zero. This result is known as *Fermat's theorem*: Namely, if $x = p$ is a local extrema point for the function $f(x)$, then $f'(p) = 0$.

A natural question to ask is: Suppose we find a point p such that $f'(p) = 0$. How can we classify it as a local minimum or a local maximum? If $f''(p) > 0$, then near the point the function will shape upward, so p would be a local minimum. If $f''(p) < 0$, then near the point the function will shape downward, so p would be a local maximum. We summarize these results as follows, known as *second derivative test*.

Suppose p is a point for the function $f(x)$ such that $f'(p) = 0$.

- If $f''(p) > 0$, then $x = p$ is a local minimum point.
- If $f''(p) < 0$, then $x = p$ is a local maximum point.
- If $f''(p) = 0$, then the test is inconclusive.

Example

We will find all the local extrema points for the function $f(x) = x^4 - x^2$.

Solution: We first find $f'(x) = 4x^3 - 2x$. The local extrema are found by solving $f'(x) = 0$, so we need to solve $4x^3 - 2x = 0$, which factors $2x(2x^2 - 1) = 0$. One root is $x = 0$. Other roots are when $2x^2 - 1 = 0$ so that $x^2 = \frac{1}{2}$, which solves to $x = \pm\frac{1}{\sqrt{2}}$. To test if these points are local maximum or local minimum, we first compute $f''(x) = 8x^2 - 2$. Then we see that $f''(0) < 0$ while $f''(\pm\frac{1}{\sqrt{2}}) > 0$ so that $x = 0$ is a local maximum point, while $x = -\frac{1}{\sqrt{2}}$ and $x = \frac{1}{\sqrt{2}}$ are local minimum points.

Mean-Value Theorem

The mean-value theorem relates the derivative, which is the instantenous rate of change, with the average rate of change. Given a function $f(x)$ and an interval $[a,b]$, then there exists a number c inside the interval such that $f'(c) = \frac{f(b) - f(a)}{b - a}$. This is known as the *mean-value theorem*.

Example

We will verify the mean-value theorem for the function $f(x) = x^2 + x$ on the interval $[1,2]$.

Solution: The mean-value theorem says there is a point c inside the interval such that:

$$f'(c) = \frac{f(2) - f(1)}{2 - 1} = \frac{6 - 2}{1} = 4$$

Now $f'(x) = 2x + 1$; therefore, we need to solve $2c + 1 = 4 \Rightarrow c = \frac{3}{2}$, which is a point inside the interval.

Integrals

Given a function $f(x)$ and an interval $[a,b]$, the *integral* of $f(x)$ over this interval $[a,b]$ is the area under the curve $y = f(x)$. We denote this quantity by $\int_a^b f(x)\,dx$.

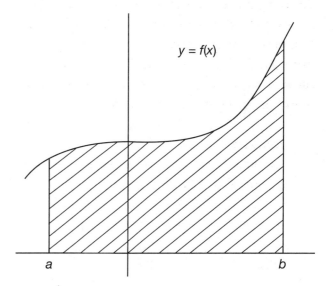

Here is a method of estimating the value of the integral. As before, $f(x)$ is our function and the interval that we want to compute the area over is $[a,b]$. Let us subdivide this interval into seven equally spaced subintervals. In order to do that, we take the length of the interval $(b - a)$ and divide it by 7, so let $D = \frac{b - a}{7}$ (the quantity D is the distance of each subinterval). In this case D is one-seventh the length of interval $[a,b]$. This partitions the interval $[a,b]$ into seven subintervals with 8 points. For convenience we label these points $x_0, x_1, \ldots, x_7$, in the order they appear, with a being x relabeled at 0, and b, the other endpoint, being relabeled at x_7. This process is shown here:

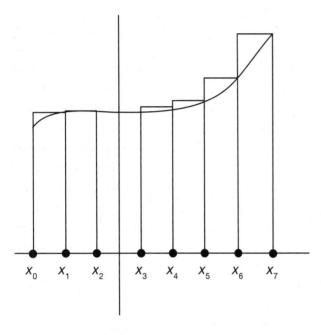

We then form rectangles with their heights determined by the right point so the first rectangle has height $f(x_1)$, the second has height $f(x_2)$, and so forth. (It is arbitrary whether to choose the right or left endpoint to draw a rectangle; we are doing it with just a right endpoint here.) The area of the first rectangle is $f(x_1)D$ (width times height). The area of the second rectangle is $f(x_2)D$, and so forth, up to the area of the seventh rectangle, which is $f(x_7)D$. The total area is then given by

$$f(x_1)D + f(x_2)D + \ldots + f(x_7)D = [f(x_1) + \ldots + f(x_7)]D$$

This quantity estimates the integral. The more rectangles we use, the more accurate it becomes. These sorts of sums for estimating the area under the curve are known as *Riemann sums*.

Example

We will estimate $\int_1^2 \frac{1}{x}\,dx$ by using seven equally subdivided rectangles.

Solution: In this case the function is $f(x) = \frac{1}{x}$, and the endpoints are $a = 1$ and $b = 2$. Since we want seven rectangles, we use the width of each of them to be $\Delta = \frac{2-1}{7} = \frac{1}{7}$. Now $x_0 = 1, x_1 = 1 + \frac{1}{7} = \frac{8}{7}, x_2 = 1 + \frac{2}{7} = \frac{9}{7}$, and so forth up to $x_7 = 2$. Thus, we compute

$$[f(x_1) + \cdots + f(x_7)]\,\Delta$$
$$= \left[\frac{7}{8} + \frac{7}{9} + \frac{7}{10} + \frac{7}{11} + \frac{7}{12} + \frac{7}{13} + \frac{7}{14}\right] \cdot \frac{1}{7}$$
$$= 0.658\ldots$$

More generally, given a function $f(x)$ and an interval $[a,b]$ we can use n rectangles of width $D = \frac{b-a}{n}$. Then $x_0 = a, x_1 = a + D, x_2 = a + 2D, \cdots, x_n = b$. The corresponding Riemann sum would be

$$[f(x_1) + f(x_2) + \cdots + f(x_n)]D$$

This quantity will approximate the value of the integral. The higher the n is, the more accurate this approximate area becomes to the true area. To get the exact area, we have to take the limit as $n \to \infty$, and the limit will be the exact area.

Example

We will compute the exact area $\int_0^1 x\,dx$. In other words, our function here is $f(x) = x$ and the endpoints are $a = 0$ with $b = 1$.

Solution: To get the exact answer, we compute the Riemann sum and send the number of rectangles to ∞. First, $D = \frac{1-0}{n} = \frac{1}{n}$ is the width of each of the n-subrectangles. Then $x_0 = 0, x_1 = \frac{1}{n}, x_2 = \frac{2}{n}, \cdots, x_n = 1$. This gives us a Riemann sum:

$$[f(x_1) + f(x_2) + f(x_3) + \cdots + f(x_n)]\Delta =$$
$$\left[\frac{1}{n} + \frac{2}{n} + \frac{3}{n} + \cdots + \frac{n}{n}\right]\frac{1}{n}$$

Factoring out, we can rewrite:

$$[1 + 2 + 3 + \cdots + n]\frac{1}{n^2} =$$

$$\frac{n(n+1)}{2} \cdot \frac{1}{n^2} = \frac{n+1}{2n} = \frac{n}{2n} + \frac{1}{2n} = \frac{1}{2} + \frac{1}{2n}$$

This is the approximate answer after using n rectangles in the Riemann sum. If we send $n \to \infty$, then the quantity $\frac{1}{2n} \to 0$ since the denominator is becoming large. Thus, in the limit we get the answer of $\frac{1}{2}$. Therefore, we say:

$$\int_0^1 x \, dx = \frac{1}{2}$$

Notice how much work we had to do to an integral computation for such a simple function! There has to be an easier way of evaluating integrals. Fortunately, there is; it is known as the fundamental theorem of calculus.

Fundamental Theorem of Calculus

Let $F(x)$ be function such that $F'(x) = f(x)$. Then,

$$\int_a^b f(x) \, dx = F(b) - F(a)$$

Example

Let us return to the previous example $\int_0^1 x \, dx$. Now we compute it the easy way.

Solution: Notice that $F(x) = \frac{1}{2}x^2$ is such a function so that $F'(x) = x$, so by the fundamental theorem we have $\int_1^1 x \, dx = F(a) - F(0) = \frac{1}{2}$.

Example

We will compute $\int_1^2 3x^2 \, dx$.

Solution: Note that $F(x) = x^3$ has the property that $F'(x) = 3x^2$, so $\int_0^2 3x^2 \, dx = F(2) - F(1) = 7$.

Example

We will compute $\int_0^\pi \cos(2x) \, dx$.

Solution: Note that $F(x) = \frac{1}{2}\sin(2x)$ is such a function so that $F'(x) = \cos(2x)$ and so $\int_0^\pi \cos(2x) \, dx = F(p) - F(0) = 0$.

This function $F(x)$ is known as an *antiderivative* of $f(x)$, because its derivative is equal to $f(x)$. Instead of finding the derivative of a function as we have been doing up to this point we rather find the antiderivative; we find a function that has the desired derivative that we seek.

Thus, the problem of evaluation of integrals reduces to the problem of computing anti-derivatives. For example, how did we know that an anti-derivative of $\cos(2x)$ was $\frac{1}{2}\sin(2x)$? We can see that it works, but by what process can we find it? We will show some useful techniques for computing antiderivatives.

Antiderivatives

Let $f(x)$ be a function. We use the notation $f(x)d(x)$ to be the antiderivatives of $f(x)$—in other words, all functions whose derivative is $f(x)$. Note, if $F(x)$ is an antiderivative of $f(x)$, then so is $F(x) + C$, where C is a constant. Thus, there is no such thing as *the* antiderivative, but rather *an* antiderivative.

Let $F(x) = \frac{x^{n+1}}{n+1}$ with $n \neq -1$ to avoid division by zero. Then by using the power rule we see that $F'(x) = x^n$. Therefore, $\int x^n \, dx = \frac{x^{n+1}}{n+1} + C$. This is known as the power rule for antiderivatives. Since the derivative of a sum and difference is the sum and difference of derivatives, the same rule is true for antiderivatives. Whenever we differentiate, we can pull out a constant; as such there is a similiar rule for antiderivatives, namely, $af(x) \, dx = af(x) \, dx$. Also, as $(\sin x)' = \cos x$ and $(\cos x)' = -\sin x$, we have the following rules:

- $\sin x\, dx = -\cos x + C$ and $\cos x\, dx = \sin x + C$
- $\int x^n\, dx = \frac{x^{n+1}}{n+1} + C$
- $f(x) + g(x)\, dx = f(x)\, dx + g(x)\, dx$
- $f(x) - g(x)\, dx = f(x)\, dx - g(x)\, dx$

Using these rules, we can compute some simple antiderivatives.

Example

$$\int x^2 - x + 3\cos x\, dx = \tfrac{1}{3}x^3 - \tfrac{1}{2}x^2 + 3\sin x + C$$

Solution: A problem, however, is that these rules are too simple. They do not allow one to compute more complicated antiderivatives. The main rule that is used more than any other rule is the analogue of the chain rule. Suppose $F(x)$ is antiderivative of $f(x)$; then by the chain rule, $[F(g(x))] = F'(g(x))g'(x) = f(g(x))g'(x)$. Thus, we have $f(g(x))g'(x)\, dx = F(g(x)) + C$.

Example

Let us say we want to find $\sin(2x)\, dx$.

Solution: This is not part of our simple table. Instead we let $f(x) = \sin x$ and $g(x) = 2x$. Then we notice that $f(g(x)) = \sin(2x)$. However, in order to use the chain rule we need a factor of $g'(x) = 2$ inside the antiderivative. Thus, we can just put in and take out that common factor:

$$\int \sin(2x)\, dx = \tfrac{1}{2}\int \underbrace{\sin(2x)}_{f(g(x))} \cdot \underbrace{2}_{g'(x)}\, dx$$

$$= \tfrac{1}{2}F(g(x)) + C = \tfrac{1}{2}F(2x) + C$$

The last step is to find $F(x)$; this is the antiderivative of $f(x) = \sin x$, which we can take to be $-\cos x$; so the answer is $-\tfrac{1}{2}\cos(2x) + C$.

There is a useful way of setting up this chain rule antiderivative method. It is typically by using a substituting $u = g(x)$ and writing $du = g'(x)\, dx$ so that the antiderivative becomes

$$\int \underbrace{f(g(x))}_{f(u)}\,\underbrace{g'(x)dx}_{du} = \int f(u)\, du = F(u) + C$$

$$= F(g(x)) + C$$

We illustrate this in a few examples:

Example

$$\int (x^2 + 1)^4 \cdot x\, dx$$

Solution: Let $u = x^2 + 1$ so that $du = 2x\, dx$, and rewrite the antiderivative to be

$$\tfrac{1}{2}\int \underbrace{(x^2 + 1)^4}_{u^4} \cdot \underbrace{2x\, dx}_{du} = \tfrac{1}{2}\int u^4\, du$$

$$= \tfrac{1}{2} \cdot \tfrac{1}{5}u^5 + C = \tfrac{1}{10}(x^2 + 1)^5 + C$$

Example

$$\int \sqrt{1 - x}\, dx$$

Solution: Let $u = 1 - x$ with $du = -dx$, and rewrite the antiderivative as

$$-\int \underbrace{(1 - x)^{\frac{1}{2}}}_{u^{\frac{1}{2}}}\underbrace{(-dx)}_{du} = -\int u^{\frac{1}{2}}\, du$$

$$= -\tfrac{2}{3}u^{\frac{3}{2}} + C = -\tfrac{2}{3}(1 - x)^{\frac{3}{2}} + C$$

Example

$$\int \frac{x^2}{(x^3 + 1)^2}\, dx$$

Solution: Let $u = x^3 + 1$, and rewrite it as

$$\int x^2 \cdot (x^3 + 1)^{-2}\, dx = \tfrac{1}{3}\int (x^3 + 1)^{-2}(3x^2\, dx)$$

Now $u = x^3 + 1$ so that $du = 3x^2 dx$, and we get

$$\tfrac{1}{3}\int u^{-2}\, du = \tfrac{1}{3}\cdot -u^{-1} + C = -\tfrac{1}{3}\cdot \frac{1}{x^3 + 1} + C$$

Example

Now, let's compute an integral, say,

$$\int_0^1 (x^2 + 1)^4 \cdot x\, dx.$$

Solution: We find the antiderivative as we did before: $F(x) = \tfrac{1}{10}(x^2 + 1)^5$, and compute by the fundamental theorem that the integral is equal to $F(1) - F(0) = \tfrac{32}{10} - \tfrac{1}{10}$.

8 ▶ GEOMETRY REVIEW

CHAPTER SUMMARY

The word *geometry* is derived from the Greek and means earth measurement. Today, geometry is the study and analysis of the size, shape, and position of objects. Geometry has also included the analysis of the mathematics of space and formal logic through the use of mathematical proofs.

This review chapter is not meant to be an exhaustive and thorough presentation of all topics and possible problems and projects in geometry. It is meant to be a review based on the Common Core Geometry Standards that will help prepare you for the Praxis II® Mathematics: Content Knowledge test.

Transformations in a Plane

An angle is the shape created by the intersection of two lines at the point of intersection called a *vertex*. The measurement of an angle in degrees or radians is the amount of turn or bending from one segment to the other. A complete turn or rotation around a point would measure 360 degrees (360°) or 2π radians. Two angles are considered equal, or congruent, if the amount of turn is equal.

Definition: A *circle* is a two-dimensional closed curved line contained in a plane in which every point is equidistant from a single point, which is called the center.

Definition: A *line segment* is a piece of a line consisting of all the points between two endpoints.

Definition: *Perpendicular lines* are intersecting lines that form right angles at the point of intersection.

Definition: *Parallel lines* are lines that never intersect. They are always the same distance apart.

Definition: A *reflection* is a mirror image of an object or a figure. The initial object is flipped over a *line of reflection* or axis. The mirror image is the same shape and size as the original object.

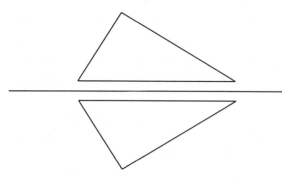

Definition: A *rotation* is a turning of an object or a figure around a fixed point. The rotated object is the same shape and size as the original object.

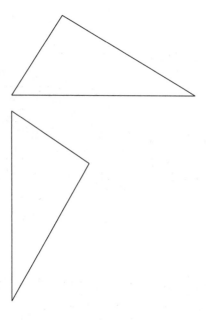

Definition: A *translation* is a moving or sliding of an object or figure to a new location. The translated object is the same shape, size, and orientation as the original object.

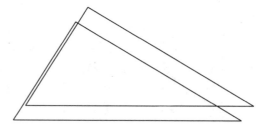

Definition: A *dilation* is an expanding or a shrinking of an object in which the shape of the object is preserved but the size of the object is not. Every dilation has a *center of dilation* and a *scale factor*.

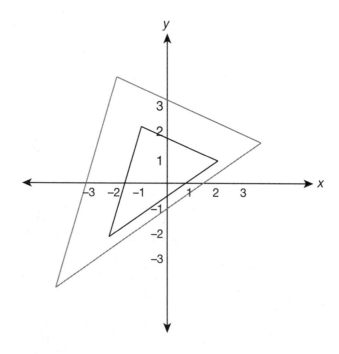

Definition: *Transformations* are functions that take points in the plane as inputs, and give other points as outputs. Transformations can be described precisely by creating two axes, an *x*-axis and a *y*-axis (which is perpendicular to the *x*-axis), and by using an ordered pair to give the exact location of a point relative to those axes.

Example

You want to translate or slide the rectangle with endpoints (–6,5), (–2,5), (–2,1), and (–6,1) up four units along the *x*-axis and down two units on the *y*-axis.

Solution: The function to translate this figure is $f(x,y) = (x + 4, y – 2)$. The translated figure is a rectangle with endpoints (–2,3), (2,3), (2,–1), (–2,–1). If you plot the two figures, you should be able to determine that distance, angle measure, and orientation of the figure are preserved.

Not all transformations preserve distance, but in the Euclidean plane they preserve angle measure. For example, a dilation can be described by the function $f(x,y) = (sx, sy)$ where *s* is the scale factor. The shape, including all angle measures, is preserved while all distances have been transformed by the scale factors.

If a rectangle is rotated 180° or 360° around the intersection of its diagonals, it will map onto itself. In addition, if the rectangle is reflected around the line that intersects at a 90-degree angle with either pair of opposite lines, it will also map onto itself.

A parallelogram can be rotated 180° around the intersection of its diagonals and map onto itself.

Unless it is isosceles, a trapezoid cannot be mapped onto itself by a reflection or a rotation less than 360°. An isosceles trapezoid can be mapped onto itself by a reflection around an axis that is a line segment whose endpoints bisect the two parallel lines of the trapezoid.

A regular polygon can be mapped onto itself by a rotation if its exterior angle is a factor of 180°. It can also be mapped onto itself by a reflection if the axis of rotation has a vertex as an endpoint and the axis bisects the angle formed by the regular polygon at that vertex.

A rotation is a rigid turning of an object in which angles, perpendicular lines, parallel lines, and length of line segments are all preserved, and circles retain their size and, if the center of the circle is the rotation, their location.

A reflection is a rigid flipping over an axis of rotation in which angles, perpendicular lines, and parallel lines are all preserved, but the original and reflected object are mirror images of each other. If the axis of rotation is a diameter of a circle, that circle will preserve its size and location.

A translation is a rigid sliding in which angles, perpendicular lines, parallel lines, and the length of line segments are all preserved. While the size of a circle is preserved, its location is altered by the mapping of the translation.

For a visual understanding of a translation, on a coordinate plane, draw the quadrilateral *ABCD* with $A(–3,–4)$, $B(1,0)$, $C(0,2)$, and $D(–2,0)$.

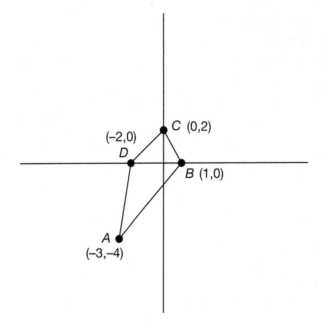

Now draw $A_1B_1C_1D_1$ on the same coordinate plane such that $F(x,y) = (x + 4, y + 3)$. Every point on *ABCD* is mapped to a unique point on $A_1B_1C_1D_1$. The coordinates of A_1 are $(1,-1)$, $B_1(5,3)$, $C_1(4,5)$, $D_1(2,3)$, and $ABCD \cong A_1B_1C_1D_1$.

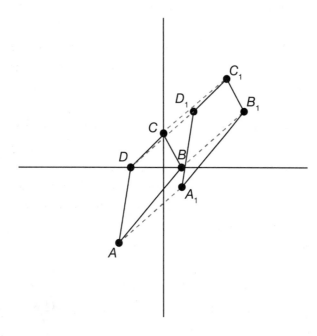

For further study, draw a rotation and a reflection. A rotation might be more easily drawn if the point of rotation is the origin of polar coordinates since each point is rotated a fixed angle. The rotated figure will be congruent to the original figure.

For every point on a reflection, draw a line from the point perpendicular to the line of reflection, and then continue the line on the opposite side of the line of reflection for exactly the same distance to map the reflected point. If you reflect the vertices of a polygon, the reflected vertices can be connected in the same order as the original polygon, with the reflected polygon being congruent to the original polygon.

If two figures are congruent, it is possible to specify a sequence of transformation that will map a given figure onto another figure.

Proving Geometric Theorems

Geometric facts can be either (1) one of a limited number of postulates or statements that are assumed to be true or (2) theorems, which can be mathematically proved from one or more postulates or previously proven theorems.

The proof of a theorem about lines and angles begins with whatever postulates and previously proved theorems are needed. Then it proceeds step-by-step to prove that if the postulates and previously proved theorems are true, then the proposed theorem is true.

Example

We want to prove that vertical angles are equal.

Solution: You will need the postulate that if the exterior rays of two adjacent angles form a straight line, then the sum of the interior angles formed by the adjacent angles is 180°. *AB* and *CD* are two straight lines that intersect at point *E*. $\angle AEC$ and $\angle BED$ are vertical angles.

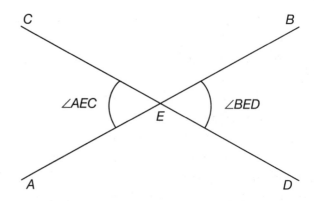

$\angle AEC$ and $\angle AED$ are adjacent angles whose exterior rays form the straight line *CD*. Therefore, $\angle AEC + \angle AED = 180°$.

$\angle BED$ and $\angle AED$ are adjacent angles whose exterior rays form the straight line *AB*. Therefore, $\angle BED + \angle AED = 180°$.

Since $\angle AEC + \angle AED = 180°$ and $\angle BED + \angle AED = 180°$, $\angle AEC + \angle AED = \angle BED + \angle AED$.

A postulate of equations states that if equals are subtracted from equals, the result is equal. Therefore, when we subtract $\angle AED$ from each side of the equation, we are left with $\angle AEC = \angle BED$, which proves the theorem that vertical angles are equal.

Theorems about triangles can also be proved using the postulates of geometry and previously proven theorems.

Example

We want to prove that the sum of the angles of a triangle is 180°.

Solution: Draw a triangle $\triangle ABC$ with base BC. Now through the vertex A, draw a line DE parallel to the base BC.

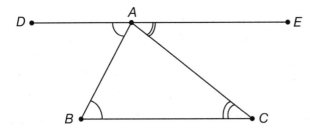

According to the postulate about the exterior sides of adjacent angles, $\angle BAD + \angle BAE = 180°$. Since $\angle BAE = \angle BAC + \angle CAE$, $\angle BAD + \angle BAC + \angle CAE = 180°$.

A theorem about parallel lines states that if two lines are parallel, the alternate interior angles are equal.

Therefore, $\angle BAD = \angle ABC$ and $\angle CAE = \angle ACB$.

Substituting $\angle ABC$ for $\angle BAD$ and $\angle ACB$ for $\angle CAE$, we get $\angle BAC + \angle ABC + \angle ACB = 180°$, which proves our theorem.

For further study, look at the proof of the most famous theorem about triangles, the Pythagorean theorem, which states that for any right triangle ABC in which $\angle C$ is a right angle, $a^2 + b^2 = c^2$.

Proving theorems about parallelograms or any other geometric figure follows a similar approach as is used to prove theorems about lines and angles. The proof includes relevant postulates and previously proven theorems that can be applied to prove the given theorem.

Example

Prove that the opposite sides of a parallelogram are of equal length.

Solution: Draw parallelogram $ABCD$. Draw diagonal BD. $\angle ABD = \angle CDB$ and $\angle ADB = \angle CBD$ since they are alternate interior angles. Side BD = side BD due to the reflexive property that states that all figures are equal to themselves. A previously proven theorem states that if two triangles have two angles and the included side congruent (angle-side-angle, or ASA), then the triangles are congruent. Therefore, $\triangle ABD \cong \triangle CDB$ and corresponding sides $AD = CB$ and $AB = CD$, proving the theorem.

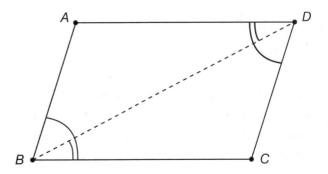

Geometric Constructions

Traditionally, geometric constructions are made with a straightedge, compass, and pencil. Some figures can be created using geometric construction, and some can't. For example, there is a procedure for bisecting any angle. However, there is no geometric construction that will trisect any angle (divide an angle into three equal angles). (Note that 90° and 180° angles can be trisected, since it is possible to construct 30° and 60° angles.)

Geometric figures can also be constructed using mirrors, paper folding, or computer software.

You can recognize a formal geometric construction since it will have only two types of figures on the page: arcs of a circle drawn using a compass and straight lines drawn using a straightedge.

Example

Using only a straightedge and compass, construct an equilateral triangle.

Solution: To make an equilateral triangle, start with a line segment *AB* and a point *C*, not on *AB*. The line segment should be short enough so that one end of the compass is at endpoint *A* and the other at endpoint *B*. Making sure that the distance between the point and pencil of the compass remains equal to line segment *AB*, place the point of the compass at point *C* and draw an arc of about a quarter of a circle. Place the point of the compass on a point *D* near one end of the arc and make another arc of radius *AB* that intersects with the first arc. Call that intersection point *E*. Now with a straightedge and pencil, draw line segments *CD*, *DE*, and *EC*. Since each of these segments is equal in length to line *AB*, they are also equal to each other, and the figure *CDE* is an equilateral triangle.

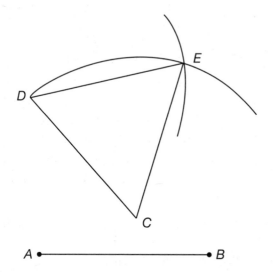

For further study, follow a similar process to create other figures such as a square or a regular hexagon inscribed in a circle.

Congruence and Similarity in Terms of Transformations

Two figures are *congruent* if they are the same shape and size. If two figures are congruent, one can be mapped onto the other using a combination of translation, which rigidly moves the figure in the plane, rotation, which rigidly turns a figure around a rotation point, and reflection, which flips a figure to its mirror image.

Two figures are similar if they are the same shape. If two figures are similar, one can be mapped onto the other using a combination of translation, rotation, reflection, and dilation, which makes a figure larger or smaller while preserving its shape using a center of dilation and a scale factor.

If two figures are congruent, they are also similar.

A translation changes the position of a figure, but does not change its shape, size, or orientation. In general, a translation does not change a figure into its mirror image.

A rotation changes the orientation of a figure by turning the figure around a center of rotation.

A reflection changes a figure to its mirror image by flipping the image along an axis of reflection.

In a dilation, the only point that is not mapped to a new location on the coordinate plane is the center of dilation. Every point $P(x,y)$ on the figure is mapped to point $P(ax,ay)$, where a is the scale factor and (x,y) is relative to the coordinates of the center of dilation. A dilation changes the size but not the shape or orientation of a figure. If the scale factor is greater than 1, the resulting figure is larger. If the scale factor is less than 1, the resulting figure is smaller. The scale factor is always greater than 0.

You can use the rigid motions to test whether two figures are congruent. Use translation to move one of the figures so that they have at least one point in common. If the figures have all points in common, they are congruent. If not, determine if there is a rotation around a center of rotation that will result in the figures having all points in common. Finally, determine whether the figures are mirror images of each other and, if so, determine an axis of reflection and flip one of the figures so that the figures have all of their points in common.

Two figures are *similar* if they are the same shape. In other words, if P is the point of dilation, Q is a point on one figure, and R is the corresponding point on the second figure such that PQR form a straight line, then if the ratio $\frac{PQ}{PR}$ equals the scale factor for all points Q on the first figure and R on the second figure, then the two figures are similar.

According to the definition of congruence in terms of rigid motions, two figures are congruent if one could be mapped onto the other using a combination of translations, rotations, and reflections. For triangles that would mean that the lengths of corresponding sides and the measures of corresponding angles are equal. If as a result of rigid transformations, one triangle can be placed directly on top of a second triangle, line segment length and angle measurements are preserved. As a result, triangles that are congruent based on the criteria of rigid transformations will also have equal sides and angles, so they will fulfill the angle-side-angle (ASA) and side-angle-side (SAS) criteria to determine triangle congruence.

To prove that if two triangles have two congruent angles then they are similar, draw triangle ABC and triangle DEF such that $\angle A \cong \angle D$ and $\angle B \cong \angle E$. Apply a dilation with scale factor $x = \frac{DE}{AB}$ to create triangle GHI.

ΔGHI is similar to ΔABC since the dilation process preserves angle measures so $\angle G \cong \angle A$, $\angle H \cong \angle B$, and $\angle I \cong \angle C$.

Side GH = side AB times x, since x is the scale factor of the dilation.

$$GH = AB \cdot \frac{DE}{AB} = DE$$

Since it was given that $\angle A \cong \angle D$ and it has been determined that $\angle G \cong \angle A$, then $\angle G \cong \angle D$. Since it was given that $\angle B \cong \angle E$ and it has been determined that $\angle H \cong \angle B$, then $\angle H \cong \angle E$.

Since $\angle G \cong \angle D$ and $\angle H \cong \angle E$, and side $GH \cong DE$, $\Delta GHI \cong \Delta DEF$ (angle-side-angle).

Therefore, there is a sequence of rigid transformations that will map ΔGHI onto ΔDEF.

If the dilation of ΔABC is followed by that sequence of rigid transformations, ΔABC will map onto ΔDEF, and $\Delta ABC \sim \Delta DEF$.

Two triangles are congruent if they are congruent in side-side-side (SSS), side-angle-side, or angle-side-angle. If two triangles are congruent, then the corresponding measures of their three sides and three angles are equal.

Two triangles are similar if their corresponding angles are equal and their corresponding sides are proportional. If two triangles have two sets of corresponding angles that are equal, then the third set of corresponding angles are equal and the triangles are similar.

If the ratio of corresponding sides of two triangles is the same for all three sets of corresponding sides, then the two triangles are similar.

Example

Look at ΔABC and ΔDEF. What is the measure of $\angle F$?

Solution:

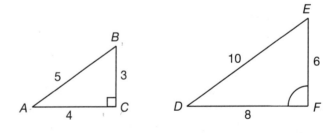

Since the two triangles are similar, the corresponding angles are equal, so $\angle F = 90°$.

Defining Trigonometric Ratios in Right Triangles

The three basic trigonometric ratios, sine, cosine, and tangent, are all defined in right triangles. All right triangles contain a 90° or right angle. Of the two remaining angles, we will call one θ. We will also name the three sides of the triangle. The side opposite the right angle is called the hypotenuse. The other side or leg that is one side of θ is called the adjacent side, while the remaining side is called the opposite side. As we learned in Chapter 6, the three ratios are:

$$\text{Sine } \theta = \frac{\text{opposite}}{\text{hypotenuse}}$$

$$\text{Cosine } \theta = \frac{\text{adjacent}}{\text{hypotenuse}}$$

$$\text{Tangent } \theta = \frac{\text{opposite}}{\text{adjacent}}$$

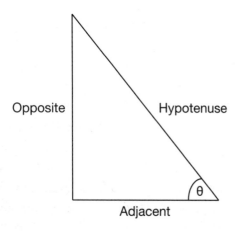

All right triangles that have an angle = θ are similar, with the three angles being the right angle, θ, and (90° − θ), since the sum of the angles of a triangle is 180°. The sides of similar triangles are proportional. In other words, for right triangles ABC and DEF with right angles at C and F, $\frac{\text{opposite } ABC}{\text{opposite } DEF} = \frac{\text{hypotenuse } ABC}{\text{hypotenuse } DEF}$ and after dividing each side by hypotenuse ABC and multiplying each side by hypotenuse DEF, $\frac{\text{opposite } ABC}{\text{hypotenuse } ABC} = \frac{\text{opposite } DEF}{\text{hypotenuse } DEF}$. The sine ratio is constant for a given

angle θ no matter what the size of the right triangle is. Similarly, the cosine and tangent ratios are constant for a given angle θ no matter what the size of the right triangle is.

For any pair of complementary angles, the sine of one is equal to the cosine of the other. In other words, for triangle ABC where C is the right angle, $\sin A = \frac{\text{side opposite } \angle A}{\text{hypotenuse}} = \frac{BC}{AB}$ and $\cos B = \frac{\text{side adjacent } \angle B}{\text{hypotenuse}} = \frac{BC}{AB}$. For any angle θ between 0° and 90°, $\sin \theta = \cos (90° − θ)$.

You can solve many practical (and not so practical) problems using this relationship.

Example

Suppose you have an adjustable extension ladder that you want to lean against a 15-foot-high wall, with a 60° angle between the level ground and the ladder. To what length should you adjust the ladder?

Solution: Since $\sin 60° = \frac{\text{side opposite } \angle A}{\text{hypotenuse}}$, and $\sin 60° \approx .87$, $.87 = \frac{15 \text{ feet}}{c}$. Solving for C results in $C = \frac{15 \text{ feet}}{.87} = 17.2$ feet. The extension ladder needs to be extended to 17.2 feet so it will form a 60° angle with the ground and reach the top of the 15-foot-high wall.

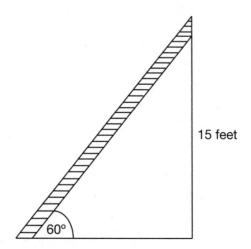

Note: You will need a scientific calculator to calculate sin 60° and other trigonometric function values.

Example

A lot in the shape of a right triangle needs to be enclosed by a fence. The legs of the right triangle measure 8 yards and 15 yards. How many running feet of fence are needed to completely enclose the lot?

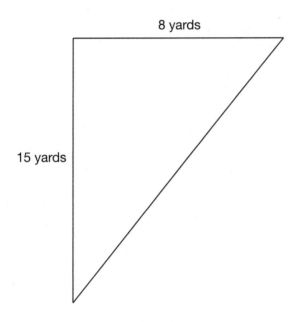

8 yards

15 yards

Solution: You can use the Pythagorean theorem to calculate the length of the third side in yards. Then add the lengths of the three sides together to get the total length in yards, and multiply by 3 to convert from yards to feet to get the total length in feet.

According to the Pythagorean theorem, for a right triangle with legs a and b and hypotenuse c, $a^2 + b^2 = c^2$. Substituting for a and b, $8^2 + 15^2 = c^2$. Calculating the squares results in $64 + 225 = c^2$. Simplify: $289 = c^2$. Take the positive square root of each side to get $17 = c$. In yards, the length of fencing needed is 8 yards + 15 yards + 17 yards = 40 yards. Convert to feet: 40 yards $\times$ 3 feet per yard = 120 feet.

Trigonometry Applied to General Triangles

Trigonometry can be applied to general triangles that do not necessarily have a right angle.

Example

Derive the formula $A = \frac{1}{2}ab \sin C$ for the area of a triangle by drawing an auxiliary line from a vertex perpendicular to the opposite side, and use it to solve problems.

Solution: Draw a triangle ABC. Draw a line from vertex B perpendicular to base b, intersecting base b or its extension at point D. The length of line segment BD is h, the height, and the area of the triangle is $\frac{1}{2}bh$.

Using the definition of sin, $\frac{\text{opposite}}{\text{hypotenuse}}$, we get $\sin C = \frac{h}{a}$.

Solve for h: $h = a \sin C$.

Substituting for h in the area formula: $A = \frac{1}{2}bh = \frac{1}{2}ba \sin C = \frac{1}{2}ab \sin C$.

You can use this formula to solve problems.

Example

A company wants to rent one floor of a triangular building. The rental cost is $3 per square foot per month. One side of the building is 24 feet, a second side is 20 feet, and the included angle is 60°. What will be the total monthly rent?

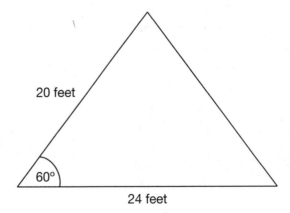

20 feet

60°

24 feet

Solution: $A = \frac{1}{2}ab \sin C$.

Substitute for a and b to get $A = \frac{1}{2}24 \times 20 \sin 60$.

Multiply and simplify to get $240 \times \sin 60 = 240 \times .87 = 208.8$ square feet.

With a monthly rental rate of $3 per square foot, the total monthly rent is 208.8 square feet $\times$ $3 per square foot = $626.40.

The Law of Sines and the Law of Cosines can be helpful in finding unknown measurements in triangles.

The Law of Sines: $\frac{\sin (A)}{a} = \frac{\sin (B)}{b} = \frac{\sin (C)}{c}$

Example

This is how the Law of Sines can be applied to find an unknown measurement in a triangle:
Triangle ABC has side $a = 15$, side $b = 20$, and $\angle B = 80°$. What is the angle measurement of $\angle A$?

Solution:

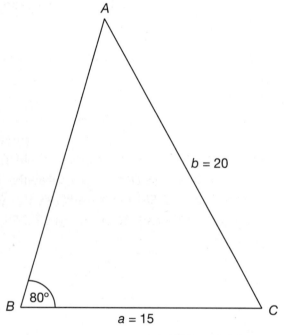

According to the Law of Sines, $\frac{\sin (A)}{a} = \frac{\sin (B)}{b}$.

Substituting for known values, $\frac{\sin (A)}{15} = \frac{\sin (80°)}{20}$.

Solving for sin (A), $\sin (A) = \frac{15 \times \sin (80°)}{20} = .74$.

Now we know that sin $(A) = .74$, and we want to know the measure of the angle with that sine. Using a scientific calculator, we use the arcsine function to get the measure of the angle.

Rounded to the nearest tenth degree, arcsin $(.74) = 47.7$ and $\angle A = 47.7$.

The Law of Cosines is: $c^2 = a^2 + b^2 - 2ab \cos (C)$.

Example

The Law of Cosines can be applied to find an unknown measurement in a triangle.

Triangle ABE has side $a = 7$, side $b = 5$, and side $c = 4$. What is the angle measurement of $\angle C$?

Solution:

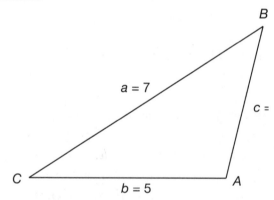

Substituting for known values,
$4^2 = 7^2 + 5^2 - 2(7 \times 5) \cos (C)$.

Simplifying: $16 = 49 + 25 - 70 \times \cos (C)$.

Subtract 74 from each side of the equation:
$16 - 74 = -70 \times \cos (C)$.

Simplify and divide by -70: $\frac{-58}{-70} = \cos (C)$.

$\frac{-58}{-70} = .83$, so $.83 = \cos (C)$.

To find the angle that has a cosine of .83, use the arccosine function, which can be found on a scientific calculator.

Arccos (.83) = 33.9°. The angle measurement of ∠*C* is 33.9°.

Theorems about Circles

Circles are one of the key figures of geometry. Understanding and applying theorems about circles have many applications.

Definition: *Radii* are line segments with one endpoint at the center of the circle and the other endpoint on the circle.

Definition: The angle formed by two radii of a circle is called a *central angle*.

Definition: A *chord* is a line segment whose endpoints both are on a circle.

Definition: If an angle has its vertex on a circle and both its rays are chords whose endpoints are on the circle, it is called an *inscribed angle*.

According to the *central angle theorem*, if an inscribed angle and a central angle intersect a circle at the same two points, the measure of the central angle is twice the measure of the inscribed angle. This relationship is true no matter where on the circle the vertex of the inscribed angle is located.

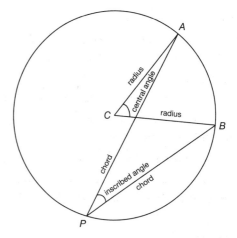

We can use what we already know to prove properties of angles for a quadrilateral inscribed in a circle.

Example
An inscribed quadrilateral is a quadrilateral whose four vertexes all lie on the same circle. The inscribed quadrilateral conjecture states that the opposite angles of an inscribed quadrilateral are supplementary.

Solution: To prove the conjecture, draw an inscribed quadrilateral *ABCD* in a circle. Point *E* is the center of the circle. Draw radii *EB* and *ED*. Central angles are equal in measure to the intercepted arc. The interior angle *DEB* + the exterior angle *DEB* = 360°, since together they form a complete rotation around the circle. The inscribed angle *DCB* has a measure that is $\frac{1}{2}$ the interior angle *DEB*, and the inscribed angle *DAB* has a measure that is $\frac{1}{2}$ the exterior angle *DEB*.

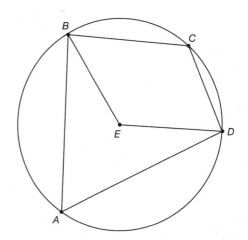

These two equalities can be combined:

$\angle DAB + \angle DCB = \frac{1}{2}$ the exterior angle $DEB + \frac{1}{2}$
     the interior angle DEB

$\angle DAB + \angle DCB = \frac{1}{2}$ (the exterior angle DEB +
     the interior angle DEB)

$\angle DAB + \angle DCB = \frac{1}{2}$ (360°)

$\angle DAB + \angle DCB = 180°$.

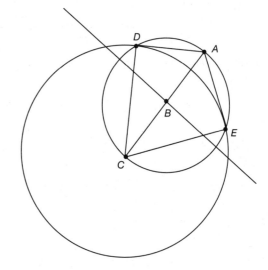

Therefore $\angle DAB$ and $\angle DCB$ are supplementary.

Draw the radii AE and EC and repeat the proof for angles ABE and ADC to prove that they are supplementary.

Definition: A line that intersects a circle at two points is called a *secant*.

Definition: A line that intersects a circle at one and only one point is called a *tangent*.

Two tangent lines can be constructed from a point outside a given circle to the circle using the following procedure:

For a circle with center C and point A outside the circle, use the straightedge to construct the line segment AC. Now use the compass to construct the perpendicular bisector of AC. The intersection of the lines is called point B. Use the compass to draw a circle with center B and radius BC. This circle will intersect the original circle at points D and E. Use the straightedge to draw triangles CDA and CEA. AC is the diameter of the constructed circle. Therefore, angles ADC and AEC are right angles, and lines AD and AE are tangent lines.

Arc Length and Area Measurements of Sectors of Circles

In addition to being measured by degrees, angles can be measured by *radians*. If a circle has radius r, and a central angle of the circle intercepts an arc length r on the circle, the measure of the angle is 1 radian.

Definition: The *diameter* of a circle is the chord that passes through the center of the circle.

Definition: The *circumference* of a circle is the distance around the circle.

Definition: π or *pi* is the ratio between the circumference and the diameter.

Therefore for any circle, the diameter can be called d, the circumference can be called C, and the relationship between d and C is described by the equation $C = \pi d$. Since $d = 2r$, where r is the radius of the circle, $C = 2\pi r$.

If the central angle of a circle is 2π radians or 360°, the arc length will be $2\pi r$.

An arc length of a circle is s. The arc s *subtends* a central angle θ; in other words, since $\pi = \frac{C}{2r}$, then angle $\theta = \frac{s}{r}$.

You can use these relationships to solve problems.

Example

For a circle of radius 4 and an angle measure $\theta = 5$, what will be subtended arc lengths?

Solution: $\theta = \frac{s}{r}$. Substitute the given values: $5 = \frac{s}{4}$. Solve for s: $s = 20$.

The area A of a circle is given by $A = \pi r^2$.

A circular sector is the portion of a circle enclosed by two radii and an arc of the circle. If the central angle θ of the sector is measured in degrees, then the area measurement of a sector of a circle would be $A = \frac{\theta}{360}\pi r^2$.

If the central angle θ of the sector is measured in radians, then the area measurement of a sector of a circle would be $A = \frac{\theta}{2\pi}\pi r^2 = \frac{\theta r^2}{2}$.

You can use these formulas to solve problems.

Example

What would be the area of a sector if $\theta = 90°$ and $r = 3$?

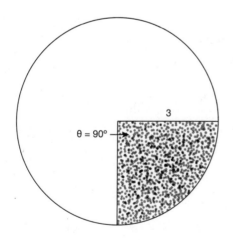

Solution: $A = \frac{\theta}{360}\pi r^2$

Substitute and reduce: $A = \frac{90}{360}\pi \times 9 = \frac{1}{4}\pi \times 9$

Multiply: $A = 2.25 \times \pi \approx 2.25 \times 3.14 = 7.065$

Example

What is the area of a slice of an 8-inch radius pizza if the central angle of the slice is 1 radian?

Solution: Substitute into the formula: $A = \frac{1 \times 8^2}{2}$ and $A = 32$ square inches.

Translating between a Geometric Description and an Equation for a Conic Section

A *conic section* is a curve that is the intersection of a cone and a plane. Conic sections include ellipses, parabolas, and hyperbolas. Circles are a special case of ellipses.

A conic section consists of a set of points whose distances to some point, called a focus, and some line, called a *directrix*, are in a fixed ratio, called the *eccentricity*. Conic sections with eccentricity less than 1 are ellipses, those with eccentricity equal to 1 are parabolas, and those with eccentricity greater than 1 are hyperbolas. Hyperbolas are bounded by lines called *asymptotes*. The hyperbola approaches the asymptote, but never reaches it. All the conic sections can be described by mathematical equations.

We can use the Pythagorean theorem to derive the equation of a circle of given center and radius. In the simplest case, the center is at the origin $(0,0)$ on the coordinate plane. The circle is the set of all points that is a given distance r from the origin. Every point on the circle is a point (a,b) where the distance from the point to the origin is r. For every point on the circle, a right triangle can be constructed with one vertex at $O(0,0)$, one vertex at $P(x,y)$, and a right angle at

$Q(x,0)$. The length of OQ is x, and the length of QP is y. According to the Pythagorean theorem, $c^2 = a^2 + b^2$.

Substituting known values, $r^2 = x^2 + y^2$ and $r^2 = x^2 + y^2$ is the equation of a circle with origin 0. If the origin is at a point (a,b), the more generalized equation is $r^2 = (x - a)^2 + (y - b)^2$.

We can use this equation to solve problems.

Example
What is the equation of a circle with radius 4 and the center at $(3,2)$?

Solution: Use the equation of a circle and substitute known values:
$$4^2 = (x - 3)^2 + (y - 2)^2$$
$$16 = (x - 3)^2 + (y - 2)^2$$

Another way to write the equation is
$$0 = x^2 - 6x + y^2 - 4y - 3.$$

Reversing the previous example, we can start with an equation in the form $0 = x^2 - ax + y^2 - by - c$ and complete the square to find the center and radius of a circle.

For example: What is the center and radius of a circle described in standard form as:
$$0 = x^2 - 8x + y^2 + 6y + 9?$$

Complete the square: $0 = (x - 4)^2 + (y + 3)^2 - 16 - 9 + 9$. Add 16 to each side of the equation to get: $16 = (x - 4)^2 + (y + 3)^2$.

Radius = 4, center = $(4,-3)$

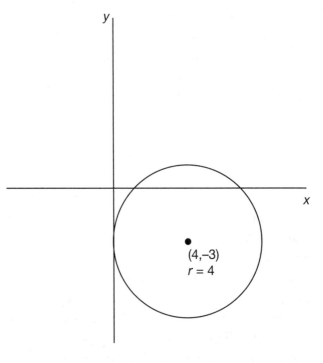

$(4,-3)$
$r = 4$

Definition: A *parabola* is the set of points that are a given distance from a point called the *focus* and a line called the *directrix*. If the directrix is a horizontal line, the parabola will open upward or downward.

Any point (x,y) on the parabola satisfies the definition of parabola, so there are two distances to calculate: the distance between point (x,y) and the focus (a,b) and the distance between point (x,y) and the line $y = c$:

The distance between point (x,y) and the focus (a,b) is $\sqrt{(x - a)^2 + (y - b)^2}$.

The distance between point (x,y) and the directrix c is the difference of their y-coordinates : $|y - c|$.

Since we need both of these distances to be positive, we use the positive square root to determine the distance between the point and the focus, and we use absolute value to indicate that we want to express the difference between the y-coordinates as a positive number.

According to the definition of a parabola, these two expressions are equal.

Therefore, $\sqrt{(x - a)^2 + (y - b)^2} = |y - c|$.

If we square both sides, we get:
$$(x - a)^2 + (y - b)^2 = (y - c)^2.$$
Expand: $(x - a)^2 + y^2 - 2by + b^2 = y^2 - 2cy + c^2.$

Simplify: $(x - a)^2 - 2by + b^2 = -2cy + c^2$, which is equivalent to: $(x - a)^2 + b^2 - c^2 = 2(b - c)y^2$, which is the equation of a parabola with focus (a,b) and directrix $y = c$.

Definition: A *conic section* is the set of all points in a plane whose distances from a particular point (the focus) and a particular line (the directrix) in the plane are a constant ratio. If the directrix is a line d, and the focus is a point F that does not lie on the directrix, and P is a point on the curve, and D is a point on the directrix such that the line segment PD is the shortest distance between the point on the curve and the directrix, then the ratio $\frac{PF}{PD}$ is a constant called e, the eccentricity of the curve. For parabolas, $e = 1$. If $e \angle 1$, then the curve is an ellipse. If $e > 1$, the curve is a hyperbola.

Definition: An *ellipse* can also be defined in relation to points F_1 and F_2, which are called *foci*. An ellipse is the set of all points such that the sum of the distances from F_1 to P and F_2 to P is a constant. The equation for an ellipse is $ax^2 + bx + cy^2 + by + f = 0$. A circle is a special case of an ellipse in which $a = c$.

The ellipse equation can be simplified if it is centered on the origin and the foci are on the x-axis.

If the sum of the distances from a point on the ellipse to the two foci is $2a$, then, $\sqrt{(x + c)^2 + y^2} + \sqrt{(x - c)^2 + y^2} = 2a$, where the coordinate of the point on the ellipse is (x,y) and the coordinates of the two foci are $(c,0)$ and $(-c,0)$.

If we set $b^2 = a^2 - c^2$, the equation simplifies to $\frac{x^2}{a^2} + \frac{y^2}{b^2} = 1$, where a is the distance from the origin to either point on the ellipse that lies on the x-axis, and b is the distance from the origin to either point on the ellipse that lies on the y-axis. If the foci $(0,-c)$ and $(0,c)$ lie on the x-axis, then that axis is called the major axis, and the points on the ellipse that are also

on the x-axis are called the vertices of the ellipse, and have coordinates $(a,0)$ and $(-a,0)$.

We can use this equation to answer questions about ellipses.

Example
Find the equation of the ellipse with foci $(-1,0)$ and $(1,0)$ and vertices $(-4,0)$ and $(4,0)$.

Solution: c is the x-coordinate of a foci, so $c = \pm1$ and $c^2 = 1$; a is the x-coordinate of a vertex, so $a = \pm4$ and $a^2 = 16$. Since $b^2 = a^2 - c^2$, $b^2 = 16 - 1 = 15$.

Substituting: $\frac{x^2}{16} + \frac{y^2}{15} = 1$.

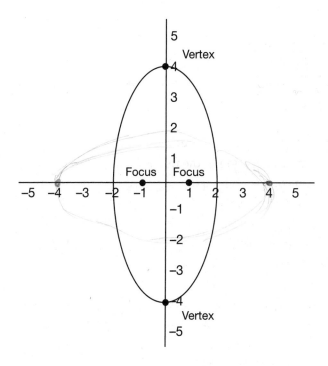

Definition: A *hyperbola* is the set of all points in the plane such that the difference between two foci is constant.

The simplified equation for a hyperbola looks very similar to the simplified equation for an ellipse, with the one change being that with a hyperbola it is a difference, not a sum, that is kept constant. The hyperbola has two parts that are bounded by intersecting straight lines called *asymptotes*. The hyperbola never intersects the asymptote.

The simplified equation for a hyperbola is $\frac{x^2}{a^2} - \frac{y^2}{b^2} = 1$, where the foci are $(\pm c, 0)$, the vertices are $(\pm a, 0)$, $c^2 = a^2 + b^2$, and the asymptotes are $y = \pm\left(\frac{b}{a}\right)x$.

We can use this equation to solve problems with hyperbolas.

Example

Find the vertices and asymptotes for the hyperbola $4x^2 - 9y^2 = 36$.

Solution: Divide both sides of the equation by 36 to get: $\frac{x^2}{9} - \frac{y^2}{4} = 1$.

$a = \pm 3$ and $b = \pm 2$. Since $c^2 = a^2 + b^2$, $c^2 = 9 + 4 = 13$. And $c = \pm\sqrt{13}$, so the foci are $(\pm\sqrt{13}, 0)$.

The vertices are $(\pm 3, 0)$ and the asymptotes are $y = \pm\left(\frac{2}{3}\right)x$.

For further study, research the orbits of the planets in our solar system. How can they be described mathematically?

Using Coordinate Geometry to Algebraically Prove Geometric Theorems

Coordinate geometry assigns an ordered pair (x, y) to every point on the plane. These ordered pairs can be used to algebraically describe geometric figures and properties and prove geometric theorems.

Using the coordinate plane, theorems that we have seen proved geometrically can be proven algebraically.

Example

A square is a quadrilateral in which all four sides are congruent, opposite sides are parallel, and adjacent sides are perpendicular.

Prove the figure $PQRS$ with vertices $P(0,0)$, $Q(a,0)$, $R(a,a)$, and $S(0,a)$ is a square.
Use the distance formula:

$d = \sqrt{(x_1 - x_2)^2 + (y_1 - y_2)^2}$ to prove that the sides are congruent.

Solution:

$$PQ = \sqrt{(-a)^2 + (0)^2} = \sqrt{a^2} = a$$

$$QR = \sqrt{(a - a)^2 + (0 - a)^2} = \sqrt{(-a)^2} = a$$

$$RS = \sqrt{(a - 0)^2 + (a - a)^2} = \sqrt{a^2} = a$$

$$SP = \sqrt{(0 - 0)^2 + (a - 0)^2} = \sqrt{a^2} = a$$

The length of all four sides is a; therefore, the sides are congruent.

Two lines are parallel if they have the same slope. The slope of a line is $\frac{\Delta y}{\Delta x}$, where $\Delta y = y_2 - y_1$ and $\Delta x = x_2 - x_1$.

Slope of $PQ = \frac{0 - 0}{a - 0} = 0$.

Slope of $RS = \frac{a - a}{a - 0} = 0$. Therefore, $PQ \| RS$.

Slope of $PS = \frac{0 - a}{0 - 0} =$ undefined. Slope of $QR = \frac{0 - a}{a - a}$ undefined. Since division by 0 is undefined, vertical lines have no defined slope and are parallel to each other. Therefore, $PS \| QR$.

The slopes of perpendicular lines are the negative reciprocal of each other. For a line with slope 0, the negative reciprocal is undefined since division by 0 is undefined.

Therefore, $PQ \perp QR$, $QR \perp RS$, $RS \perp SP$, and $SP \perp PQ$.

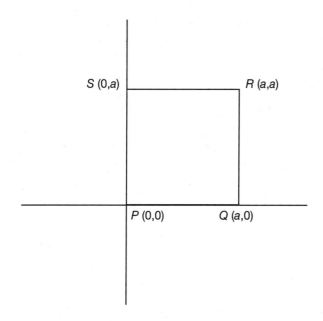

S (0,a) R (a,a)

P (0,0) Q (a,0)

All conditions are met. *PQRS* is a square.

By proving the slope criteria for parallel and perpendicular lines, we can use parallel and perpendicular lines to solve geometric problems.

Example

In the coordinate plane, the equation of a straight line is $y = mx + b$, where m is the slope of the line. The slope is the ratio of the change in y over the change in x for any two points on the line.

The equation of a line can be written as

$$y = \tfrac{\Delta y}{\Delta x}x + b.$$

We want to prove that if two lines have the same slope, then they are parallel.

Solution: Assume that two lines have the same slope, are not parallel, and cross at one and only one point.

The equation of line L_1 is $y = \tfrac{\Delta y}{\Delta x}x + b_1$.

The equation of line is L_2 is $y = \tfrac{\Delta y}{\Delta x}x + b_2$ and $b_1 \neq b_2$.

The point at which the lines cross is point (x_3, y_3) and lies on both L_1 and L_2. So for that point, $y_3 = \tfrac{\Delta y}{\Delta x}x_3 + b_1$ and $y_3 = \tfrac{\Delta y}{\Delta x}x_3 + b_2$.

Therefore, $\tfrac{\Delta y}{\Delta x}x_3 + b_1 = \tfrac{\Delta y}{\Delta x}x_3 + b_2$ and $b_1 = b_2$. This contradicts the assumption that $b_1 \neq b_2$, proving the theorem that if two lines have the same slope, they are parallel.

We can use parallel and perpendicular lines to solve geometric problems.

Example

Find the equation of a line that is perpendicular to the line with the equation $y = 3x - 4$ and passes through the point $(0,3)$.

Solution: The negative reciprocal is $-\tfrac{1}{3}$. Therefore, $y = -\tfrac{1}{3}x + b$. When $x = 0$, then $y = 3$. Therefore, $b = 3$ and $y = -\tfrac{1}{3}x + 3$.

A *directed line segment* has endpoints and a direction. A directed line segment $P(x_1, y_1)Q(x_2, y_2)$ has a slope $m = \tfrac{\Delta y - (y_2 - y_1)}{\Delta x - (x_2 - x_1)}$. In order to find the point that partitions the segment in a given ratio $\tfrac{a}{b}$, Δy and Δx must each be divided by that ratio.

For example, for directed line segment $P(1,1)$ $Q(3,9)$, we want to find the point R on the line segment that divides the segment by the ratio $\tfrac{1}{3}$. First we calculate Δy and Δx: $y_2 - y_1 = 9 - 1 = 8$, and $x_2 - x_1 = 3 - 1 = 2$. Now we must divide the directed line segment into two pieces. The relative length of the first piece is the numerator of the ratio, in this case 1. The total relative length of the line segment is the numerator + the denominator of the ratio, in this case 4. Since $\Delta y = 8$, $\Delta x = 2$, and the number of pieces is 4,

$$x_3 = x_1 + \tfrac{\Delta x}{4} = 1 + \tfrac{2}{4} = 1.5 \text{ and } y_3 = y_1 + \tfrac{\Delta y}{4} = 1 + \tfrac{8}{4} = 3$$

$R(1.5,3)$ divides directed line segment PQ by the ratio $\tfrac{1}{3}$.

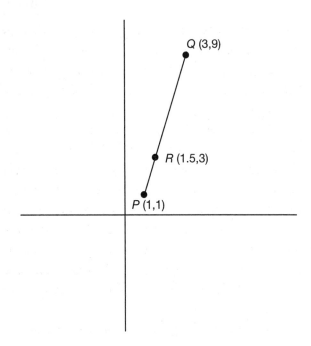

What is the area of triangle $A(3,1)B(-1,7)$ $C(0,2)$?

Solution: On the coordinate plane, draw a triangle with an obtuse angle with coordinates A (3,1), B (−1,7), C (0,2). Draw a rectangle with coordinates A (3,1), D (3,7), B (−1,7), and E (−1,1). Draw line segment $C(0,2)F(-1,2)$ and line segment $C(0,2)G(0,1)$.

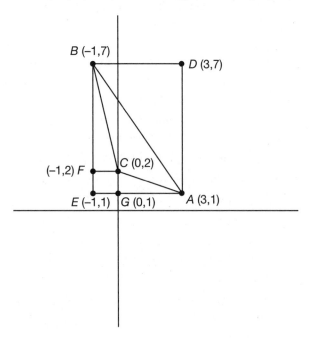

To find the perimeter of any polygon, you can use coordinates. You need to have the coordinates of every vertex. Construct right triangles between adjacent vertexes of the polygon, in which one leg is Δx and the other leg is Δy. The hypotenuse, which is part of the perimeter of the polygon, can then be calculated using the Pythagorean theorem.

For a regular polygon, this procedure needs to be done once, with the result being multiplied by the number of sides to get the perimeter of the polygon.

To find the area of a triangle ABC in which C is the largest angle, and you know the coordinates of the three vertices, draw a rectangle that circumscribes the triangle, with the two figures sharing at least one vertex, and with at least one more vertex also being a point on the rectangle. Divide the spaces within the rectangle, but outside the triangle, into right triangles and rectangles of known length by using the coordinates of the triangle. Use the area formula for right triangles and rectangles to find the area of each piece. Find the area of the large rectangle and subtract the area of the right triangles and rectangles outside the triangle of interest but inside the surrounding rectangle to indirectly calculate the area of the triangle.

We can now calculate the area of every figure except the triangle ABC.

The area of rectangle $ADBE = 24$.
The area of triangle $ADB = 12$.
The area of triangle $CBF = 2.5$.
The area of triangle $CGA = 2.$ ~~~~ $\frac{1}{2}bh = \frac{1}{2}(3)(1) = \frac{3}{2} = 1.5$
The area of square $CGEF = 1$.

Subtract the areas of the other figures from the area of the large rectangle $ADBE$ to get the area of triangle ABC.

Area of triangle $ABC = 24 - 12 - 2.5 - \overset{1.5}{\cancel{2}} - 1 = 6.5$

Perimeter, Area, Surface Area, and Volume Formulas

The formula for the circumference of a circle $C = \pi d$ comes from the definition of pi or π as the ratio between the circumference and diameter of a circle. Over the years, it has been a challenge to find increasingly accurate approximations of π, which is an irrational number. For rough calculations, 3.14 or $\frac{22}{7}$ are used as approximations of π.

Definition: *Area* is a covering of a space. The area of a rectangle is the product of the length times the width. $A = lw$. A square is a rectangle with $l = w = s$, or side, and interior angles = 90°. The area of a square is $A = s^2$.

If a square is inscribed in a circle with radius r, you can use the Pythagorean theorem to show that the length of each side of the square is equal to $\sqrt{2}r$, and that the area of the square is $\sqrt{2}r \times \sqrt{2}r = 2r^2$. If regular polygons with greater numbers of equal sides are inscribed in the circle, their areas become closer to the area of the circle. The formula for the area of a triangle is $\frac{1}{2}bh$. If a regular polygon of n sides is inscribed in a circle of radius r, as n increases, the height h will approach r, and the base b will approach 0, but there will be n triangles, and $n \times b$ will approach πd or $2\pi r$, so the total area $A = \frac{1}{2}2\pi r \times \pi r^2$.

Definition: *Volume* is a measure of three-dimensional space. The volume of a cube with length, width, and height all equal to s is $V = s^3$.

The volume of a cube can also be thought of as the product of the base times the height. A cylinder is a three-dimensional figure in which the base is a circle, rather than a square. The top of the cylinder is also a circle. The Cavalieri Principle states that the volume of an object is the sum of all its cross sections. Applying the Cavalieri Principle gives us the formula of the volume of a cylinder, which is $V = \pi r^2 h$.

We can apply the Cavalieri Principle to a process similar to what we did to find the area of a circle, which was accomplished by inscribing regular polygons with the number of sides approaching infinity in a circle. To find the volume of pyramids and cones, slice them into regular cross sections, with the number of cross sections approaching infinity. As the number of cross sections increases, the formula for the volume of a pyramid or cone approaches $V = \frac{1}{3}bh$.

The perimeter and area of geometric shapes are used to solve many practical problems.

Example

A landscaper started a new lawn on a 40-by-60-foot rectangular lot. If a pound of grass seed was used for every 800 square feet, how many pounds of seed were needed?

Solution: The area of the rectangular lot is 40 feet × 60 feet = 2,400 square feet. To find how many pounds of seed were needed, we need to divide: 2,400 square feet ÷ 800 square feet per pound = 3 pounds of seed.

Example

A gardener wants to fence in a new circular garden that would have a diameter of 45 feet. The fence would go around the entire garden, except for three running feet where the gate would be placed. How many running feet of fencing will she need?

Solution: We need to find the circumference of the garden and subtract an amount for the gate. $C = \pi d = 3.14 \times 45 = 141.3$ running feet. The amount of fencing needed is $141.3 - 3 = 138.3$ running feet.

The surface area and volume of prisms, cylinders, pyramids, cones, and spheres can be used to solve problems.

Example

A cylindrical grain elevator can be used to store grain. What is the most grain that could be stored in a 90-foot-high grain elevator with a circular base with a circumference of 314 feet, assuming it can be filled to the top?

Solution: The volume of a cylinder is the area of the base times the height. Since we are given the circumference, not the area, of the base, we need to find the radius so we can calculate the area.

The formula for circumference is $C = 2\pi r$. Substituting, we get $314 = 2 \times 3.14r$ and $100 = 2r$ and $r = 50$.

The volume of a cylinder is $V = \pi r^2 h = 3.14 \times 2{,}500$ square feet $\times 90$ feet $= 706{,}500$ cubic feet.

Visualizing Relationships between Two-Dimensional and Three-Dimensional Objects

In order to calculate surface area of a three-dimensional object, it can make sense to look at *nets*, which are made from a three-dimensional object by making cuts between surfaces so that the surfaces can be flattened and be seen in a two-dimensional plane. The same object can be unfolded in different ways to make different nets, but nets of the same object will have the same surface area.

Example

A net of a rectangular box can look like this:

or this:

This is a net of a pyramid:

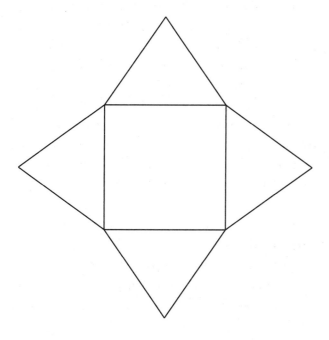

A cross section or slice can give us a picture of a three-dimensional object. Cross sections can be stacked to create a three-dimensional object.

A two-dimensional object can be rotated along an axis to generate three-dimensional objects.

Modern technology is developing new applications, such as 3-D printers that build on these mathematical concepts.

Three-dimensional solids have faces. For example, a rectangular solid has six faces. A cross section or slice of the solid has edges. The greatest number of edges a cross section can have is the number of faces of the solid, though it can have less. While a vertical slice of a rectangular solid will be in the shape of a rectangle, slicing at an angle can result in a slice in the shape of a triangle with only three edges, or even in the shape of a hexagon if the slice intersects all six faces of the rectangular solid.

Cross sections can generate a variety of two-dimensional objects. A vertical slice through the apex of a cone creates a triangle. But a vertical slice

that cuts the curved surface of a cone generates a two-dimensional curve, a parabola or a hyperbola depending on the angle of the slice. A horizontal slice creates a circle, while a diagonal slice creates an ellipse. Because these shapes can be created by taking cross sections of a cone, they are called conic sections.

Two-dimensional objects, when rotated around different axes of rotation, can create different three-dimensional objects. If a rectangle is rotated around an axis of rotation that is one of its sides, it will create a cylinder. However, if it is rotated around an axis of rotation that diagonally intersects it, the solid will be quite different.

If the axis of rotation for a circle passes through the center of the circle, the three-dimensional solid generated will be a sphere. If the axis of rotation is tangent to the circle, the three-dimensional solid generated will be the doughnut shape formally called a torus.

We can often use two-dimensional representations of three-dimensional objects to visualize and solve problems. An object such as a building can be understood and visualized by seeing what it would look like from the front, the rear, and above. An architect can use these perspectives to help visualize what a future building would look like on its site from various perspectives.

Historically, three-dimensional buildings have been described in blueprints, which represent the three-dimensional structure in a two-dimensional form.

Two-dimensional nets can also be used to understand the surface area and structure of a three-dimensional object.

Applying Geometric Concepts in Real-World Situations

Students need to know how to apply geometric concepts in real-world situations, both now and in the future. While engineers, artists, architects, and carpenters use geometry on the job, everyone will need to use some geometry skills at home. An understanding of distance, area, and volume is crucial for daily life, whether a person needs to lay out a garden, buy new carpet for a house, or design and build shelves.

Students need to connect geometric concepts to their daily lives. On a visit to a supermarket, they can estimate the volume of different containers. Which container shape is most efficient, a rectangular solid or a cylinder? How can they use their understanding of area to estimate how much paint is needed to paint an entire apartment or a house? They can look at the geometric features of traditional buildings such as the Inuit igloo, the Western Plains Indian teepee, the Mongolian yurt, the Iroquois longhouse, the Bedouin tent, the Gothic cathedral, Greek temples, and the Hopi kiva.

Projects help bring mathematics to life. Students can design a parking lot that includes parking spaces at different density levels. They can measure the area of land at risk due to sea level rise due to global warming. They can calculate the population density of various states in the United States, as well as the population density of other world nations. They can look at the packaging of food products, such as ice cream makers that change the dimensions of their packaging so that a cut in volume of the product would not be obvious. Density can also be explored in our solar system and galaxy by looking at the varying density levels of various celestial objects.

Successful projects need to be challenging but grade appropriate and contain a level of interest that would engage most students.

Geometric methods can be applied to solve design problems. Issues like slope can be used to design a handicapped ramp or a Winter Olympics bobsled run. Area, volume, and ratio can be used to frame a model of a house and scale it up to full size. A sketch on paper can be used to design a garden, while a blueprint is used to design buildings. We can also use graph paper to lay out the placement of furniture in a room. And a good understanding of angles can help in various sports, including basketball, soccer, and pool.

Using Properties of Parallel and Perpendicular Lines, Triangles, Quadrilaterals, Polygons, and Circles to Solve Problems

We can use our knowledge of parallel, perpendicular, and intersecting lines to solve problems.

Example

In much of Manhattan, the streets are numbered and laid out in a grid. The angle between 18th Street and Second Avenue is 90 degrees. The angles between 18th Street and Fifth, Sixth, Seventh, and Eighth Avenues are also all 90 degrees. If 19th Street is parallel to 18th Street, what would you predict is the angle between 19th Street and Second Avenue? Between 19th Street and Eighth Avenue?

Solution: Since the avenues all make 90-degree angles with 18th Street, they are parallel to each other. Since 19th Street is parallel to 18th Street, and Second Avenue and Eighth Avenue are transversals, the angle between 19th Street and Second Avenue is also 90 degrees, and the angle between 19th Street and Eighth Avenue is also 90 degrees.

Example

Eighteenth Street runs for 1.6 miles from First Avenue to 11th Avenue. If the distance between avenues is constant, what is the distance from First Avenue to Second Avenue?

Solution: The distance D from First Avenue to Second Avenue $= D = \frac{\text{total miles}}{\text{number of avenues}} = \frac{1.6}{10} = .16$ miles.

We can apply angle relationships to solve problems.

Example

Two road crews are assigned to work on opposite ends of Link Road, a straight connecting road that will link Town Road with the parallel Country Road. If, heading north, the angle between Link Road and Town Road is 120 degrees, what should be the angle heading south between Link Road and Town Road?

Solution: Since Town Road and Country Road are parallel, the interior angles that lie on the same side of Link Road, which is a transversal, are supplementary. Therefore, x degrees + 120 degrees = 180 degrees, and x = 60 degrees.

Geometry Basics: A Final Summary

A midpoint of a line segment is the point that divides a line segment into two equal line segments.

Example

What are the coordinates of the midpoint M of line segment AB where A is (3,2) and B is (9,8)?

Solution: The coordinates of $M = \left(\frac{x_a + x_b}{2}, \frac{y_a + y_b}{2} \right)$
$= \left(\frac{3 + 9}{2}, \frac{2 + 10}{2} \right) = (6,5)$

Definition: A *median* of a triangle is a line that connects a vertex with the midpoint of the opposite side.

Every triangle has three medians that all intersect at a point in the interior of the triangle. That intersection point is called the *centroid* of the triangle and is located $\frac{2}{3}$ of the distance from the vertex to the opposite midpoint.

Example

For triangle ABC, find the coordinates of the centroid D when A is (0,0), B is (6,0), and C is (0,8).

Solution: We need to find the midpoint of one of the sides of the triangle. The midpoint E of side CB is

$$\left(\frac{x_c + x_b}{2}, \frac{y_c + y_b}{2} \right) = \left(\frac{0 + 6}{2}, \frac{8 + 0}{2} \right) = (3,5)$$

(3,4)

Now calculate the coordinates of the point $\frac{2}{3}$ of the distance from point A on median AE.

$$(\tfrac{2}{3}x_a + x_e, \tfrac{2}{3}y_a + y_e) = \left(\tfrac{2}{3}(0 + 3) \right), \left(\tfrac{2}{3}(0 + 5) \right) = (1, 3\tfrac{1}{3})$$

The coordinates of centroid D are $(1, 3\tfrac{1}{3})$. $\left(2, \tfrac{8}{3}\right)$

Definition: An *altitude* of a triangle is a line that is perpendicular to a side of a triangle and has the opposite vertex of the triangle as one endpoint.

Angle C of triangle ABC is 140°. Can we determine whether the altitude BD is drawn inside or outside the triangle?

Definition: *Obtuse angles* of a triangle are angles that are greater than 90° and less than 180°. The altitude drawn from either of the other two vertices will lie outside the triangle.

Special triangles have some unique properties that allow us to solve many geometric problems.

Definition: An *isosceles triangle* is a triangle with two equal sides and two equal angles.

Definition: An *equilateral triangle* is a triangle with three equal sides and three equal angles.

Definition: A *right triangle* is a triangle in which one of the angles of the triangle is a right angle (90°).

Definition: A *quadrilateral* is a closed figure with four straight sides and four vertices.

Definition: A *trapezoid* is a quadrilateral with one and only one pair of parallel sides.

Definition: A *parallelogram* is a quadrilateral with two pairs of parallel sides.

Definition: A *rhombus* is a quadrilateral with two pairs of parallel sides and with every side the same length. A rhombus is a special case of parallelogram. Every rhombus is a parallelogram.

Definition: A *rectangle* is a quadrilateral with two pairs of parallel sides and with a right angle at every vertex. A rectangle is a special case of parallelogram. Every rectangle is a parallelogram.

Definition: A *square* is a quadrilateral with two pairs of parallel sides, with every side the same length, and with a right angle at every vertex. A square is a special case of parallelogram, rhombus, and rectangle. Every square is a parallelogram, a rhombus, and a rectangle.

We can use our knowledge and understanding of angles and diagonals to explore various geometric figures.

Example

A kite is a quadrilateral with two pairs of adjacent sides of equal length. We can prove that the angles between the unequal sides are equal. *ABCD* is a kite in which *AB = BC* and *CD = DA*.

Solution: Draw diagonal *AC*. Triangle *ABC* is isosceles because *AB = BC*. Therefore, angle *CAB* = angle *ACB*.

Triangle *ADC* is isosceles because *AD = DC*. Therefore, angle *CAD* = angle *ACD*. Since *CAB* and *CAD* and *ACB* and *ACD* are adjacent angles, angle *BAD* = angle *BCD*.

Now draw the other diagonal, *BD*, label the intersection of the diagonals *E*, and we will prove that *BD* ⊥ *AC*.

First we will prove that triangle *ABD* ≅ *CBD* by showing that all three corresponding sides are equal. Because of the definition of a kite, *AB = BC* and *CD = DA*. Because of the reflexivity principle, *BD = BD*, so all three sides are equal and the triangles are congruent. As a result, we can also conclude that angle *ABD = CBD* since they are corresponding angles of congruent triangles.

We will now prove that triangle *ABE* is congruent to triangle *CBE*. By definition, we have already found that *AB = CD*. Because of the reflexivity principle, *BE = BE*. And since *ABD* ≅ *CBD*, we were able to conclude that angle *ABD = CBD*, and by SAS, *ABD* ≅ *CBD*.

We now conclude that angle *AEB* = angle *CEB*, since they are the corresponding angles of *ABD* and *CBD*. Since the exterior sides of these adjacent angles make a straight line, each of the angles is a right angle and *BD* ⊥ *AC*.

Problems involving the perimeter and area of regular or irregular polygons with more than four sides can be handled by breaking them into pieces with three or four sides.

Example

Suppose that you are a contractor who has been hired to spread loam on a customer's yard. The lot is shaped like a rectangle, 100 feet wide by 150 feet long. But on the lot there is a house with exterior dimensions of 80 feet by 60 feet, and there is a 3 feet wide by 30 feet long paved walkway that connects the house with the street. The truck holds a 12 feet by 6 feet by 6 feet load of loam. If the loam is spread evenly, about how deep will the loam be spread on the lawn?

Solution: To get the square footage, break the problem into pieces. The entire lot is 100×150 or 15,000 square feet. The house is 80×60 or 4,800 square feet, and the walkway is 30×3 or 90 square feet. Since the house and the walkway are not getting any loam, their square footage needs to be subtracted from the square footage of the entire lot:

$$15,000 - 4,800 - 90 = 10,110 \text{ square feet.}$$

The total amount of loam is $12 \times 6 \times 6 = 432$ cubic feet.

Divide the number of cubic feet by the number of square feet: $432 \div 10,110 \approx .043$ feet or .5 inch. The yard would be covered with about .5 inch of loam.

CHAPTER 9 ▶ PROBABILITY AND STATISTICS REVIEW

CHAPTER SUMMARY

Recognizing patterns, predicting outcomes, and interpreting and manipulating numerical and graphical data are what the study of probability and statistics is all about. We live in a world of statistics. Every day there are countless studies released and scrutinized for predictive behaviors and outcomes—some well grounded and some downright spurious. Knowing the difference requires an understanding of the principles of probability and statistics. The review that follows of the fundamentals of these disciplines will help to prepare you for the Praxis II® Mathematics: Content Knowledge exam.

Data of One Variable

Definition: *Range of data* is the difference between maximum and minimum (i.e., max − min).

Definition: *Interquartile range* is the difference between first quartile (q1) and third quartile (q3) (i.e., q3 − q1).

Definition: *Mean* is the average of all measurements; it equals the sum of all measurements divided by the number of measurements.

Definition: *Median* is the middle data when the measurements are arranged in ascending (or descending) order.

Example

Find the mean and median.

a. If 1, 2, 3, 4, 5 are the measurements, then mean = median = 3.

b. If 1, 2, 3, 4, 5, 105 are the measurements, then mean = 20 and median = $3\frac{1}{2}$.

Notice that extreme value has more influence on mean than on median.

Shapes of Graphs

Definition: The data set is *symmetric* when the left-hand side and right-hand side are mirror images of each other, for example:

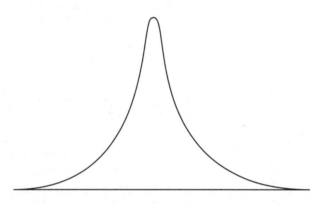

In a data set that is symmetric, the mean and the median are roughly the same.

Definition: The data set is *skewed to the right* when there is a long tail on the right-hand side, for example:

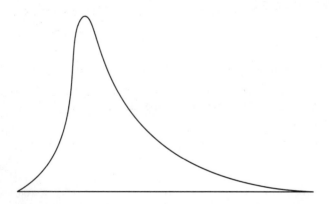

When the data set is skewed to the right, there are some measurements (the ones along the long tail) that are significantly higher than on the other side. These measurements pull up both mean and median. Extreme values, however, have more influence on the mean. Therefore, in the case of a data set skewed to the right, the mean is usually higher than the median.

Definition: The data set is *skewed to the left* when there is a long tail on the left-hand side, for example:

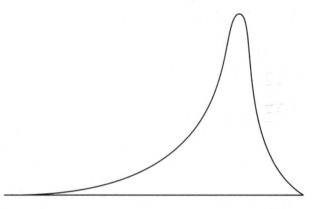

When the data set is skewed to the left, there are some measurements (the ones along the long tail) that are significantly lower than the ones on the other side. Similar to what we said about data sets that are skewed to the right, in the case of those skewed to the left, the mean is usually smaller than the median.

Definition: *Outlier* refers to unusual data, or data that is far from the other measurements. For example, if the data set included 1, 2, 2, 3, 3, 4, 4, 5, 5, 6, 6, 6, 1,095, then 1,095 would be considered an outlier.

Diagrams Summarizing Data

Definition: A *box plot* is a diagram summarizing the data by giving the maximum, minimum, first quartile, third quartile, and median.

Example

a. The following box plot summarizes the test scores of the students in test 1.

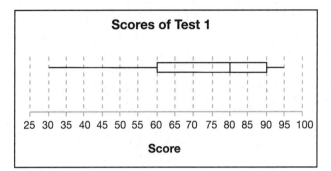

min: 30
first quartile: 60
median: 80
third quartile: 90
max: 95

Although only five numbers are provided within a box plot, more information can be generated:

Range = Max − Min = 95 − 30 = 65
Interquartile range = q3 − q1 = 90 − 60 = 30

Moreover, the data set can be separated into four regions, between 30 and 60, 60 and 80, 80 and 90, and 90 and 95; 25% of the data lies in each region.

The mean is not given in a box plot, but its comparison with the median can found in some cases. In this box plot, there is a long tail on the left-hand side, which indicates the data set is skewed to the left. The mean, therefore, is very likely to be below the median—below 80.

b. The following diagram involves two box plots.

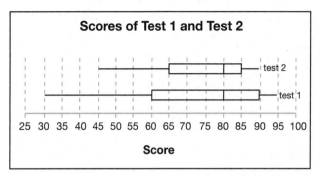

The medians of both tests are 80, but the scores in test 2 give a smaller interquartile range (20 instead of 30). Standard deviation is not given, but the one in test 2 should be lower, as the measurements are closer to the center than the ones in test 1.

c. The following diagram involves three box plots.

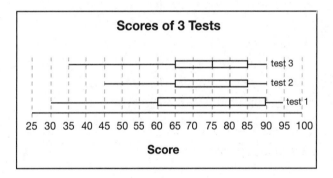

The medians of the first two tests are both 80, which is higher than the median of test 3. The interquartile range of test 2 is the same as test 3, with both of them smaller than test 1.

Definition: A *dot plot* is a diagram that uses dots to represent the measurements; each dot represents one measurement in the corresponding category.

Example

The following dot plot summarizes the results of a survey regarding the reading habits of students for the preceding year.

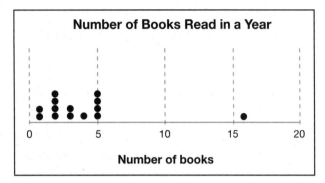

Number of Books Read in a Year

Number of books

Information based on the dot plot:

- The number of students participating the survey is 14, which is the total number of dots in the diagram. Two of them have read one book, as there are two dots listed on top of the value "1," four students have read two books, and so on.
- Median = 3 since the seventh and the eighth measurements are both 3.
- Mean can be computed by adding all the values and then dividing by 14. Mean =
$$\frac{1 + 1 + 2 + 2 + 2 + 2 + 3 + \ldots + 15}{14} =$$
$$\frac{(1 \times 2) + (2 \times 4) + (3 \times 2) + (4 \times 1) + (5 \times 4) + (16 \times 1)}{14}$$
$$= 4$$
- One student in the survey has read 16 books, which is represented by the dot on top of 16 on the right-hand side of the diagram. This can be considered an outlier because it is a number much larger than all the other measurements. This explains why the mean is higher than the median.

Definition: A *histogram* is a diagram summarizing data using a vertical bar chart.

Example

The following histogram summarizes a survey regarding classes taken by students in a college.

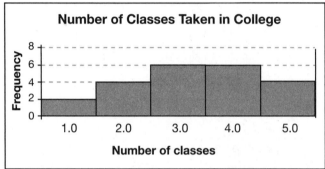

Number of Classes Taken in College

Number of classes

Information based on the histogram:

- Two students are taking one class, four students taking two classes, and so on, which can be determined from the height (frequency) of the corresponding measurement. The total number of students responding to the survey is 22 (the sum of all frequencies: 2 + 4 + 6 + 6 + 4).
- Median = 3, as the 11th and 12th measurements are both 3.
- Mean = $\frac{(1 \times 2) + (2 \times 4) + (3 \times 6) + (4 \times 6) + (5 \times 4)}{22}$
$= 2.727$ 3.2727

Normal Distribution

Normal distribution refers to a data set that is close to a bell curve.

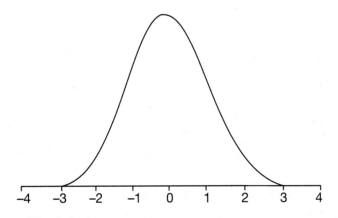

The percentages of measurements distributed in a normal distribution are shown in the following diagram.

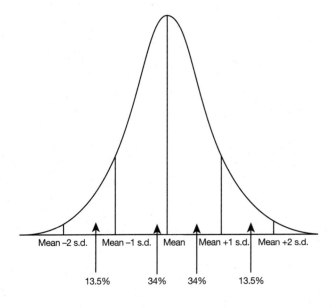

Example

If the mean and standard deviation (s.d.) of a data set are 13 and 2, respectively, and the data set is roughly normal, then approximately

13.5 percent of the measurements lie between 9 and 11.

34 percent of the measurements lie between 11 and 13.

34 percent of the measurements lie between 13 and 15.

13.5 percent of the measurements lie between 15 and 17.

In this data set, 9 is two standard deviations below the mean $(13 - 2 \times 2)$, 11 is one standard deviation below the mean $(13 - 1 \times 2)$, 15 is one standard deviation above the mean, and 17 is two standard deviations above the mean.

Definition: *Standard normal Z is a normally distributed curve with mean 0 and standard deviation 1. The area under the standard normal curve is less than or equal to a certain value that can be found in the standard normal table (the Z score table).*

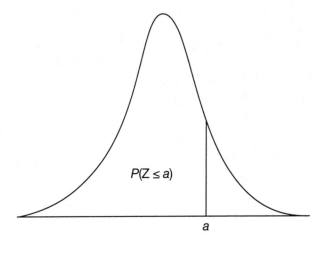

Example

The area can be found from the *Z* score table as follows:

$P(Z < 0.34) = 0.6331$
$P(Z < 1.21) = 0.8869$

With the following properties of standard normal:

1. $P(Z \geq a) = 1 - P(Z \leq a)$, and
2. $P(a \leq Z \leq b) = P(Z \leq b) - P(Z \leq a)$

The following can be found:

a. $P(Z \geq -1.1) = 1 - P(Z \leq -1.1) = 1 - 0.1357 = 0.8643$

b. $P(1.1 \leq Z \leq 2.2) = P(Z \leq 2.2) - P(Z \leq 1.1) = 0.9861 - 0.8643 = 0.1218$

General Normal Distribution

If the mean and standard deviation of a normal distribution are given, the percentage of measurements (the area under the normal curve) can be found using a Z score table after converting the normal distribution to a standard normal distribution Z by a process called *standardization*.

Standardization

If X is normal with mean μ and standard deviation σ, then $\frac{X - \mu}{\sigma}$ would be standard normal; that is, it has mean 0 and standard deviation 1.

$$Z = \frac{X - \mu}{\sigma}$$

Example
If X is normal with mean 5 and standard deviation 2, then

a. $P(X \leq 8) = P\left(\frac{X - 5}{2} \leq \frac{8 - 5}{2}\right) = P(Z \leq 1.5)$
$= 0.9332$

b. $P(3 \leq X \leq 6) = P\left(\frac{3 - 5}{2} \leq \frac{X - 5}{2} \leq \frac{6 - 5}{2}\right)$
$= P(-1 \leq Z \leq 0.5)$
$= P(Z \leq 0.5) - P(Z \leq -1)$
$= 0.6915 - 0.1587$
$= 0.5328$

In both parts, we begin with standardization and replace X with standard normal Z. Then, using the properties if necessary, we finish the questions with the numbers found in the Z score table.

Example
The GPA of a group of students is normally distributed with a mean of 3 and standard deviation of 0.4. Find the percentages of students with:

a. a GPA 3.6 or higher
b. a GPA between 2.8 and 3.4

Solution: First, define X as the GPA of the students where X would be normal with a mean of 3 and standard deviation of 0.4:

a. $P(X \geq 3.6) = P\left(\frac{X - 3}{0.4} \geq \frac{3.6 - 3}{0.4}\right)$
$= P(Z \geq 1.5) = 1 - P(Z \leq 1.5) = 1 - 0.9332$
$= 0.0668$

Thus, 6.68% of the students have a GPA of 3.6 or higher.

b. $P(2.8 \leq X \leq 3.4)$
$= P\left(\frac{2.8 - 3}{0.4} \leq \frac{X - 3}{0.4} \leq \frac{3.4 - 3}{0.4}\right)$
$= P(-0.5 \leq Z \leq 1)$
$= P(Z \leq 1) - P(Z \leq -0.5) = 0.8413 - 0.3085$
$= 0.5328$

Thus, 53.28% of the students have a GPA between 2.8 and 3.4.

This method usually works well for data sets with diagrams close to bell shape, such as a histogram similar to normal.

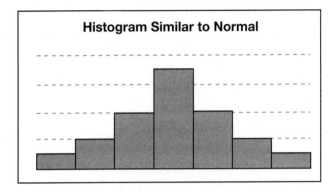

Histogram Similar to Normal

It is not a good idea, however, to use this method when the shape of the data set is not close to normal distribution.

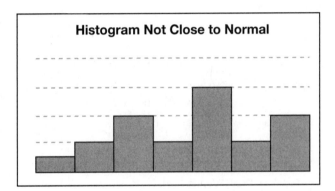

Histogram Not Close to Normal

Data of Two Variables

Categorical Data

A two-way frequency table is usually used to present categorical data with two variables.

Example

The origin of students (international vs. local) and the place they live (on campus or off campus) are being studied. The results are summarized in the following table:

	INTERNATIONAL	LOCAL
On campus	12	6
Off campus	15	27

Based on the table:

- Sixty students are being surveyed (12 + 6 + 15 + 27 = 60).
- Among these 60 students, 12 of them are international students living on campus, 6 of them are local students living on campus, 15 of them are international students living off campus, and the remaining 27 are local students living off campus.
- Total international students: 27 (12 + 15 = 27), total local students: 33 (6 + 27 = 33), total number of students living on campus: 18 (12 + 6 = 18), total number of students living off campus: 42 (15 + 27 = 42).

The frequency table can be transformed to a relative frequency table by dividing all the frequencies by the total number of measurements. In this example, there is a total of 60 measurements.

Modified table:

	INTERNATIONAL	LOCAL
On campus	0.2	0.1
Off campus	0.25	0.45

Based on the table:

- 20% of the students are international students living on campus.
- 45% of the students are local students living off campus.
- Among the international students, 44.4% of them are living on campus (conditional relative frequency of international students living on campus can be computed by $\frac{0.2}{0.2 + 0.25}$).
- Similarly, among the students living on campus, 66.7% of them are international students while 33.3% of them are local students ($\frac{0.2}{0.2 + 0.1}$ and $\frac{0.1}{0.2 + 0.1}$, respectively).

- Interpretation: 45% of the students are international students. Of the students living on campus, 66.7% of them are international students, and it is much higher than the overall number. That is to say, international students tend to live on campus. This is the association (or correlation) relationship between being international students and living on campus. In this case, the correlation is positive. The more formal introduction to correlation will be given later.

Quantitative Data

A scatter plot is usually used to present quantitative data with two variables.

Example

A study on how many hours students spent preparing for a test and the corresponding score is shown here:

Time (hours)	8	5	6	1
Score	85	95	75	60

The scatter plot would be plotted on an *xy*-coordinate plane, as time versus score, or score versus time:

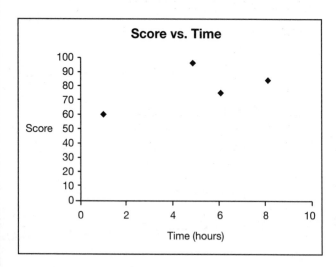

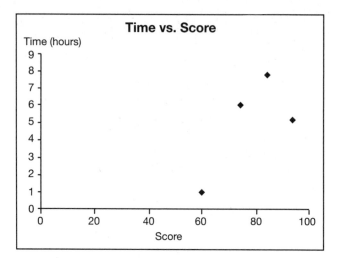

The correlation between the test score and time to study is 0.6825.

The correlation coefficient (r) between X and Y describes the association as a linear relationship between change in X and change in Y: $-1 \leq r \leq 1$

The sign of correlation coefficient:

- Positive ($r > 0$), positive correlation. An increase in X will be associated with an increase in Y, and vice versa.
- Negative ($r < 0$), negative correlation. An increase in X will be associated with a decrease in Y, and vice versa.

The magnitude of correlation coefficient:

- When r is closer to 1 (or -1), there is strong correlation. The measurements are close to a straight line.
- When r is closer to 0, there is weak correlation. The measurements are far from being a straight line.

The following diagram is a scatter plot relating the weights of different cars (in pounds) and the fuel efficiency of the cars (in miles per gallon). The data sets come from *Consumer Reports* relating the weights of automobiles and fuel mileage for selected 1996 cars. A strong negative correlation is shown in the scatter plot.

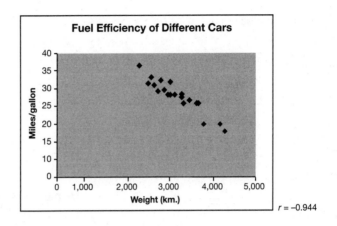

The correlation coefficient is close to −1. There is a clear downward trend of the data points, which indicates negative correlation. The data points are very close to straight line, which indicates strong correlation.

Example

Determine the correlations for scatter plots A, B, C, D, and E.

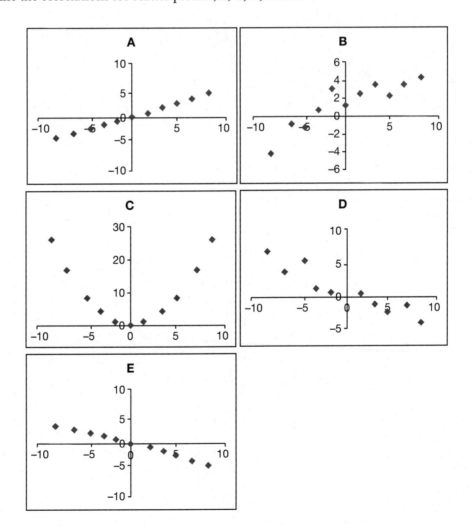

Solution: The correlations are:

- A = 1, an example of a perfect linear relationship with positive slope
- B = 0.90, an example of strong negative correlation

C = 0, an example of a nonlinear relationship

D = −0.93, an example of a strong negative correlation

E = −1, an example of a perfect linear relationship with negative slope

Linear Regression

Correlation between two variables tells whether there is a linear relationship between them. Linear regression quantifies the relationship with a linear function.

Let's return to the scatter plot about the efficiency of different cars:

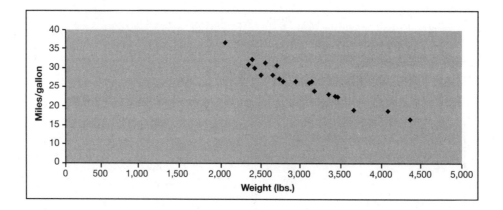

The linear relationship of the data points can be represented by adding a line:

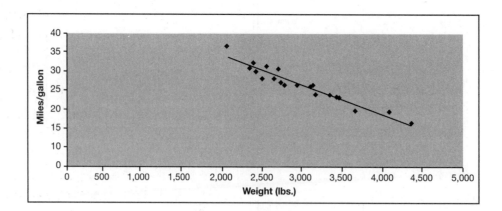

The line in the graph is called the "best fit line," which is the trend line. It can be found by the method of least squares. The details of the method are not given here, but the idea is to find the line that is closest to the data points.

Since it is a straight line, the regression line can be represented by linear function in slope-intercept form:

$$y = a + bx$$

where b is the predicted slope and a is the predicted y-intercept of the best fit line based on the data used.

Interpretation Using Linear Regression

To show how we use linear regression for interpretation, we return to the example about relative fuel efficiency of cars.

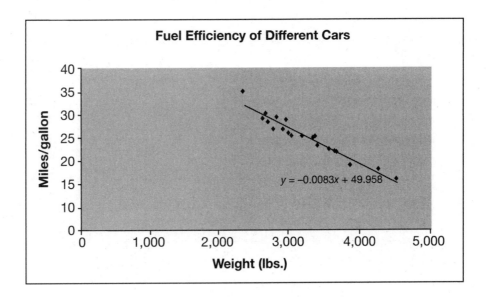

Fuel Efficiency of Different Cars

$y = -0.0083x + 49.958$

Example

If a car weighs 3,000 pounds, what is the predicted fuel efficiency of the car?

Solution: Put $x = 3,000$ into the regression equation and you will get $y = 25.066$.

Interpretation: If a car weighs 3,000 pounds, the efficiency is expected to be 25.066 miles per gallon *on average*.

Note: The result does *not* imply that all cars weighing 3,000 pounds are going to have the same efficiency at 25.066 miles per gallon. Rather, the number represents the average efficiency of the cars weighing 3,000

pounds. Therefore, the other way to interpret the result is that if a car weighing 3,000 pounds has efficiency more than 25.066 miles per gallon, its efficiency can be considered as above average; if less than 25.066 mpg, below average.

Example

If a car weighs 7,000 pounds, what is its predicted fuel efficiency?

Solution: If the same method from the previous example is applied (putting $x = 7,000$ into the regression equation), $y = -8.134$ will result. The predicted efficiency would be −8.134 miles per gallon. How could that be possible!?

Note: Prediction using a regression result is valid only for *x*-values within the range of *x* of the data points. It is not reasonable to assume the same linear trend could be observed for the *x*-values outside the range. Look at the scatter plot regarding the efficiency of cars again. The *x* (weights) values of the data points are roughly between 2,000 and 4,500. Therefore, it is not appropriate to predict the *y*-value when *x* =7,000, as 7,000 is outside the range of 2,000 and 4,500.

Example

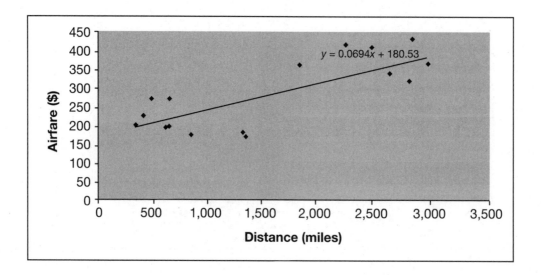

A study of the relationship between the distance of travel (*x*) and airfare (*y*) has been conducted. The regression result $y = 0.0694x + 180.53$ has been found.

a. What would be the predicted airfare if someone is traveling 2,000 miles?
b. If Bob is traveling 2,000 miles and he is paying $300 for it, is he paying above the average or below the average?

Solution:

a. 319.33
b. below average

The Residual Plot

The residual plot is the plot of *x*-values and the residual (the difference between observation and estimation).

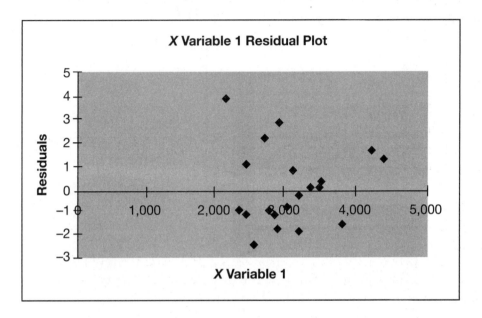

X Variable 1 Residual Plot

This diagram is the residual plot on the regression model regarding fuel efficiencies of cars. The points are located pretty randomly, so the linear model applied is likely to be appropriate.

The linear model, however, is not always appropriate in regression. For example, the following data set is part of a parabola.

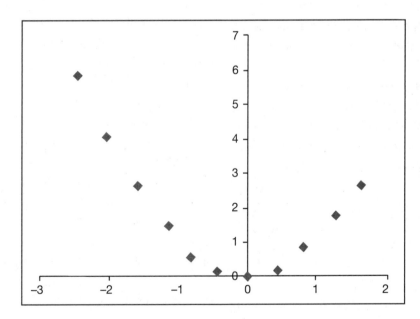

It is not reasonable to use a linear model here. If we were to use linear regression on this data set, the following residual plot would result.

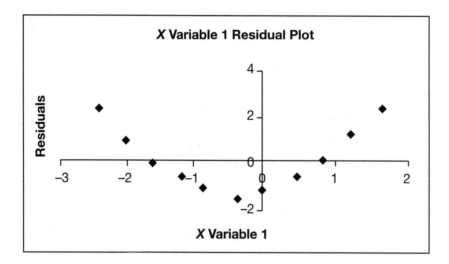

The data points on the plot clearly form a parabola, and they are not located randomly around the plot. These show that the linear regression is not the ideal model to use here.

The Slope, Intercept of Regression Line, and Correlation versus Causation

The intercept of the regression line is the y-value when $x = 0$. Since it is inappropriate to predict y-value with x-values outside the range of x of the data set, it is not common to interpret the intercept as $x = 0$ and is not usually included in the original data set. In the preceding examples regarding cars' fuel efficiency and airfare, it would not be very meaningful to consider car weights of 0 pounds or traveling 0 miles.

On the other hand, the slope of the regression line is commonly used in interpreting linear regression. The slope can be considered as the change of y with respect to 1 unit increase of x. In the example of airfare with the regression $y = 0.0694x + 180.53$, interpret the slope as follows: If the distance traveled (x) increases by 1 mile, on average the airfare would be $0.0694 higher. In the case of cars' efficiency, if the car weight (x) increases by 1 pound, on average the efficiency would be 0.0083 miles per gallon lower.

Correlation versus Causation

Slope is commonly used in interpretation, but you need to be very careful about the meaning involved. In the example of cars' efficiency, some might suggest that increasing the weights (x) causes the efficiency (y) to be lower. In the case of airfare, people might conclude that traveling longer distances (x) will result in higher prices (y).

These arguments sound reasonable, but they are true only if x and y are the cause-and-effect pair, and they cannot be shown through the scatter plot. Scatter plots show linear relation, which indicates correlation. But correlation does *not* imply causation. If two variables correlate with each other, it does not mean they are the cause-and-effect pair, unless other potential factors relating the two are being controlled.

The following is a classic example: Ice cream consumption has a strong positive correlation with the number of drownings. An increase in ice cream consumption and an increase in drowning tend to occur at the same time. Based on common sense, however, ice cream is clearly not the cause of drowning.

Scatter plots only show the relationship between two variables, but there are a lot of other unobserved factors that could impact the two variables. For example, in the case of ice cream and drowning, temperature is the important unobserved variable. Higher temperature will result in higher ice cream consumption, and at the same time more people will go swimming in hot weather, thus increasing the incidence of drowning. Mixing correlation and causation is a very common statistical fallacy.

Statistical Processes

Information regarding population is called a *parameter*. For example, the average income of all American families is a population parameter. The proportion of Americans holding college degrees is another population parameter. In a school, the average GPA of all students in the school is also a parameter, where the population refers to all students of the school.

Population parameters are usually unknown or difficult to find. The main purpose of statistics is to use information from randomized representative samples to give a good estimation of the population parameters. Samples are considered representative when the relevant characteristics of the members in the samples are similar to the ones in the population.

For example, if the average family income of a representative sample in a certain U.S. city is around $60,000 per year, we could expect the actual average family income of that city to be around $60,000 per year. We should not, however, generalize from this the average income of all U.S. families, as the situation of that city does not represent the situation of the whole country.

Here's another example: If a survey found that 65% of the people in the sample prefer movie A over movie B, we can expect that around 65% of the population would prefer movie A, as long as the sample is representative of the population as a whole. If, however, the survey targets only female audiences, the conclusion could be generalized only to the female population at most but not to the overall population, as the preferences of females are not necessarily the same as those of males.

Drawing Conclusions from Statistical Studies

There are two types of sampling:

Definition: *Simple random sampling* involves choosing a sample in such a way that all members from the population are equally likely to be chosen. Example of simple random sampling: To survey the opinions of students about a college, 200 student IDs are randomly chosen, and the corresponding students are surveyed. The sample is likely to be representative as long as the student ID numbers are randomly assigned.

Definition: *Systematic sampling* involves choosing the sample with a system, such as choosing every 10th or every 100th member of the population listing in order. Example of systematic sampling: To survey the opinions of residents about their building's facilities, the residents of every fifth apartment are surveyed. The sample could be representative if these apartments are similar to other apartments in terms of sizes, rents, and the like.

Other terms include the following:

Definition: In an *observational study*, researchers measure characteristics of samples without changing them.

An observational study is usually used to estimate a certain parameter. For example, to find the average income of American families, a random sample of different American families would be chosen and their family incomes recorded. The characteristic (income) is being observed without being affected. A similar strategy could be used to estimate the average test score of students in a school or to predict election results by using exit polls.

Definition: In *experiments*, researchers apply treatment to the sample members and measure the resulting effects. For example, experiments can be used to test medical treatments. People are randomly chosen to form a treatment group, which means they are the ones receiving the treatment. Others are randomly chosen to form a control group, which means they are not going to receive treatment and most likely would receive a placebo instead. The two groups should be selected in such a way that they are similar in all aspects except the treatment in order to ensure that the difference between the two groups at the end is due to the treatment, not other factors.

Definition: A *confidence interval* is an interval within which we are confident that the actual value lies. For example, if the 95% confidence interval of average annual income is $40,000 to $60,000, we are 95% confident that the actual average income is within that interval.

Confidence interval = estimator ± margin of error, where estimator is the estimation based on sample statistics.

The following is an example of observational study:

Example
To verify whether men and women are paid differently, a study is conducted on the income difference between the two gender groups. A group of men and a group of women are randomly selected, controlling for their educational background, working experience, and so on. The average income of men is found to be $1,000 per week, whereas the average income of women is $850 per week. The margin of error between the two groups is $120. Can we conclude from this data that men are getting paid more than women?

Solution: Difference of average incomes = 1,000 − 850 = 150, which is the estimator.

The confidence interval (estimator ± margin of error) = 150 ± 120 = 30 to 270.

Since the confidence interval does not include zero, we are confident that the difference between the two average incomes is not zero; that is to say, the two average incomes are different, and more precisely, the average income of men is higher than the average income of women.

Note: Zero is the critical value to compare with, because if the difference could be zero, the two incomes could be the same. Since we are confident that the difference is not zero, however, as zero lies outside the confidence interval, we are confident that there is a difference, which indicates higher pay for men based on the information.

Here's an example of a study involving an experiment.

Example
A school has applied an experimental teaching strategy in the current school year and would like to see whether it helps students' academic performance. Two similar groups of students are randomly chosen. For the students involved in the new teaching strategy, the average test score is 85, whereas the average score of students in the control group is 82. The margin of error of the difference between the two groups

is 5.5. Should the school be confident that the new teaching strategy is helping the students?

Solution: Difference of average scores = 85 − 82 = 3, which is the estimator.

Confidence interval = estimator ± margin of error = 3 ± 5.5 = −2.5 to 8.5.

Since the confidence interval includes zero, which represents no difference, the school should not be confident enough of the new teaching strategy. We cannot conclude that the experimental teaching strategy is an improvement over existing methods.

Independence and Conditional Probability

Definition: *Experiment* is a process from which an observation (outcome) is obtained.

Definition: *Sample space (S)* is the set of all possible outcomes.

Definition: *Event* is a collection of possible outcomes. It is a subset of sample space.

Example
Roll a die and observe the number facing up.

Experiment:
Sample space (S) = {1, 2, 3, 4, 5, 6}

Some potential events:

Event A: An even number is observed.
Event B: A prime number is observed.
Thus, A = {2, 4, 6}, B = {2, 3, 5}.

Definition: A *Venn diagram* is a visualized summary of events and sample space.

Let's return to the previous example regarding rolling a die and observing the number facing up. The Venn diagram of event A (even number) and event B (prime number) would look like this:

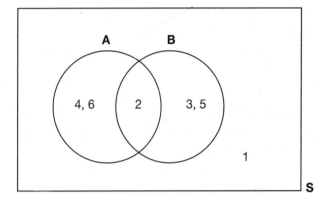

Now we'll turn to some definitions regarding event operation:

Definition: *Union (or)* is the probability that at least one of two events (A,B) will occur.

Notation: Union of events A, B: $A \cup B$

Note: Union is usually referred as "or"; thus, $A \cup B$ can be referred to as "A or B," which means event A occurs, or event B occurs, or both event A and event B occur.

Definition: *Intersection (and)* is the probability that both events (A,B) will occur.

Notation: Intersection of events A, B: $A \cap B$

Note: Intersection is usually referred as "and"; thus $A \cap B$ can be referred as "A and B," which means both A and B occur.

Definition: *Complement (not)* is the probability that an event (A) will not occur.

Notation: Complement of event A: A^C

Returning to the example of rolling a die and observing the number facing up, we can observe the concepts of union, intersection, and complement.

> Event A: An even number is observed.
> Event B: A prime number is observed.

Thus,

> A = {2, 4, 6}
> B = {2, 3, 5}

Sample space (S) = {1, 2, 3, 4, 5, 6}

> $A \cup B$ = {2, 3, 4, 5, 6}
> $A \cap B$ = {2}
> A^C = {1, 3, 5}
> B^C = {1, 4, 6}

Venn diagram:

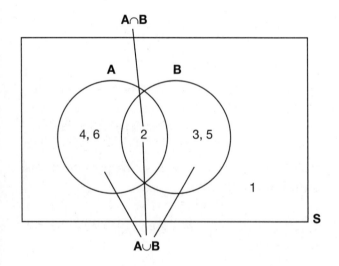

Definition: If two events (A, B) are *mutually exclusive*, they cannot both occur. If one event occurs, the other cannot.

Definition: If two events (A, B) are *independent*, one event happening or not happening does not change the probability that the other event will occur.

Example

Describe the relationship between event A and event B.

> Event A: Observe a "6" when tossing a die.
> Event B: Observe a head when flipping a coin.

Solution: Event A and event B are independent.

Consider the following questions regarding relationships between events:

> If you toss a die and observe a "6," what is the chance that a head will be observed in flipping a coin?
> If you toss a die and do not observe a "6," what is the chance that a head will be observed in flipping coin?
> Do event A (observing or not observing a "6") and event B (showing a head in a coin toss) affect the probability of each other?

Probability Calculation

Notation: $P(A)$ represents the probability that event A will occur.

Events A, B are independent if and only if $A \cap B = P(A)P(B)$.

Example

If you toss a coin two times, what is the probability that two heads will be observed?

Solution: The result of the second toss can be considered to be independent of the first toss. Therefore, the probability of observing two heads is expressed as follows:

> Probability of head in first toss × probability of head in second toss = 0.5 × 0.5 = 0.25
> If a die is tossed twice, what is the probability that the sum of the two numbers will be 10?

Solution: The results of the two tosses are independent to each other; thus we can apply $P(A \cap B) = P(A)P(B)$ again. We also need to consider, however, the different possibilities of getting a 10 in two tosses, which include 4 and 6, 5 and 5, 6 and 4.

Therefore,
$P(\text{sum} = 10) = P(4 \text{ and } 6) + P(5 \text{ and } 5) + P(6 \text{ and } 4)$
$= \left(\frac{1}{6} \times \frac{1}{6}\right) + \left(\frac{1}{6} \times \frac{1}{6}\right) + \left(\frac{1}{6} \times \frac{1}{6}\right) = \frac{3}{36} = \frac{1}{12}.$

Conditional Probability

Notation: $P(A|B)$ indicates the probability that event A will happen given that event B has occurred. The vertical line means "given"; and event B is the given information.

Notation: $P(B|A)$ indicates that probability that event B will happen given that event A has occurred. The vertical line means "given"; and event A is the given information.

Note: $P(A|B)$ and $P(B|A)$ are *not* the same.

Example
Roll a die and observe the number facing up.

Event A: An even number is observed.
Event B: A multiple of 3 is observed.
We write $A = \{2, 4, 6\}$, $B = \{3, 6\}$.

$P(A|B)$ = Probability that an even number is observed given the number is a multiple of 3.
$P(A|B) = \frac{1}{2}$. Given that the number is a multiple of 3, the number could be 3 or 6. Since 6 is even, the chance is 1 out of 2.
Similarly, $P(B|A) = \frac{1}{3}$

Calculating Conditional Probabilities

Formulas: $P(B|A) = \frac{P(A \cap B)}{P(A)}$, $P(A|B) = \frac{P(A \cap B)}{P(B)}$

Example
In a college, 34% of the students are taking a math class, 19% of the students are taking a biology class, and 8% of the students are taking both math and biology. If one student is randomly chosen from the college, find the probability that the student is taking:

a. math, given the student is taking biology
b. biology, given the student is taking math

Solution: Define event A: taking math, and event B: taking biology.
Then, $P(A) = 0.34$, $P(B) = 0.19$, $P(A \cap B) = 0.08$.
The probability that the student is taking a math class, given the student is taking a biology class, is equivalent to $P(A|B)$.
The probability that the student is taking a biology class, given the student is taking a math class, is *equivalent* to $P(B|A)$.

Therefore,

a. $P(A|B) = \frac{P(A \cap B)}{P(B)} = \frac{0.08}{0.19} = 0.421$
b. $P(B|A) = \frac{P(A \cap B)}{P(A)} = \frac{0.08}{0.34} = 0.235$

If event A and event B are independent, then $P(A \cap B) = P(A)P(B)$, and $P(B|A) = \frac{P(A \cap B)}{P(A)} = \frac{P(A)P(B)}{P(A)} = P(B)$.
Similarly, $P(A|B) = P(A)$ when event A and event B are independent.

In summary, if the events are independent, the following are equivalent:

i. A and B are independent.
ii. $P(A \cap B) = P(A)P(B)$
iii. $P(B|A) = P(B)$
iv. $P(A|B) = P(A)$

Example

One person is randomly chosen.

Event A: The person is female.
Event B: The person is elderly.

Are the two events independent?

Solution: This question can be answered using general knowledge without actual probability.

- Think about $P(A)$, the probability that the person is a female, which can be considered as the percentage of females in the population.
- Think about $P(A|B)$, the probability that the person is female given the person is elderly. If you think $P(A|B)$ is close to $P(A)$, the two events could be independent. On the other hand, if you think they are different (one of them is higher), the two events should not be independent.
- Given the person is elderly, do you think the person is more likely or less likely to be female? If the answer is more likely, the events are not independent because knowing the age of the person as elderly will change your thinking on the probability of the person's sex.

Many studies have shown females to have a longer life expectancy than males. Therefore, there are usually more females than males in the elderly population. This leads us to conclude that $P(A|B)$ is usually different from $P(A)$ (more specifically, higher); so event A (being female) and event B (being elderly) should not be considered independent events.

A similar argument could be applied to situations involving education and income. Education and income should not be considered independent events, because people with higher education levels tend to have higher income.

Events Operation and Probability Calculation

General Multiplication Rule

By the definition of conditional probability, $P(A|B) = \frac{P(A \cap B)}{P(B)}$, which, according to the general multiplication rule, can be rewritten as $P(A \cap B) = P(B)P(A|B)$.

Similarly, $P(B|A) = \frac{P(A \cap B)}{P(A)}$ can be rewritten as $P(A \cap B) = P(A)P(B|A)$.

Example

Two pieces of chalk are chosen from four pieces of chalk (three white, one red) *without replacement*. Find the probability that both of them are white.

(*Note: Without replacement* means the object will not be put back after being chosen. In the case of choosing with replacement, the chosen object will be put back after being chosen.)

Solution: Two chalks are chosen, and both of them are white. That means the first chalk is white and the second one is also white.

By the general multiplication rule, the probability of two white chalks can be interpreted as the probability that the first one is white, multiplied by the probability that the second one is white given that the first one is white.

Therefore, the probability that the first chalk is white $= \frac{3}{4}$.

The probability that the second one is white given the first one is white $= \frac{2}{3}$, as there is one less chalk, a white one, after the first pick:

$$P(2W) = \frac{3}{4} \times \frac{2}{3} = \frac{1}{2}$$

Addition Rule for Union

$$P(A \cup B) = P(A) + P(B) - P(A \cap B)$$

The addition rule is a *general rule*, which means it always works.

Example
In a college, 37% of the students are taking a math class, 17% are taking a biology class, and 9% of the students are taking both a math class and a biology class. If one student is randomly chosen from the college, find the probability that the student is taking a math class or a biology class, and then provide a Venn diagram.

Solution: Define event A: taking a math class, and event B: taking a biology class.

Then $P(A) = 0.37$, $P(B) = 0.17$, $P(A \cap B) = 0.09$.

By the formula, $P(A \cup B) = P(A) + P(B) - P(A \cap B) = 0.37 + 0.17 - 0.09 = 0.45$.

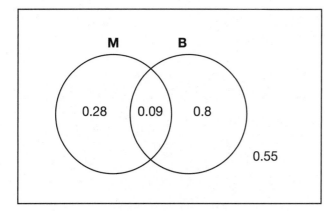

Here, the circle labeled M represents math, and 0.28 inside represents the portion of students taking math but not biology: $0.37 - 0.09$.

The circle labeled B represents biology, and 0.08 inside represents the portion of students taking biology but not math: $0.17 - 0.09$.

The number 0.55 represents the portion of students taking neither math nor biology: $1 - 0.45$.

Thus, we can conclude:

The probability that a student is taking math but not biology = 0.28.

The probability that a student is taking math or biology but not both = $0.28 + 0.08 = 0.36$.

Mutually Exclusive

Two events (A,B) are mutually exclusive if the two events cannot happen at the same time.

If events A, B are mutually exclusive, then $P(A \cap B) = 0$, and using the addition rule can be simplified to $P(A \cup B) = P(A) + P(B)$.

Example

	A	A^C
B	0.35	0.2
B^C	0.3	0.15

a. Compute: $P(A)$, $P(B)$, $P(A \cap B)$, $P(A|B)$, and $P(B|A)$.

Solution:
$P(A) = 0.35 + 0.3 = 0.65$ $P(B) = 0.35 + 0.2 = 0.55$
$P(A \cap B) = 0.35$
$P(A|B) = \frac{P(A \cap B)}{P(B)} = \frac{0.35}{0.55} = 0.636$
$P(B|A) = \frac{P(A \cap B)}{P(A)} = \frac{0.35}{0.65} = 0.538$

b. Are A, B mutually exclusive? Explain your answer.

Solution: $P(A \cap B) = 0.35$, which is not zero. Therefore, event A and event B are not mutually exclusive.

c. Are A, B independent? Explain your answer.

Solution: $P(A|B) \neq P(A)$. Therefore, event A and event B are not independent.

Rule for Complements

$P(A) = 1 - P(A^C)$ or $P(A^C) = 1 - P(A)$

Calculating Probability with Binomial Distribution

Binomial distribution refers to an experiment with repeating independent identical trials. In each trial there are two possible outcomes—success or failure.

Consider an experiment consisting of n independent identical trials. If the probability of success is p and the probability of failure is q ($q = 1 - p$), then the probability of observing k successes would be expressed as follows:

Combination

$$P(k) = C_k^n p^k q^{n-k}$$

The formula is interpreted as follows:

n = number of trials of the experiment	
k = number of successes	p = probability of success
$n - k$ = number of failures	q = probability of failure

Example

A coin is tossed five times. Find the following probabilities:

a. Two heads will be observed.
b. At most four heads will be observed.

Solution: This is an example of binomial distribution with number of trials $n = 5$, probability of heads $p = 0.5$, and probability of tails $q = 0.5$.

a. $P(2) = C_2^5(0.5)^2(0.5)^{5-2} = 10 \times 0.25 \times 0.125$
   $= 0.3125$

b. $P(\leq 4) = 1 - P(5) = 1 - C_5^5(0.5)^5(0.5)^{5-5}$
   $= 1 - (1 \times 0.03125 \times 1) = 0.96875$

Example

An arrow is shot at the following target plane, and the arrow is considered safe if it is located at least 10 meters from the edge of the plane. Assuming the position where the arrow landed is uniformly random throughout the plane, what is the probability the arrow would land on safe territory?

50 meters

80 meters

Solution: The arrow would be safe if it is at least 10 meters from the edge; so it would be safe as long as it lands on the dark region in the following diagram.

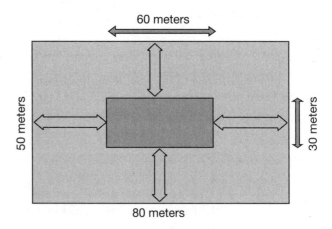

60 meters

50 meters

30 meters

80 meters

Since the landing position is uniformly random, the chance of landing on the dark region (the safe region) would be the ratio of the dark rectangle to the original rectangle $= \frac{60 \times 30}{80 \times 50} = 0.45$.

Random Variable and Expected Value

There are two important points to remember about a random variable:

1. It corresponds to the outcomes of the experiment.
2. It associates with probabilities.

Example

Roll a fair die and observe the number. Let X = the number facing up. X is a random variable.

In the case of fair dice, the six possible outcomes are equally likely to occur, which is shown in the probability distribution of X table:

X	1	2	3	4	5	6
P(X)	$\frac{1}{6}$	$\frac{1}{6}$	$\frac{1}{6}$	$\frac{1}{6}$	$\frac{1}{6}$	$\frac{1}{6}$

Note: The sum of all probabilities is the sum of all numbers in the row $P(X) = 1$.

Population Mean of a Random Variable (Expected Value)

Definition: The *expected value* (the mean) is the weighted average of the random variable.

Expected Value Formula:
$$E(X) = \mu = \Sigma xp(x) \text{ and}$$
$$\mu = \Sigma xp(x) = x_1p(x_1) + x_2p(x_2) + \ldots x_np(x_n)$$

Let's look at expected value with regard to the previous example of rolling a fair die where X = the number facing up:

$$E(X) = 1\left(\frac{1}{6}\right) + 2\left(\frac{1}{6}\right) + 3\left(\frac{1}{6}\right) + 4\left(\frac{1}{6}\right) + 5\left(\frac{1}{6}\right) + 6\left(\frac{1}{6}\right) = 3.5$$

Expected value can be thought of as the long-run average if the experiment is repeated many times. In the example of tossing the die, the expected value = 3.5, which means if the die is tossed many times, the average of all the numbers observed will be 3.5.

Example

Suppose a die is manufactured in such a way that the probability of observing an even number is two times that of observing an odd number.

a. If the die is tossed once and the number (X) is observed,
   i. Construct a table of the probability distribution of X.
   ii. Compute the expected value.
b. If the die is tossed twice and the sum of the two numbers (Y) is observed, what is the probability that the sum will be 11 or higher?

Solutions:

a. i. Since the chance of getting an even number is twice that of getting an odd number, we can put the probability of observing 1, 3, 5 as A, and the probability of observing 2, 4, 6 as $2A$.

X	1	2	3	4	5	6
P(X)	A	2A	A	2A	A	2A

$$A + 2A + A + 2A + A + 2A = 1$$

The sum of all probabilities = 1. Therefore, $9A = 1$.

$$A = \frac{1}{9}$$

And the table could be rewritten as:

X	1	2	3	4	5	6
P(X)	$\frac{1}{9}$	$\frac{2}{9}$	$\frac{1}{9}$	$\frac{2}{9}$	$\frac{1}{9}$	$\frac{2}{9}$

  ii. $E(X) = 1(\frac{1}{9}) + 2(\frac{2}{9}) + 3(\frac{1}{9}) + 4(\frac{2}{9}) + 5(\frac{1}{9}) + 6(\frac{2}{9}) = \frac{33}{9} = 3.667$

b. To generate the sum of at least 11 in two throws, the two numbers could be 5 and 6 or 6 and 5 to give 11, or 6 and 6 to give 12.

$P(11 \text{ or higher}) = P(5 \text{ and } 6) + P(6 \text{ and } 5) + P(6 \text{ and } 6)$
$= (\frac{1}{9} \times \frac{2}{9}) + (\frac{2}{9} \times \frac{1}{9}) + (\frac{2}{9} \times \frac{2}{9}) = \frac{8}{81}$

Example

A study is conducted of the number of classes taken by students in the current semester. The results are summarized in the following table:

NUMBER OF CLASSES	1	2	3	4	5
Percentage	8%	11%	24%	43%	14%

The percentages can be understood as the probabilities of picking a student at random who is taking the corresponding number of classes.

The expected value of number of classes taken = average number of classes a student is taking, which is calculated: $1(0.08) + 2(0.11) + 3(0.24) + 4(0.43) + 5(0.14) = 3.42$.

Example

Compute the expected returns of the following two investment plans:

Gain/loss	+10,000	+5,000	0	−5,000	−10,000
Probability	0.2	0.35	0.2	0.15	0.1

Gain/loss	+15,000	+5,000	−5,000	−10,000
Probability	0.2	0.2	0.3	0.3

Solution: The expected return of an investment is the expected gain or loss. By calculating the weighted averages, the expected return of the first investment plan is +2,000 whereas the expected return of the second one is −500. On average, there is a gain from the first investment and a loss from the second one. In investments, expected return is one of the indicators people usually look at. Since people want a positive return on their investments, the second plan is unattractive to investors.

Interestingly, lotteries and casino games are examples where the expected return for the players is negative. Because of the house edge, the house is making money as the players are losing in the long run. All of those games are unfair in the sense that the payoff to the player is negative.

Expected value, however, is not the only considering factor in decision making. Consider the following two investment options.

Option 1:

Profit/loss (X)	2,000
Probability	1.00

Option 2:

Profit/loss (X)	80,000	−60,000
Probability	0.45	0.55

The second option gives a higher expected return, but it also comes with a much higher risk. There's more than a 50% chance of a potential loss of $60,000. Option 2 is an example of high-risk investment.

Expected value is an important factor in making a decision, but the decision should be tempered by the risk involved.

Experimental Probability Distributions and Theoretical Probability Distribution

A die is tossed 6,000 times by simulations, and the number of times each number faces up is summarized in the following table:

1	2	3	4	5	6
1,012	966	1,002	1,034	970	1,016

Let X = the number that faces up. The probability distribution of X can be given as

X	1	2	3	4	5	6
P	0.1687	0.161	0.167	0.17233	0.16167	0.16933

P is found by dividing the number of times each number faces up by 6,000 tosses.

The distribution can be given by the following histogram:

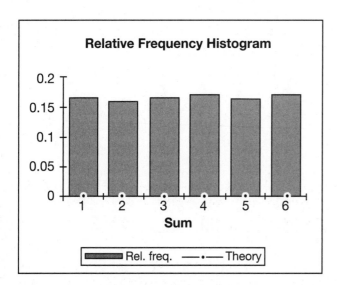

If the die is fair, the probability of observing each of the six values would be equally likely with a probability of $\frac{1}{6}$ each. The frequency of each value appearing should be close to 1,000. All six values appeared quite evenly, and the frequencies of all six are close to 1,000. Therefore, the die is a fair one or at least very close to being a fair one.

Probabilities Calculation with Independent Trials

Example
When a biased coin is flipped, there is a $\frac{3}{4}$ chance that it will land heads, and a $\frac{1}{4}$ chance it will land tails. If the coin is tossed four times, what is the probability that three heads will be observed?

Solution: First, calculate the probability that a sequence of three heads will be observed, for example, HHHT:

$$P(HHHT) = \frac{3}{4} \times \frac{3}{4} \times \frac{3}{4} \times \frac{1}{4} = \frac{27}{256}$$

Next, multiply it by the combination factor, the number of different ways that the heads and tails can be arranged. In the case of three heads, the possibilities are *HHHT, HHTH, HTHH,* and *THHH*.

Therefore, $P(3H1T) = \frac{27}{256} \times 4 = \frac{27}{64}$

Example
The same coin from the previous example is tossed four times; what is the probability that two heads will be observed?

Solution: First, calculate the probability that a sequence of two heads will be observed, for example, *HHTT*:

$$P(HHTT) = \frac{3}{4} \times \frac{3}{4} \times \frac{1}{4} \times \frac{1}{4} = \frac{9}{256}$$

Next, multiply it by the combination factor, which is 6.

Therefore, $P(2H2T) = \frac{9}{256} \times 6 = \frac{27}{128}$

Note: This kind of question can also be solved using binomial distribution.

10 ▶ DISCRETE MATHEMATICS REVIEW

CHAPTER SUMMARY

Discrete mathematics is the study of mathematical objects, structures, and patterns whose natures can be most aptly described in terms of their isolation or separateness. Discrete objects can be enumerated using the integers—in fact, the integers themselves are one of the most basic kinds of discrete mathematical structures that one can encounter. Discrete mathematics—which involves the study of things like probability, combinatorics, graph theory, set theory, and logic—can be contrasted with continuous mathematics, such as the study of continuous functions and calculus. In this chapter we cover some of the basic topics of discrete mathematics that could show up on the Praxis II® Mathematics exam, as well as discuss the contrast of discrete mathematics versus continuous mathematics.

Understanding Sequences

Our review of discrete mathematics will first take us to the study of sequences. Strictly speaking, we may define a sequence as follows:

Definition: A sequence is a function whose domain is a subset of the nonnegative (or positive) integers. We will follow the convention of using a subset of the positive integers as the domain set.

Note that a sequence may be finite or infinite. Also note that since the domain is always understood to be a set of the integers, it is often omitted, and we usually define a sequence based on its range, or output values. Thus, we may also think of a sequence as *a list of numbers or objects that follow a certain rule*. The rule may be mathematical or not, but we will of course focus on sequences where the underlying rule is a mathematical one.

Notation: A sequence is usually described in one of three forms, and the reader should be familiar with each: a list, a recursive formula, or a closed-form formula. (A list is understandable, but the reader should recall that a recursive formula is one in which new terms are determined by a formula involving one or several previous terms, while a closed-form formula is one where any term can be determined by a function of the position of the term. This will be made more clear later.) The elements of the range or the terms of the sequence may be described by a lowercase letter with a subscript indicating their position in the sequence. So, for example, the first term in a sequence could be denoted a_1, the second a_2, the fifth a_5, and so on. The reader may also recall that saying a_1, a_2, a_3, and so forth, is equivalent to saying $a(1)$, $a(2)$, $a(3)$, and so on, if we want to think of the sequence as a function. Examples of the three forms a sequence may be displayed as follows:

> **Example**
> Let's start simply and take the set of positive integers themselves as a sequence. We may describe this sequence in three ways, as:

- a list: 1, 2, 3, 4, 5, 6, …
- a recursive formula: $a_1 = 1$, $a_n = a_{n-1} + 1$ for each $n > 1$
- a closed-form formula: $a_n = n$ for all integers $n \geq 1$

Now that we have recalled what a sequence is, let's talk about the kinds of sequences and how to solve problems involving them.

Two very important kinds of sequences to know are the arithmetic sequence and the geometric sequence.

The Arithmetic Sequence

An *arithmetic sequence* is one that arises from adding a specific constant repeatedly. This constant is called the *common difference*.

A *recursive formula* for such a sequence would be:

$$a_n = a_{n-1} + d, \text{ for } n > 1$$

where a_n is the nth term of the sequence, a_{n-1} is the previous term, and d is the common difference.

A *closed-form formula* for such a sequence would be:

$$a_n = a_1 + (n-1)d$$

where a_n is the nth term of the sequence, a_1 is the first term, and d is the common difference.

The Geometric Sequence

A *geometric sequence* is one that arises from multiplying by a specific constant repeatedly. This constant is called the *common ratio*.

A *recursive formula* for such a sequence would be:

$$a_n = r \cdot a_{n-1}, \text{ for } n > 1$$

where a_n is the nth term of the sequence, a_{n-1} is the previous term, and r is the common ratio; the $\cdot$ refers to multiplication.

A *closed-form formula* for such a sequence would be:

$$a_n = a_1 \cdot r^{n-1}$$

where a_n is the nth term of the sequence, a_1 is the first term, and r is the common ratio.

Determining Arithmetic or Geometric Squence

The easy way to determine which of these sequences you are dealing with is by trying to see if there is a common difference or ratio.

You know you're dealing with an arithmetic sequence if the *difference* between successive terms is constant—that is, if $a_2 - a_1 = a_3 - a_2 = a_4 - a_3 = \ldots = d$, a constant.

You know you're dealing with a geometric sequence if the *ratio* of successive terms is a constant—that is, if $\frac{a_2}{a_1} = \frac{a_3}{a_2} = \frac{a_4}{a_3} = \ldots = r$, a constant.

Example

Identify whether the following sequences are arithmetic, geometric, or neither. If arithmetic or geometric, write down the recursive and closed-form formulas for the sequence. Otherwise, could you figure out the rule or pattern being used?

a. $-5, -2, 1, 4, 7, \ldots$

b. $\frac{1}{2}, -\frac{1}{3}, \frac{2}{9}, -\frac{4}{27}, \ldots$

c. $3, \frac{3}{2}, \frac{3}{4}, \frac{3}{8}, \frac{3}{16}, \ldots$

d. $3, 5, 8, 12, 17, \ldots$

e. $1, 4, 9, 16, 25, \ldots$

f. $57, 53, 49, 45, \ldots$

g. $1, 3, 6, 8, 16, 18, 36, \ldots$

h. $4, 31, 301, 3,001, 30,001, \ldots$

i. $1, 3, 6, 11, 18, 29, \ldots$ (what would be the next term in this sequence?)

j. $3, 9, 27, 81, 243, \ldots$

k. $3, \frac{5}{2}, \frac{7}{4}, \frac{9}{8}, \frac{11}{16}, \frac{13}{32}, \ldots$

(Try to figure these out on your own first, and then go to the solutions.)

Solution:

a. Here, the sequence is $-5, -2, 1, 4, 7, \ldots$ Note here that we have $a_1 = -5, a_2 = -2, a_3 = 1$, and so on.

Moreover, we have: $a_2 - a_1 = 3, a_3 - a_2 = 3$, $a_4 - a_3 = 3$, and so on. This means we have a common difference of 3. (We can easily check this; note that to go to the next term, we simply add 3 to the previous term.) Therefore, *this is an arithmetic sequence!* Knowing that the common difference is $d = 3$ and the first term is $a_1 = 5$, we can write down the recursive and closed-form formulas for this sequence.

Recursive: $a_1 = -5, a_n = a_{n-1} + 3$, for $n > 1$.
Closed-form: $a_n = -5 + (n-1) \cdot 3$, for all $n \geq 1$.

Or we can simplify and write $a_n = -8 + 3n$, for all $n \geq 1$.

b. Here, the sequence is $\frac{1}{2}, -\frac{1}{3}, \frac{2}{9}, -\frac{4}{27}, \ldots$ We see that $a_2 - a_1 = -\frac{1}{3} - \frac{1}{2} = -\frac{5}{6}$, while $a_3 - a_2 = \frac{2}{9} - (-\frac{1}{3}) = \frac{5}{9}$. So there is no common difference here! The difference of successive terms varies. Thus, this is not an arithmetic series. Let us see if it is geometric. $\frac{a_2}{a_1} = -\frac{2}{3} = \frac{a_3}{a_2} = \frac{a_4}{a_3} \ldots$, so it is a geometric sequence! The common ratio here is $= -\frac{2}{3}$, and one can double-check this by checking that to get to each new term, you would multiply the previous term by $-\frac{2}{3}$. Since the first term is $a_1 = \frac{1}{2}$, we can write down the recursive and closed-form formulas for this sequence.

Recursive: $a_1 = \frac{1}{2}, a_n = -\frac{2}{3} \cdot a_{n-1}$, for $n > 1$.
Closed-form: $a_n = \frac{1}{2} \cdot (-\frac{2}{3})^{n-1}$, for all $n \geq 1$.

c. Here the sequence is $3, \frac{3}{2}, \frac{3}{4}, \frac{3}{8}, \frac{3}{16}, \ldots$ There is no common difference; however, there is a common ratio of $r = \frac{1}{2}$ and a first term of $a_1 = 3$. Hence we have that this is a geometric sequence with:

Recursive: $a_1 = 3, a_n = \frac{1}{2} \cdot a_{n-1}$, for $n > 1$.
Closed-form: $a_n = 3 \cdot (\frac{1}{2})^{n-1}$, for all $n \geq 1$.

(Note that the terms of this sequence could have been written as: $\frac{3}{2^0}, \frac{3}{2^1}, \frac{3}{2^2}, \frac{3}{2^3}, \ldots$)

So we see the powers of a certain number showing up, while all other parts of the term remain the same. This happens if you're looking at a geometric sequence, so it is a pattern you should look out for.)

d. Here the sequence is 3, 5, 8, 12, 17, ... The reader can check that there is no common difference or common ratio here, so this sequence is neither an arithmetic nor a geometric sequence.

However, notice a pattern going on here. Namely, we are adding consecutive integers to arrive at new terms. To get the second term, we added 2 to the first term. To get the third term, we added 3 to the second term. We added 4 to the third term to get the fourth term, and added 5 to the fourth term to get the fifth term.

Thus, though it is not required of us to do this for problem (d), note that, based on the pattern we have seen, a recursive formula for this sequence would be:

$a_1 = 3, a_n = a_{n-1} + n$, for $n > 1$

Finding a closed-form formula would be a tad more difficult, but it could be determined that a closed-form formula would be:

$a_n = \left(n\frac{1}{2}\right)^2 + \frac{1}{2}n + 2$, for all $n \geq 1$

We will discuss a method for determining the closed form in this case shortly. It is called the *method of common differences*.

e. Here the sequence is 1, 4, 9, 16, 25, ... Since there is no common difference or ratio, this sequence is neither arithmetic nor geometric.

Again, in this case, look for a pattern. Do you see it? It's squaring! That is the rule. The closed form for this sequence is:

$a_n = n^2$, for all $n \geq 1$

You may be able to see this by inspection, but if not, the method of common differences

could be used here, as well. (Again, we'll talk about this later. Be patient!)

To write a recursive formula here would be sort of awkward or silly, but it could be done.

Recursive: $a_1 = 1, a_n = (\sqrt{a_{n-1}} + 1)^2$, for $n > 1$.

f. Here the sequence is 57, 53, 49, 45, ... It appears we always subtract 4 from the previous term to get the next term. And one can check that $a_2 - a_1 = -4$, $a_3 - a_2 = -4$, and so on, so that we have a common difference of −4. Since the first term is $a_1 = 57$, we can say that this is an arithmetic sequence with:

Recursive: $a_1 = 57, a_n = a_{n-1} - 4$, for $n > 1$.

Closed-form: $a_n = 57 + (n-1) \cdot (-4)$, for $n \geq 1$.

Or simply, $a_n = 61 - 4n$, for $n \geq 1$.

g. Here the sequence is 1, 3, 6, 8, 16, 18, 36, ... There is no common difference or common ratio; hence, this sequence is neither arithmetic nor geometric.

For fun, let's explore the pattern here. Beginning at the first term we added 2, then 3, then 2, then 8, then 2, then 18. *Hmmm*, there is a pattern of adding 2 at every other term. But for the remaining terms, what is the pattern? Well, one pattern is that for the other terms, they are always double the previous term. So the rule here would be:

Recursive: $a_1 = 1$, and

$$a_n = \begin{cases} a_{n-1} + 2, & \text{if } n \text{ is even} \\ 2 \cdot a_{n-1}, & \text{if } n \text{ is odd} \end{cases}, \text{ for } n > 1.$$

That is, we add 2 to the previous term to get to an even term and multiply the previous term by 2 to get to an odd term—a somewhat interesting, two-pronged rule (add 2 then multiply by 2, add 2 then multiply by 2, ...). Finding a closed-form rule here would be difficult, if at all possible.

h. Here the sequence is 4, 31, 301, 3,001, 30,001, . . . Again, there is no common difference or ratio, so the sequence is neither arithmetic nor geometric.

The 4 at the beginning seems sort of out of place, but let's not get thrown for a loop. There clearly seems to be a pattern for the other numbers. So let's work on that and see if we can extend the pattern to the first term as well.

There is always a 1 at the end, so let's isolate that. Note that we can write the terms as

4, 30 + 1, 300 + 1, 3,000 + 1, etc.

Ah! This can work for the first term as well, if we think of 4 as 3 + 1. Hence, the sequence is

3 + 1, 30 + 1, 300 + 1, 3,000 + 1, etc.

Things are becoming clearer! We seem to have 3 times a power of 10 plus 1 in each case.

$3 \cdot 10^0 + 1, 3 \cdot 10^1 + 1, 3 \cdot 10^2 + 1, 3 \cdot 10^3 + 1$, etc.

And voilà! We can see that the rule here can be given in closed form by

$a_n = 3 \cdot 10^{n-1} + 1$, for $n \geq 1$

So this sequence was *almost* geometric. You just added a 1 to each term.

i. Here the sequence is 1, 3, 6, 11, 18, 29, . . . And by now we're getting used to this game. We check for a common difference. None! Check for a common ratio. Zip! Hence this sequence is neither arithmetic nor geometric.

The pattern? We kept adding successive prime numbers! Beginning at the first term we added 2, then 3, then 5, then 7, then 11, and so on.

Can we write out a mathematical rule for this? Well, considering that anyone has yet to come up with a formula for the nth prime

number, we think not. We can say the rule in words, however, and, more important, we can figure out what the next term would be. The next prime number is 13, and hence the next term in the sequence is 29 + 13 = 42.

j. The sequence is 3, 9, 27, 81, 243, . . . , which is not so bad.

It is a geometric sequence with common ratio $r = 3$. So we have:

Recursive: $a_1 = 3, a_n = 3 \cdot a_{n-1}$, for $n > 1$.
Closed-form: $a_n = 3 \cdot 3^{n-1} = 3^n$, for $n \geq 1$.

We could notice this is geometric by taking the common ratio or by realizing that this sequence is simply listing powers of 3. In either case, this example was brought up to explore a pattern when using the method of finite differences. (Again, be patient, we'll get to it, and it'll be worth it!)

k. The last sequence is $3, \frac{5}{2}, \frac{7}{4}, \frac{9}{8}, \frac{11}{16}, \frac{13}{32}, \ldots$ which seems weird at first. There is no common difference or ratio, so the sequence is neither arithmetic nor geometric.

Pattern? Well, there seem to be two. First, note that we could write this as:

$$\frac{3}{2^0}, \frac{5}{2}, \frac{7}{4}, \frac{9}{8}, \frac{11}{16}, \frac{13}{32}, \ldots$$

We see that the denominators are powers of 2. So the denominators follow a geometric pattern. However, since the numerators change, it is not geometric. So, what of the numerators? They seem to follow an arithmetic pattern! The first term is 3 and the common difference is 2. It appears then, that a closed-form formula could be a combination of the arithmetic and geometric closed-form formulas. And that works! We get:

$$a_n = \frac{3 + (n-1) \cdot 2}{2^{n-1}}, \text{ for } n \geq 1$$

or, more simply,

$$a_n = \frac{1 + 2n}{2^{n-1}}, \text{ for } n \geq 1$$

Now that we're done with some basic examples of sequences, let's take a broader look at the subject.

Number Patterns That Give Rise to Sequences

Before going on to more examples involving arithmetic and geometric sequences, let's look more generally at some number patterns that give rise to them.

At the end of the day, an arithmetic sequence is simply a sequence whose closed form is given by a linear equation, whereas a geometric sequence is a sequence whose closed form is given by a single-termed exponential equation. But a linear equation is just a special case of a polynomial. And a single-termed exponential equation is a special case as well. What of the more general cases?

Suppose one encounters a sequence that is neither arithmetic nor geometric, but one wishes to find a formula for it. If the closed-form formula of the sequence is a polynomial, then it can be found by the method of common differences.

The idea: The differences between successive terms are constant for an arithmetic sequence. But suppose you don't get a constant. Then, you may try to find the common difference of the sequences of differences, and so on, until you get a constant. If you eventually get a constant, then the closed form formula for the sequence is a polynomial. The degree of the polynomial is determined by how many steps it took to get to a constant. So, if it took one step, then the degree is one—a linear polynomial, and the sequence is arithmetic. If it takes two steps, the degree is two, and the closed form is a second-degree polynomial (i.e., a quadratic). If it took three steps, then your closed form is a cubic, and so on.

Let's illustrate this with part (d) of the earlier example. Recall that the sequence is 3, 5, 8, 12, 17, . . .

The consecutive differences are 2, 3, 4, 5, . . . , so there is no common difference. However, the consecutive differences of the new sequence of differences are 1, 1, 1, 1, . . . so we get a constant (common) difference on the second step. This is how we would know we could represent this using a quadratic. To illustrate, we can look at the following figure:

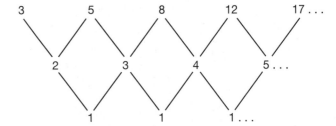

Clearly we see that the last line is just a constant sequence (there are just 1's). It doesn't matter what the constant is, just that it is constant. This means that a polynomial gives the closed form. But how do we obtain the polynomial?

Well, assume the polynomial can be written in the form

$$a_n = an^2 + bn + c$$

(Be careful not to confuse a with an a_n; in general, a is just a coefficient in our polynomial, not a term in the sequence.)

This means we have (by plugging in values for n):

$$a_1 = 3 = a + b + c$$

$$a_2 = 5 = 4a + 2b + c$$

$$a_3 = 8 = 9a + 3b + c$$

Thus, we obtain a system of three equations and three unknowns. Our discussion on matrix algebra shows us that (if a solution exists) we don't need any more equations to find it. Furthermore, we know how to solve the system using matrix algebra or some other algebraic method, like Cramer's Rule, or the elimination method or the substitution method.

Here, the solution is $a = \frac{1}{2}, b = \frac{1}{2}, c = 2$.

And that's how we obtained that the sequence was given by:

$$a_n = \frac{1}{2}n^2 + \frac{1}{2}n + 2$$

Let's look at problem (j). The method of common differences yields:

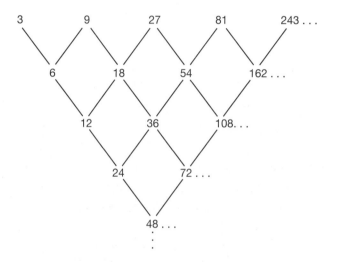

As it turns out, we will never obtain a common difference—which means this sequence cannot be represented by a polynomial. However, we have a pattern. The top-left-to-bottom-right diagonals have a multiplication pattern! Notice that to move down the diagonal, you would multiply the diagonal entries by 2 repeatedly. The rule? In geometric sequences, the said diagonals are always multiplied by a constant, namely, 1 less than the common ratio. Here, you see the diagonals are multiplied by 2; hence, we know that this sequence is a geometric sequence with common ratio $2 + 1 = 3$. This is a more complicated way to get to the answer, surely, but if you never realized in the first place that this was geometric sequence and tried the method of common differences, it would give you a second chance to figure it out.

Translating between Recursive and Closed-Form Formulas

Closed-form formulas are very convenient formulas to have. You can essentially determine any member of a sequence without knowing the values of any of the others simply by plugging in the position that you're looking for. However, there are cases where you are only given a recursive formula. This can be quite inconvenient to deal with. For example, suppose you're given a recursive formula for a sequence in which each term depends on the previous term. If you wanted to determine, say, the 1001st term of this sequence, and you had only the recursive formula at your disposal, you'd have to manually compute the first 1,000 terms using the formula in order to get to the 1001st term. Cumbersome! Wouldn't it be great if we could somehow derive the closed-form formula to obtain the nth term? So all we'd have to do is plug 1,001 into this formula to find the 1001st term. It turns out that there are cases where we can do this. We review two of the basic ones.

Case 1: Recursive Formula Involving a Previous Term and a Polynomial

Suppose you know that a recursive formula for a sequence has the form of

$$a_n = a_{n-1} + p(n)$$

where $p(n)$ is a polynomial of degree n. Then it follows that the closed form of the sequence is given by a polynomial of degree $n + 1$.

Example
Given that the recursive formula for an arithmetic sequence with first term a_1 is given by $a_n = a_{n-1} + d$, for some constant d and $n > 1$, derive a closed-form formula for an arithmetic sequence.

Solution: Since d is a constant, it can be thought of as a zero-degree polynomial. Hence, by the preceding, we can describe the arithmetic sequence by a first-degree (linear) polynomial. Thus,

$$a_n = a \cdot n + b$$

Now the recursive formula tells us that the first term is a_1, so the second term must be $a_2 = a_1 + d$. We can use these two points to set up a system of equations. We have that $n = 1 \Rightarrow a_1 = a \cdot 1 + b$ and $n = 2 \Rightarrow a_2 = a_1 + d = a \cdot 2 + b$. Thus we get the system of equations:

$$a_1 = a + b$$

$$a_1 + d = 2a + b$$

Subtracting the first equation from the second, we get:

$$a = d$$

and plugging this into the first equation, we obtain:

$$b = a_1 - d$$

This implies that the polynomial describing the nth term of the sequence is:

$$a_n = d \cdot n + (a_1 - d)$$

By combining the terms with d in them, we obtain the familiar formula:

$$a_n = a_1 + (n - 1) \cdot d, \text{ for } n \geq 1$$

Example

Given that the recursive formula for a sequence is $a_1 = 1, a_n = a_{n-1} + 2n + 1$, find a closed-form formula for the sequence.

Solution: Here, $p(n) = 2n + 1$. This is a first-degree polynomial. This means that we can write the nth term as a second-degree polynomial. So write:

$$a_n = an^2 + bn + c$$

and note that the first few terms of this sequence would be $1, 6, 13, 22, 33, 46, \ldots$

This means that by plugging $n = 1, 2, 3$ successively into the equation, we can obtain the system of equations:

$$1 = a + b + c$$

$$6 = 4a + 2b + c$$

$$13 = 9a + 3b + c$$

Solving this system yields $a = 1$, $b = 2$, and $c = -2$. Hence we may write the closed form as:

$$a_n = n^2 + 2n - 2, \text{ for } n \geq 1$$

You can check that this generates the same sequence.

Case 2: Recursive Formula Involving a Linear Combination of Some Previous Terms

Here we can describe a sequence as $a_n = b_1 a_{n-1} + b_2 a_{n-2} + b_3 a_{n-3} + \ldots + b_k a_{n-k}$ where enough information is given to determine the values of all the a_i's on the right side of the equation.

We shall spare the gory details (though you are welcome to do the research), but the theory of difference equations gives us a way to find a closed form for a_n. We assume the closed form can be written as a sum of terms of the form $c_i \cdot r_i^n$, where c_i and r_i are constants (that is, we assume each term of the sequence is a sum of geometric-like terms). This assumption forces the fact that one can rewrite the previous recursive formula as a polynomial (called a *characteristic polynomial*). Namely,

$$r^n = b_1 r^{n-1} + b_2 r^{n-2} + \ldots + b_k r^{n-k}$$

Dividing through by r^{n-k} (we can do this since we clearly do not want r to be zero), we obtain the polynomial

$$r^k = b_1 r^{k-1} + b_2 r^{k-2} + \ldots + b_k$$

and we want to solve this for r. The polynomial will have k solutions for r (counting multiplicity). And assuming each solution for r is distinct, we will finally be able to write:

$$a_n = c_1 \cdot r_1^n + c_2 \cdot r_2^n + \ldots + c_k r_k^n$$

where r_1 through r_k are the k solutions to the characteristic polynomial, and the c_i's can be determined by setting up a system of equations using known terms of the sequence as we have done several times before.

(You may also recall that if one solution, call it r, has multiplicity m, then that solution would be represented by m terms in the characteristic polynomial, taking the form $c_1 r + c_2 n r^n + c_3 n^2 r^n + \ldots + c_m n^{m-1} r^n$, as opposed to just a term of the form $c_1 r^n$.)

To avoid getting too bogged down in the theory of it all, let us look at a concrete example.

Example

A sequence is defined recursively by $a_1 = 1$, $a_2 = 2$, $a_n = 2a_{n-1} + 3a_{n-2}$, for $n > 2$. Find a closed-form formula for the nth term of the sequence.

Solution: Here, the characteristic polynomial is $r^2 = 2r + 3$. That is, $r^2 - 2r - 3 = 0$. Luckily for us, this factors, so that we obtain $(r - 3)(r + 1) = 0$. Hence, the roots are $r = 3$ and $r = -1$ (distinct).

Hence, we know we can write:

$$a_n = c_1 \cdot 3^n + c_2 \cdot (-1)^n$$

To find c_1 and c_2, we need at least two terms of the sequence. But we were already given that! We know $a_1 = 1$ and $a_2 = 2$. Hence, plugging in $n = 1$ and $n = 2$ successively, we get the pair of equations:

$$1 = c_1 \cdot 3 + c_2 \cdot (-1)$$

$$2 = c_1 \cdot 3^2 + c_2(-1)^2$$

Solving this system for c_1 and c_2, we get $c_1 = \frac{1}{4}$ and $c_2 = -\frac{1}{4}$ Hence,

$$a_n = \frac{1}{4} \cdot 3^n - \frac{1}{4} \cdot (-1)^n, \text{ for } n \geq 1$$

Again, you should verify that this generates the correct sequence—namely, the sequence $1, 2, 7, 20, 61, \ldots$

Example

A sequence is defined recursively by $a_1 = 1$, $a_2 = 2$, $a_n = 2a_{n-1} - a_{n-2}$, for $n > 2$. Find a closed-form formula for the nth term of the sequence.

Solution: Here the characteristic polynomial is $r^2 - 2r - 1$ or, more conveniently, $r^2 - 2r + 1 = 0$. This factors to $(r - 1)^2 = 0$; hence we have one root, $r = 1$, of multiplicity 2. Thus, the general term of our sequence will be given by:

$$a_n = c_1 \cdot (1)^n + c_2 n \cdot (1)^n$$

But that means,

$$a_n = c_1 + c_2 n$$

Since that's a linear equation, it means our sequence is, in fact, an arithmetic series! Now we have several options about how to proceed. One option is to revert back to our old way of doing things. We have a common difference of $a_2 - a_1 = 1$. Hence, $a_n = a_1 + (n-1) \cdot 1 = a_1 + n - 1 = 1 + n - 1 = n$. So we were in fact talking about

$$a_n = n, \text{ for } n \geq 1$$

this whole time. What a complicated way to describe the sequence of all positive integers!

The other option would be to continue in our new way of doing things, set up a system of equations, and solve for the unknowns. Doing this we would have gotten:

$$1 = c_1 + c_2$$

$$2 = c_1 + 2c_2$$

This would yield $c_1 = 0$ and $c_2 = 1$, as expected.

You can verify that the recursive formula indeed generates the sequence $1, 2, 3, 4, 5, 6, \ldots$

It is worth mentioning that the previous method could be used to obtain a closed-form formula for perhaps the most famous recursive sequence of all time—the Fibonacci sequence. Recall that this sequence is defined recursively by:

$$F_1 = 1, F_2 = 1, F_n = F_{n-1} + F_{n-2}, \text{ for } n > 2$$

That is, the sequence $1, 1, 2, 3, 5, 8, 13, 21, 34, \ldots$ (sometimes the first two values are taken to be 0 and 1, to obtain $0, 1, 1, 2, 3, 5, \ldots$).

Here is another miscellaneous example of a kind of problem you may encounter:

Example

a. The third term of an arithmetic sequence is 7. The seventh term is 15. Find the 300th term of the sequence.

b. The third term of a geometric sequence is 18. The sixth term is –486. Find the 13th term of the sequence.

Solution:

a. We are told the sequence is arithmetic. Thus it can be described by $a_n = a_1 + (n-1) \cdot d$. Plugging in $n = 3$ and $n = 7$ so that we can utilize the third and seventh terms, we obtain the system of equations:

$$7 = a_1 + 2 \cdot d$$

$$15 = a_1 + 6 \cdot d$$

Solving the system for a_1 and d, we find that $a_1 = 3$ and $d = 2$. Therefore, our sequence is defined by:

$$a_n = 3 + (n-1) \cdot 2 = 1 + 2n, \text{ for } n \geq 1$$

Hence, the 300th term is:

$$a_{300} = 1 + 2 \cdot 300 = 601$$

In this case, the answer could be obtained by more elementary means. For instance, we could realize that the difference between 15 and 7 is 8, and there are four terms between the third and the seventh. And since the jump from one term to another has to be constant, the common difference must be $\frac{8}{4} = 2$. From the third term, counting backward, we could then obtain that the first term is 3, and then proceed. However, were we given, say, the 36th term and the 75th term, this method would be more trouble than it's worth. So the standard way of setting up a system of equations would be preferable.

b. Here we know that the sequence is geometric, so we know it is described by $a_n = a_1 r^{n-1}$. Plugging in $n = 3$ and $n = 6$ so that we may utilize the third and sixth terms, we get the system of equations:

$$18 = a_1 r^2$$

$$-486 = a_1 r^5$$

By dividing the second equation by the first, we obtain

$$r^3 = -27 \Rightarrow r = -3$$

Plugging this into the first equation, we get $a_1 = 2$. Hence our sequence is defined by:

$$a_n = 2 \cdot (-3)^{n-1}$$

So, the 13th term is:

$$a_{51} = 2 \cdot (-3)^{12} = 1{,}062{,}882$$

Now that we've covered a lot to do with sequences and how to manipulate their formulas, let us move on to using our knowledge of sequences to solve problems.

Use of Recursion and Sequences to Model Various Phenomena

The famous Fibonacci sequence was initially developed to model the population growth of rabbits. As it turns out, this sequence (and the ratio of consecutive terms of the sequence) can model so many more things in nature—an astounding number of things.

The closed form for this sequence can be derived using the difference equations method of the preceding section, and it could hence be determined that the Fibonacci sequence may be defined by:

$$F_n = \frac{1}{\sqrt{5}}(\varphi^n - \psi^n)$$

where $\varphi = \frac{1 + \sqrt{5}}{2}$ is the *golden ratio* (another quantity that shows up often), and $\psi = \frac{1 - \sqrt{5}}{2}$.

But what other things can we use sequences, recursively defined or not, to model? We answer that question with some examples.

Example
A population of bacteria doubles every three hours. If you start with 100 bacteria, how many will there be after a day?

Solution: We've discussed how to solve a problem like this in Chapter 6. But let us look at this in a new light.

The size of the population of bacteria is given by a geometric series with $a_1 = 100$ and common ratio $r = 2$ (namely 100, 200, 400, 800, . . .). But the time we take to double the population moves along by 3; that is, time follows an arithmetic sequence with $a_1 = 0$ and common difference $d = 3$ (namely, 3, 6, 9, 12, . . .). Now we wish to find the size of the population after 24 hours. We set up the table (noting that the top row has a geometric sequence and the middle row has an arithmetic one) to model the situation.

POP. SIZE	100	200	400	. . .	???
Time	0 hours	3 hours	6 hours	. . .	24 hours
Term # (n)	0	1	2	. . .	???

Now the question is: What term number will we be at when we hit 24 hours? We can just follow the arithmetic sequence.

$$24 = 0 + (n-1) \cdot 3 \Rightarrow n = 9$$

(We could have also figured out by inspection that it took eight time-jumps to get to 24 hours.)

Now use $n = 9$ in the geometric sequence formula for the population,

$$a_9 = 100 \cdot (2)^{9-1} = 25,600$$

So there would be 25,600 bacteria after a day.

You can verify this answer using the methods learned in Chapter 6. And, of course, a similar problem could be asked about half-life.

Example

John suffered a shoulder injury while lifting weights and, to speed up his recovery, his personal trainer instructs him to train for a maximum of 15 minutes per day for the first week, and then increase the daily workout time by 5 minutes per day for each week thereafter. Assuming John trains for the maximum amount of time he is allowed, how long will it take John to make it to 2 hours per day training sessions?

Solution: Here the training time follows an arithmetic sequence, 15, 20, 25, 30, . . . where the a_n term describes the maximum daily workout time during the nth week. We want to know how many terms before the sequence hits the value 120 (there are 120 minutes in 2 hours).

Using $a_1 = 15$ and $d = 5$, we get that:

$$a_n = 15 + (n - 1) \cdot 5$$

$$\Rightarrow 120 = 15 + (n - 1) \cdot 5 \text{ is what we want}$$

$$\Rightarrow n = 22$$

So, counting week 1 as the 15-minute workout week, it will take John 22 weeks to get up to a 2-hour daily workout time. John won't be competing in the World's Strongest Man competition any time soon.

Example

A snowball rolling down a high hill picks up more snow as it rolls. It gains 5% more mass every minute. Assuming this trend continues and the snowball starts with a mass of 2 grams, what mass will it have when it reaches the bottom of the hill if it takes 27 minutes to get to the bottom?

Solution: Here we have a geometric sequence, since we are increasing by a percentage or proportion rather than by a fixed amount per unit time. After each minute, the new mass will be 105% of the old mass, so that the common ratio would be $r = 1.05$. Since the first term is $a_1 = 2$ and there would be 28 terms in our sequence (mass at time 0, mass at time 1 minute, mass at time 2 minutes, . . . , mass at time 27 minutes), we have:

$$a_n = 2 \cdot (1.05)^{n-1}$$

where $1 \leq n \leq 28$, and we want the 28th term of this sequence, which gives us:

$$a_{28} = 2 \cdot (1.05)^{28-1} \approx 7.47 \text{ grams}$$

Again, the methods learned in the exponential growth section of Chapter 6 could be used.

Example

How many multiples of 7 are there between 12 and 2,014?

Solution: We can use an arithmetic sequence to solve this! It would be a finite sequence, where the first term is the smallest multiple of 7 in the given range (in this case, 14) and the last term of the sequence would be the largest multiple of 7 in the range (in this case, 2,009). Thus, we wish to find out what is the value of n that corresponds to $a_1 = 14$, $d = 7$, and $a_n = 2{,}009$. The closed form is:

$$a_n = 14 + (n - 1) \cdot 7$$

and we're interested in the value of n so that

$$2{,}009 = 14 + (n - 1) \cdot 7$$

$$\Rightarrow n = 286$$

So there are 286 multiples of 7 between 12 and 2014.

Problem 36 in the diagnostic test of Chapter 3 provides another kind of example. For examples like this, you would have to be familiar with the following:

---

i. The sum of the first n terms of an *arithmetic sequence* is given by:

$$S_n = \frac{n(a_1 + a_n)}{2}$$

We can avoid the need to know the nth term by replacing a_n with its closed-form formula, to get

$$S_n = \frac{n[2a_1 + (n - 1) \cdot d]}{2}$$

(The derivation of this formula can be computed using the same method that is typically used for finding the sum of the first n positive integers.)

ii. The sum of the first n terms of a *geometric sequence* is given by:

$$S_n = \frac{a_1(1 - r^n)}{1 - r}$$

(This can be derived by writing out the polynomial that arises by summing up the first n terms and factoring it. The derivations to both of these should be easily accessible to the reader, via browsing an appropriate math text or doing a quick Internet search.)

Other problems in sequences may ask you to fill in the blanks if you're given a partial list of a sequence, or to predict the next term. The skills you have developed by making it this far should make such problems straightforward. Once you can figure out the

pattern, you can figure out what the terms are, and we've discussed figuring out patterns at length.

We now move on to another topic in discrete mathematics—sets.

Basic Set Theory

Definition: A set is a collection of objects. These objects are called the *members* or *elements* of the set.

The term *objects* here takes on a very broad meaning. The objects could be numbers, letters, names—pretty much anything. In naive set theory (which is the kind of set theory we're dealing with here), there are many objects that we declare cannot exist, because their existence would cause contradictions. Examples of such objects would be a "set of all things" or the "set of all sets" or "the largest set possible." Basically anything too grand or all-encapsulating is taboo.

Notation: Sets are usually denoted by uppercase letters. The contents of a set may be listed in {} brackets. Ellipses may also be used when the other members are understood.

Example

a. We could call the set of the first five positive integers A and write
$$A = \{1, 2, 3, 4, 5\}$$

b. The set of all positive integers is denoted by $\mathbb{N} = \{1, 2, 3, 4, 5, \ldots\}$.
Sometimes $\mathbb{N}$ is defined to include 0, so be sure to take the cue from the text you are reading.

c. Sometimes we can describe a set by writing a general form within the {} brackets and then listing necessary criteria behind the : or the |

symbol (either symbol may be read as "such that"). For example, the set of all complex numbers may be defined as

$$\mathbb{C} = \{a + ib : a \text{ and } b \text{ are real numbers}\}$$

or

$$\mathbb{C} = \{a + ib : | \, a \text{ and } b \text{ are real numbers}\}$$

In other words, the set of complex numbers is the set of numbers of the form $a + ib$ such that a and b are real numbers.

Definition: The symbol $\in$ shows membership, and can be read as "is a member (or element) of" or "belongs to."

We could then say, for example:

$$\mathbb{C} = \{a + ib \mid a, b \in \mathbb{R}\}$$

(Recall that $\mathbb{R}$ denotes the set of real numbers.)

It is often the case that we can negate the meaning of a symbol by striking through it. For example, $\notin$ means "not a member of."

Definition: A very important set is the so-called *empty set* or *null set*. It is denoted $\varnothing$ or $\{\}$, and is defined to be the set containing no elements.

Note that the objects of sets can be sets themselves. For example, the set $B = \{1, \varnothing, \{1\}\}$ contains three elements, namely, 1, $\varnothing$, and $\{1\}$ (the last two of which are sets).

Binary Operations on Sets

Given sets, we can create new sets through binary operations (recall that a binary operation is a function that uses *two* elements as inputs to create another element as an output).

(VERY) COMMON BINARY OPERATIONS ON SETS

The union—notation "$\cup$"

$A \cup B$ = set of all elements that are in A and B combined

Example: $A = \{1,3,4,5,6\}$ and $B = \{0,2,4,6,\varnothing\}$, then $A \cup B = \{0,1,2,3,4,5,6,\varnothing\}$

The intersection—notation "$\cap$"

$A \cap B$ = set of all elements that are common to both A and B

Example: $A = \{1,3,4,5,6\}$ and $B = \{0,2,4,6,\varnothing\}$, then $A \cap B = \{4,6\}$

The (set) difference—notation "$-$" or, a more archaic notation "\\"

$A - B = A \backslash B$ = set of all elements that are in A but not in B

That is, we start with the elements in A and throw away the elements that are also in B.

Example: $A = \{1, 3, 4, 5, 6\}$ and $B = \{0, 2, 4, 6, \varnothing\}$, then $A - B = \{1, 3, 5\}$

Note that if $A \cap B = \varnothing$ (that is, they have no elements in common), then the sets A and B are called *disjoint*.

Definition: A subset of a set A is a set that contains some (*some* here includes the possibility of *none* or *all*) of the elements of the set A.

Notation: We write $B \subset A$ to mean "B is a subset of A." The set A may be called a *superset* of the set B in this case. You may see $B \subseteq A$ if a writer wishes to emphasize that $B = A$ is a possibility (two sets are equal if they contain exactly the same elements).

A subset B of a set A is called a *proper subset* if it does not contain all the elements of A. That is, $B \subset A$, but $B \neq A$. In cases where an author uses $\subseteq$, the symbol $\subset$ would mean a proper subset.

Note that for any set *A* it is true that $\emptyset \subset A$. This is true even if $A = \emptyset$. That's right. The empty set is a subset of itself as well!

We often want to consider sets as subsets of a larger set. This larger set is called the universal set, and is typically denoted *U*. The universal set may be different for each situation, but is often understood. If not understood, the writer would (well, should) make it clear what the universal set is considered to be. For example, one may consider the set of all men. The universal set here may be the set of human beings, or perhaps the set of all mammals. The context would make it clear which is being considered.

Another important operation on a set is the complement. It is not a binary operation.

> The *complement* of a set *A* is defined to be the set $U - A$. It is denoted $\overline{A}$ or A^C. So we write
>
> $$A^C = \overline{A} = U - A$$
>
> That is, it is the set of all elements that are not in *A*. A^C may be read as "the complement of *A*" or "*A* complement."
>
> Example: If $U = \{1,2,3,4,5,6,7,8,9,10\}$, and $A = \{2,4,6,8,10\}$, then $A^C = \{1,3,5,7,9\}$.

Venn Diagrams

Venn diagrams are a way to pictorially represent sets. Sets are typically drawn as circles, and these circles are within a box that represents the universal set.

Example

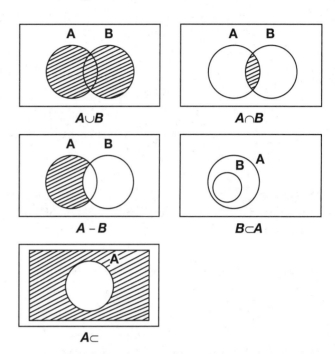

What's the point? Thinking of (groups of) objects in terms of sets and using Venn diagrams can help us solve problems.

Example

In a class of 25 students, five students take both art and science, five students take only science, and four students take neither of these classes. The other students take art but not science. How many are in this last category?

Solution: Visualizing this in a Venn diagram helps. We use *A* to represent the set of art students in the class, and *S* to represent the set of science students in the class. The box, the universal set, is the class itself—all students in this particular class.

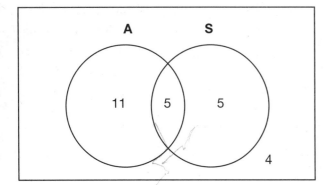

The trick to filling out a Venn diagram in a case like this is to fill in the most overlapping regions first, then the regions that are isolated (so you would fill in the number of students who take both subjects, then the number who take only science). From the diagram we can see the answer: There are 11 students who take art but not science.

Note that once we filled in the region $A \cap S$, we had to subtract the number in the intersection from the number of science students in general in order to fill out the region S–A. $(S \cup A)^c$ was given, that is the four students who take neither subject, so we placed a 4 in the universal set, but not in either of the sets A or S. Then, since the total number of students is 25, we simply subtract $25 - (5 + 5 + 4) = 11$ to find the number of students who take art but not science.

You probably could have figured out the answer without drawing a Venn diagram, but the problem becomes more complicated the more sets are thrown in, and a Venn diagram makes things a lot easier.

Example

A school has 100 students; 30 students study math (M), 40 students study English (E), and 50 students study physics (P) (20 of whom study only physics); 10 study both math and physics, 20 study math and English, 25 study physics and English, and 5 study all three subjects. How many students study none of these subjects?

Solution: Filling out the most overlapping regions first, then the physics-only region, and finally using

basic arithmetic to fill in the rest, the following Venn diagram is obtained.

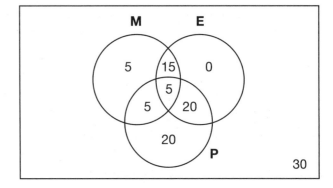

From this we see that the answer we're looking for is: *30 students take none of these subjects.*

Another kind of set worth considering is the *interval*. This applies mostly in continuous mathematics but could also apply to discrete mathematics. In either case, the reader should recall the following notation. On the right of each equation is the set notation equivalent of the interval notation on the left.

- $(a,b) = \{x \mid a < x < b\}$ This is called an *open interval*. Typically it would be assumed $x \in \mathbb{R}$, but this is not always the case.
- $(a,b] = \{x \mid a < x \leq b\}$ This, and the interval just below, are called *half-open intervals*.
- $[a,b) = \{x \mid a \leq x < b\}$
- $[a,b] = \{x \mid a \leq x \leq b\}$ This is called a *closed interval*.

Again borrowing from the continuous case, we can say that the solution to the inequality $x^2 - 1 < 0$ is the set $(-1,1)$, while the solution to $x^2 - 1 \geq 0$ is the set $(-\infty,-1] \cup [1,\infty)$.

Recall that there are, of course, more pedantic ways to write down the solutions to the foregoing. For example, the solution to $x^2 - 1 < 0$ may be written as "$-1 < x < 1$" or "all real x such that $x \in (-1,1)$" or

"$\{x \in \mathbb{R} \mid -1 < x < 1\}$" or "$\{x \in \mathbb{R} : x \in (-1,1)\}$," and so on. The reader is expected to realize that all of these are saying the same thing.

We now move on to another section of discrete mathematics one should be aware of—logic!

The Basics and Symbols of Logic

Logic refers to the objective reasoning one uses to determine whether a statement is true or false. *Statement* here refers to a declarative sentence or expression—that is, a sentence or expression whose *truth value* is either true or false (and ideally can be proven to be one or the other, based on certain premises). The idea that a statement can be both true and false is of course rejected. Knowing how to assess truth values of statements also allows us to analyze arguments. What makes an argument a good one, a reasonable one, a *logical* one? In this section, we recap the basics to make such determinations.

Definition: A *statement* is a declarative sentence or expression. Typically, a statement is denoted by an uppercase letter (the letters T and F are reserved for "true" and "false").

Typically P, Q, and R are the first three letters chosen to represent statements, sort of like how x and y are the generic go-to letters for the independent and dependent variables, respectively, of a function.

Definition: The negation of a statement is a statement that has the opposite truth value in all instances. If a statement is denoted P, then its negation is denoted by $\sim P$ or $\neg P$, and is read "the negation of P" or "not P."

Truth Tables

A truth table is a table used to keep track of the truth values of statements in one or several instances. The statements are listed along the top row. Each other row represents a given instance. Any column entry below a given statement gives its truth value in a certain instance. For example, we can represent the last definition by a truth table in the following way:

P	$\sim P$
T	F
F	T

Here we see that in the instance where P gives a value of T (true), $\sim P$ gives a value of F (false); and when P is false, $\sim P$ is true.

Recall that we can combine statements to make new statements, such as *disjunctions* ("or" statements), *conjunctions* ("and" statements), *implications* (a.k.a. conditional statements or "if-then" statements), and *bi-implications* (also known as biconditional statements or "if and only if" or "iff" statements).

As for notation:

TYPE OF COMBINATION	EXPRESSIONS IN WORDS	NOTATION IN LOGICAL SYMBOLS
Disjunction	"P or Q"	$P \vee Q$
Conjunction	"P and Q"	$P \wedge Q$
Implication	"if P, then Q," "P implies Q," "Q if P," "P only if Q," "P is sufficient for Q," "Q is necessary for P"	$P \Rightarrow Q$
Bi-implication	"P if and only if Q," "P if Q," "P is equivalent to Q," "P is necessary and sufficient for Q"	$P \Leftrightarrow Q$

It should be clear when a disjunction is true (if either or both of the statements in the disjunction are true) and it should also be clear when a conjunction is true (only when both statements in the conjunction are true); implications and bi-implications are a bit tricky, though. The complete set of truth value instances are described in these truth tables:

Disjunction

P	Q	P ∨ Q
T	T	T
T	F	T
F	T	T
F	F	F

Conjunction

P	Q	P ∧ Q
T	T	T
T	F	F
F	T	F
F	F	F

Implication

P	Q	P ⇒ Q
T	T	T
T	F	F
F	T	T
F	F	T

Bi-implication

P	Q	P ⇔ Q
T	T	T
T	F	F
F	T	F
F	F	T

It is a phenomenon of language that different statements can mean the same thing—and hence have the same truth values if they happen to be declarative. In logic, this is no different.

Definition: Two statements are said to be *equivalent* if they have the same truth values in all instances. The notation is the ≡ sign. That is, to say "*P* is equivalent to *Q*" we can write $P \equiv Q$.

Example

These truth tables show that (i) $P \Leftrightarrow Q \equiv ((P \Rightarrow Q) \wedge (Q \Rightarrow P))$ and that (ii) the negation of $P \Rightarrow Q$ is $P \wedge (\sim Q)$ ((ii) should be expected from the third truth table). Also note that (ii) here is equivalent to saying that the negation of $P \Rightarrow Q$ is equivalent to $P \wedge (\sim Q)$.

$$\text{(i) } (P \Leftrightarrow Q) \equiv ((P \Rightarrow Q) \wedge (Q \Rightarrow P))$$

P	Q	P ⇒ Q	Q ⇒ P	(P ⇒ Q) ∧ (Q ⇒ P)	P ⇔ Q
T	T	T	T	T	T
T	F	F	T	F	F
F	T	T	F	F	F
F	F	T	T	T	T

$$\text{(ii) } \sim(P \Rightarrow Q) \equiv (P \wedge (\sim Q))$$

P	Q	~Q	P ⇒ Q	~(P ⇒ Q)	P ∧ (~Q)
T	T	F	T	F	F
T	F	T	F	T	T
F	T	F	T	F	F
F	F	T	T	F	F

A couple of other important ideas in logic are those of the *tautology* and the *contradiction*.

Definition: A *tautology* is a statement that is always true; that is, its truth value is T in every instance. A *contradiction* is a statement that is always false; that is, its truth value is F in every instance.

Example

A simple contradiction is the statement $P \wedge (\sim P)$. (This is because a statement cannot be true and false at the same time.)

P	$\sim P$	$P \wedge (\sim P)$
T	F	F
F	T	F

Example

A simple tautology is the statement $P \vee (\sim P)$. (That is, a given declarative statement is certainly either true or false.)

P	$\sim P$	$P \vee (\sim P)$
T	F	T
F	T	T

The Idea of Proof

As Arthur Eddington put it: "Proof is an idol before whom the pure mathematician tortures himself." *Proof* is paramount to mathematics; it is of more importance than can be described in the space we have here. Proof allows us to *know* whether a given assertion is true. There is so much to be said about this topic, but as this is a review text, we will rush through the basics.

As it turns out, most of the statements we will want to prove can be written as conditional statements or biconditional statements. That is, given certain assumptions, we can say they imply some result. Earlier we proved that a biconditional statement is equivalent to a conjunction of conditional statements; so once we know how to prove a conditional statement, we will, in theory, know how to prove a biconditional one (we prove two implications—to prove $P \Leftrightarrow Q$ we simply prove $P \Rightarrow Q$ and $Q \Rightarrow P$ separately).

The last parenthetical statement compels us to give another definition.

Definition: The *converse* of an implication is simply the implication in the opposite direction. That is, the converse of $P \Rightarrow Q$ is $Q \Rightarrow P$.

WARNING

A statement and its converse are *not* equivalent statements! (Just look at the truth tables!) It is not uncommon for a statement to be true but its converse false.

Now, there are four major proof techniques in mathematics: direct proof, proof by contrapositive, proof by contradiction, and proof by mathematical induction. In this section, we discuss the first three—though induction can also be thought of as falling under the umbrella of discrete mathematics, it is unlikely you will need to know how to perform it on the Praxis II® exam. (For the examples in this section, the reader is expected to recall that the $\mathbb{Z}$ symbol represents the set of all integers as well as the precise definitions of an even integer and an odd integer. Namely, an integer n is called *even* if $n = 2k$ for some $k \in \mathbb{Z}$, while an integer n is called *odd* if $n = 2k + 1$ for some $k \in \mathbb{Z}$.)

Direct Proof (for Proving $P \Rightarrow Q$)

To prove $P \Rightarrow Q$ directly, one would assume the statement P is true, and then prove that this assumption forces the statement Q to be true.

Example

Prove the statement: If n is an even integer, then $3n + 5$ is an odd integer.

Proof: Assume n is even. Then we can write $n = 2k$ for some integer k. But then we have that

$$3n + 5 = 3(2k) + 5 = 6k + 5 = 6k + 4 + 1 = 2(3k + 2) + 1$$

Since $3k + 2$ is an integer (we may call it m), we have that $3n + 5 = 2m + 1$ for some integer m, so $3n + 5$ is odd.

■

The ■ symbol indicates the end of the proof. Note that if we let P be the statement "n is an even integer" and Q be the statement "$3n + 5$ is an odd integer," then the statement we want to prove is of the form $P \Rightarrow Q$. What we did was assume that P is true—that is, that n is in fact even. Then we showed that a consequence of this assumption is that the integer $3n + 5$ must be odd. *Note:* We stated that $3n + 5$ is an integer, and used the fact that $3k + 2$ is an integer if k is. The reader is expected to recall that these statements make sense since the integers are closed under multiplication and addition.

Proof by Contrapositive (for Proving P ⇒ Q)

To prove $P \Rightarrow Q$ by contrapositive, one would prove the statement $(\sim Q) \Rightarrow (\sim P)$. That is, one would assume that Q is *not* true and show that P will *not* be true as a result.

It is easy to see why a direct proof is valid—just look at the truth table for the conditional. To see why a proof by contrapositive is valid, one would only need to verify that $(P \Rightarrow Q) \equiv ((\sim Q) \Rightarrow (\sim P))$. This is an easy exercise using a truth table, and the verification is left to the reader.

Example

Prove the statement: If $3n + 5$ is odd, then n is even.

Proof: Assume, by way of the contrapositive, that n is odd. This means $n = 2k + 1$ for some $k \in \mathbb{Z}$. But then:

$$3n + 5 = 3(2k + 1) + 5 = 6k + 8 = 2(3k + 4)$$

Since $3k + 4$ is an integer, we have that $3n + 5$ is even.

■

Here P: "$3n + 5$ is odd" and Q: "n is even." We assumed Q was false (that is, we assumed n is in fact odd), and proved that P is false as a result (that is, $3n + 5$ is in fact even when n is odd).

Proof by Contradiction (for Proving P ⇒ Q)

To prove $P \Rightarrow Q$ by contradiction, one would assume $P \Rightarrow Q$ is false and show that a contradiction arises from this assumption. By doing this, one would show that assuming $P \Rightarrow Q$ is false was an error, so it actually must be the case that $P \Rightarrow Q$ is true.

But how would one go about assuming $P \Rightarrow Q$ is false? The answer: Assume its negation. Earlier, we showed that the negation of $P \Rightarrow Q$ is the statement $P \wedge (\sim Q)$. Therefore, we can rephrase the proof by contradiction technique in this way:

To prove $P \Rightarrow Q$ by the method of contradiction, one would assume that $P \wedge (\sim Q)$ is true, and show that a contradiction arises from this.

Example

Prove the statement: If n is an even integer, then $3n + 5$ is an odd integer.

Proof: Assume, for the sake of contradiction, that n is even, but $3n + 5$ is also even. Since n is even, we can write $n = 2k$ for some integer k. But then,

$$3n + 5 = 3(2k) + 5 = 6k + 5 = 6k + 4 + 1 = 2(3k + 2) + 1$$

Since $3k + 2$ is an integer, we have that $3n + 5$ is odd.

This is a contradiction, for we assumed $3n + 5$ was even.

■

Example
Prove that there is no smallest positive fraction.

Proof: Assume, to the contrary, that there is a smallest positive fraction; call it r. But consider the fraction $\frac{r}{2}$. If $0 < r$, we have that $0 < \frac{r}{2} < r$, so that $\frac{r}{2}$ is both positive and smaller than r. This contradicts the assumption that r was the smallest fraction.

■

The last example brings to the forefront the idea of an existence (or nonexistence) claim. Sometimes these can be written as implications, but sometimes they cannot. For such claims, a proof by contradiction comes in handy.

For existence proofs, note the following:

- To prove some kind of object exists, all you have to do is come up with an example of the object.
- To prove an object does not exist, you must prove that such an object cannot exist in general. A proof by contradiction is probably your safest, most straightforward technique in this case.

We already did a proof to show that a kind of object (a smallest positive fraction) cannot exist. Let's do a simple proof of an object existing.

Example
Prove that there exists a number whose square is the same as its double.

Proof: 0 is such a number. So is 2.

■

Of course, in the background, one only needs to solve the equation $x^2 = 2x$ to settle the dispute. But this need not be shown in the proof. To prove something exists, just say, "Here's an example!" Make sure your example has the necessary qualities (if this is not obvious, prove it! If it's obvious, have the reader go through the exercise), and you're done!

This also brings to light the notion of disproving something. To disprove the existence of an object or an assertion, all you have to do is find a so-called *counterexample*. A counterexample is simply an example of an object that contradicts the claim.

Example
Disprove the claim that "there is no number whose square is the same as its double."

Proof: 0 is a number where $0^2 = 0 = 2 \cdot 0$. Therefore, we have found a number whose square is equal to its double. Hence the claim is disproved.

A discussion of proof would not be complete without talking about *trivial* or *vacuous* proofs. In such proofs, you literally don't have to do anything, since the claim you're trying to prove is trivially true (due to some law of logic).

For example, we know that $P \Rightarrow Q$ is true in every instance that the statement P is false (refer to the implication truth table that appeared earlier). Therefore, it is trivial that any statement of the form $P \Rightarrow Q$ where P is false is a true statement—regardless of what Q is. A false statement implies whatever!

Example
Prove the claim that if there exists a smallest fraction, then $1 + 1 = 5$.

Proof: The claim holds vacuously, so it is trivially true.

■

Equivalence Relations

Equality is a ubiquitous relationship in mathematics; and it has some nice, dare we say even aesthetic, properties. For instance, for any number a, the fact that $a = a$ is a trivial truth. Also, if we know that $a = b$, we may, without fear, assert that $b = a$. On top of this, if we know that $a = b$ and $b = c$, then we would not be wrong to claim that $a = c$. This is so straightforward with "=" that we often take this for granted. In reality, one would not have to go far to find relationships that do not behave this way. For instance, take the usual $<$ relationship. It is *not* true that, for numbers a and b, if $a < b$ then $b < a$—in fact, that assertion is a contradiction (always false, for *every* pair of numbers a and b). The first property of "=" that we mentioned is called *reflexivity*, the second is called *symmetry*, and the last, *transitivity*. Relationships (more precisely, *relations*—which we will define shortly) that possess these three properties are called *equivalence relations*.

Definition: For sets A and B, the *Cartesian product* of A and B (denoted $A \times B$) is defined to be the set of all possible ordered pairs—where the first coordinates come from A and the second coordinates come from B. That is,

$$A \times B = \{(a,b) : a \in A \text{ and } b \in B\}$$

Note that if $A = \varnothing$ or $B = \varnothing$, then we define $A \times B = \varnothing$. Also note that in discrete mathematics we will (in theory) be able to list all the ordered pairs; in continuous mathematics, this will usually be impossible. This is similar to how we can list all the integers, in theory, but it is not possible to list all the real numbers.

Definition: A set R is called a *relation from A to B* if it is a subset of $A \times B$. (Note that $R = \varnothing$ is possible.)

If $(a,b) \in R$, then we say "a is related to b (under the relation R)," and we may write aRb. If a is not related

to b, that means $(a,b) \notin R$ and we can write $a\mathbb{R}b$. If R is a relation from A to B, then the domain of R and the range of R are, respectively, the sets

$$\text{dom}(R) = \{a \in A : (a,b) \in R \text{ for some } b \in B\}$$

$$\text{range}(R) = \{b \in B : (a,b) \in R \text{ for some } a \in A\}$$

We spoke about functions back in Chapter 6. One way to describe a function was by ordered pairs. A function is a special kind of relation. A function is a relation in which *every* element of A appears as the first coordinate of *exactly one* ordered pair in the relation.

Definition: A relation *on a set A* is simply a relation from A to A; that is, it is a subset of $A \times A$.

Note that we need not use R to represent a relation, any more than we must use f to represent a function. Even symbols are typically used instead of R. The $\sim$ symbol is often used in place of R. Now let's bring this back to equivalence relations.

Definition: Let R be a relation on a set A. There are three properties of interest.

(i) R is said to be *reflexive* if aRa for every $a \in A$. That is, $(a,a) \in R$ for every $a \in A$. Note that this could be phrased as: if $a \in A$, then $(a,a) \in R$, for every $a \in A$.

(ii) R is said to be *symmetric* if $aRb \Rightarrow bRa$ for every $a,b \in A$. That is, $(a,b) \in R \Rightarrow (b,a) \in R$ for every $a,b \in A$.

(iii) R is said to be *transitive* if $(aRb \wedge bRc) \Rightarrow aRc$ for every $a,b,c \in A$. That is, $(a,b) \in R$ and $(b,c) \in R$ implies $(a,c) \in R$ for every $a,b,c \in R$.

Definition: A relation that is reflexive, symmetric, and transitive is called an *equivalence relation*.

Note that these are the same three properties we mentioned about the "=" relation. Also note that the definitions are given in terms of implications, so that they may be fulfilled vacuously. So, for example: If $A \neq \varnothing$ and $R = \varnothing$ is a relation on A, then R is symmetric and transitive but not reflexive; call this case 1 for this discussion. Interestingly enough, if $A = \varnothing$ and $R = \varnothing$ is a relation on A, then R is an equivalence relation; call this case 2. The trick here is to note that if we phrased each of the three definitions as $P \Rightarrow Q$, then P would be false for (ii) and (iii) in case 1 and false for (i), (ii), and (iii) in case 2, thereby making all these implications true and giving R the properties it was claimed to have. Definition (i) does not hold for case 1, since $A \neq \varnothing$, so we know there exists an $a \in A$, but since $R = \varnothing$, $(a,a) \notin R$, so reflexivity is violated.

Example

Let $A = \{a,b,c,d\}$. Determine which of the properties—reflexive, symmetric, and/or transitive—the given relation R possesses.

a. $R = \{(a,a),(b,b),(c,c),(d,d)\}$
b. $R = \{(b,b),(b,c)\}$

Solution:

a. Since for every $x \in A$ we have $(x,x) \in R$, we have that R is reflexive. R is also symmetric, since in each pair if the first and second coordinate is switched, the new pair (which is really the old pair!) is also found in R. R is transitive since $(x,x) \in R$ and $(x,x) \in R$ implies $(x,x) \in R$ for each $x \in A$. (The use of x was intentional, as one can think of x as taking on any of the values a, b, c.) A very trivial example!

b. Since (a,a), (c,c), $(d,d) \notin R$, R is *not* reflexive. Since $(b,c) \in R$ but $(c,b) \notin R$, R is *not* symmetric. However, R is transitive, since $(b,b) \in R$ and $(b,b) \in R$ implies $(b,b) \in R$, and $(b,b) \in R$ and $(b,c) \in R$ implies $(b,c) \in R$.

Example

Determine whether the given relation R is an equivalence relation. If not, which of the properties—reflexive, symmetric, or transitive—is it missing?

a. R is a relation on the set of integers and is defined by aRb if $ab < 0$ for $a,b \in \mathbb{Z}$.
b. R is a relation on the set of integers and is defined by aRb if $3a + 5b$ is even, for $a,b \in \mathbb{Z}$.

Solution:

a. To be an equivalence relation, R must be reflexive, symmetric, and transitive. Let's check each.
   (i) Reflexivity: Since for any $a \in \mathbb{Z}$, $aa = a^2 \geq 0$, we have that R is *not* reflexive.
   (ii) Symmetry: Assuming $ab < 0$, it follows, since multiplication is commutative on the integers, that $ba = ab < 0$. So, R is symmetric.
   (iii) Transitivity: We must determine if $ab < 0$ and $bc < 0$ implies $ac < 0$. This is false. A counterexample would be: $a = c = 1$ and $b = -1$. Then, $ab < 0$ and $bc < 0$ but $ac = 1 > 0$. Thus, R is *not* transitive.

Conclusion: R is *not* an equivalence relation. Of the three required properties, it is only symmetric.

b. Let's jump right into checking the properties.
   (i) Reflexivity: Since $3a + 5a = 8a = 2(4a)$ is even, we have aRa; hence, R is reflexive.
   (ii) Symmetry: We need to figure out if aRb implies bRa; that is, if $3a + 5b$ is even, does this imply that $3b + 5a$ is even? So assume $3a + 5b$ is even. Then we can write $3a + 5b = 2k$ for some $k \in \mathbb{Z}$. Then we have that $3b + 5a = (3a + 5b) - 2b + 2a = 2k - 2b + 2a = 2(k - b + a)$, so that $3b + 5a$ is even. Hence, R is symmetric.

(iii) Transitivity: We need to figure out if aRb and bRc implies aRc. That is, if $3a + 5b$ and $3b + 5c$ are even, does that mean $3a + 5c$ is even? Assume $3a + 5b = 2k$ and $3b + 5c = 2l$ for integers k and l. Adding these two equations yields $3a + 8b + 5c = 2k + 2l$. But that means $3a + 5c = 2(k + l - 4b)$, which is even. Hence, R is transitive.

Conclusion: R is an equivalence relation.

Note on the last example: There are *many* variations on problems like these. In general they will require an adept use of algebra and general mathematical skill to figure out.

Now, there are many more examples we can give on this topic, and we can go even deeper into topics like equivalence classes and the integers mod n; but this is all we need for now. So we move on to a discussion about the differences between discrete and continuous representations.

Discrete versus Continuous Representations

Perhaps the most elementary way of describing the difference between discrete and continuous data is that of countability. That is, discrete data can be counted whereas continuous data can't—continuous data can be approximated, measured, and so on, but not counted. To use more math jargon, one could say that discrete data is *countable*. What this really means is *listable*. We can list each point in a discrete data set and number them using integers (even if only in theory are there such things as discrete data sets with an infinite number of data points). So, to summarize, one could say that discrete data is countable, whereas continuous data is measurable. The word *measurable* can have various meanings depending on the level and area of mathematics one is doing.

Being countable has certain consequences, and this can further showcase the difference between the discrete and the continuous. For instance, discrete data can take on only certain values, whereas continuous data can take on *any* value within some range. An example would be the number of students in a class, versus a person's height or weight. The first is an example of discrete data. You can only give an integer answer for the number of students in a class; you cannot have 0.5 students or π students. However, a function measuring the height or weight of a person would be a continuous one, because the function would be able to take on any value within some range that makes sense.

Discrete carries with it the idea of things being separate or isolated and data having gaps. When counting the number of students in a class, for example, there is a minimum gap you must respect. After "one" student, the next value you can take on is "two" students—nothing in between. Continuous data, in contrast, has no gaps. This is illustrated nicely by the kinds of graphs or charts one can use when representing discrete versus continuous data. To graph, say, the number of students taking certain classes at a college, a bar chart may be used. The bars are isolated, and each bar would represent one subject and the number of students taking that subject. Very isolated. Very "gappy." However, if you were in an algebra, precalculus, or calculus class and you were asked to draw a continuous function (perhaps a polynomial), you would realize something interesting: You would be able to draw the graph without lifting your pencil off the page. There is a smoothness and *continuity* to it. No gaps. No isolation.

We do not wish to go very deeply into this, but hope that the above will give you some idea of the differences between discrete and continuous data and what kinds of representations they can take on.

We end this section with some mind-boggling admissions. At this level, it is very weird to think of the rational numbers as discrete or continuous representations. They certainly aren't continuous, but with our current tools, you'd be hard-pressed to determine whether they are discrete, either. The rational numbers have gaps, just as the integers do—in fact, the gaps in the rational numbers are where the *irrational numbers* (such as π or e) live, and there are more irrational numbers than there are rational ones! Indeed, mind-boggling. The gaps between the rational numbers outnumber the rational numbers themselves! But it is hard to isolate a rational number. Between any two rational numbers, you can find another one (in fact, an infinite number of rational numbers); and if you plot a rational number on a number line, and make an open interval of *any* length with that rational number in the center, you are guaranteed to find another rational number in that interval. So isolation becomes tricky, but gaps are still there. And with that mind-boggling note, we move on to counting techniques.

Counting Techniques

At this point, we need not talk about the importance of counting things. That much should be clear by now: Counting is important! But counting wisely can be just as important. Sometimes counting a large number of things is not as straightforward and simple as saying "one, two, three, . . ." The challenges of counting go beyond just counting to a large number; many times, we wish to count the number of possible scenarios that can happen given a certain experiment, or the number of ways we can arrange things, or the number of ways we can make groups of things. There are techniques that can make our counting more efficient, thereby saving us time, energy, computation, and headaches. In this section, we cover three techniques: the multiplication principle, permutations, and combinations.

The Multiplication Principle

The idea behind this principle is the following: If one has a multistaged experiment and each stage has a certain number of possibilities that can happen, then the total number of possibilities for the whole experiment is the product of all these numbers. That is, if there are n_1 possible options for the first stage, and n_2 possible options for the second stage, and n_3 possible options for the third stage, and so on, then the total number of possible options for the whole experiment is $n_1 \cdot n_2 \cdot n_3 \ldots$.

Example
A man has three shirts, four pairs of pants, and two jackets. If being fashionable is not a concern and all items of clothing are distinguishable, how many different possible shirt-pants-jacket outfits can the man put together?

Solution: Here, the experiment is making an outfit. It consists of three stages: choosing a shirt to wear, choosing a pair of pants to wear, and choosing a jacket to wear. There are three possibilities for the first stage, four for the second, and two for the third; so the total number of possible outfits is:

$$3 \cdot 4 \cdot 2 = 24$$

The man can put together 24 different outfits.

Now, things can get a bit more complicated. What if the man had choices between the stages he can go through?

The Notions of "And" and "Or" in Counting
This notion can be summarized in the following way: When counting in a multistaged experiment, one can think of *and* as multiply and *or* as add or sum.

This falls in line with the multiplication rule. For example, to make an outfit, the man in the previous example had to choose a shirt *and* a pair of pants *and* a jacket. Phrasing the problem using *and* tells us we need to multiply. So we take the number of possible shirts *multiplied by* the number of possible pants *multiplied by* the number of possible jackets.

Every time an *or* is introduced, however, we have to use a sum to separate the possible options.

Example

For his work attire, a man has three shirts, four pairs of pants, two jackets, and four neckties. Where the man works, the dress code dictates that a shirt and pants must be worn, but an employee may wear either a jacket or a necktie (but not both a jacket and a necktie). How many possible work outfits could the man put together?

Solution: There are two cases here we must consider. The man can wear a jacket *or* a necktie. That tells us we have to figure out how many outfits can go with a jacket and how many outfits can go with a necktie and *sum* them together.

The number of outfits the man can put together is:

$$\underbrace{3 \cdot 4 \cdot 2}_{\text{choosing a jacket}} \underset{OR}{+} \underbrace{3 \cdot 4 \cdot 4}_{\text{choosing a tie}} = 72$$

Example

In the previous example, what if the man could choose to wear either a tie or a jacket or both? How many full work outfits could he put together?

Solution: In this case, the number of outfits he could put together is:

$$\underbrace{3 \cdot 4 \cdot 2}_{\text{choosing a jacket}} \underset{OR}{+} \underbrace{3 \cdot 4 \cdot 4}_{\text{choosing a tie}} \underset{OR}{+} \underbrace{3 \cdot 4 \cdot 2 \cdot 4}_{\text{choosing both}} = 168$$

Permutations

To understand this and the next section, we have to remind ourselves about factorials.

Definition: For a positive integer n, we define the factorial of n (read "n factorial" and denoted $n!$) to be the product of all integers between 1 and n. That is,

$$n! = n \cdot (n-1) \cdots 2 \cdot 1$$

We also define, by convention, that $0! = 1$.

Example

- $2! = 2 \cdot 1 = 2$
- $3! = 3 \cdot 2 \cdot 1 = 6$
- $5! = 5 \cdot 4 \cdot 3 \cdot 2 \cdot 1 = 120$

To permute means to arrange things in a different order. For example, you can permute the two letters a and b in two ways: ab or ba. You can permute the three letters a, b, and c in six ways: abc, acb, bac, bca, cab, or cba. That is, you can permute two objects in two ways and three objects in six ways (notice that $2! = 2$ and $3! = 6$). So a factorial tells you the number of ways you can permute a given number of objects. But not all the time do we want to permute a given number of objects. Sometimes we want to, say, take a subset of a number of objects and permute those, or arrange them in some way. To do this in a way that *order matters*, we use the *permutation*.

Definition: A permutation, denoted P_nP_r or P_r^n or something similar, gives the number of ways you can choose r objects from n objects in a way that order matters. It is computed by

$$P_r^n = \frac{n!}{(n-r)!}$$

Example

A race involves 10 people. Assuming ties are not allowed, and prizes of a gold medal, a silver medal, and a bronze medal will be awarded to the first, second, and third finishers, respectively, how many ways can the race end?

Solution: In this case, order matters. There is a first, a second, and a third. We can look at and solve this problem in two ways.

1. There are 10 possibilities for who can come first; once the first place winner is identified, there are nine possibilities for who can come second, and then eight possibilities for who can come third. By the multiplication principle, the race can end in $10 \cdot 9 \cdot 8 = 720$ ways.

2. This is a permutation problem! We want to choose three "objects" from 10 "objects" in a particular order: first, second, third. So the number of ways the race can end is:

$$P_3^{10} = \frac{10!}{(10-3)!} = \frac{10!}{7!} = 10 \cdot 9 \cdot 8 = 720$$

Notice that the 3 in this case tells you the number of factors of 10! that you want to multiply together. Using the order in which we defined the permutation, the factors of 10! are 10, 9, 8, 7, 6, 5, 4, 3, 2, 1. Simply take the first three (10, 9, 8) and multiply them. The skipped steps for the previous calculation would look like this:

$$P_3^{10} = \frac{10 \cdot 9 \cdot 8 \cdot 7 \cdot 6 \cdot 5 \cdot 4 \cdot 3 \cdot 2 \cdot 1}{7 \cdot 6 \cdot 5 \cdot 4 \cdot 3 \cdot 2 \cdot 1} = 10 \cdot 9 \cdot 8$$
$$= 720$$

The factors in 7! would cancel, leaving you with the first three factors of the 10!, and we have our answer!

Combinations

A combination is similar to a permutation in that we are counting the number of ways to choose r objects from n objects; the difference is that order does *not* matter.

Definition: A combination, denoted $\binom{n}{r}$ or $C_n C_r$ or C_r^n or something similar, gives the number of ways you can choose r objects from n objects in such a way that order does *not* matter. It is computed by:

$$\binom{n}{r} = \frac{n!}{r!(n-r)!}$$

Also, recall that $\binom{n}{r}$ is often read "n choose r." This will help you to remember you're choosing r objects from n objects—if you have n objects and choose r of them (without regard for order), you have n choose r.

Example

You wish to create a committee from 10 men and eight women, all of whom are eligible to serve on the committee. If the committee must have four men and three women serving on it, how many ways can a committee be made?

Solution: You must choose four men *and* three women. (The *and* indicates that multiplication will be at work here.) Order does not matter, since ranking positions on the committee are not considered, so we use combinations. The number of ways you can choose four men from 10 men is $\binom{10}{4} = 210$ ways. The number of ways you can choose three women from eight women is $\binom{8}{3} = 56$ ways. Hence, the number of ways you can choose this many men *and* this many women is:

$$\binom{10}{4} \cdot \binom{8}{3} = 210 \cdot 56 = \boxed{11,760}$$

So, there are 11,760 possible ways in which a committee could be made.

Here's a more complicated example using pretty much all that we've learned so far.

Example

In the previous example, suppose one of the men and one of the women are in a feud and refuse to serve on a committee with each other. How many ways could a committee be made if you wish to keep these two apart?

Solution: There would be three ways to form a committee in this case: (1) If the man is chosen, don't choose the woman he is feuding with, *or* (2) if the woman is chosen, don't choose the man she is feuding with, *or* (3) choose neither of the feuding individuals. (The *or* indicates a sum will be at play here.)

In case (1), assuming the man is chosen, you now need to choose only three more men; on top of this, you can choose from only seven women (because you don't want to pick the woman he would fight with). Thus, there is 1 way to choose the man, $\binom{9}{3}$ ways to choose the other three men, and then $\binom{7}{3}$ ways to choose three women whom the first man won't

fight with. Hence, by the multiplication rule, there are $1 \cdot \binom{9}{3} \cdot \binom{7}{3} = 2{,}940$ ways to make a committee in the first case.

Similarly, there are $1 \cdot \binom{7}{2} \cdot \binom{9}{4} = 2{,}646$ ways to make the committee in case (2).

Last, case (3) means you have only nine men and seven women to choose from, since you want to leave out one man and one woman. Hence, there are $\binom{9}{4} \cdot \binom{7}{3} = 4{,}410$ ways to make a committee in this case.

Hence, in total, the possible number of ways we can create a committee keeping the feuding man and woman separate are:

$$\underbrace{1}_{\substack{\text{choose} \\ \text{the man}}} \cdot \underbrace{\binom{9}{3}}_{\substack{\text{choose the} \\ \text{other} \\ \text{three} \\ \text{men}}} \cdot \underbrace{\binom{7}{3}}_{\substack{\text{choose the} \\ \text{women} \\ \text{other than} \\ \text{the feuding} \\ \text{one}}} \underset{\text{OR}}{+} \underbrace{1}_{\substack{\text{choose the} \\ \text{feuding woman}}} \cdot \underbrace{\binom{7}{2}}_{\substack{\text{choose the} \\ \text{other} \\ \text{two} \\ \text{women}}} \cdot \underbrace{\binom{9}{4}}_{\substack{\text{choose the} \\ \text{men} \\ \text{other than} \\ \text{the feuding} \\ \text{one}}} \underset{\text{OR}}{+} \underbrace{\binom{9}{4}}_{\substack{\text{choose four} \\ \text{nonfeuding} \\ \text{men}}} \cdot \underbrace{\binom{7}{3}}_{\substack{\text{choose three} \\ \text{nonfeuding} \\ \text{women}}}$$

That is, $1 \cdot \binom{9}{3} \cdot \binom{7}{3} + 1 \cdot \binom{7}{2} \cdot \binom{9}{4} + \binom{9}{4} \cdot \binom{7}{3} = 2{,}940 + 2{,}646 + 4{,}410 = \boxed{9{,}996}$

Another approach? Of course there is!

How about finding all the committees where we *do* put the feuding man and woman together? Then, we can subtract that from the total number of committees found in the preceding example. For a committee to have the feuding members, we must choose them (1 way each to do that, so $1 \cdot 1$), then choose the other men from the remaining nine men ($\binom{9}{3}$ ways to do that), then choose the other women from the remaining seven women ($\binom{7}{2}$ ways to do that); so there are $1 \cdot 1 \cdot \binom{9}{3} \cdot \binom{7}{2} = 1{,}764$ ways to create a com-

mittee with the feuding members. Since the total number of ways a committee can be formed is 11,760, the total number of committees where the feuding man and woman do not serve together would be:

$$11{,}760 - 1{,}764 = 9{,}996$$

which agrees with our previous answer! (*Whew!*) Okay, that does it for discrete mathematics. On to the next practice test!

C H A P T E R
11

PRAXIS II®
MATHEMATICS:
CONTENT
KNOWLEDGE
PRACTICE TEST

CHAPTER SUMMARY

Here is the second full-length practice test for Praxis II® Mathematics: Content Knowledge. Now that you have taken one exam and brushed up on your studying, take this exam to see how much your score has improved.

Like Chapter 3, this chapter contains a full-length practice test that mirrors the Praxis II® Mathematics: Content Knowledge exam. Though the actual exam you will take will be computer-based, the question types for the exam are replicated here for you in the book.

This time, as you take this practice exam, you should simulate the actual test-taking experience as closely as you can. Find a quiet place to work where you won't be disturbed. Follow the time constraint noted at the beginning of the test.

After you finish taking your practice test, you should review the answer explanations. See A Note on Scoring after the last answer explanation to find information on how to score your exam.

Good luck!

1.	ⓐ	ⓑ	ⓒ	ⓓ		21.	ⓐ	ⓑ	ⓒ	ⓓ		41.	ⓐ	ⓑ	ⓒ	ⓓ
2.	ⓐ	ⓑ	ⓒ	ⓓ		22.	ⓐ	ⓑ	ⓒ	ⓓ		42.	ⓐ	ⓑ	ⓒ	ⓓ
3.	ⓐ	ⓑ	ⓒ	ⓓ		23.	ⓐ	ⓑ	ⓒ	ⓓ		43.	ⓐ	ⓑ	ⓒ	ⓓ
4.	ⓐ	ⓑ	ⓒ	ⓓ		24.	ⓐ	ⓑ	ⓒ	ⓓ		44.	ⓐ	ⓑ	ⓒ	ⓓ
5.	ⓐ	ⓑ	ⓒ	ⓓ		25.	ⓐ	ⓑ	ⓒ	ⓓ		45.	ⓐ	ⓑ	ⓒ	ⓓ
6.	ⓐ	ⓑ	ⓒ	ⓓ		26.	ⓐ	ⓑ	ⓒ	ⓓ		46.	ⓐ	ⓑ	ⓒ	ⓓ
7.	ⓐ	ⓑ	ⓒ	ⓓ		27.	ⓐ	ⓑ	ⓒ	ⓓ		47.	ⓐ	ⓑ	ⓒ	ⓓ
8.	ⓐ	ⓑ	ⓒ	ⓓ		28.	ⓐ	ⓑ	ⓒ	ⓓ		48.	ⓐ	ⓑ	ⓒ	ⓓ
9.	ⓐ	ⓑ	ⓒ	ⓓ		29.	ⓐ	ⓑ	ⓒ	ⓓ		49.	ⓐ	ⓑ	ⓒ	ⓓ
10.	ⓐ	ⓑ	ⓒ	ⓓ		30.	ⓐ	ⓑ	ⓒ	ⓓ		50.	ⓐ	ⓑ	ⓒ	ⓓ
11.	ⓐ	ⓑ	ⓒ	ⓓ		31.	ⓐ	ⓑ	ⓒ	ⓓ		51.	ⓐ	ⓑ	ⓒ	ⓓ
12.	ⓐ	ⓑ	ⓒ	ⓓ		32.	ⓐ	ⓑ	ⓒ	ⓓ		52.	ⓐ	ⓑ	ⓒ	ⓓ
13.	ⓐ	ⓑ	ⓒ	ⓓ		33.	ⓐ	ⓑ	ⓒ	ⓓ		53.	ⓐ	ⓑ	ⓒ	ⓓ
14.	ⓐ	ⓑ	ⓒ	ⓓ		34.	ⓐ	ⓑ	ⓒ	ⓓ		54.	ⓐ	ⓑ	ⓒ	ⓓ
15.	ⓐ	ⓑ	ⓒ	ⓓ		35.	ⓐ	ⓑ	ⓒ	ⓓ		55.	ⓐ	ⓑ	ⓒ	ⓓ
16.	ⓐ	ⓑ	ⓒ	ⓓ		36.	ⓐ	ⓑ	ⓒ	ⓓ		56.	ⓐ	ⓑ	ⓒ	ⓓ
17.	ⓐ	ⓑ	ⓒ	ⓓ		37.	ⓐ	ⓑ	ⓒ	ⓓ		57.	ⓐ	ⓑ	ⓒ	ⓓ
18.	ⓐ	ⓑ	ⓒ	ⓓ		38.	ⓐ	ⓑ	ⓒ	ⓓ		58.	ⓐ	ⓑ	ⓒ	ⓓ
19.	ⓐ	ⓑ	ⓒ	ⓓ		39.	ⓐ	ⓑ	ⓒ	ⓓ		59.	ⓐ	ⓑ	ⓒ	ⓓ
20.	ⓐ	ⓑ	ⓒ	ⓓ		40.	ⓐ	ⓑ	ⓒ	ⓓ		60.	ⓐ	ⓑ	ⓒ	ⓓ

Recommended Time—150 minutes
60 questions

Directions: Read each item and select the response that best answers the question.

1. If $f(x) = e^{3x+1}$, then $f^{-1}(x) =$
   a. $3(\ln(x) - 1)$
   b. $\frac{1}{3}(\ln(x) - 1)$
   c. $3e^{3x+1}$
   d. $\frac{1}{3}e^{3x+1}$

2. Find the area of the region bounded by the curves
$$f(x) = x^2 - 5$$
$$g(x) = 3x - 1$$
   a. $\frac{95}{6}$
   b. $\frac{145}{6}$
   c. $\frac{125}{6}$
   d. $-\frac{145}{6}$

3. If the diameter of a circle has endpoints $(-3,-2)$ and $(1,-2)$, then the equation of this circle is
   a. $(x + 1)^2 + (y + 2)^2 = 4$
   b. $(x + 1)^2 + (y + 2)^2 = 16$
   c. $(x + 1)^2 + (y - 2)^2 = 4$
   d. $(x + 3)^2 + (y + 2)^2 = 8$

4. Which expression is equivalent to $\frac{1}{\sec^2 x}$?
   a. $\frac{1}{\cos^2 x}$
   b. $1 - \cos^2 x$
   c. $\sec x \tan x$
   d. $1 - \sin^2 x$

5. Solve $5x > 24 - x^2$.
   a. $(-8,3)$
   b. $(-\infty,-8) \cup (3,\infty)$
   c. $[-\infty,-8) \cup [3,\infty)$
   d. $[-8,3]$

6. Henry working alone can install wall-to-wall carpeting in a 2,000-square-foot house in 20 hours. Frank can carpet the same house in 16 hours if working alone. If Henry and Frank decide to work together, approximately how many hours will it take them to carpet a 2,000-square-foot home?
   a. 18 hours
   b. 8 hours
   c. 9 hours
   d. 2 hours

7. Find all solutions to the equation $0 = x^3 + 2x^2 - 13x + 10$. Write multiple solutions separated by commas.

   _____

8. Select all the functions that are one-to-one.
   a. $f(x) = 3x^2 + 7$
   b. $g(x) = \sin 4x$
   c. $h(x) = e^{x^2} + 1$
   d. $j(x) = \ln(x - 4)$

9. The graph of the function $f(x) = a(x - h)^2 + 1$ on the closed interval $[1,4]$ is given by

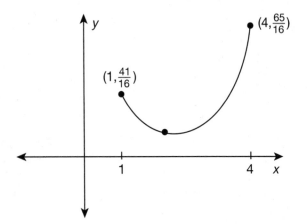

Find h, expressing your answer as a fraction.

_____

10. What is the probability that in a group of four friends at least two share the same birthday?

a. 0.99816

b. 0.01636

c. 0.01342

d. 0.04205

11. In this figure, lines l and m are parallel. What is the measure of angle θ?

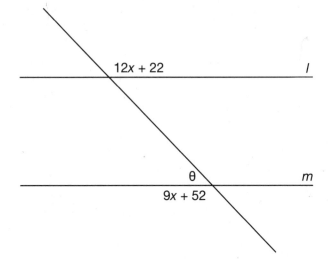

a. 38

b. 142

c. 10

d. 170

12. For what values of c is the matrix

$$A = \begin{bmatrix} 3 & 2 \\ c & 1.4 \end{bmatrix} \text{ not invertible?}$$

a. 4.3

b. 0

c. −1.4

d. 2.1

13. If $f(x) = -\dfrac{1}{\sqrt{x}}$, then $f'(4) =$

a. $\dfrac{1}{16}$

b. $\dfrac{1}{8}$

c. $-\dfrac{1}{4}$

d. $-\dfrac{3}{8}$

14. The interior of a cylindrical wading pool of radius 20 feet and depth 3 feet is showing signs of wear and needs to be repainted with a special paint that costs $280.60 for a five-gallon bucket or $60 for a one-gallon bucket. A five-gallon bucket of paint will cover approximately 650 square feet, and a one-gallon bucket will cover approximately 125 square feet. The paint is purchased so that the painters will have just enough paint to cover the interior of the pool with as little left over as possible. If the paint can be purchased only in five-gallon buckets or in one-gallon buckets, how much will it cost to paint the interior of this pool?
a. $901.80
b. $840.00
c. $741.20
d. $681.20

15. If $\cos\theta = -\frac{12}{13}$ and $\frac{\pi}{2} \leq \theta \leq \pi$, then $\csc\theta =$
a. $\frac{5}{13}$
b. $-\frac{13}{5}$
c. $\frac{13}{5}$
d. $\frac{13}{12}$

16. $i^{126} =$
a. 1
b. −1
c. i
d. $-i$

17. If the discriminant of a quadratic equation is nonzero, then which of the following graphs could be the graph of the corresponding quadratic function? Select *all* possible graphs.

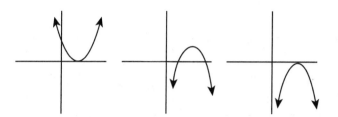

18. A particle's velocity is given by this graph. At what time does the particle have the greatest acceleration?

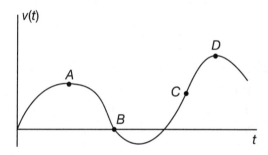

a. A
b. B
c. C
d. D

19. The number of hours a certain brand of 12-ounce scented candle can burn is normally distributed with a mean of 88.2 hours and a standard deviation of 7.8 hours. What percentage of these candles will burn for more than four days?
a. 5%
b. 1.5%
c. 32%
d. 16%

20. The half-life of a certain chemical compound is 24.7 years. How much of a 320-gram sample of this compound will be left after 50 years?
   a. 1,301.76 grams
   b. 116.30 grms
   c. 84.58 grams
   d. 78.66 grams

21. The function $f(x) = \frac{3x^2 - x - 4}{3x^2 - 7x + 4}$ has a removable discontinuity at what point?
   a. $\left(\frac{4}{3}, 0\right)$
   b. $\left(\frac{4}{3}, 1\right)$
   c. $\left(\frac{4}{3}, -1\right)$
   d. $\left(\frac{4}{3}, 7\right)$

22. Find the center of the ellipse $4x^2 + y^2 + 16x + 2y + 13 = 0$.
   a. $(2, -1)$
   b. $(-2, -1)$
   c. $(1, 2)$
   d. $(-1, -2)$

23. A rubber ball is dropped from a window 20 feet above an empty parking lot. The ball bounces and each bounce is $\frac{4}{5}$ as high as the previous bounce. Which of the following is an expression for the height of the ball on its nth bounce?
   a. $16\left(\frac{4}{5}\right)^{n-1}$
   b. $20\left(\frac{4}{5}\right)^{n-1}$
   c. $16\left(\frac{4}{5}\right)^{n}$
   d. $16\left(1 - \frac{4n}{5}\right)$

24. What is $\lim\limits_{x \to \infty} \frac{3(x - 1)(x + 1)}{5x^2 + 1}$?
   a. $\frac{1}{5}$
   b. 0
   c. ∞
   d. $\frac{3}{5}$

25. A company produces ball bearings. It takes a sample of a recent production run to measure the diameter of the ball bearings and check for defects. The diameter measurements of five of the selected bearings are 0.501 cm, 0.507 cm, 0.511 cm, 0.497 cm, and 0.492 cm.

Find the standard deviation of these measurements.

_____

26. $\frac{3 - 5i}{1 + 4i} =$
   a. $-1 - i$
   b. $1 + i$
   c. $-1 + i$
   d. $1 - i$

27. At midnight the cost of electricity provided by your power company is at a low of 2.5 cents/kWh. By noon the cost reaches a high of 24.5 cents/kWh. If this cost pattern repeats daily, then a possible formula for your cost of electricity as a function of t hours since midnight could be given by $C(t) =$
   a. $-11\sin\left(\frac{\pi}{12}t\right) + \frac{27}{2}$
   b. $11\sin(24t) + 22$
   c. $-11\cos\left(\frac{\pi}{12}t\right) + \frac{27}{2}$
   d. $11\cos(24t) + 22$

28. Suppose you are given the graph of $f(x)$. Which of the following is a list of the transformations, in the appropriate order, that must be applied to $f(x)$ to obtain the graph of $g(x) = -\frac{1}{2}f(x - 2) + 3$?
- **a.** Shift left two units, shift up three units, reflect in the x-axis, shrink by a factor of $\frac{1}{2}$.
- **b.** Shift right two units, reflect in the x-axis, shift down three units, shrink by a factor of $\frac{1}{2}$.
- **c.** Shift right two units, shrink by a factor of $\frac{1}{2}$, reflect in the x-axis, shift up three units.
- **d.** Shift left two units, reflect in the x-axis, shrink by a factor of $\frac{1}{2}$, shift up three units.

29. A bank advertises a nominal interest rate on a loan of 4.25% compounded monthly. What is the effective annual interest rate for this loan?
- **a.** 4.295%
- **b.** 4.334%
- **c.** 4.318%
- **d.** 4.341%

30. Which of the values of k makes the piecewise defined function $f(x)$ continuous at $x = 2$?

$$f(x) = \begin{cases} -x^2 + 2x + k, & x \leq 2 \\ 10x - 29, & x > 2 \end{cases}$$

_____

31. Four circles of radius r are arranged as pictured.

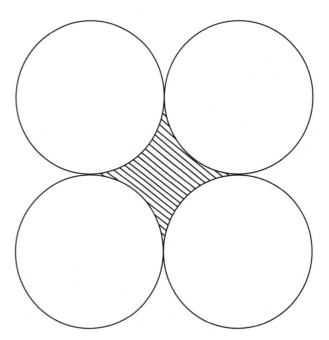

Find the area of the shaded region.
- **a.** $(4 - \pi)r^2$
- **b.** $(1 - \pi)r^2$
- **c.** $(2 - \pi)r^2$
- **d.** $(2 + \pi)r^2$

32. A 60-foot-tall telephone pole must be anchored to the ground by wires that make an angle of 30 degrees with the ground. What is the length of each of these wires?
- **a.** 120 feet
- **b.** 60 feet
- **c.** 180 feet
- **d.** 30 feet

33. Find the range of the function $f(x) = 3\cos x + 5.2$.
- **a.** [–3,3]
- **b.** [–5.2,5.2]
- **c.** [–3.2,8.6]
- **d.** [2.2,8.2]

34. If the volume of a sphere is 288π cm^3, what is its surface area?

   a. $24\pi\sqrt{6}$ cm^2

   b. 144π cm^2

   c. 24π cm^2

   d. $64\pi\sqrt[3]{36}$ cm^2

35. Triangle ABC has vertices $(4,-2)$, $(3,2)$, and $(-1,1)$. Which of the following represents a reflection of the triangle in the y-axis?

   a. $\begin{bmatrix} -1 & 0 \\ 0 & 1 \end{bmatrix}\begin{bmatrix} 4 & 3 & -1 \\ -2 & 2 & 1 \end{bmatrix}$

   b. $\begin{bmatrix} 1 & 0 \\ 0 & -1 \end{bmatrix}\begin{bmatrix} 4 & 3 & -1 \\ -2 & 2 & 1 \end{bmatrix}$

   c. $\begin{bmatrix} -1 & 0 \\ 0 & -1 \end{bmatrix}\begin{bmatrix} 4 & 3 & -1 \\ -2 & 2 & 1 \end{bmatrix}$

   d. $\begin{bmatrix} 1 & 0 \\ 0 & 1 \end{bmatrix}\begin{bmatrix} 4 & 3 & 1 \\ 2 & -2 & -1 \end{bmatrix}$

36. $\int 6x^2 e^{2x}\, dx =$

   a. $3x^2 e^{2x} + 3xe^{2x} - \frac{3}{2}e^{2x} + C$

   b. $6x^2 + 3x^2 e^{2x} + \frac{3}{2}e^{2x} + C$

   c. $3x^2 e^{2x} - 3xe^{2x} + 3e^{2x} + C$

   d. $3x^2 e^{2x} - 3xe^{2x} + \frac{3}{2}e^{2x} + C$

37. A kayaker paddled 12 miles down the Moodna Creek in two hours, but his return trip took three hours. Find the rate the kayaker can paddle in still water.

   a. 1.33 miles/hour

   b. 10 miles/hour

   c. 6 miles/hour

   d. 6.67 miles/hour

38. A customer is thinking about switching cable TV providers. He has two companies to choose from. Company A charges a one-time $520 installation fee and a monthly service charge of $120. Company B charges a one-time installation fee of $400 and $140 per month. Assuming that both companies do not adjust their monthly rates, and that the customer will always choose the least expensive option, when will the customer switch to company A?

   a. in four months

   b. in six months

   c. in eight months

   d. in two months

39. Find the exact value of $\cos\left(\arcsin\left(-\frac{2}{3}\right)\right)$.

   a. $-\frac{3}{2}$

   b. $-\frac{\sqrt{5}}{2}$

   c. $\frac{2}{3}$

   d. $\frac{\sqrt{5}}{3}$

40. Which of the following is the graph of the function?

$$f(x) = \begin{cases} -3x + 5, & x < 1 \\ x^2 - 5x + 1, & 1 \le x < 3 \\ 2x, & 3 < x \end{cases}$$

a.

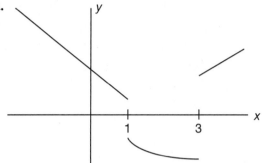

b.

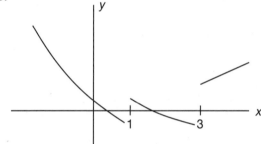

c.

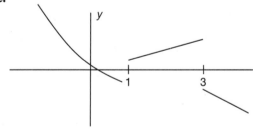

d.

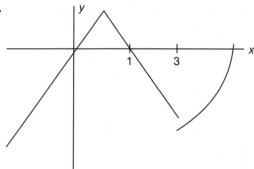

41. Solve $\frac{2x-5}{x-3} \le 4$.

a. $\left[3, \frac{7}{2}\right)$

b. $(-\infty, 3]$

c. $[-\infty, 3] \cup \left(\frac{7}{2}, \infty\right)$

d. $(-\infty, \infty)$

42. One card is selected from a standard deck of 52 playing cards. What is the probability that the card is either a diamond or a face card?

a. $\frac{13}{52}$

b. $\frac{12}{52}$

c. $\frac{3}{13}$

d. $\frac{25}{52}$

43. Find the domain of the function $f(x) = \log_2(3x - 1) + 5$.

a. $x > 0$

b. $x < -\frac{1}{3}$

c. $x > \frac{1}{3}$

d. $x > \frac{16}{3}$

44. In the figure, $\angle B \cong \angle E$ and $\overline{AD}$ bisects $\overline{BE}$. Which of the following methods proves that $\triangle BAC \cong \triangle EDC$?

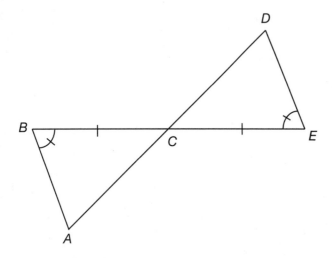

   a. SSS
   b. SAS
   c. AAS
   d. ASA

45. Solve the system of equations for z.

$$2x + 2y + z = 4$$
$$3x + y - 2z = 5$$
$$x \qquad - 3z = -2$$

   a. 4
   b. −3
   c. 0
   d. 2

46. Susan wishes to invest $15,000 into a fund that will double her money in 10 years. The fund she chooses has an annual effective interest rate of i. Find i.
   a. 17.2%
   b. 7.2%
   c. 10.7%
   d. 7.0%

47. If $f(x) = -x^3 + 1$ and $h(x) = f(2x)$, what is $h(2)$?
   a. −63
   b. −7
   c. 4
   d. −4

48. A jar contains eight blue marbles, five red marbles, 12 green marbles, and four orange marbles. Two marbles are randomly selected from the bag one after the other without replacement. What is the probability that both marbles are red?
   a. 0.0238
   b. 0.0246
   c. 0.0297
   d. 0.3153

49. For the binomial expansion of $(2x - 3y)^9$, the coefficient of the term $x^4 y^5$ is
   a. −3,888
   b. −489,888
   c. 326,592
   d. 2,592

50. Find the area of the triangle with two sides of length 62 and 20 and included angle 130°.
   a. 474.948
   b. 398.528
   c. 62.816
   d. 52.709

51. The graph of f', the derivative of f, is given here. The x-coordinate of a relative maximum of f is $x =$ _____.

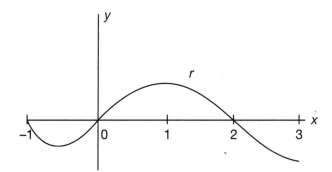

52. In how many ways can a team consisting of four men and five women be chosen from a group of seven men and nine women?

a. $\begin{pmatrix} 7 \\ 4 \end{pmatrix}\begin{pmatrix} 9 \\ 5 \end{pmatrix}$

b. 20

c. $\begin{pmatrix} 7 \\ 5 \end{pmatrix}\begin{pmatrix} 9 \\ 4 \end{pmatrix}$

d. $_7P_4 \cdot {_9}P_5$

53. Which of the following graphs is/are the graph of a function that has positive first and second derivatives on the interval shown?

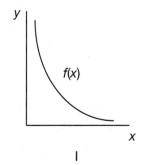

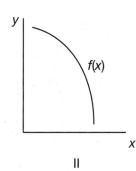

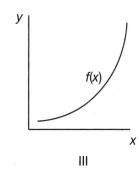

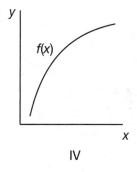

| I | II | III | IV |

a. I and III

b. II and IV

c. IV only

d. III only

54. Values for the function $f(x)$ are given in the table. Which of the following could be an estimate for $\int_{5}^{17} f(x)\ dx$?

x	5	8	11	14	17
f(x)	2	5	7	10	8

a. 80

b. 75

c. 72

d. 104

55. For the triangle given here, find cos θ.

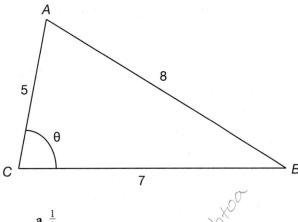

a. $\frac{1}{2}$

b. $\frac{1}{7}$

c. $\frac{11}{14}$

d. $\frac{7}{8}$

56. A study conducted by the U.S. military in World War II found that airplanes returning from combat missions were being hit by enemy fire more in certain sections of the plane than in others. As a result, these sections of U.S. combat airplanes were heavily reinforced with extra material to protect the planes from attack. Which characteristic of this study could produce a bias in the result?

a. sample size

b. population size

c. nationality of investigators

d. sample selection

57. Find the volume of the paraboloid formed by rotating the region bounded by the y-axis, x-axis, and the parabola $y = 4 - x^2$ about the y-axis.

a. 16π

b. 16

c. 4π

d. 8π

58. In this diagram, segment $\overline{AB}$ is tangent to the circle at point B. The length of segment AB is 6, and the length of segment AC is 4. What is the length of segment AD?

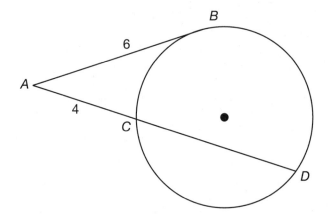

a. 9

b. 10

c. 13

d. 5

59. A conical reservoir of water with a diameter of 8 meters and a depth of 10 meters is being emptied at a rate of 5 cubic meters per hour. At what rate is the level of water decreasing when the depth of water is 6 meters?

a. −0.01 m/sec.

b. −0.28 m/sec.

c. −0.87 m/sec.

d. 0.87 m/sec.

60. For the scatter plot shown, which statement best describes the correlation between the variables x and y?

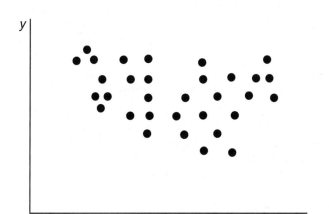

a. positive linear correlation
b. no correlation
c. negative linear correlation
d. nonlinear correlation

Answers and Explanations

1. b. The correct answer is derived as follows:
$x = e^{3y + 1}$
$\ln x = \ln e^{3y + 1}$
$\ln x = 3y + 1$ and $y = \frac{1}{3}(\ln x - 1)$. Choices **a, c,** and **d** are incorrect derivations.

2. c. The area of the region bounded by the curves is determined as follows:

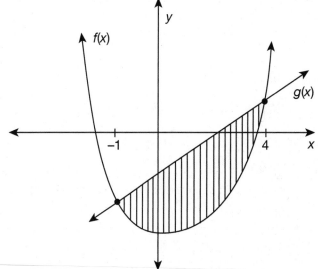

$x^2 - 5 = 3x - 1$
$x^2 - 3x - 4 = 0$
$(x - 4)(x + 1) = 0$
$x = 4, x = -1$
$\text{Area} = \int_{-1}^{4} 3x - 1 - (x^2 - 5)\, dx$

$$J_{-1} = \int_{-1}^{4} -x^2 + 3x + 4 \ \ dx \ = \frac{-x^3}{3} + \frac{3x^2}{2} + 4x \Big]_{-1}^{4}$$

$$= \frac{125}{6}$$

3. a. The equation of the circle is determined as follows:

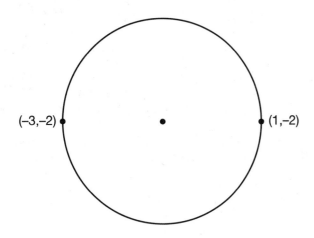

(−3,−2) •   •   • (1,−2)

Center = Midpoint of Diameter

$$= \left(\frac{(-3+1)}{2}, \frac{(-2+-2)}{2} \right)$$

$$= (-1, -2)$$

Length of diameter $= |1 - (-3)| = 4$

Radius $= \frac{4}{2} = 2$

Circle: $(x + 1)^2 + (y + 2)^2 = 4$.

4. d. The correct answer is determined as follows:

$$\frac{1}{\sec^2 x} = \frac{1}{\sec x} \cdot \frac{1}{\sec x} = \frac{1}{\left(\frac{1}{\cos^2 x} \right)} = \cos^2 x = 1 - \sin^2 x$$

5. b. The correct answer is solved as follows:

$$5x > 24 - x^2$$

$$x^2 + 5x - 24 > 0$$

$$(x - 3)(x + 8) > 0$$

$$x = 3, x = -8$$

$(x - 3)(x + 8) > 0 \qquad (x - 3)(x + 8) < 0 \qquad (x - 3)(x + 8) > 0$

⟵————————⊕————————⊕————————⟶

(−9) −8 (0) 3 (4)

Solution: $(-\infty, -8) \cup (3, \infty)$.

6. c. The correct answer is determined as follows:

Henry's work rate $= \frac{1}{20}$ job/hr.

Frank's work rate $= \frac{1}{16}$ job/hr.

Together: $\frac{1}{20} + \frac{1}{16} = \frac{1}{x}$ job/hr.

$$16x + 20x = 320$$

$$x = \frac{320}{36} = \frac{80}{9} = 9 \text{ hours}$$

7. All solutions to the equation $0 = x^3 + 2x^2 - 13x + 10$ are determined as follows:

First, we notice that $x = 1$ is a solution:

$$0 = (1)^3 + 2(1)^2 - 13(1) + 10$$

$$0 = 1 + 2 - 13 + 10$$

$$0 = 0$$

This means that $x - 1$ is a factor of $x^3 + 2x^2 - 13x + 10$.

We use synthetic division and a method for solving quadratics to find the remaining solutions.

	1	2	−13	10
		1	3	−10
1	1	3	−10	0

This shows that $x^3 + 2x^2 - 13x + 10 = (x - 1)(x^2 + 3x - 10)$.

To find the remaining solutions, we solve $x^2 + 3x - 10 = 0$:

$$x^2 + 3x - 10 = 0$$

$$(x + 5)(x - 2) = 0$$

$$x = -5, x = 2$$

8. d. This is the only function that is one-to-one. Using the fact that one-to-one functions are monotonic, we find the derivatives of the listed functions and see if these derivatives are everywhere positive or everywhere negative.

$f'(x) = 6x$, $f'(x) > 0$ for $x > 0$, and $f'(x) < 0$ for $x < 0$

Thus choice **a**, $f(x) = 3x^2 + 7$, is *not* one-to-one. Choice **b**, $g(x) = \sin 4x$, is clearly *not* one-to-one. Choice **c**, $h(x) = e^{x^2} + 1$, has derivative $h'(x) = e^{x^2}(2x)$ and is also *not* one-to-one, since $h(x) > 0$ when $x > 0$ and $h(x) < 0$ when $x < 0$. For choice **d**, $j(x) = \ln(x-4)$: $j'(x) = \frac{1}{x-4} \cdot 1$, but the domain of $j(x)$ is $x > 4$. This means that $j(x) > 0$ for all x in the domain of $j(x)$, so $j(x)$ is one-to-one.

9. The graph of the function $f(x) = a(x - h)^2 + 1$ on the closed interval $[1,4]$ is given by

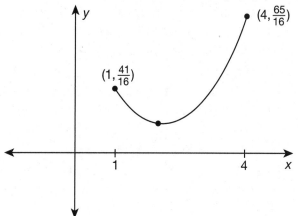

$\frac{41}{16} = a(1-h)^2 + 1$

$\frac{25}{16} = a(1-h)^2 \qquad \Rightarrow \qquad a = \frac{25}{16(1-h)^2}$

$\frac{65}{16} = \frac{25}{16(1-h)^2}(4-h)^2 + 1$

$\frac{49}{16} = \frac{25}{16} \cdot \frac{(4-h)^2}{(1-h)^2} \qquad \Rightarrow \qquad \frac{49}{25} = \frac{(4-h)^2}{(1-h)^2} = \left(\frac{4-h}{1-h}\right)^2$

Thus, $\quad \frac{4-h}{1-h} = \frac{7}{5} \quad$ OR $\quad \frac{4-h}{1-h} = -\frac{7}{5}$

$7 - 7h = 20 - 5h \quad$ OR $\quad 20 - 5h = -7 + 7h$

$-13 = 2h \qquad\qquad\qquad\qquad 27 = 12h$

$$h = \frac{27}{12} = \frac{9}{4}$$

10. b. The probability that in a group of four friends at least two share the same birthday is 0.016356. It's easier to compute this probability using the negation rule and complementary event: "not having the same birthday"

Let E = at least two share a birthday

Then $\Pr(E) = 1 - \Pr(E')$ E′ = none share a birthday

$\Pr(E')$: Choose a b-day for first person. Each person's b-day is an independent event.

$\Pr$(second has b-day different from first) = $\frac{364}{365}$

$\Pr$(third has b-day different from first and second) = $\frac{363}{365}$

$\Pr$(fourth has b-day different from first, second, and third) = $\frac{362}{365}$

Therefore, $\Pr(E) = 1 - \frac{364 \cdot 363 \cdot 362}{365^3} = .016356$

11. a. The measure of angle θ is calculated as follows:

$12x + 22 = 9x + 52$

$3x = 30$

$x = 10$

$12(10) + 22 = 142$

$180 - 142 = 38$

$\theta = 38$

12. d. We determine for what values of c the matrix $A = \begin{bmatrix} 3 & 2 \\ c & 1.4 \end{bmatrix}$ is *not* invertible as follows:

A is *not* invertible (singular) if and only if $\det A = 0$.

$\det A = 3(1.4) - 2c$

$4.2 - 2c = 0$

$c = 2.1$

13. a. The correct solution is as follows:

$f(x) = -x^{-\frac{1}{2}}$

$f'(x) = \frac{1}{2}x^{-\frac{3}{2}} = \frac{1}{2(\sqrt{x})^3}$

$f'(4) = \frac{1}{2(2)^3} = \frac{1}{16}$

14. c. To determine how much will it cost to paint the interior of this pool if the paint can be purchased only in five-gallon buckets or in one-gallon buckets:

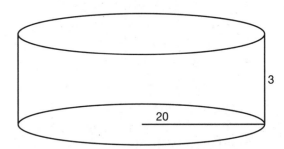

Surface area of interior = Area of bottom + Surface area of sides

$= \pi(20)^2 + 2\pi(20) \cdot 3$

$= 400\pi + 120\pi = 520\pi$ sq. ft.

$\approx 1,633.64$

$2(650) + x(125) = 1,633.64$

$125x = 333.64$

$x \approx 3$

Cost: $2(280.6) + 3(60) = \$741.20$

15. c. If $\cos \theta = -\frac{12}{13}$ and $\frac{\pi}{2} \le \theta \le \pi$, then $\csc \theta = \frac{13}{5}$. The equation is solved as follows:

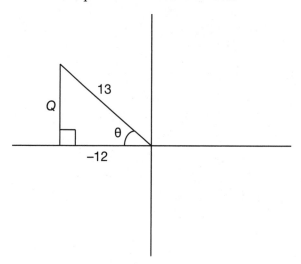

$$(13)^2 = (-12)^2 + \theta^2$$
$$\theta = \sqrt{13^2 - (-12)^2} = 5$$
$$\csc \theta = \frac{1}{\sin \theta} = \frac{13}{5}$$

16. b. The correct answer is determined as follows:

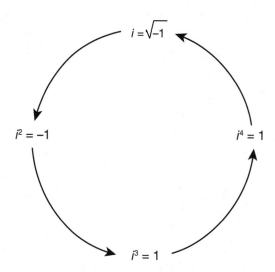

For i^{126}, 126 is even. We see from our cycles of i that an even power of i is 1 if the exponent is divisible by 4, and −1 otherwise. 126 is even, but *not* divisible by 4, so $i^{126} = -1$.

17. If the discriminant of a quadratic equation is positive, then the following two graphs could be the graph of the corresponding quadratic function:

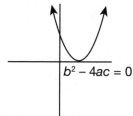

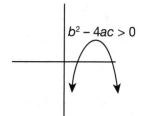

18. c. We determine at what time the particle has the greatest acceleration as follows:

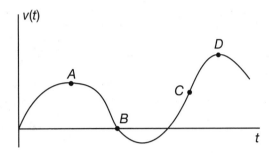

Acceleration is the slope (rate of change) of velocity with respect to time.

The graph of $v(t)$ has the steepest slope at C. Therefore, the greatest acceleration occurs at C.

19. d. The solution for the percentage of these candles that will burn for more than four days is as follows:

Let x = number of hours the candle burns.

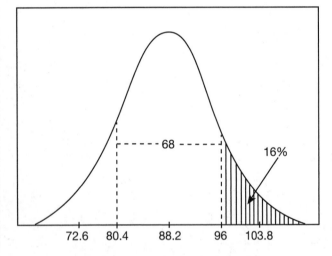

4 days = 96 hours

Using the 68–95–99.7 rule, we have:

$\Pr(x > 96) = \frac{1 - .68}{2} = .16 = 16\%$

20. d. Determine how much of a 320-gram sample of this compound will be left after 50 years as follows:

Since the half-life is 24.7 years, we have $\frac{1}{2} = e^{r(24.7)}$.

Solving for r: $\ln\frac{1}{2} = 24.7\,r$

$r = \frac{\ln\left(\frac{1}{2}\right)}{24.7} \approx -.028063$

Using this r-value and $t = 50$, we can find the desired amount:

$P = 320e^{-.028063(50)} = 78.66$ grams

21. d. The function $f(x) = \frac{3x^2 - x - 4}{3x^2 - 7x + 4}$ has a removable discontinuity at the point $\left(\frac{4}{3}, 7\right)$.

We determine this as follows:

$f(x) = \frac{(3x - 4)(x + 1)}{(3x + 4)(x - 1)}$

Since $x = \frac{4}{3}$ makes both the numerator and denominator zero, this indicates a removable discontinuity at $x = \frac{4}{3}$.

The corresponding y-coordinate is given by:

$$g\left(\frac{4}{3}\right) = \frac{\left(\frac{4}{3} + 1\right)}{\left(\frac{4}{3} - 1\right)} = \frac{\frac{7}{3}}{\frac{1}{3}} = 7$$

22. b. The center of the ellipse $4x^2 + y^2 + 16x + 2y + 13 = 0$ is $(-2, -1)$, derived as follows:

We complete the square on the equation to obtain an equation in standard form:

$4x^2 + 16x + y^2 + 2y = -13$

$4(x^2 + 4x) + (y^2 + 2y) = -13$

$4(x^2 + 4x + 4) + (y^2 + 2y + 1) = -13 + 16 + 1$

$4(x + 2)^2 + (y + 1)^2 = 4$

We now see that the center is $(-2, -1)$.

23. a. The expression for the height of the ball after its nth bounce is calculated as follows:

We can write down a sequence of bounce heights:

$\underbrace{\frac{4}{5}(20)}_{\text{1st bounce}}, \underbrace{\frac{4}{5}\left(\frac{4}{5}(20)\right)}_{\text{2nd bounce}}, \underbrace{\frac{4}{5}\left(\frac{4}{5}\left(\frac{4}{5}(20)\right)\right)}_{\text{3rd bounce}}, \cdots$

We see that this is a geometric sequence with common ratio $\frac{4}{5}$.

Thus, the height of the ball on its nth bounce is $16\left(\frac{4}{5}\right)^{n-1}$, since $16 = \frac{4}{5}(20)$.

24. d. $\frac{3}{5}$ is $\lim\limits_{x \to \infty} \frac{3(x-1)(x+1)}{5x^2+1}$.

$$\lim\limits_{x \to \infty} \frac{3(x-1)(x+1)}{5x^2+1} \approx \lim\limits_{x \to \infty} \frac{3x^2}{5x^2} = \frac{3}{5}$$

25. The standard deviation of these measurements, 0.0007583, is determined as follows:

x	$\bar{x}$	$x - \bar{x}$	$(x - \bar{x})^2$
.501	.5016	−.0006	3.6×10^{-7}
.507	.5016	.0054	.000029
.511	.5016	.0094	.000088
.497	.5016	−.0046	.000021
.492	.5016	−.0096	.000092
Sx = 2.508			S = .00023

Variance $= \frac{.00023}{4} = .000058$

Standard deviation $= \sqrt{.000058} = 0.0007583$

26. a. The correct solution is:

$$\frac{3-5i}{1+4i} \cdot \frac{1-4i}{1-4i} = \frac{3-12i-5i+20i^2}{1-4i+4i-16i^2} = \frac{-17-17i}{17} = -1-i$$

27. c. Since the minimum value occurs on the $y =$ "cost" axis, it makes sense to model this information with a function of the form $f(t) = -A \cos (Bt) + D$.

Let midnight be $t = 0$. Then $f(0) = 2.5$ (minimum) and $f(12) = 24.5$ (maximum).

The difference between 24.5 and 2.5 is twice the amplitude. Therefore $A = \frac{22}{2} = 11$.

The period is clearly 24 hours, so $B = \frac{2\pi}{24} = \frac{\pi}{12}$.

D is the average of the maximum and minimum values: $D = \frac{24.5 + 2.5}{2} = \frac{27}{2}$.

Therefore, $f(t) = -11 \cos\left(\frac{\pi}{12} t\right) + \frac{27}{2}$.

28. c. The transformations that must be applied to $f(x)$ to obtain the graph are determined as follows:

"$f(x-2)$" tells us to translate $f(x)$ two units to the right.

"$\frac{1}{2}$" indicates a horizontal shrinkage by a factor of $\frac{1}{2}$.

"−" means we reflect in the x-axis.

"+3" tells us to shift $-\frac{1}{2}f(x-2)$ up three units.

29. b. The effective annual interest rate for this loan is calculated as follows:

$$\left(1 + \frac{.0425}{12}\right)^{12} = 1 + i$$

$$i = \left(1 + \frac{.0425}{12}\right)^{12} - 1 = .043338$$

30. The value of k that makes the piecewise defined function $f(x)$ continuous at $x = 2$ is −9, determined as follows:

$$f(x) = \begin{cases} -x^2 + 2x + k, & x \le 2 \\ 10x - 29, & x > 2 \end{cases}$$

$$\lim\limits_{x \to 2^+} f(x) = \lim\limits_{x \to 2} 10x - 29 = -9$$

$$\lim\limits_{x \to 2^-} f(x) = \lim\limits_{x \to 2} -x^2 + 2x + k = -4 + 4 + k$$

$$k = -9$$

31. a. The area of the shaded region bounded by the four circles of radius r is determined as follows:

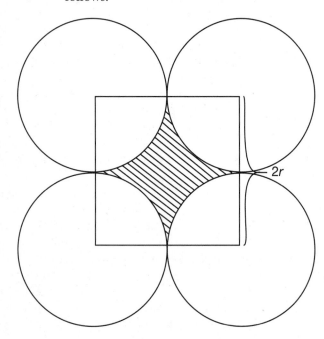

Area of shaded region = Area of square − Area of $\underbrace{\text{4 quarter-circles}}_{\text{One full circle}}$

$= (2r)^2 - \pi r^2$

$= 4r^2 - \pi r^2 = (4 - \pi)r^2$

32. a. The length of each of the wires is determined as follows:

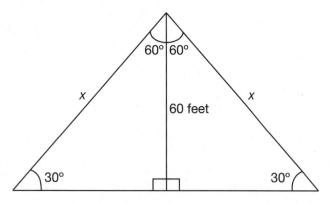

Since $\sin\theta = \frac{\text{opposite}}{\text{hypotenuse}}$, we have $\sin 30° = \frac{60}{x}$.
30° is a special angle value for which we know $\sin 30° = \frac{1}{2}$.

Thus, $\frac{1}{2} = \frac{60}{x}$ and $x = 120$

33. d. The range of the function $f(x) = 3\cos x + 5.2$ is found as follows:

5.2 gives the midline of the cosine curve.

3 is the amplitude and the distance from the midline to the maximum and minimum function values.

Therefore, the range of this function is the set of all y-values such that $5.2 - 3 > y > 5.2 + 3$ or $y \in [2.2, 8.2]$.

34. b. The surface area of a sphere with a volume of 288π cm^3 is determined as follows:

Volume of a sphere $= \frac{4}{3}\pi r^3$

$2.88\pi = \frac{4}{3}\pi r^3$

Solving for r, we get

$r = \sqrt[3]{\frac{3}{4\pi}(288\pi)} = \sqrt[3]{216} = 6.$

The surface area of a sphere is given by

$SA = 4\pi r^2$

Therefore, the surface area is $4\pi(6)^2 = 144\pi$ cm^2

35. a. The reflection in the y-axis of triangle ABC with vertices $(4,-2)$, $(3,2)$, and $(-1,1)$ is determined as follows:

The matrix that represents a reflection in the y-axis upon left multiplication is $\begin{bmatrix} -1 & 0 \\ 0 & 1 \end{bmatrix}$.

Triangle ABC can be written in matrix form $\begin{bmatrix} 4 & 3 & -1 \\ -2 & 2 & 1 \end{bmatrix}$.

A reflection in the y-axis of triangle ABC is given by $\begin{bmatrix} -1 & 0 \\ 0 & 1 \end{bmatrix}\begin{bmatrix} 4 & 3 & -1 \\ -2 & 2 & 1 \end{bmatrix}$.

36. d. The equation is solved as follows:

Here we use integration by parts.

Let $u = 6x^2$ and $dv = e^{2x}dx$.

$$\int 6x^2 e^{2x}\, dx = \underbrace{(6x^2)}_{u} \cdot \underbrace{\int e^{2x}\, dx}_{v} - \int v\, du$$

Then
$$= 6x^2\left(\frac{e^{2x}}{2}\right) - \int \frac{e^{2x}}{2}(12x\, dx)$$

$$= 3x^2 e^{2x} - \int 6x\, e^{2x}\, dx$$

We perform integration by parts again on $\int 6xe^{2x}\, dx$ with $4 = 6xdv = e^{2x}dx$.

$$\int 6xe^{2x}\, dx = 6x\left(\frac{e^{2x}}{2}\right) - \int \frac{e^{2x}}{2}6\,dx$$

$$= 3xe^{2x} - 3\cdot\frac{e^{2x}}{2} + C$$

Putting this together with our previous work, we get

$$\int 6x^2 e^{2x}\, dx = 3x^2 e^{2x} - 3xe^{2x} + \frac{3}{2}e^{2x} + C.$$

37. d. The rate the kayaker can paddle in still water is determined as follows:

We use $d = r \cdot t$, where paddling with the current $r = x + y$,

x = paddling rate in still water

y = rate of current

and paddling against the current $r = x - y$

Paddling with the current we have:

$12 = (x + y)(2)$

Paddling against the current we have:

$12 = (x - y)(3)$

We now solve this linear system for x:

$12 = 2x + 2y$

$12 = 3x - 3y$

Using the method of elimination:

$3\,(16 \not{=} 2x + 2y) \rightarrow 48 = 6x + 6y$

$\underline{2\,(16 = 3x - 3y) \rightarrow \quad 32 = 6x - 6y}$

$80 = 12x$

Therefore $x = 6\frac{2}{3} = 6.67$ miles/hour

38. b. When the customer will switch to company A is determined as follows:

The cost of choosing company A is given by $C_A(t) = 520 + 120t$, where t is measured in months.

The cost of choosing company B is given by $C_B(t) = 400 + 140t$.

The customer will choose company A when $C_A(t) < C_B(t)$. In order to determine this, we solve $C_A(t) = C_B(t)$ for t:

$520 + 120t = 400 + 140t$

$120 = 20t$

$6 = t$

39. d. The exact value of $\cos\left(\arcsin\left(-\frac{2}{3}\right)\right)$ is determined as follows:

Let $\theta = \arcsin\left(-\frac{2}{3}\right)$; that is, $\arcsin\left(-\frac{2}{3}\right)$ is the angle θ, such that $\sin\theta = \left(-\frac{2}{3}\right)$.

The range of $y = \arcsin(x)$ is $-\frac{\pi}{2} \le y \le \frac{\pi}{2}$, i.e., quadrants I and IV.

Since $\sin\theta < 0$, θ must lie in quadrant IV, as shown:

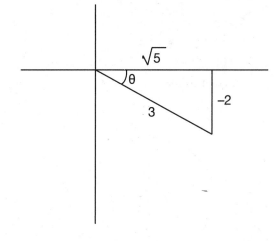

We now find the side adjacent to θ:

$\text{adj} = \sqrt{3^2 - (-2)^2} = \sqrt{5}$

Thus $\cos\left(\arcsin\left(-\frac{2}{3}\right)\right) = \cos\theta = \frac{\text{adj}}{\text{hyp}} = \frac{\sqrt{5}}{3}$

40. a. The graph of the function

$$f(x) = \begin{cases} -3x+5, & x < 1 \\ x^2 - 5x + 1, & 1 \le x < 3 \\ 2x, & 3 < x \end{cases}$$

is found as follows:

We begin by sketching an x-axis and y-axis, and labeling the x-axis with $x = 1$ and $x = 3$:

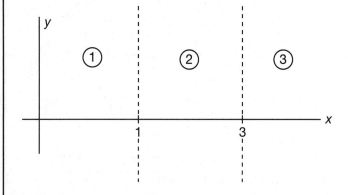

These two x-values separate the x,y-plane into three regions, as shown.

Since $f(x) = -3x + 5$ for $x < 1$, we know the graph in region 1 must be the graph of a line with negative slope:

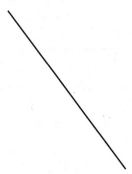

The only graph choice with that feature is choice **a**.

41. c. The inequality $\frac{2x-5}{x-3} \le 4$ is solved as follows: First we can rewrite the inequality in a more useful form.

$$\frac{2x-5}{x-3} \le 4$$

$$\frac{2x-5}{x-3} - 4 \le 0$$

$$\frac{2x-5}{x-3} - \frac{4(x-3)}{x-3} \le 0$$

$$\frac{2x-5-4x+12}{x-3} \le 0$$

$$\frac{7-2x}{x-3} \le 0$$

In this form, we see that $x = \frac{7}{2}$ makes the expression exactly 0, while $x = 3$ makes the expression undefined.

We place these two x-values on the number line and perform a sign analysis to determine the solution set.

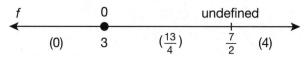

Test values appear in parentheses.

Testing $x = 0$, we see that $\frac{7-2(0)}{0-3} = \frac{+}{-} < 0$. Thus the interval $[-\infty, 3]$ is in our solution set.

Testing $x = \frac{13}{4}$, $\frac{7-2(\frac{13}{4})}{\frac{13}{4}-3} = \frac{+}{+} > 0$.

Thus the interval $(3, \frac{7}{2})$ is *not* in our solution set.

Testing $x = 4$, $\frac{7-2(4)}{(4)-3} = \frac{-}{+} < 0$.

Thus the interval $(\frac{7}{2}, \infty)$ is in our solution set.

Therefore, the solution set to this inequality is $[-\infty, 3] \cup (\frac{7}{2}, \infty)$

42. a. The probability that the card is either a diamond or a face card is determined as follows:

Let D be the event the card is a diamond.

Let F be the event the card is a face card.

Then, $\Pr[D] = \frac{13}{52}$ and $\Pr[F] = \frac{12}{52}$.

We want to compute the probability of the event $D \cup F$.

$\Pr[D \cup F] = \Pr[D] + \Pr[F] - \Pr[D \cap F]$
$= \frac{13}{52} + \frac{12}{52} - \frac{3}{13} = \frac{13}{52}$

Note: The event $D \cap F$ is the event of choosing a diamond that is a face card.

43. c. The domain of the function $f(x) = \log_2(3x - 1) + 5$ is found as follows:

The domain of the basic function $y = \log_2(x)$ is $0 < x$. This means the domain of $f(x)$ must be such that $0 < 3x - 1$. Solving this inequality for x gives the domain $\frac{1}{3} < x$.

44. d. The method that proves that $\triangle BAC \cong \triangle EDC$ is found as follows:

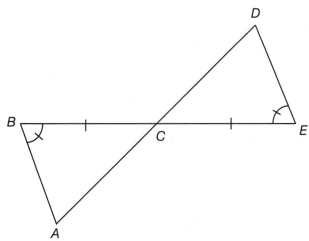

Since opposite angles are congruent, $\angle BCA \cong \angle ECD$.

We are given that $\angle B \cong \angle E$ and $\overline{BC} \cong \overline{EC}$.

Therefore, $\triangle BCA \cong \triangle ECD$ by angle-side-angle (ASA).

45. d. The system of equations for z is solved as follows.

We can solve this system using a graphing calculator, but before we do we must rewrite our system of linear equations

as an augmented matrix:
$\begin{bmatrix} 2 & 2 & 1 & 4 \\ 3 & 1 & -2 & 5 \\ 1 & 0 & -3 & -2 \end{bmatrix}$

We can now enter this matrix into the calculator so that it can help us solve this system of linear equations. The calculator keystrokes are as follows:

Type dimensions: `3` `ENTER` `4` `ENTER`

Next, type in coefficients from augmented matrix:

Press `ENTER` after each entry : `2` `2` `1` `4`
`3` `1` `-2` `5`
`1` `0` `-3` `2`

`2nd` `x⁻¹` `▷` "MATH" `◁` ... `◁` "B: rrefl" `ENTER`

"rrefl" appears on the screen

`2nd` `x⁻¹` `1:[A]` is highlighted `ENTER`

Calculator outputs:
$\begin{bmatrix} 1 & 0 & 0 & 4 \\ 0 & 1 & 0 & -3 \\ 0 & 0 & 1 & 2 \end{bmatrix}$

Row 3: "[0 0 1 2]" says $0x + 0y + 1z = 2$.

Therefore, $z = 2$.

46. b. We find i as follows:

We solve the equation $30{,}000 = 15{,}000(1 + i)^{10}$ for i.

$2 = (1 + i)^{10}$

$2^{\frac{1}{10}} = 1 + i$

$i = 2^{\frac{1}{10}} - 1 \approx .072 = 7.2\%$

47. a. The solution for $h(2)$ is derived as follows: Since $h(x) = f(2x)$ and we are given $f(x) = -x^3 + 1$, it follows that $f(2x) = -(2x)^3 + 1$ (simply substitute $2x$ for x in $f(x)$). Thus, $h(x) = -(2x)^3 + 1$, and $h(2) = -(2(2))^3 + 1$. Therefore, $h(2) = -63$.

48. b. The probability that both marbles are red is found as follows:

Let R be the event "a red marble is selected." Then $\Pr[2R]$ represents the probability two red marbles are selected. Since the selection is done "without replacement," selecting a red marble on the first try and selecting a red marble on the second try are *not* independent.

Thus, $\Pr[2R] = \Pr[R \text{ on 1st try}] \cdot \Pr[R \text{ on 2nd try} \mid R \text{ on 1st try}]$

$\Pr[2R] = \frac{5}{29} \cdot \frac{4}{28} = .0246$

49. b. The coefficient of the term x^4y^5 is found as follows:

The coefficient is $\binom{9}{4} \cdot 2^4 \cdot (-3)^5$

$= -489,888$

50. a. The area of the triangle can be found as follows:

We can picture this triangle as

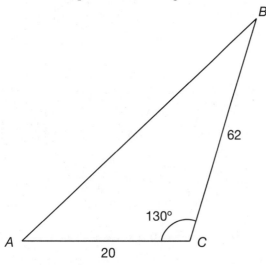

and use the formula Area $= \frac{1}{2}a \cdot b \cdot \sin C$ to compute the required area.

Area $= \frac{1}{2}(62)(20) \sin(130°)$

$= 620(.766044) = 474.948$

51. The x-coordinate of a relative maximum of f is $x = 2$ and is determined as follows:

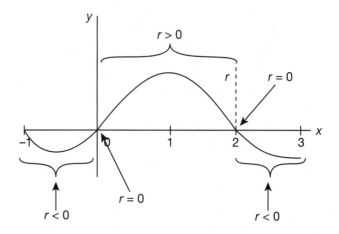

Here we use the first derivative test for relative extrema.

This test relies on recognizing the sign pattern in f that indicates a relative maximum is $f > 0, f = 0, f < 0$.

Therefore, the relative maximum occurs at $x = 2$.

52. a. We determine in how many ways a team consisting of four men and five women can be chosen from a group of seven men and nine women as follows:

We can choose four men from a group of seven men in $\binom{7}{4}$ many ways.

We can choose five women from a group of nine women in $\binom{9}{5}$ many ways.

Therefore, we can choose our team in $\binom{7}{4}\binom{9}{5}$ many ways.

53. d. We determine that only graph III is the graph of a function that has positive first and second derivatives on the interval shown:

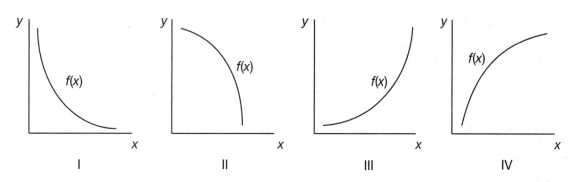

I	II	III	IV

A positive first derivative means the graph of $f(x)$ is increasing. Both III and IV are increasing. A positive second derivative means the graph of $f(x)$ is concave up. Only III is both increasing and concave up.

54. c. Given the values for the function $f(x)$ in the table, we determine which of the following could be an estimate for $\int_{5}^{17} f(x)\,dx$ as follows:

x	5	8	11	14	17
f(x)	2	5	7	10	8

Using right-hand endpoints,

$$\int_{5}^{17} f(x)\,dx \approx \sum_{i=1}^{5} f(5 + i\Delta x) \cdot \Delta x, \text{ where}$$
$$dx = x_i + 1 - x_i = 3$$
$$\approx f(8) \cdot 3 + f(11) \cdot 3 + f(14) \cdot 3 + f(17) \cdot 3$$
$$= 3(5 + 7 + 10 + 8) = 90$$

However, using left-hand endpoints,

$$\int_{5}^{17} f(x)\,dx \approx \sum_{i=1}^{5} f(5 + (1 - i)\,\Delta x) \cdot \Delta x$$
$$= 3(2 + 5 + 7 + 10) = 72$$

55. b. Cos θ is found for the triangle as follows:

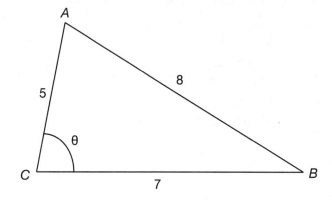

We use the law of cosines.
$$c^2 = a^2 + b^2 - 2ab \cos C$$
Thus, $\cos C = \frac{a^2 + b^2 - c^2}{2ab} = \frac{(7)^2 + (5)^2 - (8)^2}{2(7)(5)} = \frac{1}{7}$

56. d. Which characteristic of this study could produce a bias in the result is determined as follows:

We can assume from the statement that the sample and population sizes did not produce a bias, since it seems that the population was all combat airplanes, and the sample size was all combat airplanes returning from combat missions.

Clearly, the nationality of the investigators did not produce a bias in results of determining where on the body of the airplane the airplane was hit.

However, the sample selection could produce a bias, since the investigators could not consider the combat airplanes that did not return from a combat mission. It would be very useful to know where on the airplane those doomed planes were hit so that those areas on the planes could be reinforced.

57. d. The volume of the paraboloid formed by rotating the region bounded by the y-axis, x-axis, and the parabola $y = 4 - x^2$ about the y-axis is found as follows:

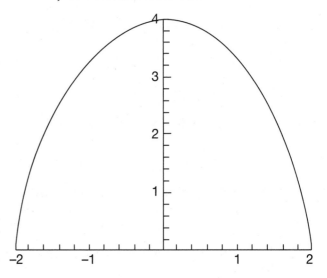

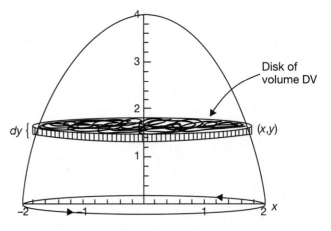

Volume of disk $= dv = \pi x^2 \cdot dy$

$y = 4 - x^2 \pi x = \sqrt{4 - y}$

Thus, $dv = \pi(4 - y)\, dy$

Therefore, $V = \int_0^4 dV = \int_0^4 \pi(4 - y)\, dy$

$$= \pi\left(4y - \frac{y^2}{2}\right)\Bigg]_0^4$$

$$= \pi\big((16 - 8) - (0 - 0)\big)$$

$$V = 8\pi$$

58. a. The length of segment AD is determined as follows:

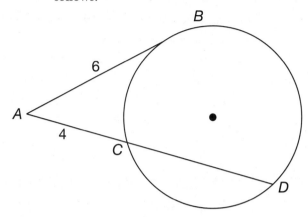

Using the theorem that states that the square of the length of the tangent segment is equal to the product of the length of the secant segment and its external segment, we have

$$6^2 = (4 + x) \cdot 4$$
$$6^2 = 16 + 4x$$
$$36 = 16 + 4x$$
$$x = 5$$
$$AD = 9$$

59. b. The rate the level of water is decreasing when the depth of water is 6 meters is found as follows:

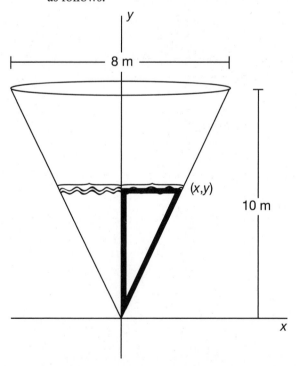

We are given that $\frac{dV}{dt} = \sim 5$.

We need to find $\frac{dy}{dt}$.

The relationship between these variables is given by the volume of a cone: $V = \frac{1}{3}\pi x^2 y$

However, this is a function of three variables. Since we want to find $\frac{dy}{dt}$ when y is 6 m, we can use similar triangles to write x in terms of y.

$$\frac{x}{4} = \frac{y}{10}$$

Thus, $x = .4y$, so,

$$V = \frac{1}{3}\pi (.4y)^2 = \frac{4}{75}\pi y^3$$

Next, we find $\frac{d}{dt}$, of $V = \frac{4}{75}\pi y^3$

$$\frac{d}{dt}V = \frac{d}{dt}\left(\frac{4}{75}\pi y^3\right)$$

$$\frac{dV}{dt} = \frac{4}{75}\pi \cdot \left(3y^2 \frac{dy}{dt}\right)$$

$$\frac{dV}{dt} = \frac{4}{25}\pi y^2 \frac{dy}{dt}$$

We substitute in the values that we know, and solve for $\frac{dy}{dt}$.

$$-5 = \frac{4}{25}\pi (6)^2 \frac{dy}{dt}$$

$$\frac{dy}{dt} \approx -0.28 \text{ m / sec.}$$

60. b. For the scatter plot shown, the statement that best describes the correlation between the variables x and y is found as follows:

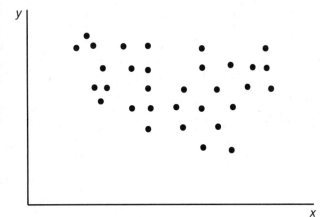

If we tried to draw a line of best fit, this line would have zero slope, so the two variables x and y have no correlation.

A Note on Scoring

Your score on this exam is based on the number of questions you answered correctly; there is no guessing penalty for incorrect answers and no penalty for unanswered questions. The Educational Testing Service does not set passing scores for these tests, leaving this up to the institutions, state agencies, and associations that use the tests.

First find the total number of questions you got right on the entire test. As noted earlier, questions you skipped or got wrong don't count; just add up how many questions you got right. Then, divide the number of questions you got right by the total number of questions (60) to arrive at a percentage. You can check your score against the passing scores in the state or organization that requires you to take the exam. If you are unsure of the passing score you will need, you can set yourself a goal of at least 70% of the answers right on the exam.

Use your percentage score in conjunction with the LearningExpress Test Preparation System guide in Chapter 2 of this book to help you devise a study plan. Then, turn to your study materials to work more on those subjects that gave you the most trouble. You should plan to spend more time on the lessons that correspond to the questions you found hardest and less time on the lessons that correspond to areas in which you did well.

12 ▶ MATHEMATICS PEDAGOGY REVIEW

CHAPTER SUMMARY

Pedagogy is the method and practice of teaching. A thorough understanding and application of mathematical pedagogy impacts every aspect of mathematics education from curriculum design and lesson planning to instruction and evaluation.

In this chapter, we review the knowledge and skills areas that are addressed in the Praxis II® Mathematics: Pedagogy test. The focus of the Pedagogy test is on planning and implementing instruction, assessment, and evaluation. The content will not go beyond first-year algebra, and the emphasis will be on the process and considerations needed for instruction, remediation, and evaluation. Each question on the Mathematics Pedagogy test is based on one or more of the knowledge or skills areas reviewed in this chapter.

Scope and Sequence

A *scope and sequence* is an outline of skills and information to be taught. The scope is the set of learning objectives, and the sequence is the order in which those objectives are taught.

Most states either have decided or are in the process of deciding whether to adopt the Common Core Standards and have developed or are in the process of developing scope and sequence documents based on these standards. Some states and individual school districts have developed or are developing their own scope and sequence documents, most of which are aligned with the Common Core Standards.

In evaluating a given scope and sequence of mathematics topics, a teacher needs to look at national, state, or local scope and sequences and judge how they align with the knowledge and skill levels of his or her students. For example, if a teacher is working in an underperforming school, the standard scope and sequence for his or her class might not be fully successful unless the instructor includes some remedial materials and activities that address any knowledge or skill deficits, as well as materials that might interest and motivate the students and connect with their neighborhood or culture. Teachers need to understand that specific lesson plans provided by their state education departments are meant to be adopted and adapted for local use rather than rigidly implemented.

When evaluating a given scope and sequence, teachers need to assess whether the proposed sequence of activities will engage the students, be in a logical and workable order, take place in a reasonable time frame, and result in students reaching the unit's learning objective. The teacher needs to be aware of prerequisites that are assumed by a given scope and sequence and possibly modify the scope and sequence to address any perceived unmet prerequisites.

For example, New York State has a website, EngageNY (www.engageny.org), that includes the New York State Common Core Mathematics Curriculum. Included on the site are numerous detailed lesson plans. These lesson plans, however, are not meant as scripts to be strictly adhered to. Instead, they are presented as complete vignettes that teachers can use as starting points for their own lessons. A lesson on dilation on the website contains a great deal of clear instruction and problems in which students can calculate dilations. But the lesson as is might be too abstract for a group of students who need actual real-life examples that connect the math to the actual world. An enhanced lesson might contain such practical applications as creating an organizational logo and shrinking it proportionally to fit on a business card, scaling it up to fit on a full-page magazine ad, or blowing it up even more to be part of a large banner to be hung at a conference.

Integrating Concepts and Connecting Topics

In the past, many math topics were taught in isolation, with the connections between them left unnoticed and unlearned. For example, traditionally, geometry and algebra were taught as two totally different subjects, often presented in different years. But when the coordinate plane is introduced into geometry, it is a natural extension to integrate concepts from algebra. For example, the distance formula on the coordinate grid is an application of geometry's Pythagorean theorem.

There are crucial unifying ideas that can help show connections among topics. The New Jersey Curriculum Frameworks provides a helpful example of such a unifying idea in the concept of proportional relationships: "Proportional relationships play a key role in a wide variety of important topics, such as ratios, proportions, rates, percent, scale, similar geometric figures, slope, linear functions, parts of a whole, probability and odds, frequency distributions and statistics, motion at constant speed, simple interest, and comparison."

Mathematics topics and concepts can also be integrated with other subjects. The use of perspective in art can be a real-life application of ratio and proportion. A comparative study of national budgets and gross domestic products uses mathematical insights to understand the wealth and priorities of various nations. Many of the insights of scientific inquiry are expressed in mathematical form. For example, in physics, the relationship of force, mass, and acceleration is given by the mathematical formula $F = ma$.

Developing a Scope and Sequence

Despite the proliferation of national, state, and local school district scope and sequences, there is still a need for individual teachers to develop their own fine-tuned scope and sequences that address individual class needs.

For example, suppose it is an election year and your eighth-grade students are very interested in the presidential election. They've been hearing a lot about standard deviation; so you decide to develop a statistics unit about standard deviation.

You research standard deviation and find out that it is the square root of the variance. Looking further, you find that the variance is the average of the squared differences from the mean or average.

So calculating and understanding standard deviation requires the following knowledge and skills:

- knowing what a mean is and how to calculate it
- knowing how to subtract the mean from each number
- knowing how to square a number
- understanding what a square root is, how to estimate it, and how to use a scientific calculator to compute square roots
- understanding the basic bell-shaped curve of a distribution graph

Looking at this list of prerequisites, you can assume that your class does not have to review subtraction. It is also likely that most eighth-grade classes do not need to review what a mean is, but you would have to judge that for your class. It is also likely that you would want to have instruction and student work on squares and square roots, focusing on estimating square roots and using the scientific calculator, particularly for numbers that are not friendly perfect squares. The variance and standard deviation can then be presented as an application of squares and square roots, with the election polls and polls of other public policies being used as real-life examples. Finally, research results can be plotted on a graph, illustrating the bell curve.

Identifying Students' Misconceptions and How to Correct Them

Addressing student errors that arise from misconceptions is a crucial activity that can have a more longstanding impact than correcting errors due to careless computation.

For example, many students are confused by dividing a number by a fraction between 0 and 1. The common image of division being cut into pieces makes the procedure of multiplying by the reciprocal of the divisor seem counterintuitive. Insisting on a rote inverting of the divisor and multiplying does not lead to any deeper understanding. One possible correction method is to have the divisor represent the size of each piece rather than the number of pieces. Say that you have three pumpkin pies and you want to divide them into pieces such that every piece is $\frac{1}{4}$ of a pie. How many pieces of pumpkin pie would you have if each pie was cut so that each piece was $\frac{1}{4}$ of a pie?

The students should be able to picture each pie being cut into four pieces, and given that there are three pies, there would be a total of $3 \times 4 = 12$ pieces of pie. In other words, $3 \div \frac{1}{4} = 3 \times 4 = 12$.

Having students describe their thought process can often help uncover misconceptions, but it is usually sufficient to look at written student work in order to identify student conceptual errors. For example, if the student's task is to simplify the expression $\frac{2x^2 + 4x + 4}{2x^2}$ and the student ends up with $4x + 4$, the teacher should be able to see that the student does not fully understand that in reducing a polynomial by a monomial, the monomial has to be reduced with each term of the polynomial. The student can be guided to find the greatest common factor of the monomial and each term of the polynomial, which in this case is 2. If the monomial and each term of the polynomial are reduced by 2, the result is: $\frac{x^2 + 2x + 2}{x^2}$.

Identifying Prerequisite Knowledge and Skills

While learning mathematics is not necessarily a linear process, for many topics there are prerequisite knowledge and skills that need to be in place prior to instruction.

For example, in the age of the calculator, students need to estimate in order to pick up on errors as well as to make predictions regarding mathematical quantities. If you were preparing a unit on estimating, you would want to know whether your students knew their times tables, rounding off, and powers of 10. You might want to have a brief preassessment, or for a few days preceding the unit, lead group mental math exercises that give extra practice in these skills.

Estimating can be taught at various levels depending on the prerequisite skills of students. Even young students should be able to understand the language used in estimating such as large, small, greater than, less than, and about, though if you have students who are learning English, you might need to confirm that they are fluent in the English language words for the mathematical concepts.

If you have a class with many English-as-a-second-language learners, you might identify the language of estimating as the first piece of knowledge your students need to master, followed by the times tables and understanding powers of 10. Students can then be taught the details of rounding off whole numbers, including understanding how to determine a reasonable level of rounding. For example, if the attendance at a professional football game is 56,782, an estimate to the nearest thousand, 57,000, gives a clear picture of the approximate size of the crowd and

is a reasonable level of rounding. By contrast, rounding to the nearest 10, 56,870, is a level of detail that does not significantly simplify the exact attendance figure. Finally, rounding decimals can complete the unit.

Developing Questions That Probe for Current Level of Understanding

Teachers can stimulate learning by asking questions that are open-ended, and that motivate students to explore and discuss topics from multiple perspectives. During such discussions or written activities, students reveal their current level of understanding of a particular topic.

Questions can also take the form of small projects that reveal students' level of understanding.

For example, you can test your students' understanding of average or mean by giving them a data set that contains the number of miles driven and the number of gallons needed to refill the tank. You could ask them to decide if the mean, median, or mode is most appropriate for the task of determining the average mileage in miles per gallon of the vehicle, and to explain how they made that choice. The data set could contain seven data points of almost all city driving and one data point with almost all highway driving. One of the city data points could represent a day the car was stuck in a massive traffic jam for hours. Drawing a graph of the data would help clarify the situation; see if the students can point to the median or mode as the more useful number since the data set contains some atypical outliers that could skew the mean, making it less useful.

Given the level of success or challenge with this activity, the rest of the unit can be structured so that students have ample opportunities to develop and present scenarios in which the mean, median, and mode each give the most useful information.

A unit on measurement could begin with an open-ended discussion in which students discuss their current understanding of the uses and needs of various measurements in one, two, and three dimensions. Such a discussion could lead the instruction in various directions, such as estimating lengths, areas, and volumes, and following up with exact measurements. Another direction might involve hands-on projects, such as reseeding a school lawn or athletic field, which might involve calculating the correct amount of seed and fertilizer to use and the correct amount of fencing to purchase and install around the seeded area to protect it until the new growth is established.

Problem-Solving Strategies

In his book, *How to Solve It* (Princeton University Press, 1945), George Polya proposed a four-step problem-solving strategy:

1. understanding the problem
2. devising a plan
3. carrying out the plan
4. looking back

Understanding the problem could include drawing a sketch or diagram to show connections and relationships, restating the problem in your own words, or making a reasonable guess at the solution. If a problem is more than a rote exercise, the solution strategy may not be obvious, necessitating the development of a plan. When the plan is carried out, it is a good idea for students to document each step so that they can retrace their steps or troubleshoot. Good documentation can help students strengthen their repertoire of problem-solving strategies. Finally, look back and see if your solution makes sense. Does the solution raise other interesting questions?

In addition to guessing and checking, reducing to a simpler problem, drawing a diagram, and working backward, other strategies could include organizing data into a table, graphing data, and comparing to similar previously solved problems.

An example of problem solving is converting to or from the metric system and the English system of weights and measures, which can be a challenge for students. They are often unsure whether they need to multiply or divide in a given situation. For example, an automobile speedometer is calibrated in kilometers per hour instead of miles per hour. The driver believes that she can drive 5 miles per hour above the speed limit without being pulled over, so she usually drives at that speed. However, she is unsure how many kilometers per hour is equivalent to that speed. She is planning to drive on a highway with a posted speed limit of 65 mph. At how many kilometers per hour can she plan to drive?

Since she understands that miles per hour can be written as $\frac{\text{miles}}{\text{hour}}$, she concludes that she can write kilometers per hour as $\frac{\text{kilometers}}{\text{hour}}$. As she plans to go 5 miles per hour over the speed limit, she is planning to drive $65 + 5 = 70$ mph or $70 \frac{\text{miles}}{\text{hour}}$. There are 1.61 kilometers in a mile or $1.61 \frac{\text{kilometers}}{\text{mile}}$. There are 0.62 miles in a kilometer or $0.62 \frac{\text{miles}}{\text{kilometer}}$. So should the kilometers per hour be 70×1.61 or 70×0.62? Her plan is to use the labels of the measurement units and cancellation of fractions to determine which conversion she should use. When she tries $1.61 \frac{\text{kilometers}}{\text{mile}}$, she gets: $70 \frac{\text{miles}}{\text{hour}} \times 1.61 \frac{\text{kilometers}}{\text{mile}} = 112.7 \frac{\text{kilometers}}{\text{hour}}$. Other strategies to solve the problem can include drawing a diagram that makes clear that each mile is longer than each kilometer.

Forms of Representation

Because students can have such a variety of learning styles, a teacher should use different forms of representation to create learning opportunities for all students. Such an approach is advocated in the Universal Design for Learning developed by the Center for

Applied Special Technology (CAST). Some students learn visually, some auditorily, some tactilely, and most through a combination of the three. By consistently employing all approaches, the teacher increases the chances that every student will find the forms of representation that most often work for that student. Teachers should use, and students should be encouraged to use, a variety of forms of representation, including written or spoken explanations; drawings, charts, and graphs; symbols (either standard or invented); and manipulatives, either physical or virtual, such as are freely available at the National Library of Virtual Manipulatives (http://nlvm.usu.edu/en/nav/vlibrary.html).

For example, if you are introducing the concept of function, you can help your students visualize what a function is by using a function machine in which every input value x produces an output value $f(x)$. In addition, to help all students develop understanding, you could have students create a table of function values and represent a function on a coordinate graph.

Teaching Strategies

Teaching strategies can be effective if they are student centered and problem focused and include a mix of group and individual work. Emphasis needs to be on the development of critical thinking skills and mathematical understanding with less stress on rote calculations. There is a place for mental math, especially in the learning of the times tables, which are very useful for estimating, but a key goal of mathematics instruction is to develop mathematical habits of mind, including creating, inventing, conjecturing, and experimenting with mathematics. When possible, mathematical instruction should develop experiential and place-based learning that taps into local resources, unique features, and specialties. Instruction should strive to make connections with local and

student culture, historical traditions, and sociocultural roots.

While traditional methods, such as lectures and worksheets, can be appropriate occasionally, a steady diet of them can stifle the learning, creativity, and engagement of students and result in classrooms that are dull and predictable. Students gain when there are group and class discussions in which alternative problem-solving strategies are presented, and students are encouraged to struggle with the mathematics rather than being given a rote procedure that they follow rigidly.

The goal is to have students think independently and develop their own questions. They need to push their limits and go beyond playing it safe.

Relating Mathematical Concepts and Ideas to Real-World Situations

There are many real-world situations in which mathematical concepts and ideas are used. Whenever possible and appropriate, these applications should be integrated into classroom instruction. Here are some of the many areas rich with mathematical examples:

- Sports provide many applications of mathematical concepts. In baseball, batting averages and earned run averages are taken as strong indicators of an athlete's ability, as are field goal percentages, free throw percentages, and assists per game in basketball. More difficult mathematics are needed to develop a safe bobsled run in which athletes can achieve record speeds without their sled leaving the track and causing severe injury.
- Health and nutrition provide many situations to use mathematics. The intake of calories through eating and the burning of calories in exercise are national obsessions. Food labels often list the percentages of daily requirements of various

nutrients in a serving. And understanding medication dosage can be important to quality of life.

- Gambling produces many opportunities to implement probability skills. The lottery, blackjack, and sports gambling, such as horse racing, can all be analyzed through probability to determine the chances of winning or losing.

- Carpentry depends on accurate measurement, including right angles when installing walls, doors, windows, and trim. If measurements are not precise, what is built might not function properly or even be safe.

- Nature and the threats to it can be the sources of many mathematical explorations. Pollution is sometimes measured in parts per billion of pollutants, an amount that is usually beyond our ability to comprehend without the use of analogies and models. The math of global warming adds an important perspective to public policy decisions, such as limiting carbon emissions. Nature is also the source of patterns such as the hexagonal honeycombs and snowflakes, and the spiral of the chambered nautilus.

- Many video games depend heavily on mathematics.

- In the areas of social studies and politics, students can use quantitative analysis to decide public policy and other political issues. Understanding the uses and limitations of polls to gauge public sentiment is another example of applying mathematics to real-world situations. Newspapers and the Internet can be used for real-world data, including sales as well as charts and graphs that attempt to explain the news of the day.

- Personal finance can include making a personal and family budget and comparison shopping using unit pricing. Students can compare the prices of online shopping, which includes shipping costs, with shopping in a store, which includes traveling costs for various items.

- Mathematics can be used to describe change. Analysis of current and past census data can be used to develop an understanding of the United States while developing mathematical abilities. Students can also mathematically analyze socioeconomic data, such as the percentage of national wealth controlled by the top 1% and the top 0.1%. Students can look at rates, such as calculating miles per gallon of an automobile or the historical rate of return of a stock or bond.

The list of real-world situations is bounded only by the limits of your and your students' imaginations. Students can develop their understanding through multiple organizations of the data, including tables, charts, and graphs, as they learn to do mathematics as an active process.

Identifying, Evaluating, and Using Curricular Materials and Resources

Teachers need to use a variety of curricular materials and resources. While textbooks are often determined by the school district, they can be used as a reference rather than a script to be followed word for word and exercise after exercise.

The teacher needs to work with students to enhance the use of technology and to help students avoid either the underuse or the overuse of technology. Computer-based materials vary widely in quality and usefulness in the classroom. There is excellent computer software available that can aid in the visualization and comprehension of important mathematical ideas; however, there are other computer-based materials that are little more than worksheets on a screen.

Manipulatives appeal to the learning style of kinesthetic learners because they allow students to actually touch the objects. Common objects, such as coins or toothpicks, can be as useful as commercially available physical manipulatives, such as base-10 blocks, Cuisenaire rods, centimeter cubes, tangrams, and geoboards, in learning to work with mathematical concepts. For visual/spatial learners, pictures or virtual manipulatives could be effective.

Teachers have the ultimate responsibility to identify, evaluate, and use curricular materials that will work for their particular students and classes. That process is enhanced, however, when input from students is encouraged and effectiveness is evaluated by the quality of the student work produced.

Controlling the Classroom without Restricting Divergent Thought

A controlled classroom is not necessarily a silent classroom. A classroom of active learners can be expected to have some level of noise as students actively participate in their learning without the classroom descending into chaos. If students are involved in more than passive listening, they are more likely to be engaged in relevant educational activities, including participating in group work, reading, writing, and discussing, and more likely to be invested in the successful functioning of the classroom.

Sometimes teachers have to deal with disruptive student behavior. Such behavior should not be tolerated, and teachers should follow school policies and procedures in dealing with such behavior. But it is crucial to separate the student from the behavior and strive to establish and maintain trust relationships with troubled students so that they remain integrated in the classroom. The ultimate goal is to have every student functioning, learning, and growing in your classroom.

To keep the classroom an exciting learning environment, encourage original and creative student thinking and create unexpected opportunities. Tailor tasks with the least amount of detail you can manage to make the key mathematical objectives of the unit clear. If students are excited by what they are learning and the process by which they are learning, they will help create and maintain a positive atmosphere. We want to develop powerful students who are comfortable with exploring mathematics, gaining a high level of understanding, and doing it in the context of dynamic, exciting classrooms.

Teaching Mathematics in a Societal Context

In a 2013 study, 29 nations and other jurisdictions outperformed U.S. students in mathematics. Other studies have returned similar results. The low level of math performance in the United States has serious long-term implications. In an increasingly technological world, the United States has been losing its dominance. In addition, the general population tends not to value mathematical and scientific knowledge, especially in areas of public policy. Negative media portrayals of people with strong mathematics and science backgrounds as socially inept nerds are an example of national disdain for mathematical analysis and scientific knowledge. Creating an educational system where more students are doing math and developing mastery of key mathematical concepts is crucial across all demographic groups.

Even given our disappointing overall performance, societal influences are having an additional negative impact on certain demographic groups. According to research by Nancy Jordan and Susan Levine, "[a]s a group, children from disadvantaged, low-income families perform substantially worse in mathematics than their counterparts from higher-income families. Minority children are disproportionately represented in low-income populations, resulting in significant racial and social-class disparities in mathematics learning linked to diminished learning opportunities."

Despite overall gains by women in academic achievement, they still lag behind their male counterparts in mathematics. This may be changing, however, as females now match males in the average number of credits of advanced math courses they earn.

Mathematics and Gender, Ethnicity, and Socioeconomic Groups

The gender gap in mathematics has been very persistent and exists across all socioeconomic levels and states in the United States. This gender gap exists in other nations as well, except those in which same-sex education is the norm. Given this reality, teachers need to be attuned to the participation level of their female students and encourage their participation and mathematical ideas.

With many well-paying jobs and careers now requiring a higher level of mathematical skills, the low performance of Hispanics and blacks continues to be a barrier to their attaining socioeconomic equality. Teachers can perpetuate these problems if they have low expectations for Hispanic and black students' achievement. Setting high expectations, along with providing extra assistance, can help. However, many black and Hispanic students are also in the lowest socioeconomic groups and attend underperforming schools that have a disproportionate amount of young, inexperienced staff. More experienced staff are often found in more affluent districts. Increased investment in staff and underperforming schools, including an investment in experienced teacher mentors, could have an impact.

The situation is dire for students from low socioeconomic status (SES) families or from the Hispanic, black, or Native American racial or ethnic groups. Even in kindergarten, these students tend to lag in basic number sense, and the gap between them and students from higher socioeconomic families and white and Asian/Pacific Island racial groups only gets wider.

Evaluation Strategies

Effective teachers use a range of evaluation strategies on an ongoing basis. They observe student participation in class discussions, examine the products of various projects and written homework, and evaluate in-class written assessments. Formal and informal assessments must be frequent and consistent. It is the only way for a teacher to know whether students are grasping the material and when to intervene with a revised or fresh approach.

And assessment is just as valuable for the feedback it provides to students. As Glenda Anthony and Margaret Walshaw wrote in the *Journal of Mathematics Education*: "Helpful feedback explains why something is right or wrong, and describes what to do next, or describes strategies for improvement. Effective teachers also provide opportunities for their students to evaluate and assess their own work. They involve students in designing test questions, writing success criteria, writing mathematical journals, and presenting portfolios as evidence of growth in mathematics."

Creating Targeted Evaluation Items
Specific evaluation items fall into one of four general types:

1. selected response and short answer, such as multiple choice, true/false, matching, fill-in-the-blank, and short answer
2. extended written response—a written answer of at least several sentences to a question or task
3. performance assessment, which can focus on the process, the product, or both
4. personal communication, which can range from informal to highly structured interactions

An evaluation can consist of a problem that calls for the use of a taught algorithm, or a brief informal interaction with a student. A quick skill check could consist of a multiple-choice item, but you need to be careful that the incorrect choices would result from conceptual errors rather than computational errors. A scenario that creates a context for the skill being evaluated and requires an extended response can often provide a richer array of insights than a selected response type of problem. On the other hand, selected response can deliver immediate, targeted feedback.

You should be aware of Webb's Depth of Knowledge (DOK) levels, which can be considered an update of Bloom's Taxonomy. In particular, you want to be careful that at least some of your evaluation tasks go beyond DOK1 (recall and reproduction), at least to DOK2 (skills and concepts). Evaluations should also include tasks that require DOK3 (strategic thinking and reasoning) and DOK4 (extended thinking).

13 ▶ PRAXIS II® MATHEMATICS: PEDAGOGY PRACTICE TEST 1

CHAPTER SUMMARY

This is the first of the three full-length practice exams in this book based on the structure and difficulty level of the Praxis II® Mathematics: Pedagogy test. Use this test to see how you would do if you were to take the exam today.

This chapter contains a practice test that mirrors the Praxis II® Mathematics: Pedagogy exam. Though the actual exam you will take might be computer-based, the question types for each exam are replicated here for you in the book.

As you take this first test, do not worry too much about timing. The actual time you will be allotted for each exam is given at the beginning of each test, but you should take this diagnostic test in as relaxed a manner as you can to find out which areas you are skilled in and which ones will need extra work.

After you finish taking this practice test, you should review the scoring criteria that will be used to grade each essay response. You will also see sample responses for each question.

Good luck!

Time: 1 hour

Three essay questions

Question 1: Planning

Student Assignment

You print out an online coupon for $10 off a pair of shoes from a local shoe store. Once in the store, you discover that all shoes are 30% off the price marked on the shoes. You find a pair of shoes marked $50 and decide to purchase them.

1. Determine the sale price of this $50 pair of shoes if you apply the $10 off coupon first, and then have the store apply the 30% discount.

2. Determine the sale price of the $50 pair of shoes if you have the store apply the 30% discount first and then use your $10 coupon.

3. Express each individual discount as a linear function and use composition of functions to show that applying the discounts in different orders leads to different functions.

Objectives/Learning Outcomes: Students in a heterogeneously grouped ninth-grade algebra class will learn about composition of functions using this student assignment as a stimulus.

Create a lesson plan that includes the following:

(a) the mathematics that the students will need to understand or learn in order to solve the problem

(b) how you would organize the class for instruction, and your reasoning for choosing this organization

(c) the specific strategies you would teach students to use in solving this problem

PRAXIS II® MATHEMATICS: PEDAGOGY PRACTICE TEST 1

Question 2: Implementation

Scenario: During a lesson on solving quadratic equations using factoring, a student correctly solves equations I and II, but cannot solve equation III.

$$\text{I. } x^2 + 3x + 2 = 0$$

$$\text{II. } x^2 + 6x = 7x + 12$$

$$\text{III. } 3x^2 - x - 4 = 0$$

(a) Give an explanation as to why the student had difficulty with equation III.

(b) Develop a set of approximately five exercises that will incrementally improve the student's understanding of factoring so that the student can successfully solve equation III.

(c) For each exercise in part (b), briefly describe (i) how the exercise can help the student understand factoring, and (ii) how each exercise follows naturally from the previous exercise and leads to the next exercise.

_____

_____

_____

_____

_____

_____

_____

_____

_____

_____

_____

Question 3: Assessment

On an end-of-unit test, students were asked the following questions about the domain and range of certain functions:

1. Find the domain of the functions:
   a. $f(x) = x^2 - 4x + 11$
   b. $d(x) = -x^3 + 5x + 1$
   c. $g(x) = \frac{1}{x-4}$
   d. $h(x) = \frac{1}{\sqrt{x-4}}$
2. Find the range of the functions:
   a. $f(x) = x^2 - 4x + 11$
   b. $d(x) = -x^3 + 5x + 1$

(a) Write a solution to each part of the two student problems, showing all work.

(b) For each part of each student problem, state the mathematical skills and knowledge that the question is designed to assess.

(c) Write two additional student problems that you think should also be asked in order to assess student understanding of the concepts of domain and range, and explain how these additional questions complement the given student problems.

Sample Answers

Scoring Criteria

Following are sample criteria for scoring pedagogy responses.

A score "5" writer will:

- Provide a complete and thorough answer to all parts of the question.
- Demonstrate a strong grasp of planning, implementing, and assessing mathematics lessons that are very likely to succeed in achieving their goals.
- Possess a strong fluency in the concepts, theories, procedures, and methodologies related to the question.
- Show a solid understanding of how to motivate various types of learners.
- Offer well-reasoned and sound explanations, supported by evidence where appropriate.

A score "4" writer will:

- Provide appropriate answers to most parts of the question.
- Demonstrate a strong grasp of planning, implementing, and assessing mathematics lessons that are likely to succeed in achieving their goals.
- Possess a satisfactory fluency in the concepts, theories, procedures, and methodologies related to the question.
- Show a satisfactory understanding of how to motivate various types of learners.
- Offer satisfactory explanations, supported by some evidence where appropriate.

A score "3" writer will:

- Provide answers to most parts of the question.
- Demonstrate an understanding of how to plan, implement, and assess mathematics lessons that are somewhat likely to succeed in achieving their goals.

- Possess a basic fluency in the concepts, theories, procedures, and methodologies related to the question.
- Show some understanding of how to motivate various types of learners.
- Offer some explanations with supporting evidence where appropriate.

A score "2" writer will:

- Provide an incomplete answer to the question.
- Demonstrate little or no grasp of planning, implementing, and assessing mathematics lessons.
- Possess weak understanding of the mathematics related to the question.
- Show little or no understanding of how to motivate students.
- Offer unclear or very weak explanations.

A score "1" writer will:

- Fail to supply a satisfactory response to any part of the question.
- Fail to show an understanding of planning, implementing, and assessing mathematics lessons.
- Misunderstand or fail to understand the mathematics related to the question.

A score "0" writer will:

- Fail to provide any response or a coherent response or a response that addresses the question.

Sample Responses for Question 1: Planning
Sample Score "5" Response

(a) The students need to understand the difference between a coupon and a percentage discount in the context of the problem. They will also need to know how to compute a percentage discount and apply this discount to a number to find a discounted value. Using the context of the given student assignment, I would review how coupons work and how percentage discounts work: coupon alone: price − coupon value = sale price; percentage discount alone: price − (price × percentage discount) = sale price. In addition, the students need to know about linear functions and how to combine functions using composition of functions, which will also require them to know about function notation. A linear function is a function of the form $y = mx + b$ where m and b are constants. Given two functions (in function notation) $f(x)$ and $g(x)$, we can compose these functions as $f(g(x))$ and $g(f(x))$.

(b) I would first discuss the prerequisite topics about using coupons and applying percentage discounts using students' own experiences as consumers and/or as employees in a retail store. I would then have the students work individually on solving problems 1 and 2. After a sufficient amount of time, I would have students pair up to share their answers and methods with one another. Before moving on to problem 3, I would review linear functions, function notation, and composition of functions with the class as a whole by giving examples of two simple linear functions (much like the ones they will be required to develop on their own in problem 3) and show how to perform composition using these two simple functions. I would then have them work as partners to complete problem 3, and upon completion have the partners share their results and methods used with the rest of the class.

(c) For problems 1 and 2, I would have the students use pen and paper to work out their results using the introductory examples we worked out together at the beginning of the lesson. For problem 3, I would have the students consider different marked prices one at a time for each type of discount (coupon or percentage discount), building on the work they

have already completed for the marked price of $50:

From problems 1 and 2, students should have:

1. Sale price = $(50 − 10) − 0.3(50 − 10) =$
   $40 − 0.3(40) = 28$
2. Sale price = $(50 − 0.3(50)) − 10 = 25$

I would encourage students to replace the original marked price ($50) with prices lower and higher than the original price for each discount type. I would emphasize that they should be looking for a pattern in the relationship between marked price and sale price in the situations from problems 1 and 2. I would encourage students to simplify their work from problems 1 and 2 so that each calculation involves only one operation on the marked price.

For the coupon, I would expect to see student work like:

$50 − 10 = 40$

$45 − 10 = 35$

$55 − 10 = 45$

I would remind them that the number we are changing (the marked price) can be represented as a variable, and I would expect them to be able to write a linear function for the coupon discount as:

$f(x) = x − 10$

For the percentage discount, I would expect to see the following student work:

$50 − 0.3(50) = 35$

$60 − 0.3(60) = 42$

$40 − 0.3(40) = 28$

And this would lead to students writing $g(x) = x − 0.3x$, which I would encourage them to simplify, if they haven't already, as $g(x) = 0.7x$. At this point, the partners would recognize (or I would remind them) that they are in a situation much like the one we had at the beginning of the lesson when we completed two examples of composition of functions. I would have them write down the composition that corresponds to problem 1 first and the composition that corresponds to problem 2 second:

Problem 1: First coupon, then percentage discount:

$$h(x) = g(f(x)) = g(x - 10) = 0.7(x - 10)$$

Problem 2: First percentage discount, then coupon:

$$p(x) = f(g(x)) = f(0.7x) = 0.7x - 10$$

Sample Score "2" Response

(a) Concepts students need to know are discounts, formulas for lines, and composition of these formulas.

(b) I would have the students work in groups of three to do all three problems. The work they do to complete problems 1 and 2 will lead them to discover the solution to problem 3. I would circulate around the room to make sure they are doing the problems correctly.

(c) I would encourage them to change the price of the shoes and look at specific examples first, and then have them generalize. This would be useful mainly for problem 3, since problems 1 and 2 can easily be done using the calculator.

Sample Responses for Question 2: Implementation
Sample Score "5" Response

(a) The student who can solve equation I knows how to factor quadratic expressions with a leading coefficient of 1. The student either knows how to factor using the method of trial and error or has some knowledge of certain clues in the quadratic expression that can help one to factor with fewer trials. In particular, the student might notice that the sign of the constant term, 2, is positive in the expression $x^2 + 3x + 2$, which means that if this expression factors, it will factor as either $(x - a)(x - b)$ or $(x + a)(x + b)$. The student can also see that the sign of the linear term, $3x$, is also positive,

which means that this expression must factor as $(x + a)(x + b)$ and to determine a and b the student need only consider factors of 2, of which there are only two possibilities: 2 and 1 (since 2 is prime). Therefore the solution to equation I is $x = -1$ and $x = -2$.

The student who can solve equation II knows that in order to solve a quadratic equation using the method of factoring, one must first rewrite the equation as

$$x^2 - x - 12 = 0$$

The quadratic expression factors as $x^2 - x - 12 = (x - 4)(x + 3)$. Therefore, the solution to equation II is $x = 4$ and $x = -3$. The fact that the student can solve equation II shows that the student is comfortable factoring quadratic expressions that factor as $(x - a)(x + b)$ or $(x + a)(x - b)$. This kind of factoring will always be needed when the constant term in the quadratic expression is negative. The student also knows how to factor quadratic expressions in which the constant term, 12 in this case, is *not* a prime number as it was in equation I. Furthermore, the student notices that since the linear term, x, is negative, the larger number in the factored form, 4, must also be negative.

Since the student can solve both equations I and II, and II in particular, this narrows down the reasons why the student had difficulty with III. The main difference between II and III is that the leading coefficient in II is 1, while the leading coefficient in III is not 1, but 3. The student may not understand that factoring a quadratic expression with a prime leading coefficient is very similar to factoring an expression with 1 as the leading coefficient, and/or the student may also have difficulty solving equation III since solutions to quadratic equations with a prime leading coefficient are often fractions rather than whole numbers as in I and II.

(b) The exercises I would give to the student are the following:

1. Factor x^2, $3x^2$, $4x^2$ as the product of two linear factors. List all possibilities for each monomial.

2. Given that $x^2 - 2x - 8 = (\_ + 2)(\_ - 4)$ and $3x^2 - 10x - 8 = (\_ + 2)(\_ - 4)$, fill in the blanks with the correct monomial.

3. Solve the equation $(3x + 2)(x - 4) = 0$.

4. Solve the equation $3x^2 - x - 4 = 0$ using factoring.

5. Solve the equation $4x^2 - 4x - 3 = 0$ by factoring.

(c) In exercise 1 the student must focus on factoring just the leading term of a quadratic expression. By completing this exercise the student will see that x^2 can only be factored as $x^2 = x \cdot x$, and that $3x^2$ can only be factored as $3x^2 = 3x \cdot x$, whereas $4x^2$ can be factored as $4x^2 = 4x \cdot x$ or $4x^2 = 2x \cdot 2x$.

Exercise 2 extends exercise 1 by asking the student again to focus on factoring only the first term, but now in the context of factoring a quadratic expression. The student can use the work done in exercise 1 to complete exercise 2: Since $x^2 = x \cdot x$ only, $x^2 - 2x - 8 = (x + 2)(x - 4)$. Since $3x^2 = 3x \cdot x$ only, $3x^2 - 10x - 8 = (3x + 2)(x - 4)$, or $3x^2 - 10x - 8 = (x + 2)(3x - 4)$, and the student can then check which factorization is correct by multiplying the two binomials in each possibility. Multiplying binomial factors is usually taught before factoring trinomials, and is usually better understood and more easily computed by students. Therefore, by using multiplication of binomials (which is just a special case of the distributive property) the student will see that $3x^2 - 10x - 8 = (3x + 2)(x - 4)$ only.

Exercise 3 gives the correct factorization from exercise 2 and puts this factored expression back into the context of solving a quadratic equation. Having the student complete exercise

3 will help me determine if the student is having difficulty only with factoring or is also having difficulty only solving linear equations with fractional answers.

For $(3x + 2)(x - 4) = 0$, either $3x + 2 = 0$ or $x - 4 = 0$.

For $3x + 2 = 0$, $x = -\frac{2}{3}$.

For $x - 4 = 0$, $x = 4$.

Exercise 4 is the culmination of exercises 1 through 3. This exercise requires the student to factor to solve a quadratic equation from start to finish. The student can use the work done in the previous exercises to assist in the completion of exercise 4.

Exercise 5 builds on exercise 1 but is meant more as a challenge exercise. Completing exercise 5 requires the student to consider all the possible cases that result from factoring $4x^2$. The student who relies solely on the method of trial and error to factor quadratic expressions may be frustrated by such an exercise and wish for a more systematic way to factor. This desire will help motivate a future lesson in which the class studies alternative methods of factoring.

Sample Score "2" Response

(a) The student could not solve equation III because the leading coefficient is 3, not 1 as in the previous two exercises.

(b) I would give the following exercises:

1. Factor $3x^2$.

2. Solve $3x^2 = 0$.

3. Factor $(3x^2 + x)$.

4. Solve $(3x^2 + x) = 0$.

5. Solve $3x^2 - x - 4 = 0$.

(c) In exercise 1 the student factors only the leading coefficient. Exercise 2 follows from exercise 1 since the student can use the factoring from 1 to solve 2. Exercise 3 adds another term to the quadratic expression and the student can factor out an x from both terms. Exercise 4 makes exercise 3 into a quadratic equation for the student to solve. Exercise 5 has the student use factoring to solve a quadratic equation with three terms, the one the student had difficulty with originally.

Sample Responses for Question 3: Assessment
Sample Score "5" Response

(a) and (b):

1a and **1b.** $f(x) = x^2 - 4x + 11$ and $d(x) = -x^3 + 5x + 1$; the domain is all real numbers since the domain of all polynomial functions is all real numbers.

These two problems test the student's basic knowledge of polynomial functions. All of the problems from problem 1 require the student to know the definition of the domain of a function: the set of all x-values that give a y-value.

1c. For $g(x) = \frac{1}{x-4}$, $g(x)$ is undefined for any x-value that makes $x - 4 = 0$. Solving $x - 4 = 0$ for x shows that $x = 4$ and is not in the domain of the function. Therefore, the domain of $g(x) = \frac{1}{x-4}$ is all real numbers *except* $x = 4$. This problem requires the student to know that an expression like $\frac{1}{0}$ is not a number and is therefore called undefined. Thus, if there is an x-value that gives such an expression when input into the function, this bad x-value cannot be included in the domain of the function. This problem tests the student's ability to find the domain of basic rational functions.

1d. $h(x) = \frac{1}{\sqrt{x-4}}$ is undefined for any x-value that makes $\sqrt{x-4} = 0$ and any x-value that makes $x - 4 < 0$. This means in order to find the domain of $h(x)$ we must solve the inequality $\sqrt{x-4} > 0$:

$$\sqrt{x-4} > 0$$
$$(\sqrt{x-4})^2 > (0)^2$$
$$x - 4 > 0$$
$$x > 4$$

This result can also be found by inspection. Therefore, the domain of the function is $x > 4$. This problem tests whether the student knows that $\sqrt{n}$ such that $n < 0$ is not a real number and any such x-value that gives a negative radicand cannot be included in the domain of a function of two real variables. This problem also tests whether or not the student can combine the ability to find the domain of rational functions with the ability of finding the domain of radical functions.

2a. The minimum y-value of the quadratic function $f(x) = x^2 - 4x + 11$ occurs at the vertex of the parabola described by this function. The x-coordinate of the vertex is given by $x = \frac{-b}{2a} = \frac{-(-4)}{2(1)} = 2$. The corresponding y-value is $y = f(2) = 2^2 - 4(2) + 11 = 7$. Therefore, the range of the function is $y \geq 7$.

This problem requires the student to know the definition of the range of a function: the set of all possible y-values that result from all x-values in the domain. The student needs to know that $f(x)$ is a quadratic function with a positive leading coefficient, which means that the graph of this function is a parabola opening up:

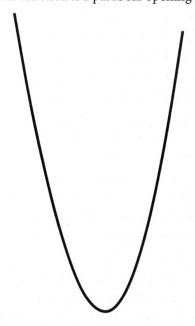

As such, the student must know that the range will be bounded below by the y-value of the vertex of the parabola. To correctly solve this problem, the student will need to know at least the formula that gives the x-coordinate of the vertex, and that evaluating the function $d(x)$ at that x-value gives the desired y-value.

2b. Since $d(x) = -x_3^2 + 5x + 1$ is a polynomial function of odd degree, the range of this function is all real numbers.

This problem requires the student to know that, in the long run, the graphs of odd-degree functions look like one of these curves:

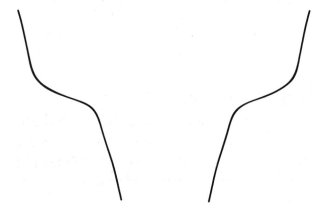

Therefore, the range of an odd-degree polynomial function must be all real numbers.

(c): The additional problems I would ask are the following:

   i. Find the domain and range of the function given by the graph:

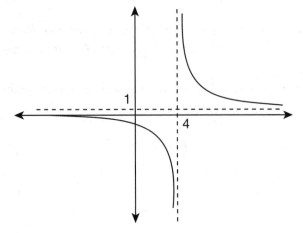

This problem would test the student's ability to determine domain and range using the graph of a function.

   ii. Find the domain and range of the function $y = f(x)$ given by the table of data:

x	−1	0	5	7	11
y	2	1	2	4	9

This problem tests the student's ability to find the domain and range of a function numerically.

Both of these problems present the student with different representations of functions than those in the given problems in which all functions were given by formulas.

Sample Score "2" Response

  (a) **1a.** All real numbers, no work needed.

     1b. All real numbers, no work needed.

     1c. $x \neq 4$, solve $x - 4 = 0$.

     1d. $x > 4$, Solve $\sqrt{x - 4} > 0$.

     2a. $y \geq 7$, found x value of the vertex, and plugged it into the formula.

     2b. All real numbers, no work needed.

  (b) **1a** and **1b** test basic facts about domains of functions.

     1c. Students need to know we can't have zero in the denominator.

     1d. Students need to know about imaginary numbers.

  (c) Problem 1: Find the domain of $t(x) = \sqrt{4 - x}$. This would give some background to problem **1d** and switches the order of the terms, which will change the answer.

Problem 2: Find the range of $g(x) = \frac{1}{x - 4}$. This completes problem **1c**.

14 ▶ PRAXIS II® MATHEMATICS: PEDAGOGY PRACTICE TEST 2

CHAPTER SUMMARY
Here is the second full-length practice test for Praxis II® Mathematics: Pedagogy. Now that you have taken one exam and brushed up on your studying, take this exam to see how much your responses have improved.

As in Chapter 13, this full-length test mirrors the Praxis II® Mathematics: Pedagogy exam. Though the actual exam you will take might be computer-based, the question types are replicated here for you in the book. You can either type your answers in a blank document on your computer or write them down on the lines provided.

This time, as you take this practice exam, you should simulate the actual test-taking experience as closely as you can. Find a quiet place to work where you won't be disturbed. Follow the time constraint noted at the beginning of the test.

After you finish taking this practice test, you should review the scoring criteria that will be used to grade each essay response. You will also see sample responses for each question.

Good luck!

Time: 1 hour

Three essay questions

Question 1: Planning

Objectives/Learning Outcomes: Students in a heterogeneously grouped grade-12 calculus class will learn about the limit concept and how to evaluate limits.

Create a lesson plan that includes the following:

(a) how you would engage your students and pique their interest in learning about the concept of a limit

(b) how you would organize the class for instruction, and your reasoning for choosing this organization

(c) the specific strategies you would teach students to use in understanding and evaluating limits

(d) specific examples, and solutions to these examples, that you would use to aid in student understanding of the topic

Question 2: Implementation

Scenario: During a lesson on solving exponential equations, a student correctly solves equation I, but cannot solve II or III.

    I. $9^x = 27^{-x+5}$

    II. $\left(\frac{1}{16}\right)^{2x+1} = 8^{x-5}$

    III. $7^x = 15$

(a) Give an explanation as to why the student had difficulty with equations II and III.

(b) Develop a set of approximately six exercises, three for equation II and three for equation III, that will incrementally improve the student's understanding of solving exponential equations (and logarithms) so the student can successfully solve equations II and III.

(c) For each exercise in part (b), briefly describe (i) how the exercise can help the student understand solving exponential equations and (ii) how the exercise follows naturally from the previous exercise and leads to the next exercise.

Question 3: Assessment

Scenario: Students in an Algebra II class are given the following problem on an end-of-unit test. This problem is to be used to answer questions (a) and (b) that follow the student problem.

Student Problem: Using what you have learned in this chapter, solve each part of the following problem. Be sure to show all of your work and/or explain your reasoning for each part. Your score will be determined by taking into account the correctness of the mathematics used and the quality of any and all explanations of your reasoning and of the problem-solving strategies used.

The Dirty Blanket Hotel has 600 rooms. At a price of $300 per room per night, all rooms are occupied. The hotel finds that if it raises the price per night for a room by $20, the demand for rooms at the hotel decreases by five rooms. The hotel has nightly fixed costs of $1,000 that cover its heat, utilities, payroll, and so on. It has a variable cost of $76 per room occupied per night, which covers the cost of cleaning and maintaining the room each night.

i. Using the information in the problem, write the formula for the function that models the demand for rooms in the hotel in the form $p = mr + b$, where p is the price per room and r is the number of rooms demanded.

ii. Use the given information to write a formula for the cost of renting a room in terms of number of rooms rented.

iii. Use your formulas from parts (i) and (ii) to determine the number of rooms that must be rented to maximize nightly profit, and determine the price that must be charged per room so that this many rooms will be rented.

You are to do the following:

(a) Write a complete solution to each part of the student problem and show all of your work.
(b) For each part of the student problem, identify the mathematical principles, skills, and abilities the problem is designed to assess.

PRAXIS II® MATHEMATICS: PEDAGOGY PRACTICE TEST 2

Sample Answers

Scoring Criteria

Following are sample criteria for scoring pedagogy responses.

A score "5" writer will:

- Provide a complete and thorough answer to all parts of the question.
- Demonstrate a strong grasp of planning, implementing, and assessing mathematics lessons that are very likely to succeed in achieving their goals.
- Possess a strong fluency in the concepts, theories, procedures, and methodologies related to the question.
- Show a solid understanding of how to motivate various types of learners.
- Offer well-reasoned and sound explanations, supported by evidence where appropriate.

A score "4" writer will:

- Provide appropriate answers to most parts of the question.
- Demonstrate a strong grasp of planning, implementing, and assessing mathematics lessons that are likely to succeed in achieving their goals.
- Possess a satisfactory fluency in the concepts, theories, procedures, and methodologies related to the question.
- Show a satisfactory understanding of how to motivate various types of learners.
- Offer satisfactory explanations, supported by some evidence where appropriate.

A score "3" writer will:

- Provide answers to most parts of the question.
- Demonstrate an understanding of how to plan, implement, and assess mathematics lessons that are somewhat likely to succeed in achieving their goals.

- Possess a basic fluency in the concepts, theories, procedures, and methodologies related to the question.
- Show some understanding of how to motivate various types of learners.
- Offer some explanations with supporting evidence where appropriate.

A score "2" writer will:

- Provide an incomplete answer to the question.
- Demonstrate little or no grasp of planning, implementing, and assessing mathematics lessons.
- Possess weak understanding of the mathematics related to the question.
- Show little or no understanding of how to motivate students.
- Offer unclear or very weak explanations.

A score "1" writer will:

- Fail to supply a satisfactory response to any part of the question.
- Fail to show an understanding of planning, implementing, and assessing mathematics lessons.
- Misunderstand or fail to understand the mathematics related to the question.

A score "0" writer will:

- Fail to provide any response or a coherent response or a response that addresses the question.

Sample Responses for Question 1: Planning
Sample Score "5" Response

(a) I would begin by asking students about their experience with limits in their own lives. Perhaps they would share things about how fast they run a mile or swim 50 meters, or how tall a human can be, or how long a person can live. I would then build on these intuitive notions of limit and move toward a more formal, mathematical definition in terms of functions and their two-dimensional graphs. I would use a specific example, like $f(x) = \dfrac{x^2(x+1)}{(x-2)(x+1)}$.

Together we would use the graphing calculator to investigate the graph of this function. I would also have the students use the Table features of the calculator to look at the behavior of the y-values of the function as the x-values approach the "interesting" x-values of $x = -1$, $x = 2$, and as x gets larger and larger. I would then ask the students to develop their own mathematical definition of the limit concept and apply this definition to come up with techniques, in their own words, for evaluating limits starting with a function like the one given and obtaining the results found using the graph and table of values. I would then discuss their results with them and formalize their definitions and techniques into the standard definition and techniques.

(b) I would have the class break up into groups of three to five students. This way students could help each other with calculator issues and discuss ideas while I circulate around the classroom to guide each group toward our common goal: a working definition of the limit of a function at a particular x-value and two computational techniques for evaluating limits, namely, substitution and the dividing-out technique.

(c) To understand limits, I would emphasize that limits are y-values that occur for specified x-values. I would have the students look at a function both graphically and numerically. Both of these techniques give the students a picture of what is happening with output values of a function when we vary the input values of a function. This type of graphical and numerical analysis will help the students when they look at different types of limits such as infinite limits, limits at infinity, and one-sided limits. In order to help students evaluate limits, I would encourage them to always start with the simplest method—the substitution method—but beware of results like $\frac{0}{0}$ or other indeterminate forms, which usually mean we must use a more advanced method, like the dividing-out technique. I would stress that the dividing-out technique works only because we are looking at x-values very close to a particular x-value, and not at the exact x-value, since that exact x-value would give us an indeterminate form. The students will also need to consider both sides of a given x-value when evaluating limits, especially of piecewise defined functions. I will emphasize to them the formal definition of limit, which requires $\lim\limits_{x \to c^+} f(x) = L = \lim\limits_{x \to c^-} f(x)$, in order for the function $f(x)$ to have a limit of L at $x = c$.

(d) I would include the following examples to make sure students understand the concept of limits graphically, numerically, and algebraically.

(i) Find the indicated limit using the graphs.

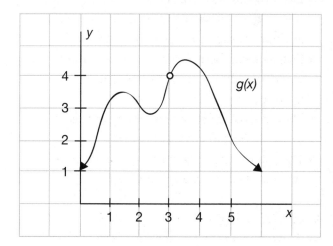

Find $\lim\limits_{x \to 3} g(x)$.

Solution: Using the graph, we see $\lim\limits_{x \to 3} g(x) = 4$.

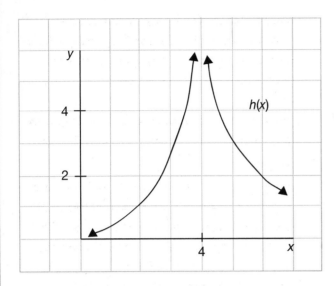

Find $\lim_{x\to 4} h(x)$.

Solution: Using the graph, we could say $\lim_{x\to 4} h(x) = \infty$; however, our answer would be that the limit does not exist, since as the x-values on either side of $x = 4$ get closer and closer to 4 the y-values increase without bound, and never achieve a finite limit.

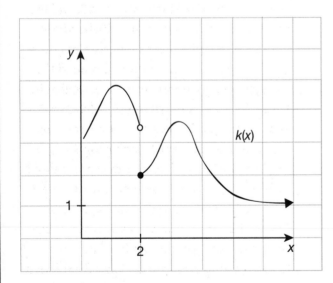

Find $\lim_{x\to 2} k(x)$ and $\lim_{x\to\infty} k(x)$.

Solution: Using the graph, we see $\lim_{x\to 2} k(x)$ does not exist, and $\lim_{x\to\infty} k(x) = 1$.

ii. Using the following tables of data, find the limit of the functions at the indicated point.

x	y1
0.9	0.45
0.99	0.495
0.999	0.4995
1.0	Undefined
1.0001	0.50005

Find $\lim_{x\to 1} y1(x)$.

Solution: $\lim_{x\to 1} y1(x) = 0.5$

x	y2
0.99	−49.5
0.999	−499.5
0.9999	−5,000.0
1.0	Undefined
1.0001	5,000.5

Find $\lim_{x\to 1} y2(x)$.

Solution: $\lim_{x\to 1} y2(x)$ does not exist.

iii. Find $\lim_{x\to -3} \dfrac{x^2 + 7x + 12}{x^2 - 2x - 15}$.

Solution: $\lim_{x\to -3} \dfrac{x^2 + 7x + 12}{x^2 - 2x - 15} = \lim_{x\to -3} \dfrac{(x+4)(x+3)}{(x-5)(x+3)}$

$= \lim_{x\to -3} \dfrac{(x+4)\cancel{(x+3)}}{(x-5)\cancel{(x+3)}} = \dfrac{1}{-8}$

Sample Score "2" Response

(a) I would teach this topic by giving several examples. I would show the students how to evaluate each limit by hand. I would write down the definition of the limit of a function at x, and discuss the definition with the students. For every example I give, I would refer back to the definition.

(b) The class would be organized as a lecture so students could take good notes, help with the examples, and ask questions. I would organize the class in this way so the students and I could interact more effectively and efficiently, and so students would not be distracted.

(c) I would show the students that no matter how we start a limit problem, it always comes down to simply evaluating the function at the specified x-value. I would emphasize the substitution method as the simplest and most common method for evaluating limits. I would show the students that if we get $\frac{0}{0}$ when performing the substitution method, we more than likely have to try a different method. I would show them two different methods and emphasize to the students that they had used these methods before in algebra class: factor canceling and rationalizing.

(d) i. Find $\lim\limits_{x \to 2} 3x - 5$.
Solution: $\lim\limits_{x \to 2} 3x - 5 = 3(2) - 5 = 1$

ii. $\lim\limits_{x \to 2} \frac{x^2 - 4}{x - 2}$
Solution: $\lim\limits_{x \to 2} \frac{x^2 - 4}{x - 2} = \lim\limits_{x \to 2} \frac{(x - 2)(x + 2)}{x - 2} = 4$

Sample Responses for Question 2: Implementation
Sample Score "5" Response

(a) The student had difficulty with equation II because he did not recognize that each side of the equation, especially the left-hand side, could be written as a power of 2. It is most likely the fraction on the left, $\frac{1}{16}$, that the student does not recognize as 2^{-4}. Once the student sees or remembers this way of rewriting fractions using negative exponents, the student can then rewite problem II in a form like problem I, and solve the equation. The student had difficulty with equation III because 7 and 15 cannot be written as powers of the same base as in equations I and II. Problem III cannot be solved without the use of logarithms. Since the student could not solve problem III, he is probably uncomfortable or unfamiliar with logarithms. In order to solve III, the student would

need to either take the log of both sides and then use properties of logarithms to solve for x, or recognize that x is the exponent on 7 that gives us 15; thus x is the number that we denote $\log_7 15$.

(b) For problem II, I would use the following three exercises: (1) solve $2^x = \frac{1}{2}$, (2) solve $2^x = 16$, and (3) solve $2^x = \left(\frac{1}{16}\right)$.
For problem III, the exercises I would give are: (1) rewrite $\log_3 9 = 2$ in exponential form, (2) describe in words what 2 is when $\log_3 9 = 2$ is written in exponential form, and (3) rewrite $\log_7 5 = x$ in exponential form.

(c) Exercise 1 for problem II, solve $2^x = \frac{1}{2}$, reminds the student that we can rewrite fractions using negative exponents. Exercise 2 reminds the student that 16 can be written as a power of 2 and begins to use numbers found in the equation in problem II, so that the student can make the connection between exercises 1 and 2 and problem II. Exercise 3 makes the connection between exercises 1 and 2, and the student's solution to exercise 3 can be directly applied to solve the equation in problem II. For problem III, exercise 1 would remind the student that logarithms are exponents; that is, the student would rewrite $\log_3 9 = 2$ as $3^2 = 9$ and see that another way of writing or saying "2" is $\log_3 9$, and a way of reading $\log_3 9$ is "the exponent on 3 that gives 9"; this exponent on 3 is, of course, 2. This is the answer to exercise 2. Exercise 3 has the student write $\log_7 5 = x$ as $7^x = 5$. The hope is that the student sees at this point that any exponent can be written as a logarithm of a given base, and that the solution to problem III is $\log_7 5$. I would give the student a few more similar examples to check his understanding of this concept: Solve $3^x = 10$, $4^x = 11$, $4^x = \frac{1}{64}$. The final example would relate problem II and problem III.

Sample Score "2" Response

(a) The student had trouble with problem II because of the fraction. The student had difficulty with problem III because $7^1 = 7$ and $7^2 = 49$; that is, the student couldn't think of a nice number that could be the solution to the equation.

(b) For problem II: (1) write $\frac{1}{2}$ as a power of 2; (2) write $\frac{1}{8}$ as a power of 2; (3) write $\frac{1}{16}$ as a power of 2.

For problem III: (1) solve $2^x = 8$; (2) solve $3^x = 9$; (3) write each solution as a logarithm.

(c) Problem II: Each exercise has the student write increasingly larger negative powers of 2. The last exercise applies directly to problem II. Problem III: Each exercise has the student solve easier exponential equations in which the solution is a whole number. The last exercise has the student write these nice whole number solutions as logarithms. The student can then use logarithms to solve problem III.

Sample Responses for Question 3: Assessment
Sample Score "5" Response

(a) and (b):

i. The first two sentences (*The Dirty Blanket Hotel has 600 rooms. At a price of $300 per room per night, all rooms are occupied.*) give us a point (600, 300). The next sentence (*The hotel finds that if it raises the price per night for a room by $20, the demand for rooms at the hotel decreases by five rooms.*) tells us that $m = \frac{\Delta p}{\Delta r} = \frac{20}{-5} = -4$, where r is number of rooms demanded and p is the price per room. We use the given point and slope to write the linear demand equation using the point-slope form of a line, which we can then easily rewrite in the form: $p = mx + b$:

$$p - 300 = -4(r - 600)$$
$$p = -4r + 2,400 + 300$$
$$p = -4r + 2,700$$

In this part, a student must recognize that we are being given enough information to write the equation of a line. The student must be able to write the equation of a line using either point-slope form or slope-intercept form using a given point and a given slope. A student must also be able to interpret price as the dependent variable and number of rooms demanded as the independent variable, as defined in the statement of this part of the problem. It would also be helpful to know that functions that model demand are decreasing functions. The student would then note that the linear function found is a decreasing function, since the slope of the line is indeed negative.

ii. The last two sentences (*The hotel has nightly fixed costs of $1,000 that cover its heat, utilities, payroll, and so on. It has a variable cost of $76 per room occupied per night, which covers the cost of cleaning and maintaining the room each night.*) tell us that the cost function is a linear function with y-intercept 1,000 and slope 76. Therefore the cost is given by the function $C(r) = 76r + 1,000$.

In this part of the problem, a student again must recognize that we are given the parameters for a linear function in slope-intercept form. A student must be able to associate the y-intercept with the fixed cost, and the slope of the line with the variable cost.

iii. Profit = revenue – cost. We see that in order to determine our profit function, we first must have a revenue function. Revenue is the amount of money we take in regardless of cost. A hotel makes money by renting a certain number of rooms r at a certain price, p. Thus revenue is given by multiplying the number of rooms rented by the price charged per room. This means that $R(r) = r \cdot p$, and p is given by the demand function we found in part (a). Therefore, our revenue function is given by $R(r) = r(-4r + 2,700) = -4r^2 + 2,700r$. Now that we have a revenue function and a cost function, we can write our profit function:

$$P(r) = -4r^2 + 2,700r - 76r - 1,000$$
$$P(r) = -4r^2 + 2,624r - 1,000$$

Since this profit function is a quadratic function with a negative leading coefficient, it follows that the maximum profit occurs at the vertex of the parabola represented by this function. The r-coordinate of the vertex can be determined using the formula $r = -\frac{b}{2a}$. Thus, the number of rooms that must be rented to maximize profit is $r = -\frac{b}{2a} = -\frac{2,624}{2(-4)} = 328$. We are also asked to find the price per room that will maximize profit. The price per room depends on the number of rooms rented according to our demand function in problem I, $p = -4r + 2,700$. We evaluate this function at 328 to find the required price, $p = -4(328) + 2,700 = 1,388$ dollars per room. (That is one high-priced hotel!)

In this problem the student must know the relationship between revenue, price, and units demanded/sold, $R = xp$. The student must also know the relationship between profit, revenue, and cost, $P = R - C$. Once these relationships are applied to this problem, the student must then be able to recognize a quadratic function and know that a quadratic function of the form $f(x) = ax^2 + bx + c$ has a maximum value when $a < 0$ and $x = -\frac{b}{2a}$.

Sample Score "2" Response
Problem I:

(a) One can read from the problem statement that the slope of the line is –4 and a point on the line is (600, 300). Demand equation is $p = -4r + 2,700$.
(b) The student needs to know how to write the equation of a line.

Problem II:

(a) It is clear from the given information that cost is $76r + 1,000$.
(b) The student needs to know how to write the equation of a line.

Problem III:

(a) Profit is revenue minus cost, so $P(r) = -4r^2 + 2,624r - 1,000$. The maximum profit occurs at $r = -\frac{b}{2a} = -\frac{2,624}{2(-4)} = 328$.
(b) The student needs to know about quadratic functions, and that the vertex of the function gives the maximum value.

PRAXIS II® MATHEMATICS: PEDAGOGY PRACTICE TEST 3

CHAPTER SUMMARY

Here is the third full-length practice test for Praxis II® Mathematics: Pedagogy. Now that you have taken two exams and brushed up on your studying, take this exam to see how much your writing has improved.

A s in Chapters 13 and 14, this contains a full-length test that mirrors the Praxis II® Mathematics: Pedagogy exam. Though the actual exam you will take might be computer-based, the question types are replicated here for you in the book. You can either type your answers in a blank document on your computer or write them down on the lines provided.

As in the previous chapter, as you take this practice exam, you should simulate the actual test-taking experience as closely as you can. Find a quiet place to work where you won't be disturbed. Follow the time constraint noted at the beginning of the test.

After you finish taking this practice test, you should review the scoring criteria that will be used to grade each essay response. You will also see sample responses for each question.

Good luck!

Time: 1 hour

Three essay questions

Question 1: Planning

Student Assignment

You are given three tables of data. You are to determine a model—in other words a function, linear or exponential—that best fits the data.

Set A:

x	5	12	17	22	27
y	7	14.7	30.87	64.827	136.137

Set B:

x	5	12	17	22	27
y	7	9.1	11.2	13.3	15.4

Set C:

x	5	12	17	22	27
y	2.5	14.4	28.9	48.4	72.9

Objectives/Learning Outcomes: Students in a heterogeneously grouped eleventh-grade precalculus class will learn about linear and exponential functions using the student assignment shown as a stimulus.

Create a lesson plan that includes the following:

(a) the mathematics that the students will need to understand or learn in order to solve the problem

(b) how you would organize the class for instruction and your reasoning for choosing this organization

(c) the specific strategies you would teach students to use in solving this problem

Question 2: Implementation

Scenario: During a lesson on solving equations using multiplication of signed numbers, a student asks, "Why is a negative number times a negative number equal to a positive number?"

(a) Describe how you would answer this question.
(b) Give an explanation as to why you would answer in this way.

Question 3: Assessment

On an end-of-unit test, students were asked the following questions about solving equations and inequalities:

1. Solve each of the following equations for x.
   a. $2x - 7 = 0$
   b. $(2x - 5)(x + 6) = 0$
   c. $2x^2 + 5x - 12 = 0$

2. Determine the solution set for each of the following inequalities.
   a. $-2x + 1 > 7$
   b. $(2x - 5)(x + 6) \leq 0$

(a) Write a solution to each part of these student problems, showing any and all work.

(b) For each part of each student problem, state the mathematical skills and knowledge that the question is designed to assess.

(c) Write two additional student problems that you think should also be asked in order to assess student understanding of the concepts of solving equations and inequalities, and explain how these additional questions complement the given student problems.

_____

_____

_____

_____

_____

_____

_____

_____

_____

_____

_____

Sample Answers

Scoring Criteria

Following are sample criteria for scoring pedagogy responses.

A score "5" writer will:

- Provide a complete and thorough answer to all parts of the question.
- Demonstrate a strong grasp of planning, implementing, and assessing mathematics lessons that are very likely to succeed in achieving their goals.
- Possess a strong fluency in the concepts, theories, procedures, and methodologies related to the question.
- Show a solid understanding of how to motivate various types of learners.
- Offer well-reasoned and sound explanations, supported by evidence where appropriate.

A score "4" writer will:

- Provide appropriate answers to most parts of the question.
- Demonstrate a strong grasp of planning, implementing, and assessing mathematics lessons that are likely to succeed in achieving their goals.
- Possess a satisfactory fluency in the concepts, theories, procedures, and methodologies related to the question.
- Show a satisfactory understanding of how to motivate various types of learners.
- Offer satisfactory explanations, supported by some evidence where appropriate.

A score "3" writer will:

- Provide answers to most parts of the question.
- Demonstrate an understanding of how to plan, implement, and assess mathematics lessons that are somewhat likely to succeed in achieving their goals.

- Possess a basic fluency in the concepts, theories, procedures, and methodologies related to the question.
- Show some understanding of how to motivate various types of learners.
- Offer some explanations with supporting evidence where appropriate.

A score "2" writer will:

- Provide an incomplete answer to the question.
- Demonstrate little or no grasp of planning, implementing, and assessing mathematics lessons.
- Possess weak understanding of the mathematics related to the question.
- Show little or no understanding of how to motivate students.
- Offer unclear or very weak explanations.

A score "1" writer will:

- Fail to supply a satisfactory response to any part of the question.
- Fail to show an understanding of planning, implementing, and assessing mathematics lessons.
- Misunderstand or fail to understand the mathematics related to the question.

A score "0" writer will:

- Fail to provide any response or a coherent response or a response that addresses the question.

Sample Responses for Question 1: Planning
Sample Score "5" Response

(a) Students will need to use the patterns that exist in linear data and exponential data. In particular, students will need to use the fact that linear functions exhibit a constant rate of change, whereas exponential functions exhibit a constant percent rate of change. In order to recall these facts, students should go back to very basic examples of linear and exponential functions and remind themselves of the patterns that exist in these function values by creating tables of values. I would encourage students to write down tables of values for the functions $f(x) = 2x$ and $g(x) = 2^x$.

x	$2x$	y
-2	2(-2)	-4
-1	2(-1)	-2
0	2(0)	0
1	2(1)	2
2	2(2)	4

x	2^x	y
-2	2^{-2}	$\frac{1}{4}$
-1	2^{-1}	$\frac{1}{2}$
0	2^0	0
1	2^1	2
2	2^2	4

From these tables, the students would be reminded that for linear functions like $f(x) = 2x$, when the difference in consecutive x-values is constant, so is the difference in consecutive y-values. In the example, students can see that $x_{n+1} - x_n = 1$, and can compute $y_{n+1} - y_n = 2$. From the table for $g(x) = 2^x$, students will be reminded that when the difference in consecutive x-values is constant, the *ratio* of consecutive y-values is constant. In particular, for $x_{n+1} - x_n = 1, \frac{y_{n+1}}{y_n} = 2$.

(b) I would have the students choose a partner and have them work together to discuss the patterns they see in each data set. I would circulate around the classroom to make sure that each group could successfully determine that data set B exhibits linear behavior, set A exhibits exponential behavior, and set C exhibits neither linear nor exponential behavior. For homework I would ask the students to see if they could find a function that could model the data in set C. I would organize the class in this way so that students could interact with one another and get practice in real-world problem solving, which most often occurs in teams, not alone. Being able to interact with one's peers during class also makes the students more engaged in the topic, and makes the lesson memorable.

(c) The specific strategies I would have the students use to solve this problem would be to first be sure that the difference between consecutive x-values is constant. In the three data sets given, they would calculate the difference between each pair of consecutive x-values to see that the difference between these values is always 5. Once the students establish the behavior of the independent variable, they can focus on the discernible patterns in the y-values. In order to find the patterns in the data, I would have students consider simpler examples of functions we had studied in class: linear, exponential, and quadratic. The hope would be that a look at the table of values of simpler functions would lead them to the correct conclusions about the given data sets. I would also have them use the scatter plot functionality of their graphing calculators to view the data sets in appropriate viewing windows and see the pattern in the data. Once the scatter plots are made, students would have further evidence that set A is exponential, set B is linear, and set C is quadratic. Once these models had been agreed upon, we would then work on creating formulas for the functions that model the exponential and linear data sets, in the form $f(x) = ab^x$ and $g(x) = mx + b$, respectively.

Sample Score "2" Response

(a) Students would need to use their knowledge of linear and exponential functions to see that set A is exponential, and set B is linear. Maybe they would even be able to see that set C is quadratic.

(b) I would have the class work in groups. This way they could solve the problem together.

(c) I would remind them that we had dealt with exponential and linear functions before. I would have them look at a table of data for $y = 2x$ and $y = 2^x$.

Sample Responses for Question 2: Implementation
Sample Score "5" Response

(a) I would begin by appealing to the student's intuition and work with the student on a series of multiplication problems that would exhibit a pattern and show that the idea of "a negative times a negative is a positive" is certainly reasonable: I would begin with: $-4 * 4 = ? (= -16)$, then proceed down the 4 times table: $-4 * 3 = -12; -4 * 2 = -8; -4 * 1 = -4; -4 * 0 = 0; -4 * -1 = ?$ I would ask the student to find the next number in the pattern, which is 4. The student would easily see this pattern, since to get from one product to the next we simply add 4. If the student was unsatisfied with this argument, I would present another argument using a number line. I would draw a number line and label it −6 through 6. I would draw a stick figure standing at 0, facing forward. I would explain that we can think of multiplication as

taking a walk on the number line a certain number of steps a certain number of times facing a certain direction (left or right). For example, suppose our stick figure walks in such a way that he takes two steps at a time. Starting at 0, if we have our stick figure face right and walk one time to the right he would be standing at 2, which is 2 steps, 1 time, or $2 * 1 = 2$. I would ask the student how we could picture walking two steps to the right three times (face right = positive 2, walk right = positive 3, stick figure winds up facing right and standing at 6). I would then ask the student how we could represent walking two steps to the left. This could be done facing to the right (+2), or facing left (−2). So, we could have the stick figure walk backward (facing right) two steps, which is the same as $2 * -1$, or he could walk facing left. We could then expand this example to give us a picture of $-2 * -3$. This product can be represented by having our stick figure face left and walk backward two steps at a time three times. The stick figure would end up standing on +6 and facing left.

(b) I would give these two answers to the student because they both give simple arguments as to why "a negative times a negative is a positive." My first answer allows the student to immediately get involved in drawing his or her own conclusions, as the number pattern in the products is easy to see and easy to compute. My second answer gives the student a way to visualize why the statement is true.

Sample Score "2" Response

(a) I would ask if the student believed that $(-1)(-1) = 1$. If the student said no, I would make some verbal statements that used a double negative, and ask them to interpret the statement. One statement could be "I don't have no money." Another could be "I can't not eat cake, if cake is served at a party." The students would then understand that a double negative is a positive, and that $(-1)(-1) = 1$. From here we could look at $(-2)(-3)$. I would show the student that we could rewrite this as $(-1)(2)(-1)$ $(3) = (-1)(-1)(2)(3) = (1)(6) = 6$.

(b) I would answer in this way because it is intuitive for the students, and easy to understand. It is also a very fast way to answer the question convincingly, and so will not take up a lot of class time.

Sample Responses for Question 3: Assessment

Sample Score "5" Response

(a), (b), and (c):

1. Solve each of the following equations for x.

a. $2x - 7 = 0$

$$2x - 7 = 0$$
$$\underline{+7 \quad +7}$$
$$2x = 7$$
$$x = \frac{7}{2}$$

This problem tests the student's ability to solve simple linear equations using rational numbers. The student must know that to solve for a specified variable, x, this variable must be isolated on one side of the equation. This is done by performing inverse operations on the values surrounding x using reverse order of operations.

b. $(2x - 5)(x + 6) = 0$

$$(2x - 5)(x + 6) = 0$$
$$2x - 5 = 0 \text{ or } x + 6 = 0$$
$$x = \frac{5}{2} \text{ or } \qquad x = -6$$

Here the student must know and take advantage of the "zero property of multiplication" that is present when multiplying real numbers. This property says that, if $ab = 0$ with $a \neq b$, then either $a = 0$ or $b = 0$. The student is given a quadratic

equation in factored form. Factoring a quadratic equation reduces solving a quadratic equation to solving two simpler linear equations. This procedure is assessed in the following question.

c. $2x^2 + 5x - 12 = 0$

$$2x^2 + 5x - 12 = 0$$
$$(2x - 3)(x + 4) = 0$$
$$2x - 3 = 0 \text{ or } x + 4 = 0$$
$$x = \frac{3}{2} \text{ or } \qquad x = -4$$

This problem tests the student's ability to solve a quadratic equation in general form using factoring. The student must first recognize that factoring will reduce this equation to the product of linear factors as in part b. Once the quadratic equation is factored, the student then must again take advantage of the zero property to solve the equation for x. In order to solve this equation using factoring, it is crucially important that the student be able to factor using the method of trial and error, or decomposing the middle term. If the student is unable to factor, the student can still solve this equation by using the quadratic formula. However, in order to use the quadratic formula the student must first recall the formula and apply it correctly to this problem.

2. Determine the solution set for each of the following inequalities.

a. $-2x + 1 > 7$

$$-2x + 1 > 7$$
$$\underline{+2x \qquad \qquad + 2x}$$
$$1 > 7 + 2x$$
$$\underline{-7 \quad -7}$$
$$-6 > 2x$$
$$-3 > x$$

This problem tests the student's ability to solve a linear inequality. In particular, it assesses the student's ability to deal with the potential of having to multiply or divide by a negative number over an inequality. If a student multiplies or divides by a negative number over an inequality, the student must remember that this operation changes the direction of the inequality symbol. This is a potential source of error for many students. The solution shown avoids this potential for error by adding $2x$ to both sides of the inequality and effectively eliminating the need to multiply or divide by a negative number over an inequality.

b. $(2x - 5)(x + 6) \leq 0$

We solve this inequality by first solving the equation $(2x - 5)(x + 6) = 0$. This was done in problem 1, part b. We see that $x = -6$ and $x = \frac{5}{2} = 2.5$. We now use these x-values and sign analysis to solve the inequality. Our solution set will consist of x-values that make the expression $(2x - 5)(x + 6)$ less than zero (i.e., negative), and exactly equal to zero. In order to perform the sign analysis we draw the x-axis and label it with the x-values that make the expression exactly equal to 0:

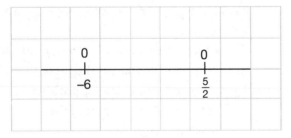

Next, we choose test x-values to represent the intervals for which we need to determine the expression positive or negative on those intervals. Specifically, we are interested in knowing if the expression is positive or

negative on the interval less than –6, on the interval between –6 and $\frac{5}{2}$, and on the interval greater than $\frac{5}{2}$. It is very easy to test for sign using the factored form of the expression. We represent the factored form of the expression with two sets of parentheses multiplied together. This factored form template that represents $(2x - 5)(x + 6)$ is written below each test value. The sign of each factor is computed and the sign of the product is placed on the number line in the corresponding interval.

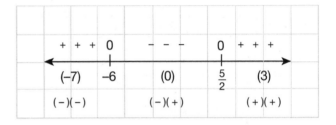

We see that $(2x - 5)(x + 6)$ is negative on the interval $-6 < x < \frac{5}{2}$. Therefore, the solution to the inequality $(2x - 5)(x + 6) \leq 0$ is $-6 \leq x \leq \frac{5}{2}$.

In order to solve this inequality, the student must have the same knowledge and skills required for problem 1, part b. In addition, the student must know that 0 is important because it separates positive numbers from negative numbers. This is the property that is taken advantage of in the sign analysis we have just done. The student must be familiar with this method of sign analysis, or recognize that $(2x - 5)(x + 6)$ is a quadratic expression with leading coefficient 2, recall that the graphs of quadratic functions are parabolas, and know that the x-values that make the expression exactly equal to 0 are x-intercepts of the graph. The student could then put these facts together to sketch the graph:

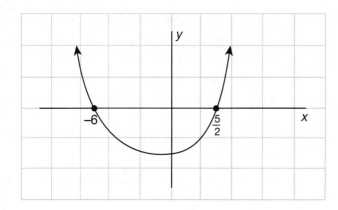

The student must recognize that the expression is less than 0 when the graph is below the x-axis. If all of this is done, then the student will have solved the inequality graphically.

c. I would include the following two problems;
  i. Solve $x^2 + 6x = 1$
  ii. Solve $|2x + 9| > 3$
Problem i will assess the student's ability to solve quadratic equations by a method other than factoring. This problem will also test whether the student can recognize when a quadratic equation can or cannot be factored over the rational numbers. Furthermore, the problem forces the student to solve a quadratic equation that is not written in the usual form $ax^2 + bx + c = 0$. Problem ii will test the student's ability to solve linear absolute value inequalities. In order to solve this problem, the student should know the definition of the absolute value function, or at least what $|a|$, absolute value of a number, a, means. This type of inequality is usually learned before solving quadratic inequalities (problem 2, part b), and a question like problem ii will assess the student's skill at solving compound inequalities that do not require knowledge of sign analysis or of quadratic equations.

Sample Score "2" Response

(a), (b), and (c):

1. Solve each of the following equations for x.
  a. $2x - 7 = 0$
$$x = \frac{7}{2}$$

This problem tests the student's ability to solve simple linear equations. The solution can be found without showing any work.

  b. $(2x - 5)(x + 6) = 0$
$$(2x - 5)(x + 6) = 0$$
$$x = \frac{5}{2} \quad \text{or} \quad x = -6$$
Here, again, the student must know how to solve linear equations.

  c. $2x^2 + 5x - 12 = 0$
$$2x^2 + 5x - 12 = 0$$
$$(2x - 3)(x + 4) = 0$$
$$x = \frac{3}{2} \quad \text{or} \quad x = -4$$
The student needs to know how to factor to solve a quadratic equation.

2. Determine the solution set for each of the following inequalities.
  a. $-2x + 1 > 7$
  $-3 > x$
This problem tests the student's ability to solve a linear inequality.

  b. $(2x - 5)(x + 6) \leq 0$
Sketch the graph of $y = (2x - 5)(x + 6)$ and see $-6 \leq x \leq \frac{5}{2}$.
The student must know about graphs of quadratic functions and x-intercepts.

  c. I would include the following problems:
    i. Solve $x^2 + 6x = 3$ for using the quadratic formula.
    ii. Solve $x(2 - 5) = 4x$ for solving linear equations using grouping symbols and variables on both sides of the equation.

ADDITIONAL ONLINE PRACTICE

Using the codes below, you'll be able to log in and access additional online practice materials!

Your free online practice access code is:
FVEVO1X0T2L17G1UDIHT

Follow these simple steps to redeem your code:

- Go to **www.learningexpresshub.com/affiliate** and have your access code handy.

If you're a new user:
- Click the **New user? Register here** button and complete the registration form to create your account and access your products.
- Be sure to enter your unique access code only once. If you have multiple access codes, you can enter them all—just use a comma to separate each code.
- The next time you visit, simply click the **Returning user? Sign in** button and enter your username and password.
- Do not re-enter previously redeemed access code. Any products you previously accessed are saved in the **My Account** section on the site. Entering a previously redeemed access code will result in an error message.

If you're a returning user:
- Click the **Returning user? Sign in** button, enter your username and password, and click **Sign In**.
- You will automatically be brought to the **My Account** page to access your products.
- Do not re-enter previously redeemed access code. Any products you previously accessed are saved in the **My Account** section on the site. Entering a previously redeemed access code will result in an error message.

If you're a returning user with a new access code:
- Click the **Returning user? Sign in** button, enter your username, password, and new access code, and click **Sign In**.
- If you have multiple access codes, you can enter them all—just use a comma to separate each code.
- Do not re-enter previously redeemed access code. Any products you previously accessed are saved in the **My Account** section on the site. Entering a previously redeemed access code will result in an error message.

If you have any questions, please contact LearningExpress Customer Support at LXHub@LearningExpressHub .com. All inquiries will be responded to within a 24-hour period during our normal business hours: 9:00 A.M.– 5:00 P.M. Eastern Time. Thank you!